God of God, Light of Light, true God of true
   God. *
Begotten, not made, *
   of one substance with the Father. *
By Whom all things were made. *
Who for us men
   down from
And He became
   Virgin Mary
   and was made
He was also cru
   suffered under Pontius Pilate, and was
   buried. *
And on the third day He rose again, according
   to the Scriptures. *
He ascended into heaven and sits at the right
   hand of the Father. *
He will come again in glory to judge the
   living and the dead. *
And of His kingdom there will be no end. *
And I believe in the Holy Spirit, the Lord and
   Giver of life, *
   Who proceeds from the Father and the Son. *
Who together with the Father and the Son
   is adored and glorified, *
   and Who spoke through the prophets. *
And one holy, Catholic, and Apostolic Church. *
I confess one baptism for the forgiveness of
   sins. *
And I await the resurrection of the dead. *
   And the life of the world to come. Amen.

Page	Sunday or Feast	1965	1966	1967	1968	1969	1970
30	Holy Name of Jesus.	3 Jan.	2 Jan.	2 Jan.	2 Jan.	5 Jan.	4 Jan.
34	Feast of Holy Family	10 Jan.	9 Jan.	8 Jan.	7 Jan.	12 Jan.	11 Jan.
38	2nd Sun. after Epiph.	17 Jan.	16 Jan.	15 Jan.	14 Jan.	19 Jan.	18 Jan.
40	3rd Sun. after Epiph.	24 Jan.	23 Jan.	....	21 Jan.	26 Jan.	....
42	4th Sun. after Epiph..	31 Jan.	30 Jan.	....	28 Jan.	....	....
42	5th Sun. after Epiph..	7 Feb.	....	....	4 Feb.	....	....
44	Septuagesima.......	14 Feb.	6 Feb.	22 Jan.	11 Feb.	2 Feb.	25 Jan.
46	Sexagesima........	21 Feb.	13 Feb.	29 Jan.	18 Feb.	9 Feb.	1 Feb.
48	Quinquagesima....	28 Feb.	20 Feb.	5 Feb.	25 Feb.	16 Feb.	8 Feb.
56	1st Sun. of Lent....	7 Mar.	27 Feb.	12 Feb.	3 Mar.	23 Feb.	15 Feb.
66	2nd Sun. of Lent....	14 Mar.	6 Mar.	19 Feb.	10 Mar.	2 Mar.	22 Feb.
74	3rd Sun. of Lent....	21 Mar.	13 Mar.	26 Feb.	17 Mar.	9 Mar.	1 Mar.
84	4th Sun. of Lent....	28 Mar.	20 Mar.	5 Mar.	24 Mar.	16 Mar.	8 Mar.
94	Passion Sunday.....	4 Apr.	27 Mar.	12 Mar.	31 Mar.	23 Mar.	15 Mar.
104	Palm Sunday.......	11 Apr.	3 Apr.	19 Mar.	7 Apr.	30 Mar.	22 Mar.
134	Easter Sunday.....	18 Apr.	10 Apr.	26 Mar.	14 Apr.	6 Apr.	29 Mar
144	1st Sun. after Easter.	25 Apr.	17 Apr.	2 Apr.	21 Apr.	13 Apr.	5 Apr.
146	2nd Sun. after Easter	2 May	24 Apr.	9 Apr.	28 Apr.	20 Apr.	12 Apr.
148	3rd Sun. after Easter	9 May	1 May	16 Apr.	5 May	27 Apr.	19 Apr.
150	4th Sun. after Easter	16 May	8 May	23 Apr.	12 May	4 May	26 Apr.
152	5th Sun. after Easter	23 May	15 May	30 Apr.	19 May	11 May	3 May
156	Ascension Day.....	27 May	19 May	4 May	23 May	15 May	7 May
158	Sun. after Ascension.	30 May	22 May	7 May	26 May	18 May	10 May
161	Pentecost Sunday...	6 June	29 May	14 May	2 June	25 May	17 May
170	Trinity Sunday.....	13 June	5 June	21 May	9 June	1 June	24 May
172	Corpus Christi......	17 June	9 June	25 May	13 June	5 June	28 May
176	2nd Sun. after Pent..	20 June	12 June	28 May	16 June	8 June	31 May
178	Sacred Heart.......	25 June	17 June	2 June	21 June	13 June	5 June
180	3rd Sun. after Pent..	27 June	19 June	4 June	23 June	15 June	7 June
182	4th Sun. after Pent..	4 July	26 June	11 June	30 June	22 June	14 June
184	5th Sun. after Pent..	11 July	3 July	18 June	7 July	29 June	21 June
186	6th Sun. after Pent..	18 July	10 July	25 June	14 July	6 July	28 June
188	7th Sun. after Pent..	25 July	17 July	2 July	21 July	13 July	5 July
190	8th Sun. after Pent..	1 Aug.	24 July	9 July	28 July	20 July	12 July
192	9th Sun. after Pent..	8 Aug.	31 July	16 July	4 Aug.	27 July	19 July
194	10th Sun. after Pent.	15 Aug.	7 Aug.	23 July	11 Aug.	3 Aug.	26 July
196	11th Sun. after Pent.	22 Aug.	14 Aug.	30 July	18 Aug.	10 Aug.	2 Aug.
198	12th Sun. after Pent.	29 Aug.	21 Aug.	6 Aug.	25 Aug.	17 Aug.	9 Aug.
200	13th Sun. after Pent.	5 Sept.	28 Aug.	13 Aug.	1 Sept.	24 Aug.	16 Aug.
202	14th Sun. after Pent.	12 Sept.	4 Sept.	20 Aug.	8 Sept.	31 Aug.	23 Aug.
204	15th Sun. after Pent.	19 Sept.	11 Sept.	27 Aug.	15 Sept.	7 Sept.	30 Aug.
206	16th Sun. after Pent.	26 Sept.	18 Sept.	3 Sept.	22 Sept.	14 Sept.	6 Sept
208	17th Sun. after Pent.	3 Oct.	25 Sept.	10 Sept.	29 Sept.	21 Sept.	13 Sept
214	18th Sun. after Pent.	10 Oct.	2 Oct.	17 Sept.	6 Oct.	28 Sept.	20 Sept
216	19th Sun. after Pent.	17 Oct.	9 Oct.	24 Sept.	13 Oct.	5 Oct.	27 Sept
218	20th Sun. after Pent.	24 Oct.	16 Oct.	1 Oct.	20 Oct.	12 Oct.	4 Oct.
222	21st Sun. after Pent.	....	23 Oct.	8 Oct.	....	19 Oct.	11 Oct.
220	Christ the King.....	31 Oct.	30 Oct.	29 Oct.	27 Oct.	26 Oct.	25 Oct.
224	22nd Sun. after Pent.	7 Nov.	3 Nov.	15 Oct.	3 Nov.	....	18 Oct.
226	23rd Sun. after Pent.	14 Nov.	6 Nov.	22 Oct.	10 Nov.	2 Nov.	....
230	24th Sun. after Pent.	....	13 Nov.	....	17 Nov.	9 Nov	1 Nov.
230	25th Sun. after Pent.	....	....	5 Nov.	....	16 Nov.	8 Nov.
230	26th Sun. after Pent.	....	....	12 Nov	....	....	15 Nov.
230	27th Sun. after Pent.	....	....	19 Nov.	....	....	....
228	Last Sun. after Pent.	21 Nov.	20 Nov.	26 Nov.	24 Nov.	23 Nov.	22 Nov.
6	1st Sun. of Advent...	28 Nov.	27 Nov.	3 Dec.	1 Dec.	30 Nov.	29 Nov.
8	2nd Sun. of Advent...	5 Dec.	4 Dec.	10 Dec.	8 Dec.	7 Dec.	6 Dec.
10	3rd Sun. of Advent...	12 Dec.	11 Dec.	17 Dec.	15 Dec.	14 Dec.	13 Dec.
15	4th Sun. of Advent...	19 Dec.	18 Dec.	24 Dec.	22 Dec.	21 Dec.	20 Dec.
22	Sun. after Christmas	26 Dec.	....	31 Dec.	29 Dec.	28 Dec.	27 Dec.

MONASTERY OF ST. ALPHONSUS
REDEMPTORISTINE NUNS
LIGUORI, MISSOURI

The People of God

together with Christ

worship the heavenly Father

✠

PARISH
MASS BOOK

"A Saint Joseph Edition"

**With all Mass prayers recited by the people
printed in boldface type and arranged in sense lines
for easy congregational recitation.**

(T-577)

"He is the true Lamb Who has taken away the sins of the world: Who by dying has destroyed our death; and by rising again has restored us to life."

(Easter Preface)

PARISH
MASS BOOK
AND HYMNAL

PEOPLE'S PARTS OF HOLY MASS
FOR EVERY DAY OF THE YEAR

Arranged for Congregational Recitation

WITH POPULAR HYMNS AND PSALMS

•

**In accordance with the
New Revised Liturgy**

254, 12
BC
Copy 2 1

CATHOLIC BOOK PUBLISHING CO.
NEW YORK

NIHIL OBSTAT:

John A. Goodwine, J.C.D.   *Censor Librorum*

IMPRIMATUR:

Terence J. Cooke, V.G.

———

This new Mass Book has been diligently prepared with the invaluable assistance of a special Board of Editors, including specialists in Liturgy, Sacred Scripture, Catechetics, Sacred Music and Art.

———

The Official Peoples texts in the Ordinary and the Proper—*Introit, Intervenient Chants, Offertory* and *Communion*— are reproduced with permission from the Roman Missal with English translations approved by the National Conference of Bishops of the United States, published by authority of the Bishops' Commission on the Liturgical Apostolate, 1312 Massachusetts Ave., N.W., Washington, D. C. 20005. © 1964 by the National Catholic Welfare Conference, Inc. Scriptural Verses adapted from the Book of Psalms © 1950 and 1955 by the Confraternity of Christian Doctrine.

All other texts, illustrations and special "sense-line arrangement" for congregational recitation (based on poetic structure) Copyright 1965 by Catholic Book Publishing Co., N.Y.

(T-577)

© 1965 by *Catholic Book Publishing Co.*, N.Y.
United States and Canada — Printed in U.S.A.

PREFACE

The Constitution on the Sacred Liturgy emphasized the communal nature of the Holy Sacrifice of the Mass and the importance of the people taking their rightful parts in the Mass.

"Mother Church earnestly desires that all the faithful should be led to that full, conscious, and active participation in liturgical celebrations which is demanded by the very nature of the liturgy. Such participation by the Christian people as a chosen race, a royal priesthood, a holy nation, a redeemed people (1 Pet. 2, 9; cf. 2, 4-5), is their right and duty by reason of their baptism . . .

"In liturgical celebrations each person, minister or layman, who has an office to perform, should do all of, but only, those parts which pertain to his office by the nature of the rite and the principles of liturgy." (Nos. 14, 28).

Guided by this principle, this new Mass book gives **all** (and only) **the people's parts** for each day of the year. To aid communal recitation, these texts are printed in easy-to-read type and in poetic (sense-line) format. The people should pause after each verse. Usually this will be one line—but in the case of some longer verses, the second part is carried over to the next line, and clearly indented to show that it belongs to the preceding verse.

The Ordinary of the Mass includes all the parts of the people, plus the Great Eucharistic Prayer of the Canon, including the Preface, to enable the faithful to join with the priest-celebrant in offering silently this most important part of the Mass.

HOW TO USE THIS MASS BOOK

1. *On Sundays:* Consult the Table of Sundays and Movable Feasts.

2. *On Weekdays:* If there is no Mass of a Saint for that particular date, the Mass of the preceding Sunday is usually said.

3. On days of low liturgical rank, the priest may celebrate a Requiem Mass (*Black Vestments*), p. 456, or Votive Mass, p. 464.

4. Mark with a ribbon or picture bookmark:

a) the Ordinary of the Mass, p. 277,

b) the Mass for Today,

c) the Hymns or Psalms of the day, p. 492.

THE PLAN OF THIS MASS BOOK

This Mass Book is arranged as follows:

THE PROPER OF THE TIME: (6-230) Contains the changeable prayers for all the Sunday Masses and for certain great festivals of the Church Year —from the 1st Sunday of Advent to the Last Sunday after Pentecost.

The COMMON OF THE SAINTS: (231-276) Contains the changeable parts common to the various classes of Saints: Popes, Martyrs, Bishops, Confessors, Confessors not Bishops, Doctors, Abbots, Virgins and Holy Women, as well as the parts common to some Feasts of our Lady, and the Masses "of the B.V.M. on Saturday."

The ORDINARY OF THE MASS: (277-298) Includes the unchangeable prayers of every Mass.

The PROPER OF THE SAINTS: (299-455) Contains the changeable parts of the Feasts of our Lord, our Blessed Mother, and of the Angels and Saints, arranged according to the civil year

MASSES FOR THE DEAD: (456-461) Contains all Masses for the Faithful Departed: All Souls' Day, Funeral Masses, Daily Mass for the Dead, etc.

NUPTIAL MASS: (462-463) Contains the Nuptial Mass.

VOTIVE MASSES: (464-491) Contains special Masses in honor of the Holy Trinity, Holy Spirit, our Blessed Lord, our Blessed Mother, and for special occasions and needs.

HYMNAL: (492-576) Contains popular Hymns and sung Masses for all occasions.

John the Baptist prepares the way for the Lord.

PROPER OF THE TIME
FIRST SUNDAY OF ADVENT

THOUGHT FOR TODAY: It is now the hour for us to rise from the sleep of sin and of religious indifference. Let us start our preparation for the blessing of Christmas with great confidence in Jesus, for "no one who waits for (Him) shall be put to shame."

BIBLE AND LITURGY: The Church sees Christ's coming to us at Christmas and at the end of the world in one perspective. What matters is Christ's coming in Grace. READ: Gen. 12, 1-9; 17, 1-8; Ex. 19, 1-8; Jer. 31, 31-33; Gal. 3, 7-9; 16, 26-29.

INTROIT Ps. 24, 1-4   [*Hope*]

To You I lift up my soul;
   in You, O God, I trust;
Let me not be put to shame;
   let not my enemies exult over me:
No one who waits for You shall be put to
     shame.

(Ps.) Your ways, O Lord, make known to me;
   teach me Your paths.
Glory be to the Father, and to the Son,
   and to the Holy Spirit.

As it was in the beginning, is now, and ever
  shall be,
  world without end. Amen.

*The Introit is repeated as far as the Psalm-verse (Ps.)
in all Masses throughout the year.*

To You I lift up my soul;
  in You, O God, I trust;
Let me not be put to shame;
  let not my enemies exult over me:
No one who waits for You shall be put to
  shame.

GRADUAL   Ps. 24, 3. 4   [*Hopes Fulfilled*]

No one who waits for You shall be put to
  shame, O Lord.
Your ways, O Lord, make known to me;
  teach me Your paths.

Alleluia, alleluia.   Ps. 84, 8   [*Mercy for All*]
Show us, O Lord, Your kindness,
  and grant us Your salvation. Alleluia.

OFFERTORY   Ps. 24, 1-3   [*Trust in God*]

To You I lift up my soul;
  in You, O my God, I trust;
Let me not be put to shame;
  let not my enemies exult over me:
No one who waits for You shall be put to
  shame.

COMMUNION   Ps. 84, 13   [*A New World*]

The Lord will give His benefits:
  and our land shall yield its increase.

While in prison, John the Baptist sends disciples to Christ.

SECOND SUNDAY OF ADVENT

THOUGHT FOR TODAY: We need not wait for another Savior. We are certain that Jesus is the Son of God become man, the Anointed Priest-Victim, Redeemer of all mankind. We want to show our love for Him by purifying our hearts.

BIBLE AND LITURGY: The History of our Salvation began with God's revelation to Abraham and reached its peak in Christ's coming. Christian Hope stems from Christ, Who came and will come ever more to save us. READ: Jer. 17, 13-18; Heb. 6, 9-20; Eph. 1, 3-23; 2, 1-22; Tit. 2, 11-14; Acts 26, 1-32.

INTROIT   Isa. 30, 30; Ps. 79. 2   [*Lord of Salvation*]

People of Sion,
    behold the Lord shall come to save the nations;
And the Lord shall make the glory of His voice to be heard,
    in the joy of your heart.

(Ps.) O Shepherd of Israel, hearken,
    O Guide of the flock of Joseph!

Glory be to the Father, and to the Son,
    and to the Holy Spirit.

As it was in the beginning, is now, and ever
   shall be,
   world without end. Amen.

People of Sion,
   behold the Lord shall come to save the
      nations;
And the Lord shall make the glory of His voice
      to be heard,
   in the joy of your heart.

GRADUAL   Ps. 49, 2-3. 5   [Beauty of God]

From Sion, perfect in beauty,
   God shines forth.
Gather His faithful ones before Him,
   those who have made a covenant with Him
      by sacrifice.

Alleluia, alleluia.   Ps. 121, 1 [Beauty of God's House]
I rejoiced because they said to me:
   "We will go up to the house of the Lord."
      Alleluia.

OFFERTORY   Ps. 84, 7-8   [Joy in God]

Will You not, O God, give us life;
   and shall not Your people rejoice in You?
Show us, O Lord, Your kindness,
   and grant us Your salvation.

COMMUNION   Bar. 5, 5; 4, 36   [A New Jerusalem]

Up, Jerusalem! stand upon the heights;
   and behold the joy that comes to you from
      your God.

John the Baptist bears witness to Christ.

THIRD SUNDAY OF ADVENT

THOUGHT FOR TODAY: While we are rejoicing "for the Lord is near," there are millions who do not know the One who should stand in the midst of them. The unbelievers must find a guiding beacon in the shining light of our Christian life.

BIBLE AND LITURGY: God is near and goes along with us on the path of life in Christ, Whose coming we shall celebrate on Christmas Eve. That is the reason why we are invited to spiritual joy. READ: Prov. 10. 28; Ex. 33, 12-19; Rom. 13, 11-14; Isa. 40, 1-11; Ps. 84.

INTROIT   Phil. 4, 4-6; Ps. 84, 2   [*The Lord Is Near*]

Rejoice in the Lord always:
  again I say, rejoice.
Let your moderation be known to all men:
  for the Lord is near.
Have no anxiety,
  but in everything by prayer
  let your petitions be made known to God.
(Ps.) You have favored, O Lord, Your land;
  You have restored the well-being of Jacob.
Glory be to the Father, and to the Son,
  and to the Holy Spirit.

As it was in the beginning, is now, and ever
    shall be,
  world without end. Amen.
Rejoice in the Lord always:
  again I say, rejoice.
Let your moderation be known to all men:
  for the Lord is near.
Have no anxiety,
  but in everything by prayer
    let your petitions be made known to God.

GRADUAL   Ps. 79, 2. 3.2   [Save Us with Power]

From Your throne, O Lord, upon the Cherubim,
  rouse Your power, and come.
O Shepherd of Israel, hearken,
  O Guide of the flock of Joseph.

Alleluia, alleluia.   [The Lord's Salvation]
Rouse, O Lord, Your power,
  and come to save us. Alleluia.

OFFERTORY   Ps. 84, 2   [Renewal]

You have favored, O Lord, Your land;
  You have restored the well-being of Jacob.
You have forgiven the guilt of your people.

COMMUNION   Isa. 35, 4   [Have No Fear]

Say to those who are frightened:
  Be strong, fear not!
Here is our God,
  He comes to save us.

EMBER WEDNESDAY IN ADVENT

INTROIT   Isa. 45, 8; Ps. 18, 2   [*Come Down Like Dew*]

**Drop down dew, you heavens, from above,
    and let the clouds rain the Just:**
**Let the earth be opened
    and bud forth a Savior.**

**(Ps.) The heavens declare the glory of God,
    and the firmament proclaims His handiwork.**
Glory be to the Father, etc.

Repeat: **Drop down dew,** etc., *as far as* (Ps.).

After the 1st Lesson:

GRADUAL   Ps. 23, 7, 3-4   [*The King Is Coming*]

**Lift up, O gates, your lintels;
    reach up, you ancient portals,
    that the King of glory may come in!**
**Who can ascend the mountain of the Lord?
    or who may stand in His holy place?**
**He whose hands are sinless, whose heart is
    clean.**

After the 2nd Lesson:

GRADUAL   Ps. 144, 18. 21   [*The Lord Is Near*]

**The Lord is near to all who call upon Him,
    to all who call upon Him in truth.**
**May my mouth speak the praise of the Lord,
    and may all flesh bless His holy Name.**

OFFERTORY   Isa. 35, 4   [*Victory in Christ*]

**Be strong, fear no longer!
    For, behold, our God will bring judgment.
    He Himself will come to save us.**

COMMUNION   Isa. 7, 14   [*Virgin and Child*]

**Behold, a Virgin shall be with child and bear
    a Son, and shall name Him Emmanuel.**

EMBER FRIDAY IN ADVENT

INTROIT Ps. 118, 151-152. 1 [*The Eternal Lord Is Near*]

You, O Lord, are near,
  and all Your ways are truth.
Of old I know from Your decrees
  that You are forever.
(Ps.) Happy are they whose way is blameless,
  who walk in the law of the Lord.
Glory be to the Father, etc.
Repeat: **You, O Lord,** etc., *as far as* (Ps.).

GRADUAL Ps. 84, 8. 2 [*Blessing of God*]

Show us, O Lord, Your kindness,
  and grant us Your salvation.
You have favored, O Lord, Your land;
  You have restored the well-being of Jacob.

OFFERTORY Ps. 84, 7-8 [*New Life*]

Will You not, O God, give us life;
  and shall not Your people rejoice in You?
Show us, O Lord, Your kindness,
  and grant us Your salvation.

COMMUNION Zach. 14, 5-6 [*Day of Light*]

Behold, the Lord shall come,
  and all His holy ones with Him:
  and there shall be in that day a great light.

EMBER SATURDAY IN ADVENT
Short Form of the Mass

INTROIT Ps. 79, 4. 2 [*Be Our Shepherd*]

Come, O Lord, from Your throne upon the
  Cherubim;

if Your face shine upon us, then we shall
   be safe.

(Ps.) O Shepherd of Israel, hearken,
   O Guide of the flock of Joseph!

Glory be to the Father, etc.

Repeat: Come, O Lord, etc., *as far as* (Ps.).

After the 1st Lesson:

GRADUAL   Ps. 18, 7. 2   [*God's Glory*]

At one end of the heavens He comes forth,
   and His course is to their other end.
The heavens declare the glory of God,
   and the firmament proclaims His handiwork.

After the 2nd Lesson:

TRACT   Ps. 79, 2-3   [*Saving Shepherd*]

O Shepherd of Israel, hearken,
   O Guide of the flock of Joseph!
From Your throne upon the Cherubim, shine
   forth
   before Ephraim, Benjamin and Manasse.
Rouse Your power, O Lord,
   and come to save us.

OFFERTORY   Zach. 9, 9   [*The King Is Coming*]

Rejoice heartily, O daughter of Sion,
   shout for joy, O daughter of Jerusalem!
See, your King shall come to you,
   a just Savior is He.

COMMUNION   Ps. 18, 6-7   [*Coming of the Champion*]

He has rejoiced as a giant to run the way:
At one end of the heavens He comes forth,
   and His course is to their other end.

John the Baptist preaches a baptism of repentance.

FOURTH SUNDAY OF ADVENT

THOUGHT FOR TODAY: As Mary is about to give her Divine Son to the world and to us, we cleanse our hearts in sincere confession to prepare the way of the Lord. The most precious Christmas gift is Christ Himself, Whom we receive in Holy Communion.

BIBLE AND LITURGY: During Advent we yearn for an ever more perfect coming of Christ in Grace. READ: Mich. 4, 1-5; 5, 2-4; 1 Cor. 1, 1-9; Eph. 4, 11-16; Ps. 144.

INTROIT   Isa. 45, 8; Ps. 18, 2   [*The Advent Plea*]

Drop down dew, you heavens, from above,
    and let the clouds rain the Just:
      let the earth be opened and bud forth a
      Savior.

(Ps.) The heavens declare the glory of God,
    and the firmament proclaims His handiwork.

Glory be to the Father, and to the Son,
    and to the Holy Spirit.

As it was in the beginning, is now, and ever
    shall be,
    world without end. Amen.

Drop down dew, you heavens, from above,
    and let the clouds rain the Just:

let the earth be opened and bud forth a
    Savior.

GRADUAL ^{Ps. 144, 18. 21} [*Praise the Lord Who Is Near*]

The Lord is near to all who call upon Him,
    to all who call upon Him in truth.
May my mouth speak the praise of the Lord,
    and may all flesh bless His holy Name.
Alleluia, alleluia.   [*Do Not Delay*]
Come, O Lord, and delay not;
    forgive the sins of Your people Israel.
        Alleluia.

OFFERTORY   Luke 1, 28. 42   [*Christ's New Paradise*]

Hail, Mary, full of grace,
    the Lord is with you,
Blessed are you among women,
    and blessed is the fruit of your womb.

COMMUNION   Isa. 7, 14   [*The Virgin-Mother*]

Behold, the virgin shall be with child and bear
    a Son,
    and shall name Him Emmanuel.

Dec. 24 — VIGIL OF CHRISTMAS

INTROIT   Ex. 16, 6. 7; Ps. 23, 1   [*Great Glory of Tomorrow*]

This day you shall know
    that the Lord will come, and save us:
    and in the morning you shall see His glory.
(Ps.) The Lord's are the earth and its fullness;
    the world and those who dwell in it.
Glory be to the Father, and to the Son,
    and to the Holy Spirit.

As it was in the beginning, is now, and ever
   shall be,
   world without end. Amen.

Repeat: **This day you,** etc., *as far as* (Ps.).

GRADUAL   Ex. 16, 6. 7; Ps. 79, 2-3

[*Salvation Made Known Today*]

**This day you shall know
   that the Lord will come and save us:
   and in the morning you shall see His glory.
O Shepherd of Israel, hearken,
   O Guide of the flock of Joseph!
From Your throne upon the Cherubim, shine
   forth
   before Ephraim, Benjamin and Manasse.**

*The following Alleluia and its versicle are said only
when the Vigil falls on a Sunday.*

Alleluia, alleluia.   [*Tomorrow the Victor*]
**Tomorrow shall the wickedness of the earth
   be abolished:
   and the Savior of the world shall reign over
   us. Alleluia.**

OFFERTORY   Ps. 23, 7   [*The Great Welcome*]

**Lift up, O gates, your lintels;
   reach up, you ancient portals,
   that the King of Glory may come in.**

COMMUNION   Isa. 40, 5   [*Glory for All*]

**The glory of the Lord shall be revealed,
   and all mankind shall see the salvation of
   our God.**

The Word is made Flesh.

CHRISTMAS DAY

THOUGHT FOR TODAY: May our hearts express our love and gratitude and our resolve to belong entirely to Jesus, as we contemplate this manifestation that God is Love, and that He so loved the world as to give us His Only-begotten Son.

BIBLE AND LITURGY: The Son of God became Man to cleanse for Himself an acceptable people. He is its Lord. This people, the Church, is the spiritualized Israel. Indeed Christ took over the throne of His ancestor David in a transcending and mysterious way. READ: 2 Kgs. 5, 1-5; Isa. 2, 6-7; Luke 1 (esp. 1, 30-33); 2, 1-20; Ps. 109.

First Mass at Midnight

INTROIT   Ps. 2, 7. 1   [*The Deep Mystery*]

The Lord said to Me, "You are My Son;
   this day I have begotten You."

(Ps.)Why do the nations rage
   and the people utter folly?

Glory be to the Father, and to the Son,
   and to the Holy Spirit.

As it was in the beginning, is now, and ever
      shall be,
   world without end. Amen.

The Lord said to Me, "You are My Son;
  this day I have begotten You."

GRADUAL   Ps. 109, 3. 1   [The Eternal Ruler]

Yours is princely power in the day of Your
    birth, in holy splendor;
  before the daystar I have begotten You.
The Lord said to my Lord: "Sit at My right
    hand,
  till I make Your enemies Your footstool."

Alleluia, alleluia. Ps. 2, 7   [Begotten of God]
The Lord said to Me, "You are My Son;
  this day I have begotten You." Alleluia.

OFFERTORY   Ps. 95, 11. 13   [Universal Rejoicing]

Let the heavens be glad and the earth rejoice
  before the Lord, for He comes.

COMMUNION   Ps. 109, 3   [Eternal Son]

In holy splendor before the daystar I have
  begotten You.

Second Mass at Dawn

INTROIT   Isa. 9, 3. 6; Ps. 92, 1   [The Hero's Arrival]

A light shall shine upon us this day:
  for the Lord is born to us:
And He shall be called wonderful, God,
  Prince of peace, Father of the world to come:
  of Whose reign there shall be no end.
(Ps.) The Lord is King, in splendor robed;
  robed is the Lord and girt about with
    strength.

Glory be to the Father, and to the Son,
   and to the Holy Spirit.
As it was in the beginning, is now, and ever
      shall be,
   world without end. Amen.
A light shall shine upon us this day:
   for the Lord is born to us:
And He shall be called wonderful, God,
   Prince of peace, Father of the world to come:
   of Whose reign there shall be no end.

GRADUAL   Ps. 117, 26, 27. 23   [*Light of the World*]

Blessed is He Who comes in the Name of the
      Lord;
   the Lord is God, and He has given us light.
By the Lord has this been done;
   it is wonderful in our eyes.

Alleluia, alleluia.   Ps. 92, 1   [*Glory of the New King*]
The Lord is King, in splendor robed;
   robed is the Lord and girt about with
      strength. Alleluia.

OFFERTORY   Ps. 92, 1-2   [*God's Eternal Throne*]

God has made the world firm,
   not to be moved.
Your throne, O God, stands firm from of old;
   from everlasting You are.

COMMUNION   Zach. 9, 9   [*The Shout of Joy*]

Rejoice heartily, O daughter Sion,
   shout for joy, O daughter Jerusalem!
See, your King shall come,
   a just Savior of the world is He.

Third Mass During the Day

INTROIT Isa. 9, 6; Ps. 97, 1 [*The Gift of God's Son*]

A Child is born to us, a Son is given to us;
  upon His shoulder dominion rests;
And His Name shall be called
  the Angel of great counsel.
(Ps.) Sing to the Lord a new song,
  for He has done wondrous deeds.
Glory be to the Father, etc.
Repeat: **A child,** etc., *as far as* (Ps.).

GRADUAL Ps. 97, 3-4. 2 [*Praise from Everywhere*]

All the ends of the earth have seen
  the salvation of our God.
Sing joyfully to God, all you lands.
The Lord has made His salvation known:
  in the sight of the nations He has revealed
    His justice.

Alleluia, alleluia. [*The Holy Light*]
A sanctified day has shone upon us;
  come, you nations, and adore the Lord:
  for this day a great light has descended upon
    the earth. Alleluia.

OFFERTORY Ps. 88, 12. 15 [*The Lord's World*]

Yours are the heavens, and Yours is the earth;
  the world and its fullness You have founded.
Justice and judgment are the foundation of
  Your throne.

COMMUNION Ps. 97, 3 [*The Vision of Salvation*]

All the ends of the earth have seen
  the salvation by our God.

Simeon foretells Mary's sorrow.

SUNDAY WITHIN OCTAVE OF CHRISTMAS

THOUGHT FOR TODAY: Through the words of Simeon, Mary and Joseph realized that their hearts would be pierced with the sword of sorrow because they were so close to the "Man of Sorrows."

BIBLE AND LITURGY: By His ready obedience first to God His Father and then to His parents, Jesus teaches us the value of obedience in our daily lives. By being obedient, He grew in wisdom and grace, and His obedience unto death was rewarded by His Father with the glory of the Resurrection. READ: Rom. 6, 15-26; Deut. 27f; Sirach 3, 1-16; Eph. 6, 1-10; Phil. 2, 5-11; Heb. 5, 7-10; 1 Pet. 2, 13-25.

INTROIT Wis. 18, 14. 15; Ps. 92, 1 [*Mystery of the Night*]

When a profound stillness compassed everything
    thing
    and the night in its swift course was half
      spent,
    Your all-powerful Word, O Lord, bounded
    from heaven's royal throne.
(Ps.) The Lord is King, in splendor robed;
    robed is the Lord, and girt about with
    strength.

Glory be to the Father, and to the Son,
 and to the Holy Spirit.
As it was in the beginning, is now, and ever
  shall be,
 world without end. Amen.

When a profound stillness compassed everything
 and the night in its swift course was half
  spent,
  Your all-powerful Word, O Lord, bounded
  from heaven's royal throne.

GRADUAL Ps. 44, 3. 2 *[Beauty of the Word]*

Fairer in beauty are You than the sons of men;
 grace is poured out upon Your lips.
My heart overflows with a goodly theme;
 as I sing my ode to the King,
  my tongue is nimble as the pen of a skillful
  scribe.

Alleluia, alleluia. Ps. 92, 1 *[Splendor of the King]*
The Lord is King, in splendor robed;
 robed is the Lord and girt about with
  strength. Alleluia.

OFFERTORY Ps. 92, 1. 2 *[God, Eternal Ruler]*

God has made the world firm,
 not to be moved.
Your throne, O God, stands firm from of old;
 from everlasting You are.

COMMUNION Matt. 2, 20 *[Back from Exile]*

Take the Child and His Mother,
 and go into the land of Israel,
  for those who sought the Child's life are
  dead.

Dec. 26 — ST. STEPHEN, First Martyr
2nd Day Within the Octave of Christmas

INTROIT   Ps. 118, 23. 86. 23   [*Plot Against the Just*]

Princes met and talked against me,
  and the wicked persecuted me wrongfully;
Help me, O Lord my God,
  for Your servant meditates on Your statutes.
(Ps.) Happy are they whose way is blameless,
  who walk in the law of the Lord!
Glory be to the Father, etc.
Repeat: **Princes met,** etc., *as far as* (Ps.).

GRADUAL   Ps. 118, 23. 86; 6, 5   [*Rescue Your Holy One*]

Princes met and talked against me,
  and the wicked persecuted me wrongfully.
Help me, O Lord my God:
  rescue me because of Your kindness.

Alleluia, alleluia.   Acts 7, 56   [*Vision of Jesus*]
I see the heavens opened,
  and Jesus standing on the right hand
  of the power of God. Alleluia.

*In Votive Masses after Septuagesima, omit "Alleluia"
at the end of the following Offertory:*

OFFERTORY   Acts 6, 5; 7, 59   [*Man of Faith and Strength*]

The apostles chose Stephen to be a levite,
  a man full of faith and of the Holy Spirit:
Whom the Jews stoned, praying and saying,
  "Lord Jesus, receive my spirit." Alleluia.

COMMUNION   Acts 7, 56. 59. 60

[Jesus Welcomes Stephen]

I see the heavens opened,
  and Jesus standing on the right hand
  of the power of God:
Lord Jesus, receive my spirit,
  and do not lay this sin against them.

Dec. 27 — ST. JOHN, Apostle, Evangelist
3rd Day Within the Octave of Christmas

INTROIT   Sir. 15, 6; Ps. 91, 2   [Wisdom]

In the midst of the assembly the Lord opened
    His mouth;
And filled him with the spirit of wisdom and
    understanding;
  He clothed him with a robe of glory.
(Ps.) It is good to give thanks to the Lord,
  to sing praise to Your Name, Most High.
Glory be to the Father, etc.
Repeat: **In the midst, etc.,** *as far as* (Ps.).

GRADUAL   John 21, 23. 22   [John Would Wait]

This saying therefore went abroad among the
    brethren,
  that that disciple was not to die.
But Jesus had not said,
  "He is not to die."
But rather,
  "So I wish him to remain until I come.
  Follow Me."

Alleluia, alleluia. John 21, 24   [*John the Witness*]
This is that disciple
   who bears witness concerning these things:
   and we know that his witness is true. Alleluia.

OFFERTORY Ps. 91, 13   [*The Just Man Flourishes*]

The just man shall flourish like the palm tree,
   like a cedar of Lebanon shall he grow.

COMMUNION John 21, 23
               [*Conjectures about John*]

A saying went abroad among the brethren,
   that that disciple was not to die.
But Jesus had not said,
   "He is not to die";
But rather,
   "So I wish him to remain until I come."

Dec. 28 — HOLY INNOCENTS, Martyrs

4th Day Within the Octave of Christmas

INTROIT Ps. 8, 3, 2   [*Praise from Babes*]

Out of the mouth of babes and of sucklings,
   O God,
   You have fashioned praise because of Your
   foes.
(Ps.) O Lord, our Lord,
   how glorious is Your Name over all the
   earth!
Glory be to the Father, etc.
Repeat: **Out of the mouth,** etc., *as far as* (Ps.).

GRADUAL   Ps. 123, 7-8   [*Rescue of the Helpless*]

We were rescued like a bird
   from the fowlers' snare.
Broken was the snare,
   and we were freed.
Our help is in the Name of the Lord,
   Who made heaven and earth.

Alleluia, alleluia.   Ps. 112, 1   [*Children's Praise*]
Praise the Lord, you children,
   praise the Name of the Lord. Alleluia.

OFFERTORY   Ps. 123, 7   [*Set Free Like Little Birds*]

We were rescued like a bird
   from the fowlers' snare.
Broken was the snare
   and we were freed.

COMMUNION   Mt. 2, 18   [*The Cry of Rachel*]

A voice was heard in Rama,
   weeping and loud lamentation;
Rachel weeping for her children,
   and she would not be comforted,
   because they are no more.

Dec. 29, 30, 31 — Days Within the Octave of Christmas

Mass: 3rd Mass of Christmas, p. 21.

Jesus is circumcised.

Jan. 1 — OCTAVE DAY OF CHRISTMAS

THOUGHT FOR TODAY: At the beginning of the new civil year we firmly resolve to live temperately and justly, and piously in the New Year, looking for the "glorious appearance of our great God."

BIBLE AND LITURGY: A Jewish boy was initiated into God's Chosen People by circumcision. Christian initiation into God's Chosen People now is effected by Faith and Baptism. READ: Gen. 17, 9-14; Acts 15, 1-12; Rom. 2, 25-29; Col. 2, 8-15; John 3, 1-8; Acts 9, 10-19.

INTROIT   Isa. 9, 6; Ps. 97, 1   [*The World's Salvation*]

A Child is born to us, a Son is given to us;
    upon His shoulder dominion rests;
And His name shall be called
    the Angel of great counsel.
(Ps.) Sing to the Lord a new song,
    for He has done wondrous deeds.
Glory be to the Father, and to the Son,
    and to the Holy Spirit.
As it was in the beginning, is now, and ever
     shall be,
    world without end. Amen.

A Child is born to us, a Son is given to us;
  upon His shoulder dominion rests;
And His name shall be called
  the Angel of great counsel.

GRADUAL   Ps. 97, 3. 4. 2   [*The Glorious Child*]

All the ends of the earth have seen
  the salvation by our God;
  sing joyfully to God, all you lands.
The Lord has made His salvation known:
  in the sight of the nations He has revealed
    His justice.

Alleluia, alleluia.Heb. 1, 1. 2[*Fulfillment of Prophecies*]
God, Who in diverse ways
  spoke in times past to the fathers
  by the prophets;
Last of all, in these days, has spoken to us
  by His Son. Alleluia.

OFFERTORY   Ps. 88, 12. 15   [*The Lord's World*]

Yours are the heavens, and Yours is the earth;
  the world and its fullness You have founded.
Justice and judgment are the foundation of
  Your throne.

COMMUNION   Ps. 97, 3   [*Salvation for All*]

All the ends of the earth have seen
  the salvation by our God.

At the Name of Jesus every knee should bend.

HOLY NAME OF JESUS

THOUGHT FOR TODAY: The Son of God made Man, was called Jesus, that is, Savior. This name recalls God's ineffable mercy for there is no other name under heaven given to men, by which we must be saved. Let us always use it with gratitude and respect.

BIBLE AND LITURGY: The Redeemer of the world, Lord of God's Chosen People, is called Jesus. There is no other name by which we must be saved. Jesus means "Savior." READ: Phil. 2, 5-11; Acts 3, 1-16; 1 Cor. 1, 10-16; 2 Thess. 1, 11-12; Rom. 10, 5-13.

INTROIT Phil. 2, 10-11; Ps. 8, 2

[*Adoration from All Creation*]

At the Name of Jesus every knee should bend
 of those in heaven, on earth, and under the
  earth,
And every tongue should confess
 that the Lord Jesus Christ
 is in the glory of God the Father.
(Ps.) **O Lord, our Lord,**
 how glorious is Your Name over all the earth!
Glory be to the Father, etc.
Repeat: **At the Name, etc.,** *as far as* (Ps.).

GRADUAL   Ps. 105, 47; Isa. 63, 16

[*Thanks to the Name of God*]

Save us, O Lord, our God,
   and gather us from among the nations,
That we may give thanks to Your holy Name
   and glory in praising You.
You, O Lord, are our Father and our Redeemer;
   from everlasting is Your Name.

Alleluia, alleluia.   Ps. 144, 21   [*Praise God's Name*]
May my mouth speak the praise of the Lord,
   and may all flesh bless His holy Name.
      Alleluia.

OFFERTORY   Ps. 85, 12. 5

[*Glory to the Name of Our God*]

I will give thanks to You, O Lord my God,
   with all my heart,
   and I will glorify Your Name forever;
For You, O Lord, are good and forgiving,
   abounding in kindness to all who call upon
      You. Alleluia.

COMMUNION   Ps. 85, 9-10

[*All Shall Praise the Holy Name*]

All the nations You have made shall come
   and worship You, O Lord,
   and glorify Your Name.
For You are great and do wondrous deeds;
   You alone are God. Alleluia.

Jan. 2-5: Mass: Octave Day of Christmas, p. 28.

Jan. 5 — ST. TELESPHORUS, Pope, Martyr

Mass: Of One or More Popes, p. 231.

*The Magi adore Jesus and offer Him gold,
frankincense and myrrh.*

Jan. 6 — THE EPIPHANY OF OUR LORD

THOUGHT FOR TODAY: Following the example of the Wise Men we adore the newborn King, and offer Him the gold of a loving heart, the frankincense of persevering prayers, and the myrrh of our readiness to labor and suffer for Him.

BIBLE AND LITURGY: Christ's Epiphany, or Manifestation, to the Gentiles teaches us about His kingdom, power and dominion, which will not be confined to the carnal offspring of Abraham. His kingdom is a spiritualized Israel. It is equally destined for all regardless of race or color. READ: Acts 10, 34-48; 13, 16-52 (esp. 46-49); 28, 17-31 (esp. 28).

INTROIT   Mal. 3, 1; 1 Par. 29, 12; Ps. 71, 1

[*The Ruler Is Here*]

Behold the Lord the Ruler is come;
and the kingdom is in His hand,
and power, and dominion.

(Ps.) **O God, with Your Judgment endow the king,**
and with Your justice, the king's son.

Glory be to the Father, and to the Son,
and to the Holy Spirit.

As it was in the beginning, is now, and ever
   shall be,
   world without end. Amen.
Behold the Lord the Ruler is come;
   and the kingdom is in His hand,
   and power, and dominion.

GRADUAL   Isa. 60, 6. 1   [*Gifts from Afar*]

All they from Saba shall come,
   bringing gold and frankincense,
   and proclaiming the praises of the Lord.
Rise up in splendor, O Jerusalem,
   for the glory of the Lord shines upon you.

Alleluia, alleluia.   Matt. 2, 2   [*The Star of Salvation*]
We have seen His star in the East:
   and have come with gifts to worship the
   Lord. Alleluia.

OFFERTORY   Ps. 71, 10-11

[*Tribute from the Whole World*]
The kings of Tharsis and the Isles shall offer
   gifts;
   the kings of Arabia and Saba shall bring
   tribute.
All kings shall pay Him homage;
   all nations shall serve Him.

COMMUNION   Matt. 2, 2   [*Led by Faith*]

We have seen His star in the East
   and have come with gifts to worship the
   Lord.

*Mary and Joseph find Jesus in the temple, listening to the
Doctors of the Law, and asking questions.*

FEAST OF THE HOLY FAMILY

FIRST SUNDAY AFTER EPIPHANY

THOUGHT FOR TODAY: The family is the smaller unit
from which society develops. As long as the love of
God binds the members of the family together, and the
Christian virtues rule in our homes, society will be
prosperous and at peace. Ask in your Mass and Holy
Communion that your conduct in family life may be
guided by the example of the Holy Family at Nazareth.

BIBLE AND LITURGY: The Church wants all Christian
families to take the Holy Family as their example. The
basic attitude toward God, each other and fellow men,
fostered in that Family, will guide all families to real
happiness. READ: Matt. 19, 3-12; Eph. 5, 22-33; 1 Cor.
7, 1-7; 1 John 4, 7-21; 2 Pet. 1, 3-11; Sirach 7, 18-36.

INTROIT   Prov. 23, 24. 25; Ps. 83, 2. 3

[*Joy of Joseph and Mary*]

**The father of the Just will exult with glee;
let Your father and mother have joy;
let her who bore You exult.**

**(Ps.) How lovely is Your dwelling place,
O Lord of hosts;**

My soul yearns and pines
  for the courts of the Lord.
Glory be to the Father, and to the Son,
  and to the Holy Spirit.
As it was in the beginning, is now, and ever
    shall be,
  world without end. Amen.
The father of the Just will exult with glee;
  let Your father and mother have joy;
  let her who bore You exult.

GRADUAL   Ps. 26, 4; 83, 5   [Happy Household]

One thing I ask of the Lord;
  this I seek:
To dwell in the house of the Lord
  all the days of my life.
Happy they who dwell in Your house, O Lord!
  continually they praise You.

Alleluia, alleluia.   Isa. 45, 15   [Hidden God]
Truly, You are a hidden God,
  the God of Israel, the Savior. Alleluia.

OFFERTORY   Luke 2, 22   [Family Worship]

The parents of Jesus took Him up to Jerusalem,
  to present Him to the Lord.

COMMUNION   Luke 2, 51   [Obedience and Love]

Jesus went down with them
  and came to Nazareth,
  and was subject to them.

FIRST SUNDAY AFTER EPIPHANY

This Mass is said on "free days" from Monday following the First Sunday after Epiphany until January 12 inclusive.

INTROIT   Ps. 99, 1   [*Eternal King*]

Upon a high throne I saw a man sitting,
  Whom a multitude of angels adore, singing in unison :
"Behold Him, the Name of Whose empire is forever."

(Ps.) **Sing joyfully to God, all you lands;**
  serve the Lord with gladness.

Glory be to the Father, etc.

Repeat: **Upon a high,** etc., *as far as* (Ps.).

GRADUAL   Ps. 71, 18. 3   [*Reign of Peace*]

Blessed be the Lord, the God of Israel,
  Who alone does wondrous deeds.
The mountains shall yield peace for the people,
  and the hills justice.

Alleluia, alleluia.   Ps. 99, 1   [*Sing with Joy*]
Sing joyfully to God, all you lands;
  serve the Lord with gladness. Alleluia.

OFFERTORY   Ps. 99, 1. 2   [*Sing and Serve*]

Sing joyfully to God, all you lands;
  serve the Lord with gladness;
  come before Him with joyful song.
Know that the Lord is God.

COMMUNION   Lk. 2, 48. 49   [*My Father's Business*]

"Son, why have You done so to us?
   In sorrow Your father and I have been seek-
    ing you."
"How is it that you sought Me?
   Did you not know that I must be about My
    father's business?"

Jan. 11 — ST. HYGINUS, Pope, Martyr

Mass: Of one or More Popes, p. 231.

Jan. 13 — THE COMMEMORATION OF THE BAPTISM OF OUR LORD

Mass: The Epiphany of Our Lord, p. 32.

Jesus changes water into wine at the Wedding Feast.

SECOND SUNDAY AFTER EPIPHANY

THOUGHT FOR TODAY: Imitating Mary's life of charity and relying on her powerful intercession, we may find a sure way out of our daily troubles, as the bridegroom did at the wedding at Cana.

BIBLE AND LITURGY: By working the miracle of changing water into wine, our Lord manifested His glory. This was the first of His many signs. The faithful reaction of His disciples should be ours. Faith is first of all a grace of God, but Jesus' signs can help those "of little Faith" to come to that complete surrender of mind and heart, which means "Faith" in the true Biblical meaning of the word. READ: Matt. 9, 1-8 (esp. 8); John 11, 1-53 (esp. 42); 1 Cor. 15, 12-19; John 3, 1-2; Matt 8, 23-27 (esp. 27).

INTROIT Ps. 65, 4. 1. 2 [*Proclaim His Glory*]

Let all on earth worship You, O God, and sing praise to You,
  sing praise to Your Name, Most High.
(Ps.) Shout joyfully to God, all you on earth,
  sing praise to the glory of His Name;
  proclaim His glorious praise.
Glory be to the Father, and to the Son,
  and to the Holy Spirit.

As it was in the beginning, is now, and ever
  shall be,
    world without end. Amen.
Let all on earth worship You, O God, and sing
  praise to You,
    sing praise to Your Name, Most High.

GRADUAL Ps. 106, 20-21 [*Thanks*]

The Lord sent forth His Word to heal them
  and to snatch them from destruction.
Let them give thanks to the Lord for His
  kindness,
    and His wondrous deeds to the children of
    men.

Alleluia, alleluia. Ps. 148, 2 [*Praise*]

Praise the Lord, all you His angels,
    praise Him, all You His hosts. Alleluia.

OFFERTORY Ps. 65, 1-2. 16 [*The Lord's Goodness*]

Shout joyfully to God, all you on earth,
    sing praise to the glory of His Name.
Hear now, all you who fear God, while I declare
  what the Lord has done for me.

COMMUNION John 2, 7. 8. 9. 10-11 [*The Sign*]

The Lord said,
    "Fill the jars with water and take to the
    chief steward."
When the chief steward had tasted the water
  after it had become wine,
He said to the bridegroom,
    "You have kept the good wine until now."
This first miracle Jesus worked
    in the presence of His disciples.

The centurion begs Jesus to come and heal his servant.

THIRD SUNDAY AFTER EPIPHANY

THOUGHT FOR TODAY: "Lord, I am not worthy to have You enter my house." Receiving Christ in frequent Holy Communion with deep humility and living faith in His Divinity is the best assurance that we shall gain eternal salvation.

BIBLE AND LITURGY: Faith, humility and confidence should mark our approach to God. Like the centurion, many persons in the Bible gave an example of faith, i.e., total self-surrender to God, Who reveals Himself to us. The most outstanding was Abraham, who is considered by the Church as the father of all the faithful. READ: Gen. 15: 1-8 (esp. 6); Gal. 3, 3-9; Rom. 4, 18-25; Matt. 17, 14-20; Luke 17, 5-6.

INTROIT   Ps. 96, 7. 8. 1   [*Adore Him*]

Adore God, all you His angels:
    Sion hears and is glad,
      and the cities of Juda rejoice.

(Ps.) **The Lord is King; let the earth rejoice;**
    let the many isles be glad.

Glory be to the Father, and to the Son,
    and to the Holy Spirit.

As it was in the beginning, is now, and ever
    shall be,
  world without end. Amen.
Adore God, all you His angels:
  Sion hears and is glad,
  and the cities of Juda rejoice.

GRADUAL   Ps. 101, 16-17   [*Revering God's Glory*]

The nations shall revere Your Name, O Lord,
  and all the kings of the earth Your glory.
For the Lord has rebuilt Sion,
  and He shall appear in His glory.

 Alleluia, alleluia. Ps. 96, 1   [*Rejoice in the King*]
The Lord is King; let the earth rejoice;
  let the many isles be glad. Alleluia.

OFFERTORY   Ps. 117, 16. 17   [*Might of the Lord*]

The right hand of the Lord has struck with
    power:
  the right hand of the Lord has exalted me;
I shall not die, but live,
  and declare the works of the Lord.

COMMUNION   Luke 4, 22   [*Marvels of the Word*]

All marveled at the words
  that came from the mouth of God.

FOURTH SUNDAY AFTER EPIPHANY

THOUGHT FOR TODAY: Our life with its temptations and struggles is often similar to a voyage on a stormy sea. If we do what is in our power and persevere in prayer, the Master of Nature will do the rest, and there will come a great calm and peace.

BIBLE AND LITURGY: Our Lord showed His power by rebuking the wind and the sea. He has that power because He is Lord of all. We must see Christ as Lord of His Church even when His power is temporarily hidden. READ: Matt. 9, 1-8; Luke 4, 33-37; Mark 13, 21-27; Apoc. 5, 9-14; 12, 10-12.

Mass: Same as on p. 40.

FIFTH SUNDAY AFTER EPIPHANY

THOUGHT FOR TODAY: God is the Creator of the world, and what He has made is good. How then do we account for the evil in the world? Because man has free will, he can misuse God's gifts and transgress His Commandments and do evil. He can become an enemy of his greatest Benefactor. It would be foolish to delay our conversion until God separates the weeds from the wheat.

BIBLE AND LITURGY: The problem of good and evil is often discussed in the Bible. Man has a free will and can misuse God's favors. God, Who is a loving Father, may also permit good people to undergo suffering and frustration to cleanse them from all attachment to evil. Often evil is a mystery. READ: Gen. 4, 1-16; Job 1-2; Ps. 50.

Mass: Same as on p. 40.

SIXTH SUNDAY AFTER EPIPHANY

THOUGHT FOR TODAY: We thank God for the shelter given us under the tree of Christ's Church. But it will not profit us if the teaching of Christ does not "leaven" our thoughts, words and deeds, and stimulate us to true Catholic Action.

BIBLE AND LITURGY: Jesus instructs us about the very nature of the Church by using parables and comparisons. The parables of the mustard seed and the leaven teach us the influence of the Church all over the world. READ: other parables and comparisons also concerning the Church: John 10, 11-18; 18, 33-37; 15, 1-7; 1 Cor. 12, 13-31; Matt. 13, 47-50; Apoc. 21, 1-4.

Mass: Same as on p. 40.

The first laborers and the last receive the same day's pay.

SEPTUAGESIMA SUNDAY

THOUGHT FOR TODAY: God holds out a great reward to us, but we must work to receive it. Unfortunately, we are by nature more inclined to endure hardships for the perishable goods of this life than we are for our eternal happiness in the Kingdom of God.

BIBLE AND LITURGY: The Church sees human nature as wounded by sin. Man is naturally inclined to evil. That is the reason why life often becomes a battle, labor and hardship. Lent and also the pre-Lenten season, which begins with this Sunday, remind us of this fact. READ: Gen. 3; Heb. 10, 32-39; 12, 1-13; 1 Cor. 9, 24-27; 2 Tim. 4, 6-8; Ps. 34.

INTROIT   Ps. 17, 5. 6. 7. 2. 3   [*My Help in Terrors*]

The terrors of death surged round about me,
    the cords of the nether world enmeshed me.
In my distress I called upon the Lord;
    from His holy temple He heard my voice.
(Ps.) I love You, O Lord, my strength,
    O Lord, my rock, my fortress, my deliverer.
Glory be to the Father, and to the Son,
    and to the Holy Spirit.
As it was in the beginning, is now, and ever
        shall be,
    world without end. Amen.

The terrors of death surged round about me,
  the cords of the nether world enmeshed me.
In my distress I called upon the Lord;
  from His holy temple He heard my voice.

GRADUAL   Ps. 9, 10. 11. 19. 20   [Trust in God's Help]

A stronghold in times of distress;
They trust in You who cherish You;
  for You forsake not those who seek You,
    O Lord.
For the needy shall not always be forgotten;
  nor shall the hope of the afflicted forever
    perish;
Rise, O Lord, let not man prevail.

TRACT   Ps. 129, 1-4   [Mercy for Sinners]

Out of the depths I cry to You, O Lord;
  Lord, hear my voice!
Let Your ears be attentive
  to the prayer of Your servant.
If You, O Lord, mark iniquities:
  Lord, who can stand it?
But with You is forgiveness,
  and by reason of Your law
  I have waited for You, O Lord.

OFFERTORY   Ps. 91, 2   [Thanks and Praise]

It is good to give thanks to the Lord,
  and to sing praise to Your Name, Most High.

COMMUNION   Ps. 30, 17. 18   [God's Kindness]

Let Your face shine upon Your servant;
  save me in Your kindness.
O Lord, let me not be put to shame,
  for I call upon You.

The sower sows his seed.

SEXAGESIMA SUNDAY

THOUGHT FOR TODAY: Jesus is the Divine Sower. His word and example will yield fruit a hundredfold in our hearts, as it did in the life of St. Paul, if we do not busy ourselves with thousands of unnecessary things which divert us from the one necessary thing, namely, the salvation of our souls.

BIBLE AND LITURGY: Man, weak in his fallen nature, can be strengthened by the strength of Christ. His Word can dwell in us. But we must receive God's Word with an open mind and cooperate in order that it may grow and bear fruit in us. Hence, regular Bible reading is extremely important. READ: Prov. 30, 5; John 5, 24; Rom. 15, 1-6; 2 Tim. 3, 10-17; 2 Pet. 1, 16-21.

INTROIT Ps. 43, 23-26 [*Come to Our Aid*]

Awake! Why are You asleep, O Lord?
  Arise! Cast us not off forever!
Why do You hide Your face,
  forgetting our oppression?
Our bodies are pressed to the earth;
  arise, O Lord, help us, and deliver us.
(Ps.) O God, our ears have heard,
  our fathers have declared to us.
Glory be to the Father, and to the Son,
  and to the Holy Spirit.

As it was in the beginning, is now, and ever
    shall be, world without end. Amen.
Awake! Why are You asleep, O Lord?
    Arise! Cast us not off forever!
Why do You hide Your face,
    forgetting our oppression?
Our bodies are pressed to the earth;
    arise, O Lord, help us, and deliver us.

GRADUAL   Ps. 82, 19. 14   [*You Are One God*]

Let the nations know that God is Your name;
    You alone are the Most High over all the
    earth.
O my God, make them like leaves in a whirl-
    wind,
    like chaff before the wind.

TRACT   Ps. 59, 4. 6   [*The God of Power*]

You have rocked the country, O Lord,
    and split it open.
Repair the cracks in it,
    for it is tottering.
That they may flee out of bowshot;
    that Your loved ones may escape.

OFFERTORY   Ps. 16, 5. 6. 7   [*God's Care of the Trustful*]

Make my steps steadfast in Your paths,
    that my feet may not falter.
Incline Your ear to me;
    hear my word.
Show Your wondrous kindness, O Lord,
    Savior of those who trust in You.

COMMUNION   Ps. 42, 4   [*Joy of God's Altar*]

I will go in to the altar of God,
    the God of my gladness and joy.

Jesus cures a blind man.

QUINQUAGESIMA SUNDAY

THOUGHT FOR TODAY: As the blind man asked sight of Jesus, so we ought to implore Christ to cure our spiritual blindness. We are spiritually blind if we do not see that our busy life on earth is worthless unless it be rooted in the love of God and of our neighbor.

BIBLE AND LITURGY: Charity is the first and most important law of the Christian Religion. It is a sign by which Christians should be recognized. We should pray often: "Lord, that I may see it that way!" READ: Luke 10, 25-37; 1 John 2, 3-11; 3, 16-18; 4, 7-21; Matt. 5, 21-26; Eph. 4, 25-32; Matt. 5, 43-48; Gal. 6, 10;

INTROIT Ps. 30, 3. 4 [*God Our Strength*]

Be my rock of refuge, O God,
 a stronghold to give me safety;
You are my strength and my fortress;
 for Your Name's sake You will lead and
  guide me.
(Ps.) In You, O Lord, I take refuge;
 let me never be put to shame.
In Your justice rescue me,
 and deliver me.
Glory be to the Father, and to the Son,
 and to the Holy Spirit.

As it was in the beginning, is now, and ever
shall be,
world without end. Amen.
Be my rock of refuge, O God,
a stronghold to give me safety;
You are my strength and my fortress;
for Your Name's sake You will lead and
guide me.

GRADUAL Ps. 76, 15. 16 [God Delivers Us]

You are the God Who alone works wonders;
among the peoples You have made known
Your power.
With Your strong arm You delivered Your
people,
the sons of Israel and Joseph.

TRACT Ps. 99, 1-2 [Sing to God]

Sing joyfully to God all you lands;
serve the Lord with gladness.
Come before Him with joyful song;
know that the Lord is God.
He made us, His we are;
His people, the flock He tends.

OFFERTORY Ps. 118, 12-13 [Learning God's Law]

Blessed are You, O Lord;
teach me Your statutes.
With my lips I declare
all the ordinances of Your mouth.

COMMUNION Ps. 77, 29-30 [All Were Filled]

They ate and were wholly surfeited;
the Lord had brought them what they craved:
they were not defrauded of that which they
craved.

ASH WEDNESDAY

BLESSING OF THE ASHES

ANTIPHON   Ps. 68, 17. 2   [*Turn in Mercy*]

Hear us, O Lord, for bounteous is Your kindness;
    in Your great mercy turn toward us, O Lord.
(Ps.) Save me, O God,
    for the waters threaten my life.
Glory be to the Father, etc.
Repeat: **Hear us, O Lord,** etc., *as far as* (Ps.).

IMPOSITION OF THE ASHES

ANTIPHON   Jl. 2, 13   [*Let Us Fast*]

Let us change our garments for ashes and sackcloth:
    let us fast and lament before the Lord:
For plenteous in mercy is our God
    to forgive our sins.

ANOTHER ANTIPHON   Jl. 2, 17; Est. 13, 17

[*Spare Your People*]

Between the porch and the altar,
    let the priests, the ministers of the Lord, weep,
    and say, "Spare, O Lord, Your people;
And close not the mouths
    of those who sing to You, O Lord."

RESPONSORY   Est. 13; Jl. 2; Ps. 78, 9   [*We Are Sinners*]

Let us amend for the better in those things
    in which we have sinned through ignorance,

Lest suddenly overtaken by the day of death,
   we seek time for repentance
   and are not able to find it.
* Attend, O Lord, and have mercy;
   for we have sinned against You. *
Help us, O God, our Savior;
   and because of the glory of Your Name,
   O Lord, deliver us.
Repeat: **Attend, O Lord,** etc.

Glory be to the Father, etc.

Repeat: **Attend, O Lord,** etc.

THE MASS

INTROIT   Wis. 11, 24. 25. 27; Ps. 56, 2

[Reject Not Your Creatures]

You have mercy on all, O Lord,
   and hate none of the things which You have
      made,
Overlooking the sins of men for the sake of
      repentance,
   and sparing them:
   because You are the Lord our God.
(Ps.) Have pity on me, O God; have pity on me,
   for in You I take refuge.
Glory be to the Father, etc.
Repeat: **You have mercy,** etc., *as far as* (Ps.).

GRADUAL   Ps. 56, 2. 4   [God's Pity]

Have pity on me, O God, have pity on me,
   for in You I take refuge.
He has sent from heaven and saved me;
He has made those a reproach who trample
   upon me.

TRACT   Ps. 102, 10; 78, 8-9   [Forget Our Sins]

O Lord, deal with us not according to our sins,
    nor requite us according to our crimes.
O Lord, remember not against us the iniquities
    of the past;
May Your compassion quickly come to us,
    for we are brought very low.
Help us, O God, our Savior,
    because of the glory of Your Name, O Lord;
Deliver us and pardon our sins
    for Your Name's sake.

OFFERTORY   Ps. 29, 2-3   [The Lord Hears Us]

I will extol You, O Lord, for You drew me clear
    and did not let my enemies rejoice over me.
O Lord,
    I cried out to You and You healed me.

COMMUNION   Ps. 1, 2. 3   [Loving Thoughtfulness]

He who shall meditate day and night
    on the law of the Lord
    shall yield his fruit in due season.

THURSDAY — After Ash Wednesday

INTROIT   Ps. 54, 17, 19, 20. 23. 2. 3   [Hear My Prayer]

When I called upon the Lord,
    He heard my voice
And freed me from those who war against me;
And He humbled them,
    He Who is before all ages
    and remains forever:
Cast your care upon the Lord,
    and He will support you.

(Ps.) **Hearken, O God, to my prayer;**
  turn not away from my pleading;
  give heed to me, and answer me.

Glory be to the Father, etc.

Repeat: **When I called,** etc., *as far as* (Ps.).

GRADUAL Ps. 54, 23, 17, 18. 19 [*Support from the Lord*]

Cast your care upon the Lord,
  and He will support you.
When I called upon the Lord,
  He heard my voice
  and freed me from those who war against me.

OFFERTORY Ps. 24, 1-3 [*Trust the Lord*]

To You, O Lord, I lift up my soul:
  in You, O my God, I trust;
Let me not be put to shame,
  let not my enemies exult over me.
No one who waits on You shall be put to shame.

COMMUNION Ps. 50, 21 [*Acceptable Sacrifice*]

You shall be pleased with due sacrifices,
  burnt offerings and holocausts on your altar,
  O Lord.

FRIDAY — After Ash Wednesday

INTROIT Ps. 29; 11. 2 [*Pity from the Lord*]

The Lord has heard, and has had pity on me;
  the Lord became my helper.

(Ps.) **I will extol You, O Lord, for You drew**
  me clear
  and did not let my enemies rejoice over me.

Glory be to the Father, etc.

Repeat: **The Lord has heard,** etc., *as far as* (Ps.).

GRADUAL   Ps. 26, 4   [*The Beauty of God's House*]

One thing I ask of the Lord;
  this I seek:
To dwell in the house of the Lord.
That I may gaze on the loveliness of the Lord
  and be protected by His holy temple.

TRACT   Ps. 102, 10; 78, 8-9   [*Forget Our Sins*]

O Lord, deal with us not according to our sins,
  nor requite us according to our crimes.
O Lord, remember not against us the iniquities
    of the past;
    may Your compassion quickly come to us,
    for we are brought very low.
Help us, O God, our Savior,
    because of the glory of Your Name, O Lord;
Deliver us and pardon our sins
    for Your Name's sake.

OFFERTORY   Ps. 118, 154. 125   [*Alert to God's Will*]

O Lord, for the sake of Your promise give me
    life,
    that I may know Your decrees.

COMMUNION   Ps. 2, 11-12   [*Serve the Lord*]

Serve the Lord with fear,
    and rejoice before Him with trembling;
Embrace discipline,
    lest you perish from the just way.

SATURDAY — After Ash Wednesday

INTROIT   Ps. 29, 11. 2   [The Lord Hears Us]

The Lord has heard, and has had pity on me;
  the Lord became my helper.
(Ps.) I will extol You, O Lord, for You drew
  me clear
  and did not let my enemies rejoice over me.
Glory be to the Father, etc.
Repeat: **The Lord has heard,** etc., *as far as* (Ps.).

GRADUAL   Ps. 26, 4   [Beauty of God's House]

One thing I ask of the Lord;
  this I seek:
To dwell in the house of the Lord.
That I may gaze on the loveliness of the Lord
  and be protected by His holy temple.

OFFERTORY   Ps. 118, 154. 125   [Alert to God's Will]

O Lord, for the sake of Your promise give me
  life,
  that I may know Your decrees.

COMMUNION   Ps. 2, 11-12   [Do Penance]

Serve the Lord with fear,
  and rejoice before Him with trembling;
Embrace discipline,
  lest you perish from the just way.

Jesus repels the temptations of Satan.

FIRST SUNDAY IN LENT

THOUGHT FOR TODAY: Christ permitted Himself to be tempted by Satan. Why, then, should we be surprised if we have to struggle against the malice and snares of the devil! Our strength to resist lies in fasting, in guarding and controlling our senses, in almsgiving, in prayer, and in uniting ourselves with Christ in Holy Mass and Communion.

BIBLE AND LITURGY: Temptation to go freely and deliberately against God's will may come at times from our nature, which is disrupted through sin. At other times, the devil and bad company may bring on temptations. READ: Apoc. 12; 1 Pet. 5, 5-11; 2 Cor. 11, 1-15 (esp. 3 and 14); 2 Tim. 2, 19-26; James 1, 12-18; 1 Cor. 10, 12-13; Matt. 6, 13.

INTROIT   Ps. 90, 15. 16   [*Glorified by Prayer*]

He shall call upon Me, and I will answer him;
   I will deliver him and glorify him;
   with length of days I will gratify him.

(Ps.) You who dwell in the shelter of the Most High,
   shall abide in the shadow of the Almighty.

Glory be to the Father, and to the Son,
  and to the Holy Spirit.

As it was in the beginning, is now, and ever
    shall be,
  world without end. Amen.

He shall call upon Me, and I will answer him;
  I will deliver him and glorify him;
    with length of days I will gratify him.

GRADUAL Ps. 90, 11-12 [Our Angel's Care]

To His angels God has given command about
    you,
  that they guard you in all your ways.
Upon their hands they shall bear you up,
  lest you dash your foot against a stone.

TRACT Ps. 90, 1-7, 11-16

[The Most High Watches Over Us]

You who dwell in the shelter of the Most High,
  shall abide in the shadow of the Almighty.
Say to the Lord, "My refuge and my fortress,
  my God, in Whom I trust."
For He will rescue you from the snare of the
    fowler,
  from the destroying pestilence.
With His pinions He will cover you,
  and under His wings you shall take refuge.
His faithfulness is a buckler and a shield;
  you shall not fear the terror of the night.
Nor the arrow that flies by day;
  nor the pestilence that roams in darkness;
  nor the devastating plague at noon.
Though a thousand fall at your side,

ten thousand at your right side,
near you it shall not come.
For to His angels He has given command about
you,
that they may guard you in all your ways.
Upon their hands they shall bear you up,
lest you dash your foot against a stone.
You shall tread upon the asp and the viper;
you shall trample down the lion and the
dragon.
Because he clings to Me, I will deliver him;
I will set him on high because he acknowl-
edges My Name.
He shall call upon Me, and I will answer him;
I will be with him in distress.
I will deliver him and glorify him;
with length of days I will gratify him
and will show him My salvation.

OFFERTORY   Ps. 90, 4. 5   [Protection of God]

With His pinions the Lord will cover you,
and under His wings you shall take refuge;
His faithfulness is a buckler and a shield.

COMMUNION   Ps. 90, 4. 5   [Protection from God]

With His pinions the Lord will cover you,
and under His wings you shall take refuge;
His faithfulness is a buckler and a shield.

MONDAY — After the 1st Sunday in Lent

INTROIT   Ps. 122, 2. 1   [*We Look up to God*]

As the eyes of servants
  are on the hands of their masters,
So are our eyes on the Lord, our God,
  till He have pity on us.
Have pity on us, O Lord, have pity on us.
(Ps.) To You I lift up my eyes,
  Who are enthroned in heaven.
Glory be to the Father, etc.
Repeat: As the eyes, etc., *as far as* (Ps.).

GRADUAL   Ps. 83, 10. 9   [*Hear Us*]

Behold, O God, our protector,
  and look upon Your servants.
O Lord God of hosts,
  hear the prayers of Your servants.

TRACT   Ps. 102, 10; 78, 8-9   [*Forget Our Sins*]

O Lord, deal with us not according to our sins,
  nor requite us according to our crimes.
O Lord, remember not against us the iniquities
    of the past;
  may Your compassion quickly come to us,
  for we are brought very low.
Help us, O God, our Savior,
  because of the glory of Your Name, O Lord;
Deliver us and pardon our sins
  for Your Name's sake.

OFFERTORY Ps. 118, 18, 26. 73 [Attentive to God's Word]

I will lift up my eyes, that I may consider
  Your wonders, O Lord;
Teach me Your statutes;
  give me discernment that I may learn Your
    commands.

COMMUNION   Matt. 25, 40. 34   [Mercy Brings Mercy]

Amen I say to you:
  What you did for one of these, the least of
    My brethren,
  you did for Me:
Come, blessed of My Father,
  take possession of the kingdom prepared for
    you from the foundation of the world.

TUESDAY — After the 1st Sunday in Lent

INTROIT   Ps. 89, 1. 2   [Our Eternal Refuge]

Lord, You have been our refuge
  through all generations;
  from everlasting to everlasting You are.
(Ps.) Before the mountains were begotten
  and the earth and the world were brought
    forth,
  from everlasting to everlasting, You are God.
Glory be to the Father, etc.
Repeat: **Lord, You have,** etc., *as far as* (Ps.).

GRADUAL   Ps. 140, 2   [The Incense of Prayer]

Let my prayer come like incense
  before You, O Lord.

The lifting up of my hands,
  like the evening sacrifice.

OFFERTORY   Ps. 30, 15-16   [*You Are My God*]

My trust is in You, O Lord;
  I say, "You are my God."
In Your hands is my destiny.

COMMUNION   Ps. 4, 2   [*Have Pity in My Distress*]

When I call, answer me, O my just God,
  You Who relieve me when I am in distress;
  have pity on me, O Lord, and hear my prayer!

EMBER WEDNESDAY IN LENT

INTROIT   Ps. 24, 6, 3. 22. 1-2   [*The Lord's Compassion*]

Remember that Your compassion, O Lord,
  and Your kindness are from of old;
Let not our enemies exult over us;
Deliver us, O God of Israel,
  from all our tribulations.
(Ps.) To You I lift up my soul, O Lord;
  in You, O my God, I trust;
  let me not be put to shame.
Glory be to the Father, etc.
Repeat: **Remember,** etc., *as far as* (Ps.).

  After the 1st Lesson:

GRADUAL   Ps. 24, 17-18   [*Relieve My Sufferings*]

Relieve the troubles of my heart,
  and bring me out of distress, O Lord.
Put an end to my affliction and my suffering
  and take away all my sins.

After the 2nd Lesson:

TRACT   Ps. 24, 17, 18. 1-4   [*I Lift Up My Soul*]

Bring me out of distress, O Lord;
Put an end to my affliction and my suffering,
   and take away all my sins.
To You, I lift up my soul, O Lord.
   In You, O my God, I trust;
Let me not be put to shame,
   let not my enemies exult over me.
No one who waits for You shall be put to
   shame;
   those shall be put to shame who heedlessly
   break faith.

OFFERTORY   Ps. 118, 47. 48   [*Delight in The Law*]

I will delight in Your commands,
   which I love exceedingly.
And I will lift up my hands to Your commands
   which I love.

COMMUNION   Ps. 5, 2-4   [*Hear My Cry*]

Attend to my sighing,
Heed my call for help,
   my King and my God!
To You, I pray, O Lord.

THURSDAY — After the 1st Sunday in Lent

INTROIT   Ps. 95, 6. 1   [*Glory of God*]

Splendor and majesty go before Him;
   praise and grandeur are in His sanctuary.
(Ps.) Sing to the Lord a new song;
   sing to the Lord, all you lands.
Glory be to the Father, etc.

Repeat: **Splendor,** etc., *as far as* (Ps.).

GRADUAL   Ps. 16, 8. 2   [*Keep Me Close*]

Keep me, O Lord, as the apple of Your eye;
  hide me in the shadow of Your wings.
From You let my judgment come;
  Your eyes behold what is right.

OFFERTORY   Ps. 33, 8-9

[*Taste the Goodness of the Lord*]

The angel of the Lord encamps
  around those who fear Him, and delivers
  them.
Taste and see how good the Lord is.

COMMUNION   John 6, 52   [*Saving Bread*]

The bread that I will give is My Flesh
  for the life of the world.

EMBER FRIDAY IN LENT

INTROIT   Ps. 24, 17. 18. 1-2   [*Take Away My Distress*]

Bring me out of distress, O Lord;
Put an end to my affliction and my suffering,
  and take away all my sins.
(Ps.) To You, O Lord, I lift up my soul.
  In You, O my God, I trust;
Let me not be put to shame.
Glory be to the Father, etc.
Repeat: **Bring me,** etc., *as far as* (Ps.).

GRADUAL   Ps. 85, 2. 6   [*Plea for Salvation*]

Save Your servant, O my God, who trusts in
    You.
Hearken, O Lord, to my prayer.

TRACT　　Ps. 102, 10; 78, 8-9　　　[*Forget Our Sins*]

O Lord, deal with us not according to our sins,
　　nor requite us according to our crimes.
O Lord, remember not against us the iniquities
　　　of the past;
　　may Your compassion quickly come to us,
　　for we are brought very low.
Help us, O God, our Savior,
　　because of the glory of Your Name, O Lord;
Deliver us and pardon our sins
　　for Your Name's sake.

OFFERTORY　　Ps. 102, 2. 5　　[*Spirit of Thankfulness*]

Bless the Lord, O my soul,
　　and forget not all His benefits;
And your youth shall be renewed like the
　　eagle's.

COMMUNION　　Ps. 6, 11　　[*Conquest of Enemies*]

All my enemies shall be put to shame in utter
　　terror;
　　they shall fall back in sudden shame.

EMBER SATURDAY IN LENT

Short Form of the Mass

INTROIT　　Ps. 87, 3. 2　　　[*Hear My Prayer*]

Let my prayer come before You;
　　incline Your ear to my call for help, O Lord.

(Ps.) **O Lord, the God of my salvation,**
  by day I cry out,
    at night I clamor in Your presence.

Glory be to the Father, etc.
Repeat: **Let my prayer,** etc., *as far as* (Ps.).

After the 1st Lesson:

GRADUAL   Ps. 78, 9. 10   [Our God Forgives]

Pardon our sins, O Lord;
Why should the nations say,
  "Where is their God?"
Help us, O God, our Savior;
  because of the glory of Your Name, O Lord,
    deliver us.

After the 2nd Lesson:

TRACT   Ps. 116, 1-2   [Give Praise]

Praise the Lord, all you nations;
  glorify Him, all you peoples!
For steadfast is His kindness toward us,
  and the fidelity of the Lord endures forever.

OFFERTORY   Ps. 87, 2-3   [Pleading Day and Night]

O Lord, the God of my salvation,
  by day I cry out,
    at night I clamor in Your presence.
Let my prayer come before You, O Lord.

COMMUNION   Ps. 7, 2   [God, My Refuge]

O Lord my God, in You I take refuge;
  save me from all my pursuers and rescue me.

*Jesus is transfigured before Peter, John and James,
who see Moses and Elia with Him.*

SECOND SUNDAY IN LENT

THOUGHT FOR TODAY: The Transfiguration of Our Lord
gives us an idea of the beauty of a soul in the state of
sanctifying grace.

BIBLE AND LITURGY: In the midst of trials and tribulations, it is well to keep our eyes on the Transfiguration
and preserve the divine life in our souls. Temptations,
sufferings, battles and penance, if accepted in Faith,
transfigure us completely and make us partakers of
Christ's glory. READ: 1 Cor. 6, 12-20; Matt. 10, 16-33;
Rom. 7, 24-25; 8, 18-23; 2 Cor. 3, 12-18; 5, 1-10.

INTROIT   Ps. 24, 6. 3. 22   [*The Lord Ever Kind*]

**Remember that Your compassion, O Lord,
and Your kindness are from of old;
Let not our enemies exult over us;
deliver us, O God of Israel, from all our
tribulations.
(Ps.) To You I lift my soul, O Lord;
in You, O my God, I trust;
let me not be put to shame.
Glory be to the Father, and to the Son,
and to the Holy Spirit.**

As it was in the beginning, is now, and ever
shall be, world without end. Amen.
Remember that Your compassion, O Lord,
and Your kindness are from of old;
Let not our enemies exult over us;
deliver us, O God of Israel, from all our
tribulations.

GRADUAL   Ps. 24, 17. 18   [Bring Calm to My Soul]

Relieve the troubles of my heart
and bring me out of my distress, O Lord.
Put an end to my affliction and my suffering,
and take away all my sins.

TRACT   Ps. 105, 1-4   [Joy of the Good]

Give thanks to the Lord, for He is good,
for His kindness endures forever.
Who can tell the mighty deeds of the Lord,
or proclaim all His praises?
Happy are they who observe what is right,
who do always what is just.
Remember us, O Lord, as You favor Your
people;
visit us with Your saving help.

OFFERTORY   Ps. 118, 47. 48   [Love of God's Law]

I will delight in Your commands,
which I love exceedingly;
And I will lift up my hands to Your commands,
which I love.

COMMUNION   Ps. 5, 2-4   [Cry to the King]

Attend to my sighing;
Heed my call for help,
my King and my God!
To You I pray, O Lord.

MONDAY — After the 2nd Sunday in Lent

INTROIT   Ps. 25, 11-12. 1   [*The Lord My Savior*]

Redeem me, O Lord,
  and have pity on me;
My foot stands on level ground;
  in the assemblies I will bless the Lord.
(Ps.) Do me justice, O Lord! for I have walked
    in integrity,
  and in the Lord I trust without wavering.
Glory be to the Father, etc.
Repeat: **Redeem me,** etc., *as far as* (Ps.).

GRADUAL   Ps. 69, 6. 3   [*Deliver Me*]

You are my help and my deliverer;
  O Lord, hold not back!
Let my enemies be put to shame and
    confounded,
  who seek my life.

TRACT   Ps. 102, 10; 78, 8-9   [*Forget Our Sins*]

O Lord, deal with us not according to our sins,
  nor requite us according to our crimes.
O Lord, remember not against us the iniquities
    of the past;
  may Your compassion quickly come to us,
  for we are brought very low.
Help us, O God, our Savior,
  because of the glory of Your Name, O Lord;
Deliver us and pardon our sins
  for Your Name's sake.

OFFERTORY   Ps. 15, 7. 8   [*The Lord at My Side*]

I bless the Lord, Who counsels me;
I set the Lord ever before me;

with Him at my right hand, I shall not be
moved.

COMMUNION   Ps. 8, 2   [*Glory of God*]

O Lord, our Lord,
    how glorious is Your Name over all the
    earth!   _____

TUESDAY — After the 2nd Sunday in Lent

INTROIT   Ps. 26, 8. 9. 1   [*Seeking the Lord*]

To You my heart speaks; You my glance seeks;
    Your presence, O Lord, I seek.
Hide not Your face from me.
(Ps.) The Lord is my light and my salvation;
    whom should I fear?
Glory be to the Father, etc.
Repeat: **To You my heart,** etc., *as far as* (Ps.).

GRADUAL   Ps. 54, 23, 17, 18. 19 [*God's Support of Us*]

Cast your care upon the Lord,
    and He will support you.
When I called upon the Lord, He heard my
    voice
    and freed me from those who war against
    me.

OFFERTORY   Ps. 50, 3   [*Forgiveness*]

Have mercy on me, O Lord,
    in the greatness of Your compassion;
    O Lord, wipe out my offense.

COMMUNION   Ps. 9, 2-3   [*Praise to God*]

I will declare all Your wondrous deeds;
I will be glad and exult in You;
    I will sing praise to Your Name, Most High.

_____

WEDNESDAY — After the 2nd Sunday in Lent

INTROIT   Ps. 37, 22-23. 2   [Hasten to Forgive]

Forsake me not, O Lord;
  my God, be not far from me!
Hasten to help me,
  O Lord, my salvation!
(Ps.) O Lord, in Your anger punish me not,
  in Your wrath chastise me not.
Glory be to the Father, etc.
Repeat: Forsake me not, etc., *as far as* (Ps.).

GRADUAL   Ps. 27, 9. 1   [Save Your People]

Save Your people, O Lord,
  and bless Your inheritance.
To You, O Lord, I call;
  O my God, be not deaf to me,
  lest I become one of those going down into
    the pit.

TRACT   Ps. 102, 10; 78, 8-9   [Forget Our Sins]

O Lord, deal with us not according to our sins,
  nor requite us according to our crimes.
O Lord, remember not against us the iniquities
    of the past;
  may Your compassion quickly come to us,
  for we are brought very low.
Help us, O God, our Savior,
  because of the glory of Your Name, O Lord;
Deliver us and pardon our sins
  for Your Name's sake.

OFFERTORY   Ps. 24, 1-3   [Unashamed Trust]

To You I lift up my soul, O Lord.
  In You, O my God, I trust;

Let me not be put to shame,
　let not my enemies exult over me.
No one who waits for You shall be put to
　shame.

COMMUNION　Ps. 10, 8　[*The Lord Loves the Just*]

The Lord is just, He loves just deeds;
　the upright shall see His face.

THURSDAY — After the 2nd Sunday in Lent

INTROIT　Ps. 69, 2. 3. 4　　　[*Victory Over Foes*]

Deign, O God, to rescue me;
　O Lord, make haste to help me;
Let my enemies be put to shame and confounded
　who seek my life.
(Ps.) Let them be turned back in disgrace
　who desire my ruin.

Glory be to the Father, etc.

Repeat: **Deign, O God,** etc., *as far as* (Ps.).

GRADUAL　Ps. 78, 9. 10　　　[*Our God Delivers Us*]

Pardon our sins, O Lord;
　why should the nations say,
　"Where is their God?"
Help us, O God, our Savior;
　because of the glory of Your Name,
　O Lord, deliver us.

OFFERTORY　Ex. 32, 11, 13. 14　　　[*Prayer of Moses*]

Moses prayed in the sight of the Lord His God,
　and said,
"Why, O Lord, are You angry with Your people?
　let the anger of Your soul be appeased;

Remember Abraham, Isaac and Jacob,
to whom You swore
that You would give the land flowing with
milk and honey."
So the Lord relented in the punishment
He had threatened to inflict on His people.

COMMUNION   John 6, 57   [Life in the Eucharist]

"He who eats My Flesh, and drinks My Blood,
abides in Me, and I in him," says the Lord.

FRIDAY — After the 2nd Sunday in Lent

INTROIT   Ps. 16, 15. 1   [Looking for God's Glory]

But I in justice shall behold Your face;
I shall be content when Your glory shall
appear.
(Ps.) Hear, O Lord, a just suit;
attend to my outcry.
Glory be to the Father, etc.
Repeat: But I in justice, etc., *as far as* (Ps.).

GRADUAL   Ps. 119, 1-2   [Prayer for Deliverance]

In my distress, I called to the Lord,
and He answered me.
O Lord, deliver me from lying lip,
from treacherous tongue.

TRACT — p. 70.

OFFERTORY   Ps. 39, 14. 15   [Rescue Me]

Deign, O Lord, to rescue me;
let all be put to shame and confusion
who seek to snatch away my life.
Deign, O Lord, to rescue me.

COMMUNION   Ps. 11, 8   [The Lord Protects]

You, O Lord, will keep us
  and preserve us always from this generation.

SATURDAY — After the 2nd Sunday in Lent

INTROIT   Ps. 18, 8. 2   [Delight of God's Law]

The law of the Lord is perfect,
  refreshing the soul;
The decree of the Lord is trustworthy,
  giving wisdom to the simple.
(Ps.) The heavens declare the glory of God,
  and the firmament proclaims His handiwork.
Glory be to the Father, etc.
Repeat: **The law of the Lord,** etc., *as far as* (Ps.).

GRADUAL   Ps. 91, 2-3   [Thanksgiving]

It is good to give thanks to the Lord,
  to sing praise to Your Name, Most High.
To proclaim Your kindness at dawn
  and Your faithfulness throughout the night.

OFFERTORY   Ps. 12, 4-5   [Watchfulness]

Give light to my eyes that I may not sleep in
    death
  lest my enemy say, "I have overcome him."

COMMUNION   Luke 15, 32   [The Lost Is Found]

You ought to rejoice, my son,
  for your brother was dead,
  and has come to life;
He was lost, and is found.

Jesus drives the devil out of a deaf and dumb man.

THIRD SUNDAY IN LENT

THOUGHT FOR TODAY: We cannot be neutral in our relationship with God. If we do not serve Him, pride and selfishness will enslave us. "Happy are they who hear the word of God, and keep it."

BIBLE AND LITURGY: Being Christians means that we made a decision. The Church teaches today that a compromise with evil is impossible. Faithful penance, abstinence and fasting will detach us from attachment to evil. Hence, they are necessary to be faithful to the decision of our Baptism. READ: 2 Esd. 1, 1-11; Dan. 9, 1-6; Jona 3; Mark 9, 24-28; 2 Cor. 6, 1-10; 1 Cor. 9,

INTROIT   Ps. 24, 15-16, 1. 2   [Looking to the Lord]

My eyes are ever toward the Lord,
  for He will free my feet from the snare.
Look toward me, and have pity on me,
  for I am alone and afflicted.
(Ps.) To You I lift up my soul,
  O Lord.
In You, O God, I trust;
  let me not be put to shame.
Glory be to the Father, and to the Son,
  and to the Holy Spirit.

As it was in the beginning, is now, and ever
shall be,
world without end. Amen.

My eyes are ever toward the Lord,
for He will free my feet from the snare.

Look toward me, and have pity on me,
for I am alone and afflicted.

GRADUAL Ps. 9, 20. 4 [Defend Us]

Rise, O Lord, let not man prevail;
let the nations be judged in Your presence.

Because my enemies are turned back,
overthrown and destroyed before You.

TRACT Ps. 122, 1-3 [Look with Pity]

To You I lift up my eyes,
Who are enthroned in heaven.

Behold, as the eyes of servants
are on the hands of their masters.

As the eyes of a maid
are on the hands of her mistress,

So are our eyes on the Lord our God,
till He have pity on us.

Have pity on us O Lord,
have pity on us.

OFFERTORY Ps. 18, 9-12 [Sweet are God's Laws]

The precepts of the Lord are right,
rejoicing the heart,

And His ordinances are sweeter than syrup
or honey from the comb;
therefore Your servant is careful of them.

COMMUNION   Ps. 83, 4. 5   [*Family of God*]

The sparrow finds a home,
  and the swallow a nest
  in which she puts her young:
Your altars, O Lord of hosts,
  my King and my God!
Happy they who dwell in Your house!
  continually they praise You.

MONDAY — After the 3rd Sunday in Lent

INTROIT   Ps. 55, 5. 2   [*Help Against Foes*]

In God, in Whose promise I glory,
  in the Lord Whose word I praise,
In God I trust without fear;
  what can flesh do against me?
(Ps.) Have pity on me, O God, for men trample
  upon me;
  all the day they press their attack against
  me.
Glory be to the Father, etc.
Repeat: **In God,** etc., *as far as* (Ps.).

GRADUAL   Ps. 55, 9. 2   [*Ever in God's Sight*]

O God, my wanderings You have counted;
  my tears are recorded in Your sight.
Have pity on me, O Lord, for men trample
  upon me;
  all the day they press their attack against
  me.

TRACT   Ps. 102, 10; 78, 8-9   [*Forget Our Sins*]

O Lord, deal with us not according to our sins,
   nor requite us according to our crimes.
O Lord, remember not against us the iniquities
      of the past;
   may Your compassion quickly come to us,
   for we are brought very low.
Help us, O God, our Savior,
   because of the glory of Your Name, O Lord;
Deliver us and pardon our sins
   for Your Name's sake.

OFFERTORY   Ps. 54, 2-3   [*Turn not Away*]

Hearken, O God, to my prayer;
   turn not away from my pleading;
   give heed to me, and answer me.

COMMUNION   Ps. 13, 7   [*Plea for Salvation*]

Oh, that out of Sion would come the salvation
      of Israel!
   When the Lord restores the well-being of
      His people,
   then shall Jacob exult and Israel be glad.

TUESDAY — After the 3rd Sunday in Lent

INTROIT   Ps. 16, 6. 8. 1   [*Protect Me*]

I call upon You, for You will answer me, O God;
   incline Your ear to me; hear my word.
Keep me, O Lord, as the apple of Your eye;
   hide me in the shadow of Your wings.
(Ps.) Hear, O Lord, a just suit;
   attend to my outcry.

Glory be to the Father, etc.
Repeat: I call upon You, etc., *as far as* (Ps.).

GRADUAL   Ps. 18, 13-14

[*Cleanse Me from What Is False*]

Cleanse me from my unknown faults, O Lord!
From wanton sin especially, restrain Your
    servant.
  Let it not rule over me.
Then shall I be blameless and innocent
  of serious sin.

OFFERTORY   Ps. 117, 16. 17   [*I Shall Live*]

The right hand of the Lord has struck with
    power:
  the right hand of the Lord has exalted me;
I shall not die, but live,
  and declare the works of the Lord.

COMMUNION   Ps. 14, 1-2   [*Living with God*]

Lord, who shall sojourn in Your tent?
  Who shall dwell on Your holy mountain?
He who walks blamelessly and does justice.

WEDNESDAY — After the 3rd Sunday in Lent

INTROIT   Ps. 30, 7-8   [*Rescue Me*]

My trust is in the Lord.
I will rejoice and be glad of Your kindness,
  when You have seen my affliction.
(Ps.) In You, O Lord, I take refuge;
  let me never be put to shame.
In Your justice rescue me
  and deliver me.

Glory be to the Father, etc.

Repeat: **My trust,** etc., *as far as* (Ps.).

GRADUAL   Ps. 6, 3-4   [Heal Me]

Have pity on me, O Lord, for I am languishing;
   heal me, O Lord.
For my body is in terror;
   my soul, too, is utterly terrified.

TRACT   Ps. 102, 10; 78, 8-9   [Forget Our Sins]

O Lord, deal with us not according to our sins,
   nor requite us according to our crimes.
O Lord, remember not against us the iniquities
      of the past;
   may Your compassion quickly come to us,
   for we are brought very low.
Help us, O God, our Savior,
   because of the glory of Your Name, O Lord;
Deliver us and pardon our sins
   for Your Name's sake.

OFFERTORY   Ps. 108, 21   [Generous Lord]

O Lord, deal kindly with me for Your Name's
      sake;
   because Your kindness is generous.

COMMUNION   Ps. 15, 11   [Joy]

You will show me the path to life,
   You will fill me with fullness of joys in Your
      presence, O Lord.

THURSDAY — After the 3rd Sunday in Lent

INTROIT   Ps. 77, 1   [The Lord Our Savior]

"I am the salvation of the people,"
  says the Lord.
"From whatever tribulation they shall cry to
    Me,
  I will hear them;
  and I will be their Lord forever."
(Ps.) Hearken, My people, to My teaching;
  incline your ears to the words of My mouth.
Glory be to the Father, etc.
Repeat: "I am the salvation, etc., *as far as* (Ps.).

GRADUAL   Ps. 144, 15-16   [Eyes of Hope]

The eyes of all look hopefully to You, O Lord,
  and You give them their food in due season.
You open your hand
  and satisfy the desire of every living thing.

OFFERTORY   Ps. 137, 7   [God Saves Me]

Though I walk amid distress, You preserve
    me, O Lord;
  against the anger of my enemies You raise
    Your hand;
  Your right hand saves me.

COMMUNION   Ps. 118, 4-5   [Make Me Steadfast]

You have commanded that Your precepts
  be diligently kept.
Oh, that I might be firm in the ways
  of keeping Your statutes!

FRIDAY — After the 3rd Sunday in Lent

INTROIT   Ps. 85, 17. 1   [Confound My Foes]

Grant me, O Lord, a proof of Your favor,
   that my enemies may see, to their confusion,
   that You, O Lord, have helped me and com-
      forted me.
(Ps.) Incline Your ear, O Lord; answer me,
   for I am afflicted and poor.
Glory be to the Father, etc.
Repeat: **Grant me,** etc., *as far as* (Ps.).

GRADUAL   Ps. 27, 7. 1   [Help from God]

In God my heart trusts, and I find help;
   then my heart exults, and with my song I
      give Him thanks.
To You, O Lord, I call;
   O my God, be not deaf to me,
   do not abandon me.

TRACT   Ps. 102, 10; 78, 8-9   [Forget Our Sins]

O Lord, deal with us not according to our sins,
   nor requite us according to our crimes.
O Lord, remember not against us the iniquities
      of the past;
   may Your compassion quickly come to us,
   for we are brought very low.
Help us, O God, our Savior,
   because of the glory of Your Name, O Lord;
Deliver us and pardon our sins
   for Your Name's sake.

OFFERTORY   Ps. 5, 3-4   [*Hear Me*]

Heed my call for help,
    my King, and my God!
To You I pray, O Lord.

COMMUNION   John 4, 13. 14   [*Living Water*]

"He who drinks of the water
    that I will give him," says the Lord.
"Shall find in himself a fountain of water,
    springing up unto life everlasting."

SATURDAY — After the 3rd Sunday in Lent

INTROIT   Ps. 5, 2-3. 4   [*Hear Me*]

Hearken to my words, O Lord,
    attend to my sighing.
Heed my call for help,
    my King and my God!
(Ps.) To You I pray, O Lord;
    at dawn You hear my voice.
Glory be to the Father, etc.
Repeat: **Hearken,** etc., *as far as* (Ps.).

GRADUAL   Ps. 22, 4   [*No Fear*]

Even though I walk in the dark valley,
    I fear no evil; for You are at my side, O Lord.
With Your rod and Your staff
    that give me courage.

OFFERTORY   Ps. 118, 133   [Steady Me]

Steady my footsteps according to Your promise,
    and let no iniquity rule over me, O Lord.

COMMUNION   John 8, 10. 11   [No Condemnation]

Has no one condemned you, woman?
    No one, Lord.
Neither will I condemn you;
    now sin no more.

*Jesus feeds a large crowd with only seven loaves
and a few fishes.*

FOURTH SUNDAY IN LENT

THOUGHT FOR TODAY: A true Christian life requires
self-denial and penance. Nevertheless, there is enough
joy in it, because self-control leads to the freedom of
the children of God. The wonderful Bread which we
receive in Holy Communion is another reason for joy
because it unites us with God Almighty, the source of
all happiness.

BIBLE AND LITURGY: Lenten observance, carried out in
Faith, will make us share ever more in the freedom,
wherewith Christ has made us free. Christ's Word and
Sacraments, especially, the Sacrament of His Precious
Body and Blood, make it possible to keep ourselves
free from the bondage of evil. READ: John 8, 31-38;
Rom. 6, 1-23; 1 Cor. 7, 17-24 (esp. 23); Ps. 125.

INTROIT   Isa. 66, 10. 11; Ps. 121, 1   [*Rejoice*]

Rejoice, O Jerusalem,
   and come together all you who love her:
Rejoice with joy,
   you who have been in sorrow:
That you may exult,
   and be filled from the breasts of your
      consolation.

(Ps.) **I rejoiced because they said to me:**
  "We will go up to the house of the Lord."

Glory be to the Father, and to the Son,
  and to the Holy Spirit.

As it was in the beginning, is now, and ever
    shall be,
  world without end. Amen.

Rejoice, O Jerusalem,
  and come together all you who love her:
Rejoice with joy,
  you who have been in sorrow:
That you may exult,
  and be filled from the breasts of your
    consolation.

GRADUAL   Ps. 121, 1. 7   [*The House of God*]

I rejoiced because they said to me:
  "We will go up to the house of the Lord."
May peace be within your walls,
  prosperity in your buildings.

TRACT   Ps. 124, 1. 2   [*The Lord Is Close to Us*]

They who trust in the Lord are like Mount
    Sion,
  which is immovable; which forever stands.
Mountains are round about Jerusalem;
  so the Lord is round about His people,
  both now and forever.

OFFERTORY   Ps. 134, 3. 6   [*Praise the Lord*]

Praise the Lord, for He is good;
  sing praise to His Name, for He is sweet;
All that He wills He does
  in heaven and on earth.

COMMUNION Ps. 121, 3. 4 [*The Heavenly Jerusalem*]

Jerusalem built as a city
  with compact unity;
To it the tribes go up,
  the tribes of the Lord,
    to give thanks to Your Name, O Lord.

MONDAY — After the 4th Sunday in Lent

INTROIT   Ps. 53, 3-4. 5   [*Save Me*]

O God, by Your Name save me,
  and by Your might deliver me.
O God, hear my prayer;
  hearken to the words of my mouth.
(Ps.) For haughty men have risen up against
    me,
  and fierce men seek my life.
Glory be to the Father, etc.
Repeat: **O God,** etc., *as far as* (Ps.).

GRADUAL   Ps. 30, 3; 70, 1   [*God My Refuge*]

Be my rock of refuge, O God,
  a stronghold to give me safety.
In You, O God, I take refuge;
  O Lord, let me never be put to shame.

TRACT   Ps. 102, 10; 78, 8-9   [*Forget Our Sins*]

O Lord, deal with us not according to our sins,
  nor requite us according to our crimes.
O Lord, remember not against us the iniquities
    of the past;
  may Your compassion quickly come to us,
  for we are brought very low.

Help us, O God, our Savior,
  because of the glory of Your Name, O Lord;
Deliver us and pardon our sins
  for Your Name's sake.

OFFERTORY   Ps. 99, 1-2   [*Come Joyfully*]

Sing joyfully to God, all you lands;
  serve the Lord with gladness;
come before Him with joyful song:
  know that the Lord is God.

COMMUNION   Ps. 18, 13. 14   [*Restrain Me*]

Cleanse me from my unknown faults, O Lord!
  From wanton sin especially, restrain Your
    servant.   _____

TUESDAY — After the 4th Sunday in Lent

INTROIT   Ps. 54, 2-3. 3-4   [*Take Heed of Me*]

Hearken, O God, to my prayer;
  turn not away from my pleading;
  give heed to me, and answer me.
(Ps.) I rock with grief, and am troubled
  at the voice of the enemy and the clamor of
    the wicked.
Glory be to the Father, etc.
Repeat: **Hearken, O God,** etc., *as far as* (Ps.).

GRADUAL   Ps. 43, 26. 2   [*Redeem Us*]

Arise, O Lord, help us!
  Redeem us for Your Name's sake.
O God, our ears have heard,
  our fathers have declared to us
The deeds You did in their days,
  in days of old.

OFFERTORY   Ps. 39, 2. 3. 4   [He Rescued Me]

I have waited, waited for the Lord,
  and He stooped toward me and heard my cry.
And He put a new song into my mouth,
  a hymn to our God.

COMMUNION   Ps. 19, 6   [Victory]

May we shout for joy at Your victory
  and raise the standards in the Name of the
    Lord our God.

WEDNESDAY — After the 4th Sunday in Lent

INTROIT   Ezech. 36, 23-26; Ps. 33, 2   [A New Spirit]

When I prove My holiness through you,
  I will gather you from all the foreign lands;
And I will sprinkle clean water upon you
  to cleanse you from all your impurities;
  and I will give you a new spirit.

(Ps.) I will bless the Lord at all times;
  His praise shall be ever in my mouth.

Glory be to the Father, etc.

Repeat: **When I prove,** etc., *as far as* (Ps.).

  After the 1st Lesson:

GRADUAL   Ps. 33, 12. 6   [Fear of the Lord]

Come, children, hear me;
  I will teach you the fear of the Lord.
Look to Him that you may be radiant with joy,
  and your faces may not blush with shame.

After the 2nd Lesson:

GRADUAL   Ps. 32, 12. 6   [God Our Possession]

Happy the nation whose God is the Lord,
  the people whom He has chosen for His
    own inheritance.
By the word of the Lord the heavens were
    made;
  by the breath of His mouth all their host.

TRACT   Ps. 102, 10; 78, 8-9   [Forget Our Sins]

O Lord, deal with us not according to our sins,
  nor requite us according to our crimes.
O Lord, remember not against us the iniquities
    of the past;
  may Your compassion quickly come to us,
  for we are brought very low.
Help us, O God, our Savior,
  because of the glory of Your Name, O Lord;
Deliver us and pardon our sins
  for Your Name's sake.

OFFERTORY   Ps. 65, 8-9. 20   [Sound His Praise]

Bless the Lord our God, you peoples,
  loudly sound His praise;
He has given life to my soul,
  and has not let my feet slip.
Blessed be God, Who refused me not
  my prayer or His kindness.

COMMUNION   John 9, 11   [The Light of Faith]

The Lord made clay of spittle,
  and anointed my eyes:
And I went, and I washed, and I saw,
  and I have believed in God.

THURSDAY — After the 4th Sunday in Lent

INTROIT   Ps. 104, 3-4. 1   [*Defend Us*]

Rejoice, O hearts
  that seek the Lord!
Look to the Lord, and be strengthened;
  seek His face evermore.
(Ps.) Give thanks to the Lord, invoke His Name;
  make known among the nations His deeds.
Glory be to the Father, etc.
Repeat: **Rejoice, O hearts,** etc., *as far as* (Ps.).

GRADUAL   Ps. 73, 20. 19. 22 [*Make Haste to Help Us*]

Look, O Lord, to Your covenant;
  be not forever unmindful of the lives of Your
    afflicted ones.
Arise, O Lord; defend Your cause;
  remember the reproaches of Your servants.

OFFERTORY   Ps. 69, 2. 3. 4   [*Help Through Life*]

O Lord, make haste to help me.
Let all those be put to shame
  who desire the ruin of Your servants.

COMMUNION Ps. 70, 16-17. 18[*Joy in Seeking the Lord*]

O Lord, I will tell of Your singular justice.
O God, You have taught me from my youth;
  and now that I am old and gray,
    O God, forsake me not.

FRIDAY — After the 4th Sunday in Lent

INTROIT   Ps. 18, 15. 2   [*Acceptable Minds*]

Let the thought of my heart find favor before
   You,
   O Lord, my rock and my redeemer.
(Ps.) The heavens declare the glory of God,
   and the firmament proclaims his handiwork.
Glory be to the Father, etc.
Repeat: Let the thought, etc., *as far as* (Ps.).

GRADUAL Ps. 117, 8-9 [*Trust the Lord above All Others*]

It is better to take refuge in the Lord
   rather than to trust in man.
It is better to take refuge in the Lord
   than to trust in princes.

TRACT   Ps. 102, 10; 78, 8-9   [*Forget Our Sins*]

O Lord, deal with us not according to our sins,
   nor requite us according to our crimes.
O Lord, remember not against us the iniquities
     of the past;
   may Your compassion quickly come to us,
   for we are brought very low.
Help us, O God, our Savior,
   because of the glory of Your Name, O Lord;
Deliver us and pardon our sins
   for Your Name's sake.

OFFERTORY Ps. 17, 28. 32 [*God's Love for the Humble*]

Lowly people you save, O Lord,
   but haughty eyes you bring low;
For who is God except You, O Lord?

COMMUNION John 11, 33. 35. 43. 44. 39 [*Lazarus Arose*]

The Lord, seeing the sisters of Lazarus weeping
    at the tomb,
        wept before the Jews, and cried out:
    "Lazarus, come forth";
And he who had been dead four days came
    forth,
        bound hands and feet.

SATURDAY — After the 4th Sunday in Lent

INTROIT   Isa. 55, 11; Ps. 77, 1   [*Come and Drink*]

"All who thirst, come to the waters,"
    says the Lord;
"And you who have no money,
    come and drink with joy."
(Ps.) Hearken, My people, to My teaching;
    incline your ears to the words of My mouth.
Glory be to the Father, etc.
"All who thirst, come to the waters,"
    says the Lord;
"And you who have no money,
    come and drink with joy."

GRADUAL   Ps. 9, 14. 1-2   [*Father of the Helpless*]

On You, O Lord, the unfortunate man depends;
    of the fatherless You are the helper.
Why, O Lord, do You stand aloof?
    Why hide in times of distress?
While the wicked man is proud,
    the afflicted is set on fire.

OFFERTORY   Ps. 17, 3   [*The Lord, My Deliverer*]

The Lord is become my rock, my fortress, my
    deliverer;
  and in Him will I put my trust.

COMMUNION   Ps. 22, 1-2   [*My Shepherd: the Lord*]

The Lord is my shepherd; I shall not want.
  In verdant pastures He gives me repose;
Beside restful waters He leads me.

*The Jews attempt to stone Jesus for declaring
Himself to be God.*

FIRST SUNDAY OF THE PASSION

THOUGHT FOR TODAY: The misled Jewish people tried
to stone Christ after He had proclaimed His Divinity.
But this was not yet the hour in which Jesus was going
to die for us. He proved Himself to be the Master of
time and of His life when He "hid Himself, and slipped
out of the Temple precincts."

BIBLE AND LITURGY: The Church wants to focus our attention and appreciation upon the tremendous fact that
Christ became the eternal High Priest of mankind, and
at the same time the Victim Who took away the sin of
the world. READ: Ex. 24, 4-8; 29, 1-9; Lev. 16, 1-19;
Heb. 9, 11-15 (*Ep.*); Heb. 10, 1-18; 1 Cor. 11, 23-26;
John 18, 4-11.

INTROIT   Ps. 42, 1. 2. 3   [*God my Strength*]

Do me justice, O God, and fight my fight
    against a faithless people;
      from the deceitful and impious man rescue
        me;
For You are my God
    and my strength.

(Ps.) Send forth Your light and Your fidelity;
    they shall lead me on

And bring me to Your holy mountain,
to Your dwelling-place.
Do me justice, O God, and fight my fight
against a faithless people;
from the deceitful and impious man rescue
me;
For You are my God
and my strength.

GRADUAL   Ps. 142, 9. 10   [*Come to My Rescue*]

Rescue me from my enemies, O Lord;
teach me to do Your will.
O Lord, my deliverer from the angry nations:
truly above my adversaries You exalt me
and from the violent man You have rescued
me.

TRACT   Ps. 128, 1-4   [*My Afflictions*]

Much have they oppressed me from my youth;
let Israel say:
Much have they oppressed me from my youth,
yet they have not prevailed against me;
Upon my back the plowers plowed.
Long did they make their furrows.
But the just Lord has severed
the cords of the wicked.

OFFERTORY   Ps. 118, 17. 107   [*Give Me Life*]

I praise You, O Lord,
with all my heart;
Be good to Your servant, that I may live
and keep Your words.
O Lord, give me life according to Your word.

COMMUNION   1 Cor. 11, 24. 25   [*This Is Life*]

"This is My Body which shall be given up for
   you:
   this is the cup of the new covenant in My
      Blood,"
   says the Lord;
"Do this as often as you receive it,
   in remembrance of Me."

MONDAY — After the 1st Sunday
in Passiontide

INTROIT   Ps. 55, 2. 3   [*Trampled by Foes*]

Have pity on me, O Lord, for men trample
   upon me;
   all the day they press their attack against
      me.
(Ps.) My adversaries trample upon me all the
   day;
   yes, many fight against me.
Repeat: **Have pity on me,** etc., *as far as* (Ps.).

GRADUAL   Ps. 53, 4. 3   [*Save Me*]

O God, hear my prayer;
   hearken to the words of my mouth.
O God, by Your Name save me,
   and by Your might deliver me.

TRACT   Ps. 102, 10; 78, 8-9   [*Forget Our Sins*]

O Lord, deal with us not according to our sins,
   nor requite us according to our crimes.

O Lord, remember not against us the iniquities
  of the past;
  may Your compassion quickly come to us,
  for we are brought very low.
Help us, O God, our Savior,
  because of the glory of Your Name, O Lord;
Deliver us and pardon our sins
  for Your Name's sake.

OFFERTORY   Ps. 6, 5   [*Save Me in Your Kindness*]

Return, O Lord, save my life;
  rescue me because of Your kindness.

COMMUNION   Ps. 23, 10   [*The King*]

The Lord of hosts,
  He is the king of glory.

TUESDAY — After the 1st Sunday
in Passiontide

INTROIT   Ps. 26, 14. 1   [*Wait for the Lord*]

Wait for the Lord with courage;
  be stouthearted, and wait for the Lord.
(Ps.) The Lord is my light and my salvation;
  whom should I fear?
Repeat: Wait for the Lord, etc., *as far as* (Ps.).

GRADUAL   Ps. 42, 1. 3   [*Your Light, O Lord*]

Fight my fight, O Lord;
  from the deceitful and impious man rescue
    me.

Send forth Your light and Your fidelity;
 they shall lead me on
 and bring me to Your holy mountain.

OFFERTORY Ps. 9, 11-12. 13 [*God Does Not Forsake Us*]

They trust in You who cherish Your Name,
 O Lord,
 for You forsake not those who seek You.
Sing praise to the Lord enthroned in Sion,
 for He has not forgotten the cry of the
 afflicted.

COMMUNION Ps. 24, 22 [*Relief from Sorrow*]

Redeem me, O God of Israel,
 from all my distress.

WEDNESDAY — After the 1st Sunday
in Passiontide

INTROIT Ps. 17, 48-49. 2-3 [*Exalt Me*]

My deliverer from the angry nations;
 truly above my adversaries You exalt me
 and from the violent man You have rescued
 me, O Lord.
(Ps.) I love You, O Lord, my strength,
 O Lord, my rock, my fortress, my deliverer.
Repeat: **My deliverer,** etc., *as far as* (Ps.).

GRADUAL Ps. 29, 2-4 [*God, My Savior*]

I will extol You, O Lord, for You drew me
 clear
 and did not let my enemies rejoice over me.

O Lord, my God,
   I cried out to You and You healed me.
O Lord, You brought me up from the nether
      world;
   You preserved me from among those going
      down into the pit.

TRACT   Ps. 102, 10; 78, 8-9   [*Forget My Sins*]

O Lord, deal with us not according to our sins,
   nor requite us according to our crimes.
O Lord, remember not against us the iniquities
      of the past;
   may Your compassion quickly come to us,
   for we are brought very low.
Help us, O God, our Savior,
   because of the glory of Your Name, O Lord;
Deliver us and pardon our sins
   for Your Name's sake.

OFFERTORY   Ps. 58, 2   [*Defend Me*]

Rescue me from my enemies, O my God;
   from my adversaries defend me, O Lord.

COMMUNION   Ps. 25, 6-7 [*Praise from the Innocent*]

I wash my hands in innocence,
   and I go around Your altar, O Lord,
giving voice to my thanks,
   and recounting all Your wondrous deeds.

THURSDAY — After the 1st Sunday in Passiontide

INTROIT   Dan. 3, 31; Ps. 118, 1   [*Mercy Undeserved*]

All that You have done to us, O Lord,
  You have done in true judgment:
Because we have sinned against you,
  and have not obeyed Your commandments:
But give glory to Your Name,
  and deal with us according to the multitude
    of Your mercy.

(Ps.) Happy are they whose way is blameless,
  who walk in the law of the Lord.

Repeat: **All that You,** etc., *as far as* (Ps.).

GRADUAL   Ps. 95, 8-9; 28, 9   [*Glory to God*]

Bring gifts and enter His courts;
  worship the Lord in His holy court.
The Lord strips the forests,
  and in His temple all say, "Glory!"

OFFERTORY   Ps. 136, 1   [*The Days of Sion*]

By the streams of Babylon
  we sat and wept
  when we remembered Sion.

COMMUNION   Ps. 118, 49-50   [*God's Promise*]

Remember Your word to Your servant, O Lord,
  since You have given me hope.
This is my comfort in my affliction.

FRIDAY — After the 1st Sunday
in Passiontide

INTROIT   Ps. 30, 10. 16. 18. 2   [*The Lord, My Refuge*]

Have pity on me, O Lord, for I am in distress;
  rescue me from the clutches of my enemies
    and my persecutors.
O Lord, let me not be put to shame,
  for I call upon You.
(Ps.) In You, O Lord, I take refuge;
  let me never be put to shame.
In Your justice rescue me.
Repeat: **Have pity on me,** etc., *as far as* (Ps.).

GRADUAL   Ps. 34, 20. 22   [*You Can See, Lord*]

My enemies spoke peaceably to me:
  and in anger they afflicted me.
You, O Lord, have seen; be not silent;
  be not far from me!

TRACT   Ps. 102, 10; 78, 8-9   [*Forget Our Sins*]

O Lord, deal with us not according to our sins,
  nor requite us according to our crimes.
O Lord, remember not against us the iniquities
    of the past;
  may Your compassion quickly come to us,
  for we are brought very low.
Help us, O God, our Savior,
  because of the glory of Your Name, O Lord;
Deliver us and pardon our sins
  for Your Name's sake.

OFFERTORY   Ps. 118, 12. 121. 42   [Answer from God]

Blessed are You, O Lord;
  teach me Your statutes.
Let not the proud oppress me;
  so shall I have an answer for those who
    reproach me.

COMMUNION   Ps. 26, 12   [False Witnesses]

Give me not up, O Lord, to the wishes of my
  foes;
  for false witnesses have risen up against me,
  and such as breathe out violence.

SATURDAY — After the 1st Sunday
in Passiontide

INTROIT   Ps. 30, 10. 16. 18. 2   [Rescue Me]

Have pity on me, O Lord, for I am in distress;
  rescue me from the clutches of my enemies
    and my persecutors.
O Lord, let me not be put to shame, for I call
  upon You.
(Ps.) In You, O Lord, I take refuge;
  let me never be put to shame.
In Your justice rescue me.
Repeat: **Have pity on me,** etc., *as far as* (Ps.).

GRADUAL   Ps. 34, 20. 22   [Duplicity]

My enemies spoke peaceably to me:
  and in anger they afflicted me.
You, O Lord, have seen; be not silent;
  be not far from me!

OFFERTORY   Ps. 118, 12. 121. 42

[*My Answer Is from the Lord*]

Blessed are You, O Lord;
   teach me Your statutes.
Let not the proud oppress me;
   so shall I have an answer for those who
   reproach me.

COMMUNION   Ps. 26, 12   [*Protect Me*]

Give me not up, O Lord, to the wishes of my
   foes;
   for false witnesses have risen up against me,
   and such as breathe out violence.

Jesus enters Jerusalem in triumph.

SECOND SUNDAY OF THE PASSION OR PALM SUNDAY

THOUGHT FOR TODAY: Joy and sorrow are found closely joined in today's Mass. The triumphal entry of Jesus into Jerusalem and the sorrowful recollection of His Passion are both expressed in the Liturgy of today. The Hosannas of the people will soon yield to the "Crucify Him." It is safer for us to follow Christ along the hard way of fulfilled duties than to walk along the easy road of the world.

BLESSING OF THE PALMS

ANTIPHON Matt. 21, 9 [*Hail, Christ, Our King!*]

Hosanna to the Son of David!

Blessed is He Who comes in the Name of the Lord.

O King of Israel:

hosanna in the highest.

DISTRIBUTION OF THE PALMS

ANTIPHON [*The Children's Acclaim*]

The children of the Hebrews, bearing olive branches,

went to meet the Lord, crying aloud and
saying,
"Hosanna in the highest."

PSALM   Ps. 23, 1. 2. 7-10   [*The King of Glory*]

The Lord's are the earth and its fullness;
the world and those who dwell in it.
For He founded it upon the seas
and established it upon the rivers.

The Antiphon is repeated:

The children of the Hebrews, bearing olive
branches,
went to meet the Lord, crying aloud and
saying,
"Hosanna in the highest."

Lift up, O gates, your lintels;
reach up, you ancient portals,
that the king of glory may come in!
Who is this king of glory?
The Lord, strong and mighty,
the Lord, mighty in battle.

The Antiphon is repeated:

The children of the Hebrews, bearing olive
branches,
went to meet the Lord, crying aloud and
saying,
"Hosanna in the highest."

Lift up, O gates, your lintels;
reach up, you ancient portals,
that the king of glory may come in!
Who is this king of glory?
The Lord of hosts; He is the king of glory.

The Antiphon is repeated:

The children of the Hebrews, bearing olive branches,
   went to meet the Lord, crying aloud and saving,
   "Hosanna in the highest."

Glory be to the Father and to the Son,
   and to the Holy Spirit.

As it was in the beginning, is now, and ever shall be,
   world without end. Amen.

The Antiphon is repeated:

The children of the Hebrews, bearing olive branches,
   went to meet the Lord, crying aloud and saving,
   "Hosanna in the highest."

The above psalm and antiphon are repeated, if necessary.

THE PROCESSION WITH THE BLESSED PALMS

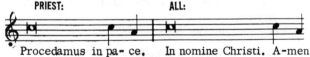

PRIEST: ALL:

Procedamus in pa- ce.   In nomine Christi. A-men
Let us go forth in   peace. In Christ's name. A-men

The procession now takes place. The servers and celebrant lead; the people follow, carrying palms.

During the procession, all sing the following hymn.

HYMN: All Glory, Laud, and Honor

[*Hail to Christ Our King*]

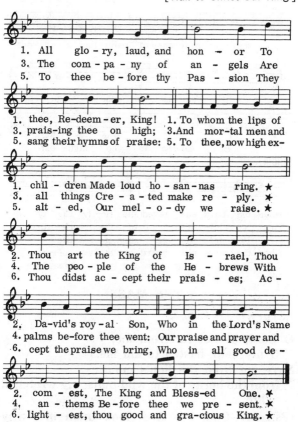

1. All glo - ry, laud, and hon - or To
3. The com - pa - ny of an - gels Are
5. To thee be - fore thy Pas - sion They

1. thee, Re - deem - er, King! 1. To whom the lips of
3. prais - ing thee on high; 3. And mor - tal men and
5. sang their hymns of praise: 5. To thee, now high ex -

1. chil - dren Made loud ho - san - nas ring. ★
3. all things Cre - a - ted make re - ply. ★
5. alt - ed, Our mel - o - dy we raise. ★

2. Thou art the King of Is - rael, Thou
4. The peo - ple of the He - brews With
6. Thou didst ac - cept their prais - es; Ac -

2. Da - vid's roy - al Son, Who in the Lord's Name
4. palms be - fore thee went: Our praise and prayer and
6. cept the praise we bring, Who in all good de -

2. com - est, The King and Bless - ed One. ★
4. an - thems Be - fore thee we pre - sent. ★
6. light - est, thou good and gra - cious King. ★

★ The first stanza is repeated wherever the star occurs.

As the procession enters the church, all jubilantly sing the following antiphon. The antiphon is repeated after each choir verse.

Bear-ing bran-ches of palm they cried out

Ho - san-na in the high - est!

Ho- san-na in the high- est !

CHOIR

When the	Lord	en-	tered the	Ho- ly	Ci- ty
The	chil-	dren	of the	He-	brews
Fore-tel-	ling	re-	turn of	life	
When the peo-	ple	heard Je-	sus was com-	ing	
They all	went	out to	meet Him		

THE MASS

INTROIT   Ps. 21, 20. 22

O Lord, be not far from me;
   O my help, hasten to aid me.
Save me from the lion's mouth;
   from the horns of the wild bulls, my wretched life.
(Ps.) My God, My God, look upon me, why have you forsaken me?
   Far from my salvation are the words of my sins.

O Lord, be not far from me;
  O my help, hasten to aid me.
Save me from the lion's mouth;
  from the horns of the wild bulls, my wretched
    life.

GRADUAL Ps. 72, 24. 1-3 [*God's Goodness to His Own*]

You have hold of my right hand;
  with Your counsel You guide me;
  and in the end You will receive me in glory.
How good God is to Israel,
  to those who are clean of heart!
But, as for me, I almost lost my balance;
  my feet all but slipped,
Because I was envious of sinners
  when I saw them prosper though they were
    wicked.

TRACT Ps. 21, 2-9. 18. 19. 22. 24. 32 [*The Powers of Evil*]

My God, My God, look upon me, why have
  You forsaken me?
  Far from my salvation are the words of my
    sins.
O my God, I cry out by day, and You answer
  not;
  by night, and there is no relief.
But You are enthroned in the holy place,
  O glory of Israel!
In You our fathers trusted;
  they trusted, and You delivered them.
To You they cried, and they escaped;
  in You they trusted, and they were not put
    to shame.

But I am a worm, not a man;
  the scorn of men, despised by the people.
All who see me, scoff at me;
  they mock me with parted lips, they wag
    their heads.
"He relied on the Lord; let Him deliver him,
  let Him rescue him, if he loves Him."
But they look on and gloat over me;
  they divide my garments among them,
  and for my vesture they cast lots.
Save me from the lion's mouth;
  from the horns of the wild bulls, my wretched
    life.
You who fear the Lord, praise Him;
  all you descendants of Jacob, give glory to
    Him.
There shall be declared to the Lord a gener-
    ation to come:
  and the heavens shall show forth His justice.
To a people that shall be born,
  which the Lord has made.

OFFERTORY   Ps. 68, 21-22   [I Found None to Help]

Insult has broken my heart, and I am weak;
  I looked for sympathy, but there was none;
  for comforters, and I found none;
Rather they put gall in my food,
  and in my thirst they gave me vinegar to
    drink.

COMMUNION   Matt. 26, 42   [Christ Accepts]

Father, if this cup cannot pass away,
  unless I drink it,
  Your will be done.

———

MONDAY IN HOLY WEEK

INTROIT   Ps. 34, 1-2. 3   [*Come to My Defense*]

Judge, O Lord, those who wrong me;
  war against those who make war upon me.
Take up the shield and buckler,
  and rise up in my defense,
  O Lord, the strength of my salvation.
(Ps.) Brandish the lance, and block the way
  in the face of my pursuers;
Say to my soul, "I am your salvation."
Repeat: **Judge, O Lord,** etc., *as far as* (Ps.).

GRADUAL   Ps. 34, 23. 3   [*Protect Me*]

Awake, O Lord, and be vigilant in my defense,
  my God and my Lord.
Brandish the lance, and block the way
  in the face of my pursuers.

TRACT   Ps. 102, 10; 78, 8-9   [*Forget Our Sins*]

O Lord, deal with us not according to our sins,
  nor requite us according to our crimes.
O Lord, remember not against us the iniquities
    of the past;
  may Your compassion quickly come to us,
  for we are brought very low.
Help us, O God, our Savior,
  because of the glory of Your Name, O Lord;
Deliver us and pardon our sins
  for Your Name's sake.

OFFERTORY   Ps. 142, 9-10   [*Save Me for My Trust*]

Rescue me from my enemies, O Lord,
  for in You I hope.
Teach me to do Your will,
  for You are my God.

COMMUNION   Ps. 34, 26   [*Rout My Enemies*]

Let all be put to shame and confounded
  who are glad at my misfortune.
Let those be clothed with shame and disgrace
  who glory over me.

TUESDAY IN HOLY WEEK

INTROIT   Gal. 6, 14; Ps. 66, 2   [*Glory in the Cross*]

But it behooves us to glory in the cross of our
    Lord Jesus Christ:
  in Whom is our salvation, life, and
    resurrection;
  by Whom we are saved and delivered.
(Ps.) **May God have pity on us and bless us;**
  may He let His face shine upon us;
  and may He have pity on us.
Repeat: **But it behooves us,** etc., *as far as* (Ps.).

GRADUAL   Ps. 34, 13. 1-2   [*Undeserved Pain*]

But as for me, when they were troublesome to
    me,
  I was clothed with haircloth,
And I humbled my soul with fasting,
  and poured forth prayers within my bosom.
Judge, O Lord, those who wrong me;
  war against those who make war upon me.
Take up the shield and buckler,
  and rise up in my defense.

OFFERTORY   Ps. 139, 5 [*Preserve Me from Violence*]

Save me, O Lord, from the hands of the wicked;
  preserve me from violent men.

COMMUNION   Ps. 68, 13-14   [*Reviled by Sinners*]

They who sit at the gate gossip about me;
   and the drunkards make me the butt of their
      songs.
But I pray to You, O Lord;
For the time of Your favor, O God,
   in Your great kindness answer me.

WEDNESDAY IN HOLY WEEK

INTROIT   Phil. 2, 10, 8. 11; Ps. 101, 2 [*Obedient unto Death*]

At the Name of Jesus every knee should bend,
   of those in heaven, on earth and under the
      earth,
For the Lord became obedient unto death,
   even to death on a cross.
Therefore our Lord Jesus Christ
   is in the glory of God the Father.
(Ps.) O Lord, hear my prayer,
   and let my cry come to You.

Repeat: **At the Name,** etc., *as far as* (Ps.).

GRADUAL   Ps. 68, 18. 2-3   [*Hide Not from Me*]

Hide not Your face from Your servant;
   in my distress, make haste to answer me.
Save me, O God,
   for the waters threaten my life;
I am sunk in the abysmal swamp
   where there is no foothold.

TRACT   Ps. 101, 2-5. 14   [*Answer Quickly*]

O Lord, hear my prayer,
   and let my cry come to you.

Hide not Your face from me;
   in the day of my distress, incline Your ear
     to me.
In the day when I call,
   answer me speedily.
For my days vanish like smoke,
   and my bones burn like fire.
Withered and dried up like grass is my heart;
   I forget to eat my bread.
You will arise, O Lord, and have mercy on
     Sion,
   for it is time to pity her.

OFFERTORY   Ps. 101, 2-3   [*My Cry*]

O Lord, hear my prayer,
   and let my cry come to You.
Hide not Your face from me.

COMMUNION   Ps. 101, 10, 13. 14 [*Pity Your People*]

I mingle my drink with tears,
   for You lifted me up only to throw me down,
   and I wither like grass;
But You, O Lord, endure forever.
You will arise and have mercy on Sion,
   for it is time to pity her.

HOLY THURSDAY
Solemn Evening Mass

INTROIT   Gal. 6, 14; Ps. 66, 2   [*Glory in the Cross*]

But it behooves us to glory in the cross of our
  Lord Jesus Christ:
  in Whom is our salvation, life and
  resurrection:
  by Whom we are saved and delivered.

(Ps.) **May God have pity on us and bless us;**
  may He let His face shine upon us;
  and may He have pity on us.

Repeat: **But it behooves us,** etc., *as far as* (Ps.).

GRADUAL   Phil. 2, 8-9   [*Obedient Sacrifice*]

Christ became obedient for us unto death,
  even to death on a cross.
Therefore, God also has exalted Him
  and has given Him the Name that is above
  every name.

WASHING OF THE FEET

8th ANTIPHON   [*Let Love Abound*]

Where charity and love are, there is God.
The love of Christ has gathered us together.
  Let us rejoice in Him and be glad.
Let us fear and love the living God.
  And let us love one another with a sincere
  heart.

The Antiphon is repeated:

Where charity and love are, there is God.
When, therefore, we are assembled together.

Let us take heed, that we be not divided in mind.
Let malicious quarrels and contentions cease.
  And let Christ our God dwell among us.

The Antiphon is repeated:

Where charity and love are, there is God.
Let us also with the blessed see.
  Your face in glory, O Christ our God.
There to possess immeasurable and happy joy.
  For infinite ages of ages. Amen.

———

OFFERTORY   Ps. 117, 16. 17   [God's Loving Power]

The right hand of the Lord has struck with power:
  the right hand of the Lord has exalted me;
I shall not die, but live,
  and declare the works of the Lord.

At the threefold "Agnus Dei," p. 291, the answer is, "have mercy on us," three times.

COMMUNION   John 13, 12. 13. 15   [Example of Love]

The Lord Jesus,
  after He had supped with His disciples,
  washed their feet, and said to them,
"Do you know what I,
  your Lord and Master, have done to you?
I have given you an example,
  that so you also should do."

Hymn: "Sing My Tongue," p. 514.

For Ps. 21, see p. 550.

———

GOOD FRIDAY
Solemn Commemoration of the Passion and Death of Our Lord

1st PART OF THE LITURGICAL SERVICE — THE READINGS

After the 1st Reading:

RESPONSORY Hb. 3, 2-3   [Awe at God's Word]

O Lord, I have heard Your hearing and was afraid;
  I have considered Your works and trembled.
In the midst of two animals You shall be made
    known;
  when the years shall draw near.
You shall be known;
  when the time shall come, You shall be manifested.
When my soul shall be in trouble,
  You will remember mercy, even in Your wrath.
God will come from Lebanon,
  and the Holy One from the shady and thickly
    covered mountain.
His majesty covered the heavens;
  and the earth is full of His praise.

After the 2nd Reading:

RESPONSORY Ps. 139, 2-10. 14   [Save Us]

Deliver me, O Lord, from evil men;
  preserve me from violent men.
From those who devise evil in their hearts,
  and stir up wars every day.
They make their tongues sharp as those of serpents;
  the venom of asps is under their lips.
Save me, O Lord, from the hands of the wicked;
  preserve me from violent men.
Who plan to trip up my feet—
  the proud who have hidden a trap for me.

They have spread cords for a net;
   by the wayside they have laid snares for me.
I say to the Lord, you are my God;
   hearken, O Lord, to my voice of supplication.
O Lord, my Lord, my strength and my salvation;
   You are my helmet in the day of battle!
Give me not up from my desire to the wicked:
   they have plotted against me.
Do not forsake me
   lest at any time they should triumph.
Those who surround me lift up their heads;
   may the mischief which they threaten overwhelm
       them.
Surely the just shall give thanks to Your Name;
   the upright shall dwell in Your presence.

2nd PART OF THE LITURGICAL SERVICE —
THE PRAYER OF THE FAITHFUL
The people respond Amen to each prayer.

3rd PART OF THE LITURGICAL SERVICE—
SOLEMN ADORATION OF THE HOLY CROSS

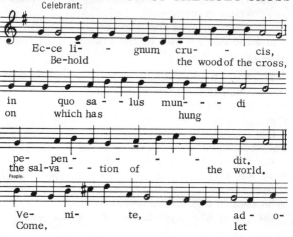

Celebrant:

Ec-ce li - gnum cru - cis,
Be-hold   the wood of the cross,

in   quo sa - lus mun - di
on   which has   hung

pe - pen - - - - dit.
the sal-va - - tion of   the world.

People:

Ve - ni - te, ad - o -
Come,   let

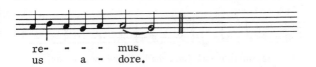

re - - - mus.
us a - dore.

REPROACHES

The parts sung by the People are indicated by the numbers 1 (first Choir) and 2 (second Choir); those sung by both are indicated 1 and 2.

1 and 2

My peo - ple, what have I done to you? In what have I of-fend-ed you, answer me. Be- cause I led you from the land of Egypt, you have pre-pared a cross for your Sav - ior.

1   2

Ho- ly God.   Ho- ly God.

1   2

Ho- ly Al- migh- ty God. Ho- ly Al-migh-ty God.

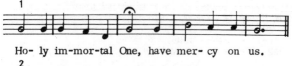

Ho- ly im-mor-tal One, have mer- cy on us.

Ho- ly im-mor-tal One, have mer- cy on us.

1 and **2** Because I led you out through the desert
    forty years,
and fed you with manna,
and brought you into a very good land,
you have prepared a cross for your Savior.

1 Holy God, *etc., as above.*

1 and **2** What more should I have done,
    and did it not?
Behold I have planted you as My fairest vine,
    and you have become very bitter to Me,
For you have quenched My thirst with vinegar,
    and with a lance you have pierced your Savior's
        side.

1 Holy God, *etc., as above.*

1 For you I scourged Egypt and its firstborn,
    and you have given Me over to be scourged.

2 My people . . . answer Me, as above.

1 I led you out of Egypt, overwhelming Pharao in
    the Red Sea,
and you have delivered Me to the chief priests.

2 My people . . . answer Me, as above.

1 I opened the sea before you,
    and you have opened My side with a lance.

2 My people . . . answer Me, as above.

1 I went before you in a pillar of cloud,
  and you have haled Me to the judgment hall of
    Pilate.

2 My people . . . answer Me, as above.

1 I fed you with manna through the desert
  and you have smitten Me with buffets and with
    lashes.

2 My people . . . answer Me, as above.

1 I gave you the water of salvation to drink from
    the rock,
  and you have given Me gall and vinegar to drink.

2 My people . . . answer Me, as above.

1 For you I smote the kings of the Chanaanites,
  and you have smitten My head with a reed.

2 My people . . . answer Me, as above.

1 I gave you a royal sceptre,
  and you have given My head a crown of thorns.

2 My people . . . answer Me, as above.

1 With great power I lifted you up,
  and you have hung Me upon the gibbet of the
    cross.

2 My people . . . answer Me, as above.

ANTIPHON   [Adoration of the Cross]

1 and 2 We adore Your cross, O Lord;
  we praise and glorify Your holy resurrection.
For behold, by reason of that wood,
  joy has come into all the world.

PSALM Ps. 66, 2   [May God Have Pity]

1 May God have pity on us
  and bless us.

2 May He let His face shine upon us;
  and have pity on us.

ANTIPHON [Adoration of the Cross]

1 and 2 We adore Your cross, O Lord;
  we praise and glorify Your holy resurrection.
For behold, by reason of that wood;
  joy has come into all the world.

ANTIPHON

1 and 2

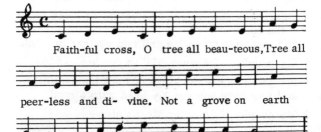

Faith-ful cross, O tree all beau-teous, Tree all peer-less and di- vine. Not a grove on earth

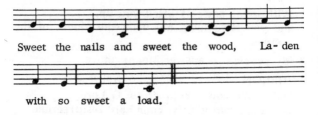

can show us Such a flow'r and leaf as thine.

Sweet the nails and sweet the wood, La- den with so sweet a load.

HYMN: PANGE LINGUA [Song of the Cross]

1 Sing, my tongue, the Savior's glory;
  tell His triumph far and wide;
Tell aloud the famous story
  of His body crucified;
How upon the cross a Victim,
  vanquishing in death, He died.

2 Faithful Cross . . . **thine,** as above.

1 Eating of the tree forbidden,
  man had sunk in Satan's snare,
When our pitying Creator did
  this second tree prepare;
Destined, many ages later,
  that first evil to repair.

2 Sweet the nails . . . **load,** as above,

1 Such the order God appointed
  when for sin He would atone;
To the serpent thus opposing
  schemes yet deeper than His own;
Thence the remedy procuring,
  whence the fatal wound had come.

2 Faithful Cross . . . **thine,** as above.

1 So when now at length the fullness
  of the sacred time drew nigh,
Then the Son, the world's Creator,
  left His Father's throne on high;
From a virgin's womb appearing,
  clothed in our mortality.

2 Sweet the nails . . . **load,** as above,

1 All within a lowly manger,
  lo, a tender babe He lies!
See His gentle Virgin Mother
  lull to sleep His infant cries!
While the limbs of God incarnate
  round with swathing bands she ties.

2 Faithful Cross . . . **thine,** as above.

1 Thus did Christ to perfect **manhood**
  in our mortal flesh attain:

Then of His free choice He goeth
  to a death of bitter pain;
And as a lamb, upon the altar of the cross,
  for us is slain.

2 Sweet the nails . . . load, as above,

1 Lo, with gall His thirst He quenches!
  See the thorns upon His brow!
Nails His tender flesh are rending!
  See, His side is opened now!
Whence, to cleanse the whole creation,
  streams of blood and water flow.

2 Faithful Cross . . . thine, as above.

1 Lofty tree, bend down thy branches,
  to embrace thy sacred load;
Oh, relax the native tension
  of that all too rigid wood;
Gently, gently bear the members
  of thy dying King and God.

2 Sweet the nails . . . load, as above,

1 Tree, which solely wast found worthy
  the world's great victim to sustain.
Harbor from the raging tempest!
  Ark, that saved the world again!
Tree, with sacred blood anointed
  of the Lamb for sinners slain.

2 Faithful Cross . . . thine, as above.

The conclusion is never omitted:

1 Blessing, honor everlasting,
  to the immortal Deity;
To the Father, Son, and Spirit,
  equal praises ever be;
Glory through the earth and heaven
  to Trinity in Unity. Amen.

2 Sweet the nails . . . load, as above,

4th PART OF THE LITURGICAL SERVICE — THE COMMUNION

We a- dore you, O Christ,
By a tree we were made slaves,
    and by the holy cross
Sav- ior of the world, save us: you, who
    by your cross and blood

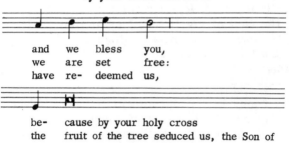

and we bless you,
we are set free:
have re- deemed us,

be- cause by your holy cross
the fruit of the tree seduced us, the Son of
help us,

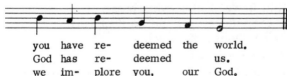

you have re- deemed the world.
God has re- deemed us.
we im- plore you, our God.

The People say the "Lord's Prayer" with the Celebrant and add "Amen" at the end of the prayer following it.

The Deacon recites the "Confiteor." Then the Celebrant pronounces the absolution, to which all respond: "Amen." Then holding up a Sacred Host and turning toward the people, he says: "Behold the Lamb," etc., and "Lord, I am not worthy," etc., as usual.

Finally, the Celebrant says three prayers to which the people answer: "Amen."

HOLY SATURDAY — THE PASCHAL VIGIL
THE READINGS

After the 2nd Lesson:

CANTICLE Ex. 15, 1. 2   [*Triumph*]

I will sing to the Lord, for He is gloriously
    triumphant;
  horse and chariot He has cast into the sea.
My strength and my courage is the Lord,
  and He has been my Savior.
He is my God, I praise Him;
  the God of my father, I extol Him.
The Lord crushes hostile attacks,
  Lord is His Name!

After the 3rd Lesson:

CANTICLE Isa. 5, 1. 2   [*The Nuptial Vineyard*]

My friend had a vineyard on a fertile hillside;
He spaded it, cleared it of stones,
  and planted the choicest vines;
Within it he built a watchtower,
  and hewed out a wine press.
For the vineyard of the Lord of Hosts
  is the house of Israel.

After the 4th Lesson:

CANTICLE Deut. 32, 1-4   [*Proclaim God's Greatness*]

Give ear, O heavens, while I speak;
  let the earth hearken to the words of my
    mouth!
May my instruction soak in like the rain,
  and my discourse permeate like the dew,
Like a downpour upon the grass,
  like a shower upon the crops:
For I will sing the Lord's renown.
  Oh, proclaim the greatness of our God!

The Rock— how faultless are His deeds,
 how right all His ways!
A faithful God, without deceit,
 how just and upright is the Lord!

FIRST PART OF LITANY OF THE SAINTS

Lord, have mercy.
All: Christ, have mercy.
Lord, have mercy.
Christ, hear us.
All: Christ, graciously hear us.
God, the Father of heaven,
All: Have mercy on us.
God the Son, Redeemer of the world,
All: Have mercy on us.
God the Holy Spirit,
All: Have mercy on us.
Holy Trinity, one God,
All: Have mercy on us.
Holy Mary,
All: Pray for us.
Holy Mother of God,
Holy Virgin of virgins,
St. Michael,
St. Gabriel,
St. Raphael,
All you holy angels and archangels,
All you holy ranks of blessed spirits,
St. John the Baptist,
St. Joseph,
All you holy patriarchs and prophets,
St. Peter,
St. Paul,
St. Andrew,
St. John,
All you holy apostles and evangelists,
All you holy disciples of the Lord,
St. Stephen,
St. Lawrence,
St. Vincent,
All you holy martyrs,
St. Sylvester,
St. Gregory,
St. Augustine,
All you holy bishops and confessors,
All you holy doctors,
St. Antony,
St. Benedict,
St. Dominic,
St. Francis,
All you holy priests and clerics,
All you holy monks and hermits,
St. Mary Magdalen,
St. Agnes,
St. Cecilia,
St. Agatha,
St. Anastasia,
All you holy virgins and widows,
All you holy men and women, saints of God,
All: Intercede for us.

Following the Blessing of Baptismal Water:

CANTICLE   Ps. 41, 2-4   [*Thirsting People*]

As the hind longs for the running waters,
  so my soul longs for You, O God.
Athirst is my soul for God, the living God.
  When shall I go and behold the face of God?
My tears are my food day and night,
  as they say to me day after day, "Where is
  your God?"

RENEWAL OF BAPTISMAL VOWS

[*Time for Genuine Renewal*]

Celebrant: Do you renounce Satan?

All: We do renounce him.

Celebrant: And all his works?

All: We do renounce them.

Celebrant: And all his allurements?

All: We do renounce them.

Celebrant: Do you believe in God, the Father
  almighty, creator of heaven and earth?

All: We do believe.

Celebrant: Do you believe in Jesus Christ, His
  only Son, our Lord, Who was born into this
  world and Who suffered?

All: We do believe.

Celebrant: Do you believe also in the Holy
  Spirit, the Holy Catholic Church, the communion of saints, the forgiveness of sins,
  the resurrection of the body and life everlasting?

All: We do believe.

Celebrant: Now let us pray to God together,
  as our Lord Jesus Christ has taught us to
  pray:

All: **Our Father, who art in heaven,
hallowed be Thy name;
Thy kingdom come;
Thy will be done on earth as it is in heaven.
Give us this day our daily bread;
and forgive us our trespasses
as we forgive those who trespass against us;
and lead us not into temptation,
but deliver us from evil.
Amen.**

Celebrant: And may almighty God, the Father of our Lord Jesus Christ, Who has given us new birth by means of water and the Holy Spirit and forgiven all our sins, keep us by His grace in the same Christ Jesus our Lord, so that we may have life everlasting.

All: **Amen.**

SECOND PART OF LITANY OF THE SAINTS

Be merciful,
All: Spare us, Lord.
Be merciful,
All: Hear us, Lord.
From every evil,
All: Deliver us, Lord.
From every sin,
From everlasting death,
Through the mystery of your holy Incarnation,
Through your coming,
Through your birth,
Through your baptism and holy fasting,
Through your cross and passion,
Through your death and burial,

Through your holy resurrection,
Through your wonderful ascension,
Through the coming of the Holy Spirit, the consoler,
In the day of judgment,
Sinners that we are,
All: We ask You to hear us.
That You would pardon us,
All: This we ask You, hear our prayer.
That You would govern and preserve You holy Church,

That You would preserve the Apostolic Pope and all ranks in the Church in holy religion,

That You would humble the enemies of Holy Church,

That You would give peace and true union of hearts to Christian kings and rulers,

That You would strengthen and keep us in Your holy service,

That you would repay with everlasting goods all who have done good to us,

That You would give and preserve the fruits of the earth,

That You would grant eternal rest to all the faithful departed,

That You would listen to us,

Lamb of God, Who take away the sins of the world,

All: Spare us, Lord.

Lamb of God, Who take away the sins of the world,

All: Hear us, Lord.

Lamb of God, Who take away the sins of the world,

All: Have mercy on us.

Christ, hear us.

Christ, graciously hear us.

THE MASS

AL-LE - - - LU- - IA.

Ps. 117, 1; 116, 1-2

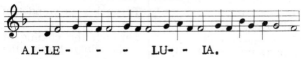

1. Give thanks to the Lord, for He is good,
2. Praise the Lord, all you na - tions;

1. for his mercy endures forev- er.
2. glorify him all you peo- ples!

1. ---------
2. For steadfast is his kind-ness toward us,

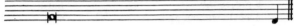

1. --------
2. and the fidelity of the Lord endures forev- er.

The "Agnus Dei," p. 291, is omitted. After Communion Lauds is sung, as follows:

Antiphon

Al-le-lu-ia, al- le-lu-ia, al- le- lu- ia.

Psalm Ps. 150

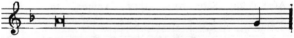

1 Praise the Lord in his sanctuar- y,
2 Praise him with the blast of the trum- pet,
3 Praise him with sounding cym- bals,
4 Glory be to the Father and to the Son,

1 praise him in the firmament of his strength.
2 praise him with lyre and harp,
3 praise him with clanging cym- bals.
4 and to the Holy Spi- rit.

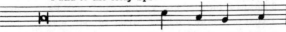

1 Praise him for his migh-ty deeds,
2 Praise him with tim- brel and harp,
3 Let every- thing that has breath
4 As it was in the
   beginning, is now and ev- er shall be,

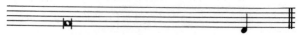

1 praise him for his sovereign majes- ty.
2 praise him with strings and   pipe.
3 praise the   Lord!
4 world without end. A-   men.

The Antiphon, "Alleluia, alleluia, alleluia," p. 131,
is repeated.

Antiphon

And ve- ry ear-ly in the   morn- ing

Af-ter the Sab- bath, they   came   to

the se-pul- chre at sun- rise al -   le- lu- ia.

Canticle of Zachary   Luke 1, 68-79

[*Salvation from Our God*]

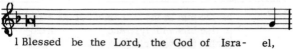

1 Blessed be the Lord, the God of Isra-   el,
2 As he promised through the mouths of his holy ones,
3 He has fulfilled his kindness to our Fa-   thers,
4 That delivered from the hands of our ene-   mies,
5 And you, O child,   shall be   called.
6 To give to his people knowledge of salva-   tion
7 To shine on those who sit in darkness and
                        the shadow of   death,
8 Glory be to the Father and to the   Son

1 because he has visited and wrought
 redemption for his peo- ple,
2 the prophets from of old:
3 and been mindful of his holy coven- ant
4 we should serve him without fear
5 the prophet of the Most High;
6 through forgiveness of their sins,
7 to guide our feet into the way of peace.
8 and to the Holy Spi- rit.

1 And has raised up a horn of sal- va- tion for us
2 Salvation from our en-em-ies
3 In the oath to Abra- ham our fa- ther,
4 In holiness and just- ice be- fore him
5 For you shall go be- fore the Lord
6 Because of the compassionate kind-ness of our God
7 (choir begins "Glory be, etc.")
8 As it was in the beginning, is now,
 and ev- er shall be.

1 in the house of David his ser- vant,
2 and from the hands of all our foes.
3 by which he swore to grant us.
4 all our days.
5 to prepare his ways.
6 with which the Orient from on high has visited us.
7
8 world without end. A- men.

The Antiphon, "And very early, etc.," p. 132, is repeated.

Go, the Mass is ended, al-le-lu-ia, al - le - - - lu - - ia.
Thanks be to God, al-le-lu-ia, al - le - - - lu - - ia.

On the third day Jesus rises from the dead.

EASTER SUNDAY

THOUGHT FOR TODAY: The Resurrection of Christ is a historical fact. When His enemies believed that they had destroyed Him, His real triumph began. To die to sin and to live with Christ is our way to victory and glorious resurrection.

BIBLE AND LITURGY: The Jews celebrated the Feast of "Passover" because the Lord "passed over" the houses of the Israelites, whose doorposts were sprinkled with the blood of the "passover" (paschal) lamb. Our Passover Lamb is Christ. His Blood, shed on Calvary, keeps the devil from harming us and makes us partakers of His glorious Resurrection. READ: Ex. 12, 21-28; 1 Cor. 5, 7-8 (*Ep.*); Rom. 6, 1-11; 1 Cor. 15, 12-58; 1 Thess. 4, 13-18.

INTROIT   Ps. 138, 18. 5. 6. 1. 2   [*Christ is Risen*]

I arose, and am still with You, alleluia;
   You rest Your hand upon Me, alleluia;
      Your knowledge is too wonderful, alleluia, alleluia.

(Ps.) **O Lord, You have probed Me and You know Me;**
   You know when I sit and when I stand.

Glory be to the Father, and to the Son,
   and to the Holy Spirit.
As it was in the beginning, is now, and ever
      shall be,
   world without end. Amen.
I arose, and am still with You, alleluia;
   You rest Your hand upon Me, alleluia;
   Your knowledge is too wonderful, alleluia,
      alleluia.

GRADUAL   Ps. 117, 24. 1   [*This Is the Day*]

This is the day the Lord has made;
   let us be glad and rejoice in it.
Give thanks to the Lord, for He is good,
   for His mercy endures forever.

Alleluia, alleluia.   1 Cor. 5, 7   [*The Miracle*]
Christ, our Passover, has been sacrificed.

SEQUENCE

Christians, to the Paschal victim
   Offer your thankful praises!
A lamb the sheep redeemeth: Christ, Who only
      is sinless,
   Reconcileth sinners to the Father.
Death and life have contended in that combat
      stupendous:
   The Prince of life, Who died, reigns immortal.
Speak, Mary, declaring
   What thou sawest, wayfaring.
"The tomb of Christ, Who is living,
   The glory of Jesus' resurrection;
Bright angels attesting,
   The shroud and napkin resting.

Yea, Christ my hope is arisen:
    To Galilee He goes before you."
Christ indeed from death is risen, our new life
        obtaining.
    Have mercy, victor King, ever reigning'
        Amen. Alleluia.

OFFERTORY   Ps. 75, 9. 10   [*Triumph*]

The earth feared and was silent,
    when God arose for judgment. Alleluia.

COMMUNION   1 Cor. 5, 7. 8   [*The Paschal Victim*]

Christ our passover, has been sacrificed,
    alleluia:
    therefore let us keep festival with the un-
        leavened bread of sincerity and truth,
    alleluia, alleluia, alleluia.

———————

MONDAY — Within the Octave of Easter

INTROIT   Ex. 13, 5. 9; Ps. 104, 1   [*The New Life*]

The Lord has brought you into a land
    flowing with milk and honey, alleluia:
Thus the law of the Lord
    will ever be on your lips, alleluia, alleluia.
(Ps.) Give thanks to the Lord, invoke His Name;
    make known among the nations His deeds.
Glory be to the Father, etc.
Repeat: **The Lord has,** etc., *as far as* (Ps.).

GRADUAL   Ps. 117, 24. 2   [*His Mercy Endures*]

This is the day the Lord has made;
    let us be glad and rejoice in it.

Let the house of Israel say that He is good,
   that His mercy endures forever.

Alleluia, alleluia.   Matt. 28, 2   [*Empty Tomb*]

An angel of the Lord came down from heaven,
   and drawing near, rolled back the stone,
   and sat upon it.

SEQUENCE — **p. 135.**

OFFERTORY   Matt. 28, 2, 5. 6   [*Risen As He Said*]

An angel of the Lord came down from heaven,
   and said to the women,
"He Whom you seek
   is risen as He said." Alleluia.

COMMUNION   Luke 24, 34   [*Peter Saw Him*]

The Lord has risen,
   and has appeared to Peter. Alleluia.

TUESDAY — Within the Octave of Easter

INTROIT   Sir. 15, 3. 4; Ps. 104, 1   [*Living Water*]

He gave them the water of learning to drink,
   alleluia;
It shall be made strong in them,
   and shall not be moved, alleluia,
And it shall exalt them forever, alleluia, alleluia.
(Ps.) Give thanks to the Lord, invoke His Name;
   make known among the nations His deeds.
Glory be to the Father, etc.
Repeat: **He gave them,** etc., *as far as* (Ps.).

GRADUAL Ps. 117, 24; 106, 2   [*Redeemed*]

This is the day the Lord has made;
 let us be glad and rejoice in it.
Thus let the redeemed of the Lord say,
 those whom He has redeemed from the hand
  of the foe
And gathered from the lands.

Alleluia, alleluia.   [*Risen*]
The Lord is risen from the sepulchre,
 Who for us hung upon a tree.

SEQUENCE — p. 135.

OFFERTORY Ps. 17, 14. 16   [*The Great Voice*]

The Lord thundered from heaven,
 and the Most High gave forth His voice:
 and the fountains of waters appeared, alleluia.

COMMUNION Col. 3, 1-2   [*Seek What Is Above*]

If you have risen with Christ,
 seek the things that are above,
Where Christ is seated at the right hand of
  God, alleluia;
 mind the things that are above, alleluia.

WEDNESDAY — Within the Octave of Easter

INTROIT Matt. 25, 34; Ps. 95, 1   [*Receive the Kingdom*]

Come, blessed of my Father,
 receive the kingdom, alleluia,
Which was prepared for you
 from the foundation of the world, alleluia,
  alleluia, alleluia.

(Ps.) **Sing to the Lord a new song;**
   sing to the Lord, all you lands.
Glory be to the Father, etc.
Repeat: **Come, blessed,** etc., *as far as* (Ps.).

GRADUAL   Ps. 117, 24. 16   [*Power of the Lord*]

This is the day the Lord has made;
   let us be glad and rejoice in it.
The right hand of the Lord has struck with
   power:
   the right hand of the Lord has exalted me.

Alleluia, alleluia.   Luke 24, 34   [*Risen Indeed*]
The Lord is risen indeed,
   and has appeared to Peter.

SEQUENCE — p. 135.

OFFERTORY   Ps. 77, 23-25   [*Manna from Heaven*]

The Lord opened the doors of heaven;
   He rained manna upon them for food
   and gave them heavenly bread.
The bread of angels was eaten by men, alleluia.

COMMUNION   Rom. 6, 9   [*Death No More*]

Christ, having risen from the dead,
   dies now no more, alleluia;
Death shall no longer have dominion over Him,
   alleluia, alleluia.

THURSDAY — Within the Octave of Easter

INTROIT Wis. 10, 20-21; Ps. 97, 1 [The New Song]

They praised in unison Your conquering hand,
  O Lord, alleluia,
Because wisdom opened the mouths of the
  dumb,
    and gave ready speech to infants, alleluia,
    alleluia.
(Ps.) Sing to the Lord a new song,
  for He has done wondrous deeds.
Glory be to the Father, etc.
Repeat: **They praised,** etc., *as far as* (Ps.).

GRADUAL Ps. 117, 24. 22-23 [The Cornerstone]

This is the day the Lord has made;
  let us be glad and rejoice in it.
The stone which the builders rejected
  has become the cornerstone.
By the Lord has this been done;
  it is wonderful in our eyes.

Alleluia, alleluia. [Creator and Lover]
Christ is risen,
  Who created all things,
    and Who had compassion upon the human
    race.

SEQUENCE — p. 135.

OFFERTORY Ex. 13, 5 [The New World]

"In the day of your solemnity,"
  says the Lord,

"I will bring you into a land
  flowing with milk and honey." Alleluia.

COMMUNION   1 Pet. 2, 9   [Out of Darkness]

O purchased people,
  proclaim the perfections of Him, alleluia,
Who has called you out of darkness
  into His marvelous light, alleluia.

FRIDAY — Within the Octave of Easter

INTROIT   Ps. 77, 53. 1   [Rescue]

The Lord led them on in hope, alleluia,
  while He covered their enemies with the sea,
    alleluia, alleluia, alleluia.
(Ps.) Hearken, My people, to My teaching:
  incline your ears to the words of My mouth.
Glory be to the Father, etc.
Repeat: **The Lord led them,** etc., *as far as* (Ps.).

GRADUAL   Ps. 117, 24. 26-27   [Blessed Is He]

This is the day the Lord has made;
  let us be glad and rejoice in it.
Blessed is He Who comes in the Name of the
    Lord;
  the Lord is God, and He has given us light.
Alleluia, alleluia.   Ps. 95, 10   [Cross of the King]
Say among the nations:
  the Lord has reigned from a tree.

SEQUENCE — p. 135.

OFFERTORY Ex. 12, 14 [*Ever-memorable Day*]

This day shall be a memorial feast for you,
    alleluia;
    and you shall celebrate it as a solemn feast
    to the Lord
    from generation to generation:
    an everlasting legal day, alleluia, alleluia,
    alleluia.

COMMUNION Matt. 28, 18-19 [*Save All Nations*]

All power in heaven and on earth
    has been given to Me, alleluia.
Go and make disciples of all nations,
    baptizing them in the Name of the Father,
    and of the Son,
    and of the Holy Spirit, alleluia, alleluia.

SATURDAY — Within the Octave of Easter

INTROIT Ps. 104, 43. 1 [*The Lord, Our Leader*]

The Lord led forth His people with joy, alleluia;
    with shouts of joy, His chosen ones, alleluia,
    alleluia.
(Ps.) **Give thanks to the Lord, invoke His Name;**
    make known among the nations His deeds.
Glory be to the Father, etc.
Repeat: **The Lord led forth,** etc., *as far as* (Ps.).

ALLELUIA Ps. 117, 24; 112, 1 [*Praise God*]

Alleluia, alleluia.
This is the day the Lord has made;
    let us be glad and rejoice in it.

Alleluia. Praise, you servants of the Lord, praise the name of the Lord.

SEQUENCE — p. 135.

OFFERTORY   Ps. 117, 26-27   [*Giver of Light*]

Blessed is He Who comes in the Name of the Lord;
  we bless you from the house of the Lord.
  The Lord is God, and He has given us light,
    alleluia, alleluia.

COMMUNION   Gal. 3, 27   [*Put on Christ*]

All you who have been baptized into Christ, have put on Christ, alleluia.

St. Thomas expresses his faith in the risen Jesus.

FIRST SUNDAY AFTER EASTER

THOUGHT FOR TODAY: Despite all convincing proofs, many doubting Thomases are still saying "I'll never believe." We should repeat the words of the believing Thomas, "My Lord and My God," as often as we lift our eyes up to the Blessed Sacrament.

BIBLE AND LITURGY: It is through Baptism, sealing and perfecting a beginning Faith, that man is initiated into God's Holy People. Through Faith and Baptism man undergoes a mysterious rebirth and shares in God's life. READ: Acts 8, 26-39; John 3, 1-6; Acts 2, 37-41; 8, 4-13; 16, 11-15; 18, 1-11; 19, 1-7.

INTROIT   1 Pet. 2, 2; Ps. 80, 2   [*New Life*]

Crave as newborn babes, alleluia:
  pure spiritual milk: alleluia, alleluia, alleluia.
(Ps.) Sing joyfully to God our strength;
  acclaim the God of Jacob.
Glory be to the Father, and to the Son,
  and to the Holy Spirit.
As it was in the beginning, is now, and ever
    shall be,
  world without end. Amen.

Crave as newborn babes, alleluia:
   pure spiritual milk: alleluia, alleluia, alleluia.

ALLELUIA   Matt. 28, 7; John 20, 26   [*I will go Before You*]

"On the day of My Resurrection," says the
      Lord,
   "I will go before you into Galilee."
Alleluia. After eight days, the doors being
      closed,
   Jesus stood in the midst of His disciples,
      and said,
   "Peace be to you!" Alleluia.

OFFERTORY   Matt. 28, 2. 5. 6   [*Risen As He Said*]

An angel of the Lord came down from heaven,
      and said to the women,
"He Whom you seek has risen,
   even as He said," alleluia.

COMMUNION   John 20, 27   [*Believe*]

Put in your hand,
   and know the place of the nails, alleluia;
And be not unbelieving,
   but believing, alleluia, alleluia.

Jesus the Good Shepherd brings back the lost sheep.

SECOND SUNDAY AFTER EASTER

THOUGHT FOR TODAY: Our good example and prayers must help to bring the straying sheep back to Christ, that there may be one flock, one shepherd.

BIBLE AND LITURGY: Christ used examples, taken from the rural life of His audience, to explain heavenly truth. The writers of both the Old and the New Testament did the same. READ: John 10, 1-19; Jer. 31, 1-13; Ezech. 34; John 21, 15-17.

INTROIT Ps. 32, 5. 6. 1 [*God's Kindness Everywhere*]

Of the kindness of the Lord the earth is full, alleluia;
> by the word of the Lord the heavens were made, alleluia, alleluia.

(Ps.) Exult, you just, in the Lord;
> praise from the upright is fitting.

Glory be to the Father, and to the Son,
> and to the Holy Spirit.

As it was in the beginning, is now, and ever shall be,
> world without end. Amen.

Of the kindness of the Lord the earth is full, alleluia;

by the word of the Lord the heavens were
made, alleluia, alleluia.

ALLELUIA   Luke 24, 35; John 10, 14   [*It Is the Lord*]

Alleluia, alleluia.
The disciples recognized the Lord Jesus
in the breaking of the bread.
Alleluia. I am the Good Shepherd:
and I know My sheep,
and Mine know Me. Alleluia.

OFFERTORY   Ps. 62, 2. 5   [*Longing for God*]

O God, my God, to You do I watch at break
of day,
and in Your Name I will lift up my hands,
alleluia.

COMMUNION   John 10, 14   [*I Know Mine*]

I am the Good Shepherd, alleluia:
and I know My sheep
and Mine know Me: alleluia, alleluia.

Jesus tells His disciples that He will return.

THIRD SUNDAY AFTER EASTER

THOUGHT FOR TODAY: All those who resolve to live up to their Christian principles will meet with opposition and persecution. But our life on earth is only "a little while," and our sorrow shall be turned into joy.

BIBLE AND LITURGY: We must regard suffering, pain, frustration, opposition and disillusionment in the same perspective as Christian abstinence and penance. God permits the former and Christians freely embrace the latter for the same end—an ever more perfect detachment from evil and a greater freedom to unite themselves to God in a bond of love. READ: Matt. 5, 10; Luke 6, 20-26; Rom. 8, 35-39; 2 Cor. 4, 7-18; 2 Thess. 1, 3-10; 2 Tim. 3, 10-17.

INTROIT   Ps. 65, 1. 2. 3   [Sing Joyfully]

Shout joyfully to God, all you on earth, alleluia;
   sing praise to the glory of His Name, alleluia;
     proclaim His glorious praise, alleluia, alleluia,
     alleluia.

(Ps.) Say to God, "How tremendous are Your
     deeds, O Lord!

   For Your great strength Your enemies fawn
     upon You."

Glory be to the Father, and to the Son,
and to the Holy Spirit.

As it was in the beginning, is now, and ever
shall be,
world without end. Amen.

Shout joyfully to God, all you on earth, alleluia;
sing praise to the glory of His Name, alleluia;
proclaim His glorious praise, alleluia, alleluia,
alleluia.

ALLELUIA   Ps. 110, 9; Luke 24, 46

[Salvation through Suffering]

Alleluia, alleluia.
The Lord has sent deliverance
to His people.
Alleluia. It behooved Christ to suffer
and to rise again from the dead,
and so to enter into His glory. Alleluia.

OFFERTORY   Ps. 145, 2   *[Lifelong Praise]*

Praise the Lord, O my soul;
I will praise the Lord all my life;
I will sing praise to my God while I live.
Alleluia.

COMMUNION   John 16, 16   *[I Go to the Father]*

A little while, and you shall not see Me, alleluia;
and again a little while, and you shall see Me:
because I go to the Father, alleluia, alleluia.

Jesus promises the Holy Spirit to His disciples.

FOURTH SUNDAY AFTER EASTER

THOUGHT FOR TODAY: The Holy Spirit, promised by Christ to His Church, continues to prove the world wrong concerning sin, justice, and condemnation. Only among those people who follow this teaching, can a lasting peace be secured.

BIBLE AND LITURGY: The typical attitude of an unbeliever is scepticism. All knowledge is uncertain to him. Pilate asked: "What is truth?" (John 18, 38). We know the truth through God's Spirit, Who has been poured into our souls by Faith, Baptism and Confirmation. READ: John 18, 37-38; 1, 1-18 (esp. 14); 8, 12-33 (esp. 32); 8, 42-47; 15, 26-27.

INTROIT   Ps. 97, 1. 2. 1   [*Deeds of the Lord*]

Sing to the Lord a new song, alleluia;
> for the Lord has done wondrous deeds, alleluia
> in the sight of the nations, He has revealed His justice, alleluia, alleluia.

(Ps.) His right hand has won victory for Him, His holy arm.

Glory be to the Father, and to the Son, and to the Holy Spirit.

As it was in the beginning, is now, and ever
   shall be,
   world without end. Amen.
Sing to the Lord a new song, alleluia;
   for the Lord has done wondrous deeds,
      alleluia
   in the sight of the nations, He has revealed
      His justice, alleluia, alleluia.

ALLELUIA   Ps. 117, 16; Rom. 6, 9   [Power of God]

Alleluia, alleluia.
The right hand of the Lord has struck with
   power;
   the right hand of the Lord has exalted me.
Alleluia. Christ, having risen from the dead,
   dies now no more;
   death shall no longer have dominion over
      Him. Alleluia.

OFFERTORY   Ps. 65, 1. 2. 16   [Declaring the Lord]

Shout joyfully to God, all you on earth,
   sing praise to the glory of His Name;
Hear now, all you who fear God, while I declare
   what the Lord has done for me. Alleluia.

COMMUNION   John 16, 8   [Work of the Holy Spirit]

When the Paraclete has come, the Spirit of
   truth,
   He will convict the world
   of sin, and of justice, and of judgment,
      alleluia, alleluia.

Jesus foretells His Ascension to heaven.

FIFTH SUNDAY AFTER EASTER

THOUGHT FOR TODAY: At the opening of the Rogation Week we are reminded of Christ's promise that our petitions will be granted if we ask anything in His Name. To speak in His Name we must be "doers," not "hearers" only, of the word of God.

BIBLE AND LITURGY: Being God's children through Faith and Baptism, we can preserve our relationship with our heavenly Father by prayer. Praying means to direct our heart to God. This is possible only with God's help. That is the reason why Jesus teaches and helps us. READ: Luke 11, 1-13; Matt. 6, 5-15; 7, 7-11; Gen. 19, 16-33; Acts 12, 1-17 (esp. 5 and 13); Tobias 3; Ps. 140.

INTROIT   Isa. 48, 20; Ps. 65, 1. 2

[*Proclaiming God's Goodness*]

Declare the word of joy,
and let it be heard, alleluia:
Declare it even to the ends of the earth;
the Lord has delivered His people: alleluia,
alleluia.
(Ps.) Shout joyfully to God, all you on earth,
sing praise to the glory of His Name;
proclaim His glorious praise.

Glory be to the Father, and to the Son,
   and to the Holy Spirit.
As it was in the beginning, is now, and ever
      shall be,
   world without end. Amen.
Declare the word of joy,
   and let it be heard, alleluia:
Declare it even to the ends of the earth;
   the Lord has delivered His people: alleluia,
      alleluia.

ALLELUIA   John 16, 28   [*The Redeeming Christ*]

Alleluia, alleluia.
Christ is risen, and has shone upon us,
   whom He redeemed with His Blood.
Alleluia. I came forth from the Father,
   and have come into the world.
Again I leave the world,
   and go to the Father. Alleluia.

OFFERTORY Ps. 65, 8. 9. 20 [*Giver of Life and Protector*]

Bless the Lord our God, you peoples,
   loudly sound His praise;
He has given life to my soul,
   and has not let my feet slip.
Blessed be the Lord, Who refused me not
   my prayer, or His kindness. Alleluia.

COMMUNION   Ps. 95, 2   [*Sing of Salvation*]

Sing to the Lord, alleluia;
   sing to the Lord;
Bless His Name;
   announce His salvation day after day, alleluia,
      alleluia.

MAJOR AND MINOR LITANIES
ROGATION MASS

INTROIT Ps. 17,7, 2-3   [*God Hears Us*]

From His holy temple He heard my voice;
my cry to Him reached His ears. Alleluia.
alleluia.
(Ps.) I Love You, O Lord, my strength,
O Lord, my rock, my fortress, my deliverer.
Glory be to the Father, etc.
Repeat: **From His holy,** etc., *as far as* (Ps.).

In Paschaltime: Ps. 78, 9-10; 30, 8
Alleluia, alleluia.   [*Proof of God's Presence*]
Pardon our sins, O Lord;
Why should the nations say,
"Where is their God?"
Alleluia. I will rejoice and be glad of Your
kindness,
when You have seen my affliction
and watched over me in my distress. Alleluia.

Outside Paschaltime:
GRADUAL Ps. 43, 8-9   [*God's Salvation*]

You saved us, O Lord, from our foes,
and those who hated us You put to shame.
In God we gloried day by day;
Your Name we praised always.

Alleluia, alleluia.   Ps. 78, 9-10
Pardon our sins, O Lord;
Why should the nations say,
"Where is their God?" Alleluia.

TRACT   Ps. 24, 17-18. 1-4   [*Trust*]

Bring me out of distress, O Lord;
Put an end to my affliction and my suffering,
   and take away all my sins.
To You I lift up my soul, O Lord.
In You, O my God, I trust; let me not be put
   to shame,
   let not my enemies exult over me.
No one who waits for You shall be put to
   shame;
   those shall be put to shame who heedlessly
   break faith.

OFFERTORY   Ps. 108, 30-31   [*Thanks for God's Help*]

I will speak my thanks earnestly to the Lord,
   and in the midst of the throng I will praise
   Him,
For He stood at the right hand of the poor man,
   to save me from those who would condemn
   me. (P.T. Alleluia.)

COMMUNION   Luke 11, 9-10   [*Confidence*]

Ask, and you shall receive;
   seek, and you shall find;
   knock, and it shall be opened to you.
For everyone who asks receives;
   and he who seeks finds;
   and to him who knocks, it shall be opened.
   (P.T. Alleluia.)

VIGIL OF THE ASCENSION

Mass: As on 5th Sunday after Easter, p. 152.

After forty days with His disciples, Jesus ascends to heaven.

ASCENSION DAY

THOUGHT FOR TODAY: Our Lord ascended into heaven to prepare a place for us. His apostles were sent to teach all nations what He had commanded them. We must now cleanse our hearts from sin, which cannot enter heaven, and store up good deeds, performed in the state of grace. These will speak for us when we appear before God.

BIBLE AND LITURGY: The Bible theme of the First Passion Sunday teaches the Christian vision on Christ's eternal priesthood. Christ went up into heaven, sits at the right hand of God the Father (i.e., shares power with Him) and is constantly interceding for us. He is our Mediator and High Priest in heaven. READ: John 14, 1-24; Heb. 7, 11-28 (esp. 25); 8, 1-13; 1 John 2, 1-2; Apoc. 21, 22-27; 22, 3-5.

INTROIT   Acts 1, 11; Ps. 46, 2   [*Why Look Up?*]

Men of Galilee,
> why do you stand looking up to heaven? Alleluia.

He shall come in the same way
> as you have seen Him going up to heaven: alleluia, alleluia, alleluia.

(Ps.) **All you peoples, clap your hands.**
shout to God with cries of gladness.

Glory be to the Father, and to the Son,
and to the Holy Spirit.

As it was in the beginning, is now, and ever shall be,
world without end. Amen.

Men of Galilee,
why do you stand looking up to heaven? Alleluia.

He shall come in the same way
as you have seen Him going up to heaven: alleluia, alleluia, alleluia.

ALLELUIA   Ps. 46, 6; 67, 18. 19
[*Glory and Christ's Mission*]

Alleluia, alleluia.

God mounts His throne amid shouts of joy;
the Lord, amid trumpet blasts.

Alleluia. The Lord advances from Sinai to the sanctuary;
ascending on high,
He has led captivity captive. Alleluia.

OFFERTORY   Ps. 46, 6   [*Triumph*]

God mounts His throne amid shouts of joy;
the Lord, amid trumpet blasts. Alleluia.

COMMUNION   Ps. 67, 33. 34
[*Praise to Christ in Triumph*]

Chant praise to the Lord,
Who rides on the heights of the heavens to the East. Alleluia.

Jesus declares the Holy Spirit will bear witness to Him.

SUNDAY AFTER THE ASCENSION

THOUGHT FOR TODAY: Fervent prayers are being said during this week in preparation for Pentecost. To make these prayers more acceptable to God, "maintain constant charity toward each other, because charity does away with a multitude of sins."

BIBLE AND LITURGY: Jesus promised to send the Spirit, Who proceeds from the Father. The Spirit is God just as the Father and the Son. He sanctifies us into the image of God. It is the Spirit also Who gives wisdom, understanding, fortitude and godliness to God's Chosen People. READ: Isa. 11, 1-10; Matt. 3, 13-17; Rom. 8, 1-17; 8, 26-27; 1 Cor. 2, 6-16; 3, 10-17.

INTROIT Ps. 26, 7. 8. 9. 1   [*My Heart Speaks*]

Hear, O Lord, the sound of my call, alleluia;
  to You my heart speaks, Your glance I seek;
Your presence, O Lord, I seek.
  Hide not Your face from me, alleluia, alleluia.
(Ps.) The Lord is my light and my salvation;
  whom should I fear?
Glory be to the Father, and to the Son,
  and to the Holy Spirit.

As it was in the beginning, is now, and ever
    shall be,
  world without end. Amen.
Hear, O Lord, the sound of my call, alleluia;
  to You my heart speaks, Your glance I seek;
Your presence, O Lord, I seek.
  Hide not Your face from me, alleluia, alleluia.

ALLELUIA   Ps. 46, 9; John 14, 18   [*Children of a King*]

Alleluia, alleluia.
The Lord reigns over all the nations,
  God sits upon His holy throne.
Alleluia. I will not leave you orphans;
  I go away and I come to you,
    and your heart shall rejoice. Alleluia.

OFFERTORY   Ps. 46, 6.   [*Triumph*]

God mounts His throne amid shouts of joy;
  the Lord, amid trumpet blasts. Alleluia.

COMMUNION   John 17, 12. 13. 15

[*Keep Them from Evil*]

Father, while I was with them,
  I kept them whom You have given Me,
    alleluia;
But now I am coming to You:
  I do not pray that You take them out of the
    world,
    but that You keep them from evil, alleluia,
    alleluia.

SATURDAY — THE VIGIL OF PENTECOST

INTROIT   Ezech. 36, 23. 24. 25-26: Ps. 33, 2   *[A New Spirit]*

When I prove My holiness through you,
  I will gather you from all foreign lands;
And I will sprinkle clean water upon you
  to cleanse you from all your impurities;
  and I will give you a new spirit, alleluia, alleluia.

(Ps.) **I will bless the Lord at all times;**
  His praise shall be ever in my mouth.

Glory be to the Father, etc.

Repeat: **When I prove,** etc., *as far as* (Ps.).

ALLELUIA   Ps. 116, 1-2   *[Give Thanks]*

Give thanks to the Lord, for He is good,
  for His kindness endures forever!

TRACT   Ps. 116, 1-2   *[Praise the Lord]*

Praise the Lord, all you nations;
  glorify Him, all you peoples!
For steadfast is His kindness toward us,
  and the fidelity of the Lord endures forever.

OFFERTORY   Ps. 103, 30-31   *[Re-created by the Spirit]*

Send forth Your spirit, and they shall be created,
  and You shall renew the face of the earth.
May the glory of the Lord endure forever, alleluia.

COMMUNION   John 7, 37-39   *[Diffusion of the Spirit]*

On the last day of the feast, Jesus said,
"He who believes in Me, from within him
  there shall flow rivers of living water."
He said this, however, of the Spirit,
  Whom they who believed in Him were to receive,
  alleluia, alleluia.

The Holy Spirit descends on the disciples.

PENTECOST SUNDAY

THOUGHT FOR TODAY: Jesus had instructed His disciples on several occasions about the coming of the Holy Spirit. The marvelous events which accompanied His arrival were signs of the far greater effects of grace He produces in the souls of those who receive Him. We pray with the Church: "Come, Holy Spirit, fill the hearts of Your faithful, and kindle in them the fire of Your love."

BIBLE AND LITURGY: The Spirit of God, another Advocate and Consoler, worked marvels in the Apostles and continues to do so in the Church. Faith, Baptism and Confirmation gave us this Spirit of God. Our constant prayer should be the prayer after the Epistle of this Mass: "Come, Holy Spirit, fill the hearts of Your faithful!" READ: Joel 2, 28-32; Acts 2, 14-21; 2, 37-41; 1 Cor. 12, 1-16; Eph. 4, 25-32; Acts 10, 34; 42-48; 8, 14-17.

INTROIT   Wis. 1, 7; Ps. 67, 2   [*Spirit Fills the World*]

The Spirit of the Lord fills the world, alleluia, is all-embracing, and knows man's utterance, alleluia, alleluia, alleluia.

(Ps.) **God arises, His enemies are scattered, and those who hate Him flee before Him.**

Glory be to the Father, and to the Son,
   and to the Holy Spirit.

As it was in the beginning, is now, and ever
      shall be,
   world without end. Amen.

The Spirit of the Lord fills the world, alleluia,
   is all-embracing, and knows man's utterance,
      alleluia, alleluia, alleluia.

ALLELUIA   Ps. 103, 30   [*Fire of New Love*]

Alleluia, alleluia.

Send forth Your Spirit, and they shall be
      created;
   and You shall renew the face of the earth.

Alleluia. Come, Holy Spirit, fill the hearts of
      Your faithful:
   and kindle in them the fire of Your love.

SEQUENCE   [*Cry of Mankind to the Lifegiver*]

Come Thou Holy Spirit, come!
And from Thy celestial home
   Shed a ray of light divine!

Come, Thou Father of the poor!
Come, Thou source of all our store!
   Come, within our bosoms shine!

Thou, of comforters the best;
Thou, the soul's most welcome Guest;
   Sweet refreshment here below;

In our labor, rest most sweet;
Grateful coolness in the heat;
   Solace in the midst of woe.

O most blessed Light divine,
Shine within these hearts of Thine,
   And our inmost being fill!

Where Thou art not man hath naught,
Nothing good in deed or thought,
  Nothing free from taint of ill.

Heal our wounds, our strength renew;
On our dryness pour Thy dew;
  Wash the stains of guilt away:

Bend the stubborn heart and will;
Melt the frozen, warm the chill;
  Guide the steps that go astray.

On the faithful, who adore
And confess Thee, evermore
  In Thy sev'nfold gift descend;

Give them virtue's sure reward;
Give them Thy salvation, Lord;
  Give them joys that never end. Amen,
    Alleluia.

OFFERTORY Ps. 67, 29. 30

[*Continue the Work of the Spirit*]

Confirm, O God,
  what You have wrought in us;
From Your temple, which is in Jerusalem,
  kings shall offer gifts to You. Alleluia.

COMMUNION Acts 2, 2. 4

[*Filled with the Holy Spirit*]

Suddenly there came a sound from heaven,
  as of a violent wind blowing,
    where they were sitting, alleluia:
And they were all filled with the Holy Spirit,
  speaking of the wonderful works of God,
    alleluia, alleluia.

MONDAY — Within the Octave of Pentecost

INTROIT   Ps. 80, 17. 2   [Fed by the Holy Spirit]

He fed them with the best of wheat, alleluia:
  and filled them with honey from the rock,
    alleluia, alleluia.

(Ps.) **Sing joyfully to God our strength;**
  acclaim the God of Jacob.

Glory be to the Father, etc.

Repeat: **He fed them,** etc., *as far as* (Ps.)

ALLELUIA   Acts 2, 4   [Come, Holy Spirit]

Alleluia, alleluia.

The apostles spoke in foreign tongues
  the wonderful works of God.

Alleluia. Come, Holy Spirit, fill the hearts of
    Your faithful;
  and kindle in them the fire of Your love.

SEQUENCE — p. 162.

OFFERTORY   Ps. 17, 14. 16   [Life-giving Water]

The Lord thundered from heaven,
  the Most High gave forth His voice;
  and the fountains of waters appeared, alleluia.

COMMUNION   John 14, 26   [Taught by the Spirit]

The Holy Spirit will teach you, alleluia:
  Whatever I have said to you, alleluia, alleluia.

TUESDAY — Within the Octave of Pentecost

INTROIT   4 Ezr. 2, 36. 37; Ps. 77, 1

[Joyful Message of the Spirit]

Receive the joy of your glory, alleluia:
  giving thanks to God, alleluia,

Who has called you to the heavenly kingdom,
alleluia, alleluia, alleluia.

(Ps.) **Hearken, My people to My teaching;**
incline your ears to the words of My mouth.

Glory be to the Father, etc.

Repeat: **Receive the joy,** etc., *as far as* (Ps.).

ALLELUIA   John 14, 26   [*Heavenly Teacher*]

Alleluia, alleluia.
The Holy Spirit will teach you
whatever I have said to you.
Alleluia. Come, Holy Spirit, fill the hearts of
Your faithful;
and kindle in them the fire of Your love.

SEQUENCE — p. 162.

OFFERTORY   Ps. 77, 23-25   [*Bread of Angels*]

The Lord opened the doors of heaven;
He rained manna upon them for food
and gave them heavenly bread.
The bread of the angels was eaten by men,
alleluia.

COMMUNION   John 15, 26; 16, 14
[*Glorified by the Spirit*]

The Spirit Who proceeds from the Father,
alleluia:
He will glorify Me, alleluia, alleluia.

EMBER WEDNESDAY AFTER PENTECOST

INTROIT   Ps. 67, 8. 9. 2   [*God - with - Us*]

O God, when you went forth at the head of
Your people,
making a passage for them,
dwelling in their midst, alleluia:

The earth quaked;
   it rained from heaven, alleluia, alleluia.

(Ps.) **God arises; His enemies are scattered,
   and those who hate Him flee before Him.**

Glory be to the Father, etc.

Repeat: **O God,** etc., *as far as* (Ps.).

After the 1st Lesson:

Alleluia. Ps. 32, 6   [*Creating Spirit*]

**By the word of the Lord the heavens were
   made;
   by the breath of His mouth all their host.**

   After the 2nd Lesson:

Alleluia, alleluia.   [*Enkindle the Fire*]

**Come, Holy Spirit, fill the hearts of Your
   faithful;
   and kindle in them the fire of Your love.**

SEQUENCE — p. 162.

OFFERTORY   Ps. 118, 47-48   [*Obedient Sacrifice*]

**I will delight in Your commands,
   which I love exceedingly.
And I will lift up my hands to Your commands,
   which I love, alleluia.**

COMMUNION   John 14, 27   [*Christ's Peace*]

**Peace I leave with you, alleluia;
   My peace I give to you, alleluia, alleluia.**

THURSDAY — Within the Octave of Pentecost

Mass: As on Pentecost Sunday, p. 161.

EMBER FRIDAY AFTER PENTECOST

INTROIT   Ps. 70, 8. 23. 1-2   [*Joyfully Sing to God*]

Let my mouth be filled with Your praise,
alleluia:
   that I may sing, alleluia.
My lips shall shout for joy
   as I sing Your praises, alleluia, alleluia.
(Ps.) In You, O Lord, I take refuge;
   let me never be put to shame.
In Your justice rescue me, and deliver me.
Glory be to the Father, etc.
Repeat: Let my mouth, etc., *as far as* (Ps.).

ALLELUIA   Wis. 12, 1   [*Spirit of Sweetness*]

Alleluia, alleluia.
O how good and sweet
   is Your Spirit, O Lord, within us!
Alleluia. Come, Holy Spirit, fill the hearts of
Your faithful;
   and kindle in them the fire of Your love.

SEQUENCE — p. 162.

OFFERTORY   Ps. 145, 2   [*Life-long Praise*]

Praise the Lord, O my soul;
   I will praise the Lord all my life;
   I will sing praise to my God while I live,
     alleluia.

COMMUNION   John 14, 18   [*Reunion in Joy*]

I will not leave you orphans;
   I will come to you again, alleluia:
   and your hearts shall rejoice, alleluia.

EMBER SATURDAY AFTER PENTECOST

Short Form of the Mass

INTROIT Rom. 5, 5; Ps. 102, 1 [*Pouring Out of the Spirit*]

The charity of God is poured forth in our hearts,
  alleluia:
  by His Spirit dwelling in us, alleluia, alleluia.
(Ps.) **Bless the Lord, O my soul;**
  and all my being, bless His holy Name.
Glory be to the Father, etc.
Repeat: **The charity,** etc., *as far as* (Ps.).

After the 1st Lesson:

Alleluia. John 6, 64   [*Spirit of Life*]

It is the Spirit that gives life;
  but the flesh profits nothing.

After the 2nd Lesson:

Alleluia, alleluia.   [*Enkindle Our Hearts*]

Come, Holy Spirit, fill the hearts of Your
  faithful;
  and kindle in them the fire of Your love.

SEQUENCE — p. 162.

OFFERTORY Ps. 87, 2-3   [*Cry for Salvation*]

O Lord, the God of my salvation,
  by day I cry out,
  at night I clamor in Your presence.
Let my prayer come before You, O Lord,
  alleluia.

COMMUNION John 3, 8   [*Spirit's Breath*]

The Spirit breathes where He will,
  and you hear His voice, alleluia, alleluia;
But do not know whence He comes
  or where He goes, alleluia, alleluia, alleluia.

FIRST SUNDAY AFTER PENTECOST

This Mass is said only on "free days" between the First and Second Sundays after Pentecost.

INTROIT Ps. 12, 6. 1   [Do Not Forget Us, O Lord]

O Lord, I trusted in Your kindness.
Let my heart rejoice in Your salvation;
> let me sing of the Lord, "He has been good to me."

(Ps.) How long, O Lord? will You utterly forget me?
> How long will You hide Your face from me?

Glory be to the Father, etc.

Repeat: **O Lord,** etc., *as far as* (Ps.)

GRADUAL Ps. 40, 5. 2   [The Lord Loves Compassion]

I said, "O Lord, have pity on me;
> heal my soul, for I have sinned against You."

Happy is he who has regard for the lowly and the poor;
> in the day of misfortune the Lord will deliver him.

Alleluia alleluia.   Ps. 5, 2   [Hear Us]
Hearken to my words, O Lord,
> attend to my sighing. Alleluia.

OFFERTORY   Ps. 5, 3-4   [Our Cry to God]

Heed my call for help,
> my King and my God!

To you I pray, O Lord.

COMMUNION   Ps. 9, 2-3   [Glory to God's Name]

I will declare all Your wondrous deeds;
I will be glad and exult in You;
> I will sing praise to Your Name, Most High.

One God in Three Persons.

TRINITY SUNDAY

THOUGHT FOR TODAY: Our intellect is too limited to comprehend the inner life of the infinite God, the Mystery of One God in three Divine Persons. But we know that everything in our Christian Religion is related to the Holy Trinity: Creation, Sanctification and Salvation. The "Glory be to the Father, and to the Son, and to the Holy Spirit" is an expression of our reverence and gratitude.

BIBLE AND LITURGY: Divine Revelation teaches us about the Father, the Son, and the Holy Spirit. These three Persons: Father, Son, and Holy Spirit—all of them are God. "One God in three Persons" is also called the "Blessed Trinity." We cannot understand this mystery in God. We should approach it in Faith and profound adoration. READ: Acts 17, 16-34; Matt. 3, 13-17; 2 Cor. 13, 1-13; 1 Pet. 1, 1-12; Jude 20-24.

INTROIT   Tob. 12, 6; Ps. 8, 2   [*Glorious Trinity*]

Blessed be the Holy Trinity and undivided Unity:

We will give glory to Him,
    because He has shown His mercy to us.

(Ps.) O Lord, our Lord,
    how glorious is Your Name over all the earth!

Glory be to the Father, and to the Son,
   and to the Holy Spirit.
As it was in the beginning, is now, and ever
     shall be,
   world without end. Amen.
Blessed be the Holy Trinity and undivided
     Unity:
We will give glory to Him,
   because He has shown His mercy to us.

GRADUAL   Dan. 3, 55. 56   [*Reigning Supreme*]

Blessed are You, O Lord,
   Who look into the depths
   from Your throne upon the Cherubim.
Blessed are You, O Lord,
   in the firmament of heaven,
   and praiseworthy forever.

Alleluia, alleluia.   Dan. 3, 52   [*Eternal Praise*]
Blessed are You, O Lord, the God of our fathers,
   and praiseworthy forever. Alleluia.

OFFERTORY   Tob. 12, 6   [*Mercy from the Trinity*]

Blessed be God the Father,
   and the Only-begotten Son of God,
   and also the Holy Spirit:
Because He has shown His mercy to us.

COMMUNION   Tob. 12, 6   [*Bless God*]

We bless the God of heaven,
   and before all living we will praise Him;
Because He has shown His mercy to us.

FEAST OF CORPUS CHRISTI
THURSDAY AFTER TRINITY SUNDAY

THOUGHT FOR TODAY: The joy of the institution of the Holy Eucharist is not fully expressed on Holy Thursday because of the nearness of Good Friday. Hence, wherever possible, public homage and adoration are paid to Jesus in the Blessed Sacrament on this feast.

BIBLE AND LITURGY: This feast expresses the joy of God's people, because Christ is with us in the Holy Eucharist. READ: Gen. 14, 18-20 and Heb. 7; Mal. 1, 10-11; John 6; Mark 14, 17-21.

INTROIT   Ps. 80, 17. 2   [*Food for God's People*]

He fed them with the best of wheat, alleluia;
  and filled them with honey from the rock,
    alleluia, alleluia, alleluia.

(Ps.) Sing joyfully to God our strength;
  acclaim the God of Jacob.

Glory be to the Father, and to the Son,
  and to the Holy Spirit.

As it was in the beginning, is now, and ever
    shall be,
  world without end. Amen.

He fed them with the best of wheat, alleluia;
  and filled them with honey from the rock,
    alleluia, alleluia, alleluia.

GRADUAL   Ps. 144, 15-16   [*Hope*]

The eyes of all look hopefully to You, O Lord;
  and You give them their food in due season.
You open Your hand;
  and satisfy the desire of every living thing.

Alleluia, alleluia.   John 6, 56-57   [*The Heavenly Food*]
My Flesh is food indeed,
  and My Blood is drink indeed.

He who eats My Flesh and drinks My Blood,
   abides in Me, and I in him.

SEQUENCE [*Song of the Eucharist*]

Laud, O Sion, thy salvation,
Laud with hymns of exultation,
   Christ, Thy King and Shepherd true:

Bring Him all the praise thou knowest,
He is more than thou bestowest,
   Never canst thou reach His due.

Special theme for glad thanksgiving
Is the quick'ning and the living
   Bread today before thee set:

From His hands of old partaken,
As we know, by faith unshaken,
   Where the twelve at supper met.

Full and clear ring out thy chanting,
Joy nor sweetest grace be wanting,
   From thy heart let praises burst:

For today the feast is holden,
When the institution olden
   Of that supper was rehearsed.

Here the new law's new oblation,
By the new King's revelation,
   Ends the form of ancient rite:

Now the new the old effaceth,
Truth away the shadow chaseth,
   Light dispels the gloom of night.

What He did at supper seated,
Christ ordained to be repeated,
   His memorial ne'er to cease:

And His rule for guidance taking,
Bread and wine we hallow, making
   Thus our sacrifice of peace.

This the truth each Christian learneth,
Bread into His Flesh He turneth,
　To His Precious Blood the wine:

Sight hath fail'd, nor thought conceiveth,
But a dauntless faith believeth,
　Resting on a pow'r divine.

Here beneath these signs are hidden
Priceless things to sense forbidden;
　Signs, not things are all we see:

Blood is poured and Flesh is broken,
Yet in either wondrous token
　Christ entire we know to be.

Whoso of this food partaketh,
Rendeth not the Lord nor breaketh
　Christ is whole to all that taste:

Thousands are, as one, receivers,
One, as thousands of believers,
　Eats of Him Who cannot waste.

Bad and good the feast are sharing,
Of what divers dooms preparing,
　Endless death, or endless life.

Life to these, to those damnation,
See how like participation
　Is with unlike issues rife.

When the sacrament is broken,
Doubt not, but believe 'tis spoken,
　That each sever'd outward token doth the
　　very whole contain.

Nought the precious gift divideth,
Breaking but the sign betideth
　Jesus still the same abideth, still unbroken
　　doth remain.

Lo the Angels' Food is given
To the pilgrim who hath striven;
    See the children's bread from heaven, which
        on dogs may not be spent.

Truth the ancient types fulfilling,
Isaac bound, a victim willing,
    Paschal lamb, its life blood spilling, manna
        to the fathers sent.

Very bread, Good Shepherd, tend us,
Jesu, of Thy love befriend us,
    Thou refresh us, Thou defend us,
    Thine eternal goodness send us
In the land of life to see.

Thou Who all things canst and knowest,
Who on earth such food bestowest,
    Grant us with Thy saints, though lowest,
    Where the heav'nly feast Thou showest,
Fellow heirs and guests to be. Amen. Alleluia.

OFFERTORY   Lev. 21, 6   [Solemn Liturgy]

The priests of the Lord
    offer incense and loaves to God,
And therefore they shall be sacred to their God
    and not profane His Name. Alleluia.

COMMUNION   1 Cor. 11, 26-27 [The Divine Command]

As often as you shall eat this bread
    and drink the cup,
You proclaim the death of the Lord,
    until He comes.
Therefore whoever eats this bread
    or drinks the cup of the Lord unworthily,
Will be guilty
    of the Body and Blood of the Lord. Alleluia.

*The poor and the crippled and the lame
are invited to the banquet.*

SECOND SUNDAY AFTER PENTECOST

THOUGHT FOR TODAY: The Communion-Banquet to which we are invited is not only for the just, but for all who acknowledge that they are poor, feeble, blind, and lame in their religious life and sincerely desire to be cured. We must, however, first, pass from the death of sin to the life of grace through the Sacrament of Penance before Christ can welcome us at the Eucharistic Table.

BIBLE AND LITURGY: Faith and eternal happiness in the future life are a favor and an invitation of God. We should gratefully accept this invitation. To refuse it by carelessly losing our Faith may result in eternal punishment. READ: Matt. 23, 37-39; John 8, 43-59; 9 (*Pay attention to the attitude toward Faith of parents, Pharisees and blind man.*); 12, 37-50.

INTROIT   Ps. 17, 19. 20. 2. 3   [Act of Love]

The Lord came to my support;
  He set me free in the open,
    and rescued me, because He loves me.
(Ps.) I love You, O Lord, my strength,
  O Lord, my rock, my fortress, my deliverer.

Glory be to the Father, and to the Son,
   and to the Holy Spirit.
As it was in the beginning, is now, and ever
      shall be,
   world without end. Amen.
The Lord came to my support;
   He set me free in the open,
   and rescued me, because He loves me.

GRADUAL   Ps. 119, 1-2   [*Deliver Me*]

In my distress I called to the Lord,
   and He answered me.
O Lord, deliver me from dying lip,
   from treacherous tongue.

Alleluia, alleluia.   Ps. 7, 2   [*Rescue Me*]
O Lord, my God, in You I take refuge;
   save me from all my pursuers and rescue me.
      Alleluia.

OFFERTORY   Ps. 6, 5   [*Protecting Love*]

Return, O Lord, save my life;
   rescue me because of Your kindness.

COMMUNION   Ps. 12, 6   [*Sing to God's Goodness*]

I will sing of the Lord,
   "He has been good to me";
And I will sing to the Name
   of the Lord the Most High.

The Heart of Christ burns with love for mankind.

FEAST OF THE SACRED HEART OF JESUS

FRIDAY BEFORE 3rd SUNDAY AFTER PENTECOST

On First Friday, see p. 476.

THOUGHT FOR TODAY: The Sacred Heart of Jesus is always eager to forgive whenever a sinner sincerely repents, and desires to return to God, to the source of joy and peace. Why then hesitate? "Cast your care upon the Lord, and He will support you."

BIBLE AND LITURGY: God is love. All love in this world merely springs forth from God's abundance of love. His love and goodness became visible in Christ, Whose Sacred Heart is a symbol of that Love. READ: Cant. (*Read first the Introduction!*); John 15, 1-11; Rom. 8, 35-39; Ps. 17, 1-4; John 20, 11-18.

INTROIT   Ps. 32, 11. 19. 1   [*Love for All*]

**The thoughts of His Heart
   are to all generations:
To deliver them from death
   and preserve them in spite of famine.
(Ps.) Exult, you just, in the Lord;
   praise from the upright is fitting.**

Glory be to the Father, and to the Son,
  and to the Holy Spirit.

As it was in the beginning, is now, and ever
    shall be,
  world without end. Amen.

The thoughts of His Heart
  are to all generations:

To deliver them from death
  and preserve them in spite of famine.

GRADUAL   Ps. 24, 8-9   [The Guide]

Good and upright is the Lord;
  thus He shows sinners the way.

He guides the humble to justice;
  He teaches the humble His way.

Alleluia, alleluia.   Matt. 11, 29   [Learn]

Take My yoke upon you,
  and learn from Me,

For I am meek, and humble of heart:
  and you will find rest for your souls. Alleluia.

OFFERTORY   Ps. 68, 21   [No One to Comfort]

My heart expected reproach and misery;
  I looked for sympathy, but there was none;
  for comforters, and I found none.

COMMUNION   John 19, 34   [Blood and Water]

One of the soldiers opened His side with a
    lance,
  and immediately there came out blood and
    water.

Jesus finds the lost sheep.

THIRD SUNDAY AFTER PENTECOST

THOUGHT FOR TODAY: The Catholic Church is a hospice for souls that are spiritually ill. Some people are scandalized because she is kind to sinners and forgives them over and over again. They forget that she obeys the merciful Heart of the Physician of souls.

BIBLE AND LITURGY: Since we are inclined to evil and fall into it again and again, we should strive as Christians to be constantly converted (turned back) to God. READ: 2 Kgs. 11; 12, 1-13; Luke 7, 36-50; 22, 54-62 and Matt. 27, 3-5; Ps. 50.

INTROIT   Ps. 24, 16. 18. 1. 2   [*I Lift My Soul*]

Look toward me, and have pity on me, O Lord,
    for I am alone and afflicted.
Put an end to my affliction and my suffering,
    and take away all my sins, O my God.
(Ps.) To You, I lift up my soul, O Lord.
    In You, O my God, I trust;
    let me not be put to shame.
Glory be to the Father, and to the Son,
    and to the Holy Spirit.

As it was in the beginning, is now, and ever
   shall be,
   world without end. Amen.

Look toward me, and have pity on me, O Lord,
   for I am alone and afflicted.

Put an end to my affliction and my suffering,
   and take away all my sins, O my God.

GRADUAL   Ps. 54, 23. 17. 19   [*God Our Helper*]

Cast your care upon the Lord,
   and He will support you.

When I called upon the Lord,
   He heard my voice
   and freed me from those who war against me.

Alleluia, alleluia.   Ps. 7, 12   [*A Strong God*]

A just judge is God, strong and patient;
   is He angry every day? Alleluia.

OFFERTORY   Ps. 9, 11. 12. 13   [*He Forgets Not*]

They trust in You who cherish Your Name,
   O Lord,
   for You forsake not those who seek You.

Sing praise to the Lord enthroned in Sion,
   for He has not forgotten the cry of the
   afflicted.

COMMUNION   Luke 15, 10   [*Joy over Repentance*]

I say to you:
   there is joy among the angels of God
   over one sinner who repents.

*Peter and his followers make a great catch
of fish at Jesus' suggestion.*

FOURTH SUNDAY AFTER PENTECOST

THOUGHT FOR TODAY: Let us always work as Christians laboring in union with, and for, the honor of Christ. We must also be fishers of men, eager to draw them into the boat of Peter, the Catholic Church.

BIBLE AND LITURGY: God's wisdom is not our wisdom. We should learn to adapt our way of thinking to God's way of thinking by frequent contact with His word in the Bible. Simon Peter achieved success by heeding the Word of Christ, the Son of God. READ: Prov. 2, 1-22; 3, 1-24; Wisd. 6, 1-21; Rom. 8, 5-11; 12, 9-21 (esp. 17); 1 Cor. 1, 17-31.

INTROIT   Ps. 26, 1. 2. 3   [*My Light and Strength*]

The Lord is my light and my salvation;
  whom should I fear?
The Lord is my life's refuge;
  of whom should I be afraid?
My enemies that trouble me
  themselves stumble and fall.
(Ps.) Though an army encamp against me,
  my heart will not fear.
Glory be to the Father, and to the Son,
  and to the Holy Spirit.

As it was in the beginning, is now, and ever
     shall be,
  world without end. Amen.
The Lord is my light and my salvation;
  whom should I fear?
The Lord is my life's refuge;

  of whom should I be afraid?
My enemies that trouble me
  themselves stumble and fall.

GRADUAL   Ps. 78, 9. 10   [*We Have Pardon*]

Pardon our sins, O Lord;
  why should the nations say,
  "Where is their God?"
Help us, O God our Savior;
  because of the glory of Your Name,
  O Lord, deliver us.

Alleluia, alleluia.   Ps. 9, 5. 10   [*We Have Defense*]
O God, seated on Your throne, judging justly:
  be a stronghold for the oppressed in times
  of distress. Alleluia.

OFFERTORY   Ps. 12, 4. 5   [*Keep Me Alive*]

Give light to my eyes that I may never sleep
  in death,
  lest my enemy say, "I have overcome him."

COMMUNION   Ps. 17, 3   [*Refuge*]

O Lord, my rock, my fortress, my deliverer:
  my God, my rock of refuge!

Jesus demands brotherly love before sacrifice.

FIFTH SUNDAY AFTER PENTECOST

THOUGHT FOR TODAY: Purely external practices of devotion like those of the Pharisees have no value in God's eyes. We must first "revere the Lord Christ in (our) hearts." From this inner grace and pure intention will spring patience and readiness to help and forgive even an offending neighbor.

BIBLE AND LITURGY: The Christian ideal is to be honest with oneself, with God and His commandments. "Unless your justice exceeds that of the Scribes and Pharisees . . ." In the life of a Christian there should be no room for hypocrisy and self-satisfaction. **READ:** Job 20, 1-29; Matt. 6, 1-34; 23; Luke 11, 29-54; 12, 1-3; James 2, 14-26.

INTROIT   Ps. 26, 7. 9. 1   [*Hear Us*]

Hear, O Lord, the sound of my call;
   be my helper:
Forsake me not:
   despise me not, O God my Savior.
(Ps.) The Lord is my light and my salvation;
   whom should I fear?
Glory be to the Father, and to the Son,
   and to the Holy Spirit.

As it was in the beginning, is now, and ever
   shall be,
   world without end. Amen.
Hear, O Lord, the sound of my call;
   be my helper:
Forsake me not:
   despise me not, O God my Savior.

GRADUAL   Ps. 83, 10. 9   [Look upon Us]

Behold, O God, our protector,
   and look on Your servants.
O Lord God of Hosts,
   hear the prayers of Your servants.

Alleluia, alleluia.   Ps. 20, 1   [God's Strength]
O Lord, in Your strength the king is glad;
   in Your victory how greatly he rejoices!
   Alleluia.

OFFERTORY   Ps. 15, 7. 8   [Eyes on God]

I bless the Lord Who counsels me;
   I set God ever before me;
With Him at my right hand
   I shall not be disturbed.

COMMUNION   Ps. 26, 4   [God's House]

One thing I ask of the Lord;
   this I seek:
To dwell in the house of the Lord
   all the days of my life.

Jesus feeds a great multitude of people with a few loaves and fishes.

SIXTH SUNDAY AFTER PENTECOST

THOUGHT FOR TODAY: Having risen with Christ from sin, let us strive to live with Christ the new life of holiness, sustaining ourselves by the Eucharist prefigured in the miracle of the multiplication of the loaves.

BIBLE AND LITURGY: Death to sin, symbolized by immersion into the Baptismal water, and a new life with Christ should be our constant concern through a close contact with Christ, His Word and His Holy Signs, especially frequent Communion. READ: Ezech. 18; Mark 2, 13-17; Col. 2, 20-23; Rom. 3, 21-26; 5, 1-19; 8, 1-4; Gal. 3, 23-29.

INTROIT   Ps. 27, 8. 9. 1   [*Saving Refuge*]

The Lord is the strength of His people,
   the saving refuge of His anointed.
Save Your people, O Lord, and bless Your
      inheritance;
   and rule them forever!
(Ps.) To You, O Lord, I call;
   O my God, be not deaf to me,
Lest, if You heed me not,
   I become one of those going down into the
      pit.

Glory be to the Father, and to the Son,
   and to the Holy Spirit.
As it was in the beginning, is now, and ever
      shall be,
   world without end. Amen.
The Lord is the strength of His people,
   the saving refuge of His anointed.
Save Your people, O Lord, and bless Your
      inheritance;
   and rule them forever!

GRADUAL   Ps. 89, 13. 1   [Return to Us]

Return, O Lord! How long?
   Have pity on Your servants!
O Lord, You have been our refuge
   through all generations.

Alleluia, alleluia.   Ps. 30, 2. 3   [Save Me]

In You, O Lord, I take refuge;
   let me never be put to shame.
In Your justice rescue me and release me;
   incline Your ear to me,
      make haste to deliver me! Alleluia.

OFFERTORY   Ps. 16, 5. 6. 7   [Direct Us]

Make my steps steadfast in Your paths,
   that my feet may not falter.
Incline Your ear to me; hear my word.
Show Your wondrous kindness, O Lord,
   O Savior of those who trust in You.

COMMUNION   Ps. 26, 6   [Sacrifice and Song]

I will go round and offer in His tent,
   sacrifices with shouts of gladness;
I will sing and chant praise to the Lord.

People, like trees, are known by their fruit.

SEVENTH SUNDAY AFTER PENTECOST

THOUGHT FOR TODAY: As good trees we must bring forth good fruit. We hear enough pious words, but we do not see enough good deeds. Thus, we pray, "O Lord, lead us to do that which is right before You."

BIBLE AND LITURGY: Christians should be known "by their fruit" in this life and will be known by this fruit in the future life. Heaven is not just a pay check for a good life. Heaven is what we now make of it, just as the exertion of youth is rewarded in later life. READ: Eph. 4, 7-16; Matt. 13, 24-30; Eph. 2, 1-22 (esp. 22); 1 Pet. 2, 1-10 (esp. 2); 2 Pet. 3, 18; Gal. 6, 8-10; Col. 1, 1-14.

INTROIT   Ps. 46, 2. 3   [*Gladness*]

All you peoples, clap your hands,
   shout to God with cries of gladness.

(Ps.) For the Lord, the Most High, the awesome,
   is the great King over all the earth.

Glory be to the Father, and to the Son,
   and to the Holy Spirit.

As it was in the beginning, is now, and ever
   shall be,
   world without end. Amen.

All you peoples, clap your hands,
shout to God with cries of gladness.

GRADUAL Ps. 33, 12. 6 [*Fear with Hope*]

Come, children, hear me;
I will teach you the fear of the Lord.
Look to Him that you may be radiant with joy,
and your faces may not blush with shame.

Alleluia, alleluia. Ps. 46, 2 [*Rejoice*]
All you peoples, clap your hands,
shout to God with cries of gladness. Alleluia.

OFFERTORY Dan. 3, 40 [*Pleasing Sacrifice*]

As though it were holocausts of rams and
bullocks,
or thousands of fat lambs,
So let our sacrifice be in Your presence today,
that it may please You;
For those who trust in You
cannot be put to shame, O Lord.

COMMUNION Ps. 30, 3 [*Save Us*]

Incline Your ear to me,
make haste to deliver me.

Jesus praises the prudence of the unjust steward who plans for his future.

EIGHTH SUNDAY AFTER PENTECOST

THOUGHT FOR TODAY: The parable of the steward shows how "the children of the light" neglected so many opportunities to gain a happy eternity by not participating in the Holy Sacrifice of the Mass and letting other means of sanctification go by unused.

BIBLE AND LITURGY: The cleverness and devotion of "the children of this world" should shame quite a few Christians. Inertia does not fit into the mentality of Christ, Who said: "I have come to bring a sword, not peace" (Matt. 10, 34). **READ:** Matt. 10, 16-42; 1 Cor. 9, 24-27; Apoc. 2, 1-11; 2 Mach. 7; Acts 7, 54-60.

INTROIT Ps. 47, 10. 11. 2 [*Glorify God in His Sanctuary*]

O God, we ponder Your kindness
　　within Your temple.
As Your Name, O God, so also Your praise
　　reaches to the ends of the earth.
Of justice Your right hand is full.
(Ps.) Great is the Lord, and wholly to be praised;
　　in the city of our God, His holy mountain.
Glory be to the Father, and to the Son,
　　and to the Holy Spirit.

As it was in the beginning, is now, and ever
   shall be,
   world without end. Amen.

O God, we ponder Your kindness
   within Your temple.
As Your Name, O God, so also Your praise
   reaches to the ends of the earth.
Of justice Your right hand is full.

GRADUAL   Ps. 30, 3; 70, 1   [Make Me Safe]

Be my rock of refuge, O God,
   a stronghold to give me safety.
In You, O God, I take refuge;
   O Lord, let me never be put to shame.

Alleluia, alleluia. Ps. 47, 2 [Praise in the Sanctuary]
Great is the Lord, and wholly to be praised
   in the city of our God, His holy mountain.
      Alleluia.

OFFERTORY   Ps. 17, 28. 32   [Love for the Humble]

Lowly people You save, O Lord,
   but haughty eyes You bring low;
For who is God except You, O Lord?

COMMUNION   Ps. 33, 9   [Taste and See]

Taste and see how good the Lord is;
   happy the man who takes refuge in Him.

Jesus chases the money-changers out of the temple.

NINTH SUNDAY AFTER PENTECOST

THOUGHT FOR TODAY: The Holy Scriptures prove that God rewards and punishes even here on earth. Jerusalem rejected the Savior and it was destroyed. No temptation is so strong that we cannot conquer it with the grace of God, "Who will not let you be tested beyond your strength."

BIBLE AND LITURGY: What really matters in life is the worship we give to God. We must worship God by doing our daily duties and by saying our private prayers, but its peak should be our weekly community worship in the parish church. What the temple was for the Jews, the parish church is for a Christian community. Every Catholic is responsible for the Church and public worship. READ: Ex. 25, 1-40; 27, 1-2; 28, 1; 29, 38-42; Heb. 10, 8-9; Matt. 18, 19-20; 1 Cor. 11, 17-34; Deut, 14, 22-29; 1 Cor. 9, 13-14; Ps. 150.

INTROIT   Ps. 53, 6. 7. 3   [*Sustain My Life*]

Behold, God is my helper,
   the Lord sustains my life.
Turn back the evil upon my foes;
   in Your faithfulness destroy them, O Lord,
      my protector.

(Ps.) **O God, by Your Name save me,**
and by Your might deliver me.

Glory be to the Father, and to the Son,
and to the Holy Spirit.

As it was in the beginning, is now, and ever
shall be,
world without end. Amen.

Behold, God is my helper,
the Lord sustains my life.

Turn back the evil upon my foes;
in Your faithfulness destroy them, O Lord,
my protector.

GRADUAL   Ps. 8, 2   [Glorious Lord]

O Lord, our Lord,
how glorious is Your Name over all the earth!
You have elevated Your Majesty above the
heavens.

Alleluia, alleluia.   Ps. 58, 2   [Defend Us]
Rescue me from my enemies, O my God;
from my adversaries defend me. Alleluia.

OFFERTORY   Ps. 18, 9. 10. 11. 12   [The Law Is Sweet]

The precepts of the Lord are right,
rejoicing the heart,
And His ordinances sweeter than syrup
or honey from the comb;
therefore Your servant is careful of them.

COMMUNION   John 6, 57   [Union with Christ]

"He who eats My Flesh, and drinks My Blood,
abides in Me, and I in him,"
says the Lord.

The Pharisee exalts himself before God.

TENTH SUNDAY AFTER PENTECOST

THOUGHT FOR TODAY: Humility is the foundation of all Christian virtues. God reveals Himself to the humble and despises arrogance and pride.

BIBLE AND LITURGY: We should be humble. Everything we possess: faith, our very existence, health, career and happiness in life, is a favor of God. Moreover, being sinners, we have God's mercy as our hope. READ: Jud. 9; Ps. 33; Matt. 11, 25-30; 18, 1-4; 20, 20-28; Luke 22, 24-40.

INTROIT Ps. 54, 17. 18. 20. 23. 2. 3 [*The Lord Our Support*]

When I called upon the Lord,
  He heard my voice,
    and freed me from those who war against me;
And He humbled them,
He Who is before all ages,
  and remains forever;
Cast your care upon the Lord,
  and He will support you.
(Ps.) Hearken, O God, to my prayer;
  turn not away from my pleading;
    give heed to me, and answer me.
Glory be to the Father, and to the Son,
  and to the Holy Spirit.

- 194 -

As it was in the beginning, is now, and ever
   shall be, world without end. Amen.

When I called upon the Lord,
   He heard my voice,
   and freed me from those who war against me;
And He humbled them,
   He Who is before all ages,
   and remains forever;
Cast your care upon the Lord,
   and He will support you.

GRADUAL   Ps. 16, 8. 2   [Guard Me]

Keep me, O Lord, as the apple of Your eye;
   hide me in the shadow of Your wings.
From You let judgment come;
   Your eyes behold what is right.

Alleluia, alleluia. Ps. 64, 2   [Debt of Praise]

To You we owe our hymn of praise,
   O God, in Sion;
To You must vows be fulfilled in Jerusalem.
   Alleluia.

OFFERTORY   Ps. 24, 1-3   [Patient Prayer]

To You I lift up my soul, O Lord.
   in You, O my God, I trust;
Let me not be put to shame,
   let not my enemies exult over me.
No one who waits for You shall be put to
   shame.

COMMUNION   Ps. 50, 21   [Appeasing Sacrifice]

You shall be pleased with due sacrifices,
   burnt offerings and holocausts
   on Your altar, O Lord.

Jesus opens the lips of a dumb man.

ELEVENTH SUNDAY AFTER PENTECOST

THOUGHT FOR TODAY: If we would not take so many things as a matter of course, we would marvel at the beauty of our Religion, and we could speak intelligently about our religious belief to others.

BIBLE AND LITURGY: What Christ did to the deaf and dumb man, the priest did to us on the day of our Baptism, also saying: "Ephphatha" that is, "Be opened." We should pray always to have an openminded willingness for God, Who approaches us with His favors. St. Paul did so finally and became a great saint. READ: Deut. 32, 1-14; Gen. 1 and Acts 17, 22-34; 1 Tim. 6, 11-16; Titus 2, 11-15; Matt. 22, 1-14.

INTROIT   Ps. 67, 6. 7. 36. 2   [*God Brings Unity*]

God is in His holy dwelling,
God Who makes men of one mind
    to dwell in a house;
He shall give power and strength to His people.
(Ps.) God arises; His enemies are scattered,
    and those who hate Him flee before Him.
Glory be to the Father, and to the Son,
    and to the Holy Spirit.

As it was in the beginning, is now, and ever
    shall be,
   world without end. Amen.

God is in His holy dwelling,
God Who makes men of one mind
    to dwell in a house;
He shall give power and strength to His people.

GRADUAL   Ps. 27, 7. 1   [*Exult in Trust*]

In God my heart trusts, and I find help;
    then my heart exults, and with my song I
      give Him thanks.
To You, O Lord, I call;
    O my God, be not deaf to me;
    depart not from me.

Alleluia, alleluia.   Ps. 80, 2. 3   [*Sing with Joy*]
Sing joyfully to God our strength;
    acclaim the God of Jacob.
Take up a pleasant psalm with the harp.
    Alleluia.

OFFERTORY   Ps. 29, 2-3   [*Prayer Answered*]

I will extol You, O Lord, for You drew me clear
    and did not let my enemies rejoice over me;
O Lord, I cried out to You
    and You healed me.

COMMUNION   Prov. 3, 9-10   [*Offer Sacrifice*]

Honor the Lord with your wealth,
    with first fruits of all your produce.
Then will your barns be filled with grain,
    with new wine your vats will overflow.

The Good Samaritan takes care of a wounded neighbor.

TWELFTH SUNDAY AFTER PENTECOST

THOUGHT FOR TODAY: Personally and actively to participate in the Mass makes us love God, and increases in us a spirit of kindness in dealing with others.

BIBLE AND LITURGY: Christ teaches us through His Church to love our neighbor regardless of race or color. And a Catholic who does not have the courage to translate the word "charity-love" into "justice" is a hypocrite, just as so many so-called Christians who try to prove segregation from the Bible. READ: 4 Kgs. 17, 1-6 and 24-28; John 4, 1-45 (esp. 9); Luke 10, 30-37 (*Ep.*); Num. 12, 1-16; Philemon (esp. 15-17); Gal. 3, 27-28.

INTROIT   Ps. 69, 2-3. 4   [*Conquer My Foes*]

Deign, O God, to rescue me;
   O Lord, make haste to help me.
Let them be put to shame and confounded
   who seek my life.
(Ps.) Let them be turned back in disgrace
   who desire my ruin.
Glory be to the Father, and to the Son,
   and to the Holy Spirit.
As it was in the beginning, is now, and ever
   shall be, world without end. Amen.

Deign, O God to rescue me;
O Lord, make haste to help me.
Let them be put to shame and confounded
who seek my life.

GRADUAL Ps. 33, 2. 3 [*Bless the Lord Always*]

I will bless the Lord at all times;
His praise shall be ever in my mouth.
Let my soul glory in the Lord;
the lowly will hear and be glad.

Alleluia, alleluia. Ps. 87, 2 [*Call upon God*]

O Lord, the God of my salvation, by day I cry
out,
at night I clamor in Your presence. Alleluia.

OFFERTORY Ex. 32, 11. 13. 14 [*Mediator*]

Moses prayed in the sight of the Lord his God,
and said,
"Why, O Lord, is Your indignation enkindled
against Your people?
let the anger of Your mind cease;
Remember Abraham, Isaac, and Jacob,
to whom You swore to give a land flowing
with milk and honey."
And the Lord was appeased from doing the evil
which He had spoken of doing against His
people.

COMMUNION Ps. 103, 13. 14. 15 [*God's Favors*]

The earth is replete
with the fruit of Your works, O Lord;
You produce bread from the earth,
and wine to gladden men's hearts,
So that their faces gleam with oil,
and bread fortifies the hearts of men.

One of the ten lepers cured by Jesus returns to thank Him.

THIRTEENTH SUNDAY AFTER PENTECOST

THOUGHT FOR TODAY: Ten lepers "were made clean." Only one returned to give thanks and glory to God. We send many petitions to heaven, but we often forget our prayers of thanksgiving. A grateful soul may always hope for more and greater blessings.

BIBLE AND LITURGY: We should be thankful for the tremendous favors God has bestowed upon us. The best way to thank God is to join often in the Great Prayer of Thanksgiving and Adoration, which is the very core of the Mass. READ: Num. 15, 13-21; Deut. 4, 9-14 (esp. 9); Acts 4, 23-31; Eph. 5, 1-20 (esp. 19); Phil. 4, 4-9; Matt. 26, 26-29 (esp. 27); Ps. 117.

INTROIT   Ps. 73, 20. 19. 23. 1   [*Be Not Angry, Lord*]

Look to Your covenant, O Lord,
> forsake not forever the lives of Your afflicted ones.

Arise, O Lord; defend Your cause;
> be not unmindful of the voices of those who ask You.

(Ps.) Why, O God, have You cast us off forever?
> Why does Your anger smolder against the sheep of Your pasture?

Glory be to the Father, and to the Son,
  and to the Holy Spirit.
As it was in the beginning, is now, and ever
    shall be,
  world without end. Amen.
Look to Your covenant, O Lord,
  forsake not forever the lives of Your afflicted
    ones.
Arise, O Lord; defend Your cause;
  be not unmindful of the voices of those who
    ask You.

GRADUAL Ps. 73, 20. 19. 22 [*Remember Us, Lord*]

Look to Your covenant, O Lord,
  be not unmindful of the lives of Your af-
    flicted ones.
Arise, O Lord; defend Your cause;
  remember the reproach of Your servants.

Alleluia, alleluia. Ps. 89, 1 [*Ever the Refuge*]
Lord, You have been our refuge
  through all generations. Alleluia.

OFFERTORY Ps. 30, 15. 16 [*We Belong to God*]

My trust is in You, O Lord;
  I say, "You are my God."
  In Your hands is my destiny.

COMMUNION Wis. 16, 20 [*Food from Heaven*]

You have given us, O Lord, bread from heaven,
  endowed with all delights
  and the sweetness of every taste.

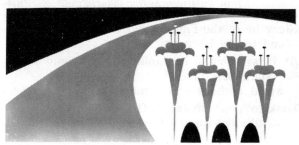

Jesus urges us to trust God who clothes the lilies.

FOURTEENTH SUNDAY AFTER PENTECOST

THOUGHT FOR TODAY: We "of little faith" attend with such anxiety to our temporal affairs that we neglect our religious duties. If we seek the supernatural first, we may confidently rely on God's help in our daily affairs.

BIBLE AND LITURGY: A Christian must try so to pass through temporal things as not to lose those which are eternal. Trying to make a living or finding a way out of trouble should never absorb us so much that we forget God and lose our confidence in Him. We should be known by the fruits of the Spirit we bear! (*Ep.*) READ: Pss. 26; 45; 124; Jer. 17, 5-8; Sirach 11, 20-28.

INTROIT   Ps. 83, 10. 11. 2. 3   [*Courts of the Lord*]

Behold, O God, our Protector,
    and look upon the face of Your Anointed.
Better is one day in Your courts
    than a thousand elsewhere.
(Ps.) How lovely is Your dwelling place;
    O Lord of Hosts!
My soul yearns and pines
    for the courts of the Lord.
Glory be to the Father, and to the Son,
    and to the Holy Spirit.

As it was in the beginning, is now, and ever
    shall be,
  world without end. Amen.

Behold, O God, our Protector,
  and look upon the face of Your Anointed.
Better is one day in Your courts
  than a thousand elsewhere.

GRADUAL   Ps. 117, 8. 9   [*Trust Not in Man*]

It is better to take refuge in the Lord
  than to trust in man.
It is better to take refuge in the Lord
  than to trust in princes.

Alleluia, alleluia.   Ps. 94, 1   [*God of Salvation*]
Come, let us sing joyfully to the Lord;
    let us acclaim the God of our salvation.
    Alleluia.

OFFERTORY   Ps. 33, 8. 9   [*Protection by Angels*]

The Angel of the Lord encamps
  around those who fear Him, and delivers
    them.
Taste and see
  how good the Lord is.

COMMUNION   Matt. 6, 33   [*Kingdom of God First*]

"Seek first the Kingdom of God;
  and all things shall be given you besides,"
  says the Lord.

Jesus raises the widow's son to life.

FIFTEENTH SUNDAY AFTER PENTECOST

THOUGHT FOR TODAY: Physical and spiritual health are not always found together. If your conscience tells you that you are spiritually dead, do not delay to arise in sincere confession. Life is too short to be wasted. "A man will surely reap what he sows," life or death.

BIBLE AND LITURGY: Christian tradition sees in the mother of Naim another Mother, who weeps over the spiritual death of so many of her children. Holy Mother Church prays constantly for those children and keeps urging them to repent. READ: Mark 2, 1-10; Isa. 1, 1-31 (esp. 18); Jer. 9; Phil. 3, 17-21; James 5, 13-18.

INTROIT   Ps. 85, 1. 2. 3. 4   [*Hear My Prayer*]

Incline Your ear, O Lord; answer me;
   save Your servant, O my God, who trusts in You.
Have pity on me, O Lord,
   for to You I call all the day.
(Ps.) Gladden the soul of Your servant,
   for to You, O Lord, I lift up my soul.
Glory be to the Father, and to the Son,
   and to the Holy Spirit.

As it was in the beginning, is now, and ever
   shall be,
   world without end. Amen.
Incline Your ear, O Lord; answer me;
   save Your servant, O my God, who trusts in
      You.
Have pity on me, O Lord,
   for to You I call all the day.

GRADUAL   Ps. 91, 2. 3   [Thanks]

It is good to give thanks to the Lord,
to sing to Your Name, Most High.
To proclaim Your kindness at dawn
   and Your faithfulness throughout the night.

Alleluia, alleluia.   Ps. 94, 3   [Great Is the Lord]
For the Lord is a great God,
   and a great King over all the earth. Alleluia.

OFFERTORY   Ps. 39, 2. 3. 4   [God Hears Me]

I have waited, waited for the Lord,
   and He stooped toward me and heard my cry.
And He put a new song into my mouth,
   a hymn to our God.

COMMUNION   John 6, 52   [Heavenly Food]

The bread that I will give
   is My Flesh for the life of the world.

Jesus advises us always to take the last place.

SIXTEENTH SUNDAY AFTER PENTECOST

THOUGHT FOR TODAY: The supernatural life which we receive in baptism is like a seed that must be developed. Rooted and grounded in love, we pray that God may increase our faith and hope, and that His grace may stir up in us zeal for good works.

BIBLE AND LITURGY: Human nature will constantly try to seduce us to pride and selfishness. Only when we are rooted and grounded in love can we avoid it. "Love is not pretentious!" (1 Cor. 13, 4). READ: Tob. 4, 1-23 (esp. 14); 1 Cor. 13, 1-13; Sirach 10, 6-30; 1 Pet. 5, 5-7; James 4, 11-17.

INTROIT   Ps. 85, 3. 5. 1   [*Have Pity*]

Have pity on me, O Lord,
    for to You I call all the day;
For You, O Lord, are good and forgiving,
    abounding in kindness to all who call upon
       You.
(Ps.) Incline Your ear, O Lord; answer me,
    for I am afflicted and poor.
Glory be to the Father, and to the Son,
    and to the Holy Spirit.

As it was in the beginning, is now, and ever
   shall be,
 world without end. Amen.

Have pity on me, O Lord,
 for to You I call all the day;

For You, O Lord, are good and forgiving,
 abounding in kindness to all who call upon
   You.

GRADUAL   Ps. 101, 16-17   [All Revere the Lord]

The nations shall revere Your Name, O Lord,
 and all the kings of the earth Your glory.

For the Lord has rebuilt Sion,
 and He shall appear in His glory.

Alleluia, alleluia. Ps. 97, 1   [God's Wondrous Works]
Sing to the Lord a new song,
 for the Lord has done wondrous deeds.
   Alleluia.

OFFERTORY   Ps. 39, 14. 15   [Rescue Me]

Deign, O Lord, to rescue me;
Let all be put to shame and confusion
 who seek to snatch away my life.
Deign, O Lord, to rescue me.

COMMUNION   Ps. 70, 16. 17. 18   [In God's Keeping]

O Lord, I will tell of Your singular justice;
 O God, You have taught me from my youth;
And now that I am old and gray,
 O God, forsake me not.

Jesus urges love of neighbor.

SEVENTEENTH SUNDAY AFTER PENTECOST

THOUGHT FOR TODAY: We all have "one Lord, one faith, one Baptism, one God and Father of all." This supernatural unity encourages us to "avoid every contamination of the devil," and to perform works of charity. By the grace of the Sacraments we curb our passions that they may not separate us from our holy union in the Mystical Body of Christ.

BIBLE AND LITURGY: Again Charity is emphasized as basic in the Christian Religion. READ: Prov. 10, 12; 1 Cor. 13, 1-13; Gen. 13, 1-13; 1 Kgs. 18, 1-16; 19, 1-7; 20, 1-43; 23, 16-18; Luke 6, 27-38.

INTROIT   Ps. 118, 137. 124. 1   [God's Law]

You are just, O Lord,
    and Your ordinance is right.
Deal with Your servant according to Your
    kindness.
(Ps.) Happy are they whose way is blameless
    who walk in the law of the Lord.
Glory be to the Father, and to the Son,
    and to the Holy Spirit.

As it was in the beginning, is now, and ever
   shall be,
   world without end. Amen.

You are just, O Lord,
   and Your ordinance is right.

Deal with Your servant according to Your
   kindness.

GRADUAL   Ps. 32, 12. 6   [God's People]

Happy the nation whose God is the Lord,
   the people the Lord has chosen for His own
      inheritance.

By the word of the Lord the heavens were
   made;
   by the breath of His mouth all their host.

Alleluia, alleluia.   Ps. 101, 2   [Hear Our Prayer]

O Lord, hear my prayer,
   and let my cry come to You. Alleluia.

OFFERTORY   Dan. 9, 17. 18. 19   [Look Down on Us]

I, Daniel, prayed to my God, saying,
   "Hear, O Lord, the prayers of Your servant;

Show Your face upon Your sanctuary,
   and favorably look down upon this people,
   upon whom Your Name is invoked, O God."

COMMUNION   Ps. 75, 12-13 [Acclaim the Great Lord]

Make vows to the Lord, your God, and fulfill
   them;
   let all round about Him bring gifts to the
      terrible Lord

Who checks the pride of princes,
   Who is terrible to the kings of the earth.

EMBER WEDNESDAY IN SEPTEMBER

INTROIT   Ps. 80, 2, 3, 4. 5. 6   [*Sing to the Lord*]

Sing joyfully to God our strength;
acclaim the God of Jacob.
Take up a pleasant psalm with the harp;
blow the trumpet in the beginning of the
month;
For it is a statute in Israel,
an ordinance of the God of Jacob.
(Ps.) He made it a decree for Joseph,
when he came forth from the land of Egypt:
he heard an unfamiliar speech.
Glory be to the Father, etc.
Repeat: **Sing joyfully,** etc., *as far as* (Ps.).

After the 1st Lesson:

GRADUAL   Ps. 112, 5-7   [*None Like the Lord*]

Who is like the Lord, our God, Who is en-
throned on high
and looks upon the heavens and the earth
below?
He raises up the lowly from the dust;
from the dunghill He lifts up the poor.

After the 2nd Lesson:

GRADUAL   Ps. 32, 12. 6   [*Happy Are God's People*]

Happy the nation whose God is the Lord,
the people the Lord has chosen for His own
inheritance.
By the word of the Lord the heavens were
made;
by the breath of His mouth all their host.

OFFERTORY   Ps. 118, 47. 48   [*Delight in Obedience*]

I will delight in Your commands,
  which I love exceedingly.
And I will lift up my hands to Your commands,
  which I love.

COMMUNION   2 Esd. 8, 10   [*The Day of the Lord*]

Eat fat meats, and drink sweet wine,
  and send portions to those
  who have not prepared for themselves:
Because it is the holy day of the Lord,
  be not sad,
  for the joy of the Lord is our strength.

EMBER FRIDAY IN SEPTEMBER

INTROIT   Ps. 104, 3-4. 1   [*Seek the Lord in Joy*]

Rejoice, O hearts that seek the Lord!
Look to the Lord, and be strengthened;
  seek His face evermore.

(Ps.) Give thanks to the Lord, invoke His Name;
  make known among the nations His deeds.

Glory be to the Father, etc.

Repeat: **Rejoice, O hearts,** etc., *as far as* (Ps.).

GRADUAL   Ps. 89, 13. 1   [*Return, O Lord*]

Return, O Lord! How long?
  Have pity on Your servants.
O Lord, You have been our refuge
  through all generations.

OFFERTORY Ps. 102, 2. 5 [Youth Renewed]

Bless the Lord, O my soul,
  and forget not all His benefits;
And your youth shall be renewed like the
  eagle's.

COMMUNION Ps. 118, 22. 24 [Delight in the Law]

Take away from me reproach and contempt,
  for I observe Your decrees, O Lord.
Your decrees are my delight.

EMBER SATURDAY IN SEPTEMBER

Short Form of the Mass

INTROIT Ps. 94, 6-7. 1 [Acknowledge the Lord]

Come, let us bow down in worship to God;
  let us kneel before the Lord.
Let us weep before Him Who made us;
  for He is the Lord our God.
(Ps.) Come, let us sing joyfully to the Lord;
  let us acclaim God our Savior.
Glory be to the Father, etc.
Repeat: Come, let us bow, etc., *as far as* (Ps.).

After the 1st Lesson:

GRADUAL Ps. 78, 9. 10 [Pardon for Us]

Pardon our sins, O Lord;
Why should the nations say,
  "Where is their God?"

Help us, O God our Savior;
  because of the glory of Your Name,
  O Lord, deliver us.

After the 2nd Lesson:

TRACT   Ps. 116, 1-2   [Praise to God]

Praise the Lord, all you nations;
  glorify Him, all you peoples!
For steadfast is His kindness toward us,
  and the fidelity of the Lord endures forever.

OFFERTORY   Ps. 87, 2-3   [Persistent Prayer]

O Lord, the God of my salvation,
  by day I cry out,
  at night I clamor in your presence.
Let my prayer come before You, O Lord.

COMMUNION   Lev. 23, 41. 43   [Feast of Deliverance]

In the seventh month
  you shall keep this feast,
As I made the Israelites dwell in booths,
  when I led them out of the land of Egypt.
I, the Lord, am your God.

Jesus cures a paralytic and forgives his sins.

EIGHTEENTH SUNDAY AFTER PENTECOST

THOUGHT FOR TODAY: "Your sins are forgiven." We also hear the identical words, "I absolve you from your sins," when, after due preparation, we humbly confess our sins. Let us be grateful to God for the Sacrament of Penance and use it frequently to restore or to increase the supernatural life of our souls, which is so pleasing to Him.

BIBLE AND LITURGY: God, our Father, approaching us in Christ, is willing to forgive our human weakness over and over again, if we are sorry. Indeed, in everything we have been enriched in Him (*Ep.*). READ: Matt. 18, 21-35; Luke 15, 11-32; Matt. 16, 13-20; John 20, 19-23;

INTROIT   Sir. 36, 18; Ps. 121, 1   [Peace]

Give peace, O Lord to those who have hoped in
   You,
      and let Your Prophets be proved true.
Hear the prayers of Your servant,
   and of Your people Israel.

(Ps.) I rejoiced because they said to me,
   "We will go up to the house of the Lord."

Glory be to the Father, and to the Son,
   and to the Holy Spirit.
As it was in the beginning, is now, and ever
      shall be,
   world without end. Amen.
Give peace, O Lord to those who have hoped in
      You,
   and let Your Prophets be proved true.
Hear the prayers of Your servant,
   and of Your people Israel.

GRADUAL   Ps. 121, 1. 7   [The House of the Lord]

I rejoiced because they said to me,
   "We will go up to the house of the Lord."
May peace be within your walls,
   prosperity in your buildings.

Alleluia, alleluia.   Ps. 101, 16   [Glory from All]
The nations shall revere Your Name, O Lord,
   and all the kings of the earth Your glory.
      Alleluia.

OFFERTORY   Ex. 24, 4. 5   [Evening Sacrifice]

Moses consecrated an altar to the Lord,
   offering upon it holocausts,
   and sacrificing victims:
He made an evening sacrifice to the Lord God
   for an odor of sweetness,
   in the sight of the Israelites.

COMMUNION   Ps. 95, 8. 9   [Worship]

Bring gifts and enter His courts;
   worship the Lord in His holy court.

*The man without the wedding suit is cast out
of the wedding feast.*

NINETEENTH SUNDAY AFTER PENTECOST

THOUGHT FOR TODAY: Without the garment of sanctifying grace, we cannot enter the kingdom of heaven. To die in the state of grace is a special gift for which we must pray and which God will certainly not deny us if we keep His commandments.

BIBLE AND LITURGY: The Church teaches us to put on the new man, keeping our baptismal robe unstained and our candle lighted till the Lord comes to His marriage feast (*Rites of Baptism*). READ: Luke 16, 19-31; Matt. 8, 10-12; Luke 13, 22-30; Apoc. 14, 6-11.

INTROIT   Ps. 77, 1   [*God, Our Savior*]

"I am the salvation of the people,"
    says the Lord,
"In whatever tribulation they shall cry to Me,
    I will hear them;
    and I will be their Lord forever."
(Ps.) Hearken, My people, to My teaching;
    incline your ears to the words of My mouth.
Glory be to the Father, and to the Son,
    and to the Holy Spirit.

As it was in the beginning, is now, and ever
    shall be,
  world without end. Amen.

"I am the salvation of the people,"
  says the Lord,
"In whatever tribulation they shall cry to Me,
  I will hear them;
    and I will be their Lord forever."

GRADUAL   Ps. 140, 2   [Incense of Prayer]

Let my prayer come like incense before You,
  O Lord,
  the lifting up of my hands, like the evening
    sacrifice.

Alleluia, alleluia.   Ps. 104, 1   [Proclaim the Lord]
Give thanks to the Lord, invoke His Name;
  make known among the nations His deeds.
    Alleluia.

OFFERTORY Ps. 137, 7 [The Lord Makes Us Fearless]

Though I walk amid distress, You preserve me,
  O Lord;
  against the anger of my enemies You raise
    Your hand;
  Your right hand saves me.

COMMUNION   Ps. 118, 4-5   [Steadfast Obedience]

You have commanded that Your precepts
  be diligently kept.
Oh, that I might be firm in the ways
  of keeping Your statutes!

Faith is rewarded.

TWENTIETH SUNDAY AFTER PENTECOST

THOUGHT FOR TODAY: Numberless sins, committed daily on earth, cry to heaven for punishmen. Let us appease God by leading a good Christian life.

BIBLE AND LITURGY: The Church deals again with Faith (i.e., the total surrender of ourselves to God, Who reveals Himself to us) and the motives for belief. Faith is a grace of God. Fulfilled prophecies and miracles help those "of little Faith" to come to the complete surrender of mind and heart, which means "Faith" in the Biblical meaning of the word. READ: John 20, 24-29; Luke 24, 13-35 (esp. 27); Matt. 2, 1-6; 11, 7-19; Luke 1, 67-79 (esp. 70); 18, 31-43; John 20, 30-31.

INTROIT   Dan. 3, 31. 29. 35; Ps. 118, 1   [We Are Guilty]

All that You have done to us, O Lord,
   You have done in true judgment;
Because we have sinned against You,
    and we have not obeyed Your command-
       ments;
But give glory to Your Name,
    and deal with us according to the multitude
      of Your mercy.
(Ps.) Happy are they whose way is blameless,
  who walk in the law of the Lord.

Glory be to the Father, and to the Son,
  and to the Holy Spirit.
As it was in the beginning, is now, and ever
    shall be,
  world without end. Amen.
All that You have done to us, O Lord,
  You have done in true judgment;
Because we have sinned against You,
  and we have not obeyed Your command-
    ments;
But give glory to Your Name,
  and deal with us according to the multitude
    of Your mercy.

GRADUAL   Ps. 144, 15-16   [Hopeful Eyes]

The eyes of all look hopefully to You, O Lord,
  and You give them their food in due season.
You open Your hand
  and satisfy the desire of every living thing.

Alleluia, alleluia.   Ps. 107, 2   [Steady of Heart]

My heart is steadfast, O God; my heart is stead-
    fast;
  I will sing and chant praise to You, my glory.
    Alleluia.

OFFERTORY   Ps. 136, 1   [Fears for the Fatherland]

By the streams of Babylon
  we sat and wept
  when we remembered You, O Sion.

COMMUNION   Ps. 118, 49. 50 [Hope in God's Word]

Remember Your word to Your servant, O Lord,
  since You have given me hope.
  This is my comfort in my affliction.

Jesus is King of kings and Lord of lords.

FEAST OF CHRIST THE KING

THOUGHT FOR TODAY: Jesus said: "My kingdom is not of this world," but it is in this world. He came to establish a kingdom of truth for our intellect; a kingdom of justice and holiness for our will; a kingdom of love and peace for our heart. If we follow Him, He will lead us into His eternal kingdom.

BIBLE AND LITURGY: At the very moment of His incarnation, Christ (i.e., the Anointed One) was anointed Eternal High Priest and King by His Father. The Church deals today with Christ, our King, and His Kingdom, i.e., a spiritualized Israel, the Church. READ: 2 Kgs. 5, 1-5; Luke 1, 30-33; Matt. 21, 1-9; John 6, 14-15; 18, 33-37 (*Gosp.*); Matt. 16, 18-19; Heb. 1, 1-14.

INTROIT   Apoc. 5, 12; 1, 6; Ps. 71, 1   [*Glory to the King*]

Worthy is the Lamb Who was slain
   to receive power, and divinity,
      and wisdom, and strength, and honor.
To Him belong glory and dominion
   forever and ever.
(Ps.) **O God, with Your judgment endow the King,**
   and with Your justice, the King's son.

Glory be to the Father, and to the Son,
  and to the Holy Spirit.
As it was in the beginning, is now, and ever
    shall be,
  world without end. Amen.
Worthy is the Lamb Who was slain
  to receive power, and divinity,
  and wisdom, and strength, and honor.
To Him belong glory and dominion
  forever and ever.

GRADUAL   Ps. 71, 8. 11   [*The Ruler*]

He shall rule from sea to sea,
  and from the River to the ends of the earth.
All kings shall pay Him homage,
  all nations shall serve Him.

Alleluia, alleluia. Dan. 7, 14   [*Everlasting Reign*]
His dominion is an everlasting dominion
  that shall not be taken away,
  and His kingdom shall not be destroyed.
    Alleluia.

OFFERTORY   Ps. 2, 8   [*All Power*]

Ask of Me and I will give You
  the nations for an inheritance
  and the ends of the earth for Your possession.

COMMUNION   Ps. 28, 10. 11   [*Enthroned*]

The Lord is enthroned as King forever;
  may the Lord bless His people with peace!

The master hands the wicked servant over to the torturers.

TWENTY-FIRST SUNDAY AFTER PENTECOST

THOUGHT FOR TODAY: We say in the Our Father: "Forgive us our trespasses as we forgive those who trespass against us." But those who do not forgive think only of revenge, and never forget an offense.

BIBLE AND LITURGY: To nourish hatred is to go against the very basic laws of our Religion. READ: Lev. 19, 17-18; Matt. 5, 1-26; Luke 11, 14; 6, 37-38; Matt. 18, 21-22; Luke 23, 33-34.

INTROIT Esther 13, 9. 10. 11; Ps. 118, 1 [*God's Sacred Will*]

In Your will are all things, O Lord,
   and there is none that can resist Your will;
For You have made all things,
      heaven and earth, and all things that are
      under the cope of heaven.
   You are Lord of all.
(Ps.) Happy are they whose way is blameless,
   who walk in the law of the Lord.
Glory be to the Father, and to the Son,
   and to the Holy Spirit.
As it was in the beginning, is now, and ever
      shall be, world without end. Amen.
In Your will are all things, O Lord
   and there is none that can resist Your will;

For You have made all things,
heaven and earth, and all things that are
under the cope of heaven.
You are Lord of all.

GRADUAL   Ps. 89, 1-2   [*Everlasting God*]

O Lord, You have been our refuge
through all generations.
Before the mountains were begotten
and the earth and the world were brought
forth,
from everlasting to everlasting You are God.

Alleluia, alleluia.   Ps. 113, 1   [*Liberator*]

When Israel came forth from Egypt,
the house of Jacob from a people of alien
tongue. Alleluia.

OFFERTORY   Job 1   [*Trials before Victory*]

There was a man in the land of Us,
whose name was Job,
simple, and upright, and fearing God,
Whom Satan besought that he might tempt:
and power was given him from the Lord
over his possessions and his flesh;
And he destroyed all his substance and his
children,
and wounded his flesh also with a grievous
ulcer.

COMMUNION   Ps. 118, 81. 84. 86   [*Plea for Defense*]

My soul pines for Your salvation;
I hope in Your word.
When will You do judgment on my persecutors?
The wicked persecuted me wrongfully;
help me, O Lord my God!

*Jesus urges us to render to secular authorities
what is due them.*

TWENTY-SECOND SUNDAY AFTER PENTECOST

THOUGHT FOR TODAY: Man was made by God and continually needs His sustaining hand. Hence he does not possess absolute dominion over his life. It is our obligation to take reasonable care of our body and to use it in the service of God and our fellowmen, and to cultivate our spiritual life, so that we may be "without offense unto the day of Christ."

BIBLE AND LITURGY: "There exists no authority except from God" (Rom. 13, 1). We should give due respect and obedience to all legal authority, except when it commands us to do something that is surely against God's will. READ: Rom. 13, 1-7; Sirach 3, 1-16; Heb. 13, 7-17; Eph. 6, 5-9; Luke 2, 41-52 (esp. 51).

INTROIT   Ps. 129, 3. 4. 1. 2   [*A Forgiving God*]

**If You, O Lord, mark iniquities,
    Lord, who can stand?
But with You is forgiveness,
    O God of Israel.
(Ps.) Out of the depths I cry to You, O Lord;
    Lord, hear my voice!**

Glory be to the Father, and to the Son,
  and to the Holy Spirit.
As it was in the beginning, is now, and ever
    shall be,
  world without end. Amen.
If You, O Lord, mark iniquities,
  Lord, who can stand?
But with You is forgiveness,
  O God of Israel.

GRADUAL   Ps. 132, 1-2   [Brotherly Love]

Behold how good it is, and how pleasant
  where brethren dwell at one!
It is as when the precious ointment upon the
    head
  runs down over the beard, the beard of
    Aaron.

Alleluia, alleluia.   Ps. 113, 11   [Trust in the Lord]
Those who fear the Lord trust in the Lord;
  He is their help and their shield. Alleluia.

OFFERTORY   Esther 14, 12. 13

                 [Put the Right Prayer on My Lips]

Remember me, O Lord,
  You Who rule above all power:
And give a well-ordered speech in my mouth,
  that my words may be pleasing in the sight
    of the prince.

COMMUNION   Ps. 16, 6   [Hear My Words]

I call upon You, for You will answer me, O God;
  incline Your ear to me; hear my word.

Jesus raises the daughter of Jairus to life.

TWENTY-THIRD SUNDAY AFTER PENTECOST

THOUGHT FOR TODAY: The same Jesus Who raised the maid to life again, will make our body "an image of His Own glorified Body." Therefore, let us not yield to blind passions, but rather let us consider all that we do in the light of eternity.

BIBLE AND LITURGY: "We are citizens of heaven. And it is from there that we hopefully await the coming of our Savior, the Lord Jesus Christ." (*Ep.*) Waiting for Christ's final coming is a typical Christian attitude. READ: Apoc. 22, 16-21; Luke 12, 35-48; 1 Thess. 5, 1-11; 1 Cor. 1, 4-9; Matt. 24, 36-51; Jude 20-25.

INTROIT Jer. 29, 11. 12. 14; Ps. 84, 2 [*Thoughts of Peace*]

The Lord says:
   "I think thoughts of peace, and not of affliction.
You shall call upon Me,
   and I will hear you;
   and I will bring back your captivity from all places."

(Ps.) You have favored, O Lord, Your land;
   You have restored the well-being of Jacob.

Glory be to the Father, and to the Son,
and to the Holy Spirit.

As it was in the beginning, is now, and ever shall be,
world without end. Amen.

The Lord says:
"I think thoughts of peace, and not of affliction.

You shall call upon Me,
and I will hear you;
and I will bring back your captivity from all places."

GRADUAL   Ps. 43, 8-9   [*Grateful Praise*]

You saved us, O Lord, from our foes,
and those who hated us You put to shame.

In God we gloried day by day;
Your Name we praised always.

Alleluia, alleluia.   Ps. 129, 1. 2   [*Cry from the Depths*]
Out of the depths I cry to You, O Lord;
Lord, hear my prayer! Alleluia.

OFFERTORY   Ps. 129, 1. 2   [*Earnest Prayer*]

Out of the depths I cry to You, O Lord;
Lord, hear my prayer!
Out of the depths I cry to You, O Lord.

COMMUNION   Mark 11, 24   [*Power of Prayer*]

Amen I say to you,
all things whatever you ask for in prayer,
Believe that you shall receive,
and it shall be done to you.

The Angels announce the coming of Jesus on the last day.

LAST SUNDAY AFTER PENTECOST

THOUGHT FOR TODAY: At the end of the ecclesiastical year the Church earnestly reminds us of the judgment that we must pass before the all-knowing God. It is wise to anticipate that judgment in frequent and contrite confession, and always to live in friendly union with Jesus in the Blessed Sacrament Who will be our Judge.

BIBLE AND LITURGY: The History of our Salvation began with the calling of Abraham, our Patriarch, and reached its speak in the Death and Resurrection of our Lord and the descent of the Holy Spirit; it will be finished at Jesus' second coming, when He delivers the Kingdom to God the Father. READ: Matt. 25, 31-46; Apoc. 7, 13-17; 1 Cor. 15, 20-28 (esp. 24); Apoc. 21, 1-4.

INTROIT Jer. 29, 11. 12. 14; Ps. 84, 2   [*Thoughts of Peace*]

The Lord says:

  "I think thoughts of peace, and not of affliction.

You shall call upon Me, and I will hear you;

  and I will bring back your captivity from all places."

(Ps.) You have favored, O Lord, Your land,

  You have restored the well-being of Jacob.

Glory be to the Father, and to the Son,
    and to the Holy Spirit.
As it was in the beginning, is now, and ever
     shall be,
    world without end. Amen.
The Lord says:
    "I think thoughts of peace, and not of af-
     fliction.
You shall call upon Me,
    and I will hear you;
    and I will bring back your captivity from all
     places."

GRADUAL   Ps. 43, 8-9   [*Grateful Praise*]

You saved us, O Lord, from our foes,
    and those who hated us You put to shame.
In God we gloried day by day;
    Your Name we praised always.

Alleluia, alleluia.   Ps. 129, 1. 2   [*Cry from the Depths*]
Out of the depths I cry to You, O Lord;
    Lord, hear my prayer! Alleluia.

OFFERTORY   Ps. 129, 1. 2   [*Earnest Prayer*]

Out of the depths I cry to You, O Lord,
    Lord, hear my prayer!
Out of the depths I cry to You, O Lord.

COMMUNION   Mark 11, 24   [*Power of Prayer*]

Amen I say to you,
    all things whatever you ask for in prayer,
Believe that you shall receive,
    and it shall be done to you.

MASS FOR 24th, 25th, 26th, and 27th SUNDAYS AFTER PENTECOST

INTROIT   Jer. 29, 11. 12. 14; Ps. 84, 2 [*Thoughts of Peace*]

The Lord says:

"I think thoughts of peace, and not of affliction.

You shall call upon Me, and I will hear you;
and I will bring back your captivity from all places."

(Ps.) You have favored, O Lord, Your land;
You have restored the well-being of Jacob.

Glory be to the Father, etc.

Repeat: The Lord says , etc.,*as far as* (Ps.).

GRADUAL   Ps. 43, 8-9   [*Grateful Praise*]

You saved us, O Lord, from our foes,
and those who hated us You put to shame.

In God we gloried day by day;
Your Name we praised always.

Alleluia, alleluia.   Ps. 129, 1. 2   [*Out of the Depths*]

Out of the depths I cry to You, O Lord;
Lord, hear my prayer! Alleluia.

OFFERTORY   Ps. 129, 1. 2   [*Earnest Prayer*]

Out of the depths I cry to You, O Lord;
Lord, hear my prayer!
Out of the depths I cry to You, O Lord.

COMMUNION   Mark 11, 24   [*Power of Prayer*]

Amen I say to you,
all things whatever you ask for in prayer,
Believe that you shall receive,
and it shall be done to you.

COMMON OF THE SAINTS

COMMON OF ONE OR MORE POPES

INTROIT   John 21, 15-17; Ps. 29, 1   [*Loving Shepherd*]

If you love Me, Simon Peter,
  feed My lambs, feed My sheep. (P.T. Alleluia,
    alleluia.)
(Ps.) I will extol You, O Lord, for You drew
  me clear
  and did not let my enemies rejoice over me.
Glory be to the Father, etc.
Repeat: If you love Me, etc., *as far as* (Ps.).

GRADUAL   Ps. 106, 32, 31   [*Praise from the Church*]

Let them extol him in the assembly of the
  people;
  and praise him in the council of the elders.
Let them give thanks to the Lord for His
  kindness
  and His wondrous deeds to the children of
  men.

Alleluia, alleluia.   Matt. 16, 18   [*The Rock*]
You are Peter,
  and upon this rock I will build My Church.
  Alleluia.

*After Septuagesima, the Alleluia and versicle are
omitted and the following Tract is said:*

TRACT   Ps. 39, 10-11   [Witness of the Lord]

I announced Your justice in the vast assembly;
  I did not restrain my lips as You, O Lord,
    know.
Your justice I kept not hid within my heart;
  Your faithfulness and Your salvation I have
    spoken of.
I have made no secret of Your kindness and
    Your truth
  in the vast assembly.

*During Paschaltime, the Gradual is omitted and the
following Alleluia is said:*

Alleluia, alleluia.   Matt. 16, 18; Ps. 44, 17. 18   [Princes]

You are Peter,
  and upon this rock I will build My Church.
Alleluia. You shall make them princes through
    all the land;
  they shall remember Your Name, O Lord,
    through all generations. Alleluia.

OFFERTORY   Jer. 1, 9-10   [Authority]

See, I place My words in your mouth!
  behold, I set you over nations and over
    kingdoms,
To root up and to tear down,
  and to build and to plant. (P.T. Alleluia.)

COMMUNION   Matt. 16, 18   [The Rock]

You are Peter,
  and upon this rock I will build My Church.
    (P.T. Alleluia.)

COMMON OF ONE MARTYR
Outside Paschaltime

I. FOR A MARTYR BISHOP

INTROIT   Sir. 45, 30; Ps. 131, 1   [An Eternal Priest]

The Lord made a covenant of friendship with
   him,
   and made him a prince;
   that he should possess the dignity of priesthood forever.

(Ps.) **Remember, O Lord, David**
   and all his meekness.

Glory be to the Father, etc.

Repeat: **The Lord made,** etc., *as far as* (Ps.).

GRADUAL   Ps. 88, 21-23   [Anointed]

I have found David, My servant;
   with My holy oil I have anointed him,
That My hand may be always with him,
   that My arm may make him strong.
No enemy shall have an advantage over him,
   nor shall the son of iniquity have power to
   hurt him.

Alleluia, alleluia.   Ps. 109, 4   [Priest Forever]

You are a priest forever, according to the order
   of Melchisedec. Alleluia.

*After Septuagesima, the Alleluia and versicle are
omitted and the following Tract is said:*

TRACT   Ps. 20, 3-4   [Crown]

You have granted him his heart's desire;
   You refused not the wish of his lips.

For You welcomed him with goodly blessings.
You placed on his head a crown of precious
stones.

OFFERTORY   Ps. 88, 25   [Exaltation]

My faithfulness and My kindness shall be with
him,
and through My Name shall his horn be
exalted.

COMMUNION   Ps. 88, 36. 37-38   [Faithful Witness]

Once by My holiness have I sworn:
His posterity shall continue forever,
and his throne shall be like the sun before
me,
Like the moon perfect forever—
a faithful witness in the sky.

II. FOR A MARTYR BISHOP

INTROIT   Dan. 3, 84. 87. 57   [Priestly Praise]

Priests of the Lord, bless the Lord,
holy men of humble heart, praise God.
(Ps.) Bless the Lord, all you works of the Lord,
praise and exalt Him above all forever.
Glory be to the Father, etc.

Repeat Priests of the Lord, etc., *as far as* (Ps.).

GRADUAL   Ps. 8, 6-7   [Crowned]

You crowned him with glory and honor.
You have given him rule over the works of
Your hands, O Lord.

Alleluia, alleluia.   [*Glory*]

**This is the priest whom the Lord has crowned.
    Alleluia.**

*After Septuagesima, the Alleluia and versicle are
omitted and the following Tract is said:*

TRACT   Ps. 111, 1-3   [*Eternal Kingdom*]

**Happy the man who fears the Lord,
    who greatly delights in His commands.
His posterity shall be mighty upon the earth;
    the upright generation shall be blessed.
Wealth and riches shall be in his house;
    his generosity endures forever.**

OFFERTORY   Ps. 88, 21-22   [*Anointed*]

**I have found David, My servant;
    with My holy oil I have anointed him,
That My hand may be always with him,
    and that My arm may make him strong.**

COMMUNION   Ps. 20, 4   [*Golden Crown*]

**You placed on his head, O Lord,
    a crown of precious stones.**

III. FOR A MARTYR NOT A BISHOP

INTROIT   Ps. 20, 2-3. 4   [*God' Victor*]

**O Lord, in Your strength the just man is glad;
    in Your salvation how greatly he rejoices!
You have granted him his heart's desire.
(Ps.) For You welcomed him with goodly
    blessings,**

You placed on his head a crown of precious
  stones.

Glory be to the Father, etc.

Repeat: **O Lord,** etc., *as far as* (Ps.).

GRADUAL   Ps. 111, 1-2   [*Happy the Just Man*]

Happy the man who fears the Lord,
  who greatly delights in His commands.
His posterity shall be mighty upon the earth;
  the upright generation shall be blessed.

Alleluia, alleluia.   Ps. 20, 4   [*Golden Crown*]
You placed on his head, O Lord,
  a crown of precious stones. Alleluia.

*After Septuagesima, the Alleluia and versicle are
omitted and the following Tract is said:*

TRACT   Ps. 20, 3-4   [*Glorified*]

You have granted him his heart's desire:
  You refused not the wish of his lips.
For You welcomed him with goodly blessings.
  You placed upon his head a crown of precious
    stones.

OFFERTORY   Ps. 8, 6-7   [*Crowned*]

You crowned him with glory and honor;
You have given him rule over the works of
  Your hands, O Lord.

COMMUNION   Matt. 16, 24   [*The Cross*]

Whoever wishes to come after Me,
  let him deny himself,
And take up his cross,
  and follow Me.

IV. FOR A MARTYR NOT A BISHOP

INTROIT   Ps. 63, 11. 2   [*Happiness of the Just*]

The just man is glad in the Lord and takes
    refuge in Him;
  all the upright of heart shall be praised.
(Ps.) Hear, O God, my voice in my lament;
  from the dread enemy preserve my life.
Glory be to the Father, etc.
Repeat: **The just man,** etc., *as far as* (Ps.).

GRADUAL   Ps. 36, 24. 26   [*Sustained by the Lord*]

Though the just man fall,
  he does not lie prostrate,
    for the hand of the Lord sustains him.
All the day he is kindly and lends,
  and his descendants shall be blessed.

Alleluia, alleluia.   John 8, 12   [*Eternal Life*]
He who follows Me does not walk in darkness,
  but will have the light of life eternal. Alleluia.

*After Septuagesima, the Alleluia and versicle are
omitted and the following Tract is said:*

TRACT   Ps. 111, 1-3   [*Glory of the Just*]

Happy the man who fears the Lord,
  who greatly delights in His commands.
His posterity shall be mighty upon the earth;
  the upright generation shall be blessed.
Wealth and riches shall be in his house;
  his generosity shall endure forever.

*After Septuagesima "Alleluia" is omitted at the end
of the following Offertory.*

OFFERTORY   Ps. 20, 4-5   [Golden Crown]

O Lord, You placed on his head
  a crown of precious stones.
He asked life of You.
  and You gave it to him. Alleluia.

COMMUNION   John 12, 26   [God and His Servant]

Whoever serves me, let him follow me;
  and where I am there also shall my servant
    be.

_____

COMMON OF SEVERAL MARTYRS

Outside Paschaltime

I. FOR SEVERAL MARTYRS

INTROIT   Ps. 78, 11, 12. 10. 1   [God the Avenger]

Let the prisoners' sighing come before You,
  O Lord;
Repay our neighbors sevenfold into their
    bosoms;
  avenge the blood of Your saints which has
    been shed.
(Ps.) O God, the nations have come into Your
    inheritance;
  they have defiled Your holy temple,
  they have made Jerusalem as a place to keep
    fruit.
Glory be to the Father, etc.
Repeat: Let the prisoners', etc., *as far as* (Ps.).

GRADUAL   Ex. 15, 11. 6   [God and His Saints]

God is glorious in His saints,
  wonderful in majesty, a worker of wonders.
Your right hand, O Lord, is magnificent in
  power;
  Your right hand has shattered the enemy.

Alleluia, alleluia.   Sir. 44, 14   [Eternal Memory]
The bodies of the saints are buried in peace,
  but their name lives on and on. Alleluia.

*After Septuagesima, the Alleluia and versicle are
omitted and the following Tract is said:*

TRACT   Ps. 125, 5-6   [Back in Triumph]

Those that sow in tears
  shall reap rejoicing.
Going, they went and wept,
  casting their seeds.
But coming, they shall come with joyfulness,
  carrying their sheaves.

*After Septuagesima "Alleluia" is omitted at the end
of the following Offertory.*

OFFERTORY   Ps. 67, 36   [Wonderful in His Saints]

God is wonderful in His saints;
  the God of Israel is He
Who gives power and strength to His people.
  Blessed be God! Alleluia.

COMMUNION   Wis. 3, 4. 5. 6   [Sacrificial Offering]

For if before men they were punished,
  God tried them;

As gold in the furnace He proved them,
and as sacrificial offerings He took them to
Himself. _____

II. FOR SEVERAL MARTYRS

INTROIT   Sir. 44, 15. 14; Ps. 32, 1   [*Praises of the Saints*]

At gatherings the wisdom of the saints is retold,
and the assembly sings their praises;
their name lives on and on.

(Ps.) Exult, you just, in the Lord;
praise from the upright is fitting.

Glory be to the Father, etc.

Repeat: **At gatherings,** etc., *as far as* (Ps.).

GRADUAL   Ps. 123, 7-8   [*Rescue*]

We were rescued like a bird
from the fowlers' snare.
Broken was the snare,
and we were freed;
Our help is in the Name of the Lord,
Who made heaven and earth.

Alleluia, alleluia.   Ps. 67, 4   [*Rejoice and Exult*]
The just feast and exult before God;
and they are glad and rejoice. Alleluia.

*After Septuagesima, the Alleluia and versicle are
omitted and the following Tract is said:*

TRACT   Ps. 125, 5-6   [*Back in Triumph*]

Those that sow in tears
shall reap rejoicing.

Going, they went and wept,
  casting their seeds.
But coming, they shall come with joyfulness,
  carrying their sheaves.

*After Septuagesima "Alleluia" is omitted at the end
of the following Offertory.*

OFFERTORY   Ps. 149, 5-6   [Exult]

Let the faithful exult in glory;
  let them sing for joy upon their couches;
  let the high praises of God be in their throats.
    Alleluia.

COMMUNION   Luke 12, 4   [Fear Not]

But I say to you, My friends:
  do not be afraid of those who persecute you.

III. FOR SEVERAL MARTYRS

INTROIT   Ps. 36, 39. 1   [God, Our Savior]

The salvation of the just is from the Lord;
  He is their refuge in time of distress.
(Ps.) Be not vexed over evildoers,
  nor jealous of those who do wrong.
Glory be to the Father, etc.
Repeat: The salvation, etc., *as far as* (Ps.)

GRADUAL   Ps. 33, 18-19   [The Lord Hears the Just]

The just cry out and the Lord hears them,
  and from all their distress He rescues them.
The Lord is close to those who are broken-
    hearted;
  and those who are crushed in spirit He saves.

Alleluia, alleluia. [Praise from Martyrs]
The white-robed army of Martyrs
praises You, O Lord. Alleluia.

*After Septuagesima, the Alleluia and versicle are
omitted and the following Tract is said:*

TRACT Ps. 125, 5-6 [Find Joy]

Those that sow in tears
shall reap rejoicing.
Going, they went and wept,
casting their seeds.
But coming, they shall come with joyfulness,
carrying their sheaves.

*After Septuagesima "Alleluia" is omitted at the end
of the following Offertory.*

OFFERTORY Wis. 3, 1, 2. 3 [Peace, At Last]

The souls of the just are in the hand of God,
and no torment of death shall touch them.
They seemed, in the view of the foolish, to be
dead;
but they are in peace. Alleluia.

COMMUNION Matt. 10, 27 [Preach Openly]

"What I tell you in darkness,
speak it in the light," says the Lord,
"And what you hear whispered,
preach it on the housetops."

I. FOR ONE MARTYR

INTROIT Ps. 63, 3. 2 [*Shelter by God*]

You have sheltered me, O God, against the
   council of malefactors, alleluia,
   against the multitude of the workers of in-
      iquity, alleluia, alleluia.

(Ps.) Hear, O God, my voice in lament;
   from the dread enemy preserve my life.

Glory be to the Father, etc.

Repeat: You have sheltered, etc., *as far as* (Ps.).

Alleluia, alleluia. Ps. 88, 6; 20, 4 [*God's Wonders*]

The heavens proclaim Your wonders, O Lord,
   and Your faithfulness in the assembly of the
      holy ones.

Alleluia. You placed on his head, O Lord,
   a crown of precious stones. Alleluia.

OFFERTORY Ps. 88, 6 [*Heavenly Acclaim*]

The heavens proclaim Your wonders, O Lord,
   and Your faithfulness in the assembly of the
      holy ones, alleluia, alleluia.

COMMUNION Ps. 63, 11 [*Joy of the Upright*]

The just man is glad in the Lord and takes
   refuge in Him;

all the upright of heart shall be praised, alleluia, alleluia.

II. FOR SEVERAL MARTYRS

INTROIT   Ps. 144, 10-11. 1   [*Glory of the Kingdom*]

Let Your faithful ones bless You, O Lord;
   let them discourse of the glory of Your
   kingdom, alleluia, alleluia.

(Ps.) I will extol You, O my God and King,
   and I will bless Your Name forever and ever.

Glory be to the Father, etc.

Repeat: **Let Your faithful,** etc., *as far as* (Ps.).

Alleluia, alleluia. Ps. 115, 15 [*God's Joy in the Saints*]
Your faithful shall flourish like the lily, O Lord,
   and be as the odor of balsam before You.
Alleluia. Precious in the eyes of the Lord
   is the death of His faithful ones. Alleluia.

OFFERTORY   Ps. 31, 11   [*Exult*]

Be glad in the Lord, and rejoice, you just;
   and exult, all you upright of heart, alleluia,
   alleluia.

COMMUNION   Ps. 32, 1   [*Praise from the Upright*]

Exult, you just, in the Lord, alleluia;
   praise from the upright is fitting, alleluia.

COMMON OF A CONFESSOR BISHOP

I. FOR A CONFESSOR BISHOP

INTROIT   Sir. 45, 30; Ps. 131, 1   [*Priestly Dignity*]

The Lord made a covenant of friendship with
  him,
  and made him a prince,
  that he should possess the dignity of priesthood forever. (P.T. Alleluia, alleluia.)

(Ps.) Remember, O Lord, David
  and all his meekness.

Glory be to the Father, etc.

Repeat: **The Lord made,** etc., *as far as* (Ps.).

GRADUAL   Sir. 44, 16. 20   [*Devotion and Salvation*]

Behold, a great priest,
  who in his days pleased God.
There was not found the like to him,
  who kept the law of the Most High.

Alleluia, alleluia.   Ps. 109, 4   [*Priest Forever*]
You are a priest forever, according to the order
  of Melchisedec. Alleluia.

*After Septuagesima, the Alleluia and versicle are
omitted and the following Tract is said:*

TRACT   Ps. 111, 1-3   [*Glory of the Just*]

Happy the man who fears the Lord,
  who greatly delights in His commands.
His posterity shall be mighty upon the earth;
  the upright generation shall be blessed.
Wealth and riches shall be in his house:
  his generosity shall endure forever.

During Paschaltime, the Gradual is omitted and the following Alleluia is said:

Alleluia, alleluia.   Ps. 109, 4   [*Priestly Crown*]
**You are a priest forever, according to the order
    of Melchisedec.
Alleluia. This is the priest whom the Lord has
    crowned. Alleluia.**

OFFERTORY   Ps. 88, 21-22   [*Anointed*]

**I have found David, My servant;
    with My holy oil I have anointed him,
That My hand may be always with him,
    and that My arm may make him strong.
        (P.T. Alleluia.)**

COMMUNION   Luke 12, 42   [*Faithful Servant*]

**The faithful and prudent servant
    whom the master will set over his household
    to give them their ration of grain in due
    time. (P.T. Alleluia.)**

II. FOR A CONFESSOR BISHOP

INTROIT   Ps. 131, 9-10. 1   [*Priestly Justice*]

**May Your priests, O Lord, be clothed with
    justice;
    let Your faithful ones shout merrily for joy.
For the sake of David Your servant,
    reject not the plea of Your anointed. (P.T.
    alleluia, alleluia.)
(Ps.) Remember, O Lord, David
    and all his meekness.**

Glory be to the Father, etc.

Repeat: **May Your priests,** etc., *as far as* (Ps.).

GRADUAL   Ps. 131, 16-17   [*A Saving Priesthood*]

Her priests I will clothe with salvation,
and her faithful ones shall shout merrily for
joy.
In her will I make a horn to sprout forth for
David;
I will place a lamp for My anointed.

Alleluia, alleluia.   Ps. 109, 4   [*Priest Forever*]

The Lord has sworn, and He will not repent:
"You are a priest forever, according to the
order of Melchisedec." Alleluia.

After Septuagesima, the Alleluia and versicle are
omitted and the following Tract is said:

TRACT   Ps. 111, 1-3   [*Glory of the Just*]

Happy the man who fears the Lord,
who greatly delights in His commands.
His posterity shall be mighty upon the earth;
the upright generation shall be blessed.
Wealth and riches shall be in his house;
his generosity shall endure forever.

During Paschaltime, the Gradual is omitted and the
following Alleluia is said:

Alleluia, alleluia. Ps. 109, 4; Sir. 45, 9 [*Clothed in Glory*]

The Lord has sworn, and He will not repent:
"You are a priest forever, according to the
order of Melchisedec."
Alleluia. The Lord loved him and adorned him;
He clothed him with a robe of glory. Alleluia.

OFFERTORY   Ps. 88, 25   [*Exalted*]

My faithfulness and My kindness shall be with
   him,
     and through My Name shall his horn be
     exalted. (P.T. Alleluia.)

COMMUNION   Matt. 24, 46-47   [*Watchfulness*]

Blessed is that servant whom his master,
   when he comes, shall find watching.
Amen I say to you,
   he will set him over all his goods. (P.T.
   Alleluia.)

COMMON OF DOCTORS

INTROIT   Sir. 15, 5; Ps. 91, 2   [*Wisdom*]

In the midst of the assembly He opened his
   mouth;
And the Lord filled him with the spirit of wis-
   dom and understanding;
     He clothed him with a robe of glory. (P.T.
     Alleluia, alleluia.)
(Ps.) It is good to give thanks to the Lord,
   to sing praise to Your Name, Most High.
Glory be to the Father, etc.
Repeat: In the midst, etc., *as far as* (Ps.).

GRADUAL   Ps. 36, 30-31   [*Law of God*]

The mouth of the just man tells of wisdom,
   and his tongue utters what is right.
The law of his God is in his heart,
   and his steps do not falter.

Alleluia, alleluia. Sir. 45, 9   [Adorned]
The Lord loved him and adorned him;
    He clothed him with a robe of glory. Alleluia.

After Septuagesima, the Alleluia and versicle are omitted and the following Tract is said:

TRACT Ps. 111, 1-3   [Glory of the Just]

Happy the man who fears the Lord,
    who greatly delights in His commands.
His posterity shall be mighty upon the earth;
    the upright generation shall be blessed.
Wealth and riches shall be in his house;
    his generosity shall endure forever.

During Paschaltime, the Gradual is omitted and the following Alleluia is said:
                    Sir. 45, 9; Osee 14, 6

Alleluia, alleluia.   [The Just Man Flourishes]
The Lord loved him and adorned him;
    He clothed him with a robe of glory.
Alleluia. The just man shall blossom like a lily;
    and shall flourish forever before the Lord.
        Alleluia.

OFFERTORY Ps. 91, 13   [Growth]

The just man shall flourish like the palm tree,
    like a cedar of Lebanon shall he grow. (P.T. Alleluia.)

COMMUNION Luke 12, 42   [Faithful Servant]

The faithful and prudent servant
    whom the Master will set over His household
    to give them their ration of grain in due time.
        (P.T. Alleluia.)

COMMON OF A CONFESSOR
NOT A BISHOP

I. FOR A CONFESSOR NOT A BISHOP

INTROIT   Ps. 36, 30-31. 1   [Wisdom]

The mouth of the just man tells of wisdom,
 and his tongue utters what is right.
The law of his God is in his heart. (P.T. Alleluia,
 alleluia.)
(Ps.) Be not vexed over evildoers,
 nor jealous of those who do wrong.
Glory be to the Father, etc.
Repeat: The mouth, etc.. *as far as* (Ps.).

GRADUAL   Ps. 91, 13. 14. 3 [Witness to God's Kindness]

The just man shall flourish like the palm tree,
 like a cedar of Lebanon shall he grow
 in the house of the Lord.
To proclaim Your kindness at dawn
 and Your faithfulness throughout the night.

Alleluia, alleluia.   James 1, 12   [Perseverance]
Blessed is the man who endures temptation;
 for when he has been tried,
 he will receive the crown of life. Alleluia.

*After Septuagesima, the Alleluia and versicle are
omitted and the following Tract is said:*

TRACT   Ps. 111, 1-3   [Glory of the Just]

Happy the man who fears the Lord,
 who greatly delights in His commands.

His posterity shall be mighty upon the earth;
  the upright generation shall be blessed.
Wealth and riches shall be in his house;
  his generosity shall endure forever.

*During Paschaltime, the Gradual is omitted and the
following Alleluia is said:*
James 1, 12; Sir. 45, 9

Alleluia, alleluia.   [*Crowned and Adorned*]

Blessed is the man who endures temptation;
  for when he has been tried,
  he shall receive the crown of life.
Alleluia. The Lord loved him and adorned him;
  He clothed Him with a robe of glory. Alleluia.

OFFERTORY   Ps. 88, 25   [*Exaltation*]

My faithfulness and My kindness shall be with
    him,
  and through My Name shall his horn be
    exalted. (P.T. Alleluia.)

COMMUNION   Matt. 24, 46-47   [*Watchfulness*]

Blessed is that servant whom his master,
  when He comes, shall find watching.
Amen I say to you,
  He will set him over all His goods. (P.T.
    Alleluia.)
———————

II. FOR A CONFESSOR NOT A BISHOP

INTROIT   Ps. 91, 13-14. 2   [*The Just Man Flourishes*]

The just man shall flourish like the palm tree,
  like a cedar of Lebanon shall he grow,
Planted in the house of the Lord,

in the courts of the house of our God. (P.T. Alleluia, alleluia.)

(Ps.) **It is good to give thanks to the Lord, to sing praise to Your Name, Most High.**

Glory be to the Father, etc.

Repeat: **The just man,** etc., *as far as* (Ps.).

GRADUAL   Ps. 36, 30-31   [Wisdom]

The mouth of the just man tells of wisdom, and his tongue utters what is right. The law of his God is in his heart, and his steps do not falter.

Alleluia, alleluia.   Ps. 111, 1   [Delight in God's Law]
Happy the man who fears the Lord, who greatly delights in His commands. Alleluia.

After Septuagesima, the Alleluia and versicle are omitted and the following Tract is said:

TRACT   Ps. 111, 1-3   [Glory of the Just]

Happy the man who fears the Lord, who greatly delights in His commands. His posterity shall be mighty upon the earth; the upright generation shall be blessed. Wealth and riches shall be in his house; his generosity shall endure forever.

During Paschaltime, the Gradual is omitted and the following Alleluia is said:
         Ps. 111, 1; Osee 14, 6

Alleluia, alleluia.   [The Just Flourishes]
Happy the man who fears the Lord, who greatly delights in His commands.

Alleluia. **The just man shall blossom like the lily,**
  and flourish forever before the Lord. Alleluia.

OFFERTORY   Ps. 20, 2-3   [*Joy in God*]

O Lord, in Your strength the just man is glad;
  in Your victory how greatly he rejoices!
You have granted him his heart's desire. (P.T. Alleluia.)

COMMUNION   Matt. 19, 28. 29   [*The Reward*]

Amen I say to you that you,
  who have left all things and followed Me,
Shall receive a hundredfold,
  and shall possess life everlasting. (P.T. Alleluia.)

COMMON OF ABBOTS

INTROIT   Ps. 36, 30-31. 1   [*Wisdom*]

The mouth of the just man tells of wisdom,
  and his tongue utters what is right.
The law of his God is in his heart. (P.T. Alleluia, alleluia.)
(Ps.) Be not vexed over evildoers,
  nor jealous of those who do wrong.
Glory be to the Father, etc.
Repeat: The mouth, etc., *as far as* (Ps.).

GRADUAL   Ps. 20, 4-5   [*Crowned*]

O Lord, You welcomed him with goodly blessings,
  You placed on his head a crown of precious stones.

He asked life of You and You gave him
    length of days forever and ever.

Alleluia, alleluia.   Ps. 91, 13   [Growth]
The just man shall flourish like the palm tree
    like a cedar of Lebanon shall he grow.
    Alleluia.

*After Septuagesima, the Alleluia and versicle are
omitted and the following Tract is said:*

TRACT   Ps. 111, 1-3   [Glory of the Just]

Happy the man who fears the Lord,
    who greatly delights in His commands.
His posterity shall be mighty upon the earth;
    the upright generation shall be blessed.
Wealth and riches shall be in his house;
    his generosity shall endure forever.

*During Paschaltime, the Gradual is omitted and the
following Alleluia is said:*

Ps. 91, 13; Osee 14, 6
Alleluia, alleluia.   [The Just Man Flourishes]
The just man shall flourish like the palm tree,
    like a cedar of Lebanon shall he grow.
Alleluia. The just man shall blossom like the
    lily,
    and flourish forever before the Lord. Alleluia.

OFFERTORY   Ps. 20, 3. 4   [Golden Crown]

You have granted him his heart's desire, O Lord;
    You refused not the wish of his lips;
You placed on his head a crown of precious
    stones. (P.T. Alleluia.)

COMMUNION   Luke 12, 42   [*Faithful Servant*]

The faithful and prudent servant
  whom the master will set over his household
  to give them their ration of grain in due time.
    (P.T. Alleluia.)

COMMON OF VIRGINS

I. FOR A VIRGIN MARTYR

INTROIT   Ps. 118, 46-47   [*Joyful Witness*]

I will speak of Your decrees before kings
  without being ashamed.
And I will delight in Your commands,
  which I love exceedingly. **(P.T. Alleluia,
    alleluia.)**

(Ps.) Happy are they whose way is blameless,
  who walk in the law of the Lord.

Glory be to the Father, etc.

Repeat: I will speak, etc., *as far as* (Ps.).

GRADUAL   Ps. 44, 8   [*Oil of Gladness*]

You love justice and hate wickedness.
  Therefore God, your God, has anointed you
  with the oil of gladness.

Alleluia, alleluia. Ps. 44, 15. 16 [*Glory Before the King*]
Behind her the virgins of her train are brought
    to the King.
  Her neighbors are brought to You with
    gladness. Alleluia.

After Septuagesima, the Alleluia and versicle are omitted and the following Tract is said:

TRACT Ps. 44, 8. 5 [Receive the Crown]

**Come, O spouse of Christ,
  receive the crown
Which the Lord has prepared for you forever,
  for the love of Whom you shed your blood.
You love justice and hate wickedness;
  therefore God, your God, has anointed you
  with the oil of gladness above your fellows.
In your splendor and your beauty
  ride on triumphant, and reign.**

During Paschaltime, the Gradual is omitted and the following Alleluia is said:

Alleluia, alleluia. Ps. 44, 15. 16. 5 [Triumph]
**Behind her the virgins of her train are brought
    to the King.
  Her neighbors are brought to You with
    gladness.
Alleluia. In your splendor and your beauty
  ride on triumphant, and reign. Alleluia.**

OFFERTORY Ps. 44, 15. 16 [Eternal Glory]

**Behind her the virgins of her train are brought
    to the King.
  Her neighbors are brought to You with
    gladness and joy;
    they enter the palace of the Lord, the King.
    (P.T. Alleluia.)**

COMMUNION Ps. 118, 78. 80 [Judgment of God]

Let the proud be put to shame for oppressing
   me unjustly;
  I will meditate on Your precepts, on Your
    statutes,
   that I be not put to shame. (P.T. Alleluia.)

II. FOR A VIRGIN MARTYR

INTROIT Ps. 118, 95-96. 1 [Trust in God]

Sinners wait to destroy me,
  but I pay heed to Your decrees, O Lord.
I see that all fulfillment has its limits;
  broad indeed is Your command. (P.T. Alle-
    luia, alleluia.)

(Ps.) Happy are they whose way is blameless,
  who walk in the law of the Lord.

Glory be to the Father, etc.

Repeat: Sinners wait, etc., *as far as* (Ps.).

GRADUAL Ps. 45, 6. 5 [City of Delight]

God will help her with His countenance;
  God is in her midst,
  she shall not be disturbed.
There is a stream whose runlets gladden the
   city of God;
  the Most High has sanctified His dwelling.

Alleluia, alleluia. [Wise Virgin]

This is a wise virgin,
  and one of the number of the prudent.
  Alleluia.

After Septuagesima, the Alleluia and versicle are omitted and the following Tract is said:

TRACT   Ps. 44, 8. 5   [Receive the Crown]

Come, spouse of Christ,
   receive the crown,
Which the Lord has prepared for you forever,
   for the love of Whom you shed your blood.
You love justice and hate wickedness,
   therefore God, your God, has anointed you
   with the oil of gladness above your fellows.
In your splendor and your beauty
   ride on triumphant, and reign.

During Paschaltime, the Gradual is omitted and the following Alleluia is said:

Alleluia, alleluia.   Wis. 4, 1   [Beauty of the Chaste]
This is a wise virgin,
   and one of the number of the prudent.
Alleluia. Oh, how beautiful is the chaste generation with glory! Alleluia.

OFFERTORY   Ps. 44, 3   [Grace]

Grace is poured out upon your lips;
   thus God has blessed you forever and ever.
   (P.T. Alleluia.)

COMMUNION   Ps. 118, 121, 122. 128   [Strength]

I have done judgment and justice, O Lord,
   let not the proud slander me.
I was directed toward all Your commandments;
   I have hated all wicked ways. (P.T. Alleluia.)

III. FOR A VIRGIN ONLY

INTROIT   Ps. 44, 8. 2   [*Love of Justice*]

You love justice and hate wickedness;
> therefore God, your God has anointed you
> with the oil of gladness above your fellows.
> **(P.T. Alleluia, alleluia.)**

(Ps.) My heart overflows with a goodly theme;
> as I sing my ode to the King.

Glory be to the Father, etc.

Repeat: **You love,** etc., *as far as* (Ps.).

GRADUAL   Ps. 44, 5   [*Splendor of Virginity*]

In your splendor and your beauty
> ride on triumphant, and reign.

Because of truth, and meekness, and justice;
> may your right hand show you wondrous
> deeds.

Alleluia, alleluia.   Ps. 44, 15. 16   [*Triumph*]

Behind her the virgins of her train are brought
> to the King.

> Her neighbors are brought to You with
> gladness. Alleluia.

*After Septuagesima, the Alleluia and versicle are
omitted and the following Tract is said:*

TRACT   Ps. 44, 11. 12. 13. 10. 15-16   [*Loved by the King*]

Hear, O daughter, and see, and turn your ear;
> for the King shall desire your beauty.

All the rich among the people seek Your favor;
> the daughters of kings come in Your honor.

Behind her the virgins of her train are brought
> to the king.

Her neighbors are brought to You.
They are brought with gladness and joy;
  they enter the palace of the King.

*During Paschaltime, the Gradual is omitted and the
following Alleluia is said:*

Alleluia, alleluia. Ps. 44, 15. 16. 5   [*Triumph*]

**Behind her the virgins of her train are brought
    to the King.**

> **Her neighbors are brought to You with
>   gladness.**

**Alleluia. In your splendor and beauty
  ride on triumphant, and reign. Alleluia.**

OFFERTORY   Ps. 44, 10   [*Beauty*]

**The daughters of kings come in Your honor;
    the queen takes her place at Your right hand
      in gold and colored clothing. (P.T. Alleluia.)**

COMMUNION   Matt. 25, 4. 6   [*Go Forth*]

**The five virgins took oil in their vessels with
    the lamps;
  and at midnight a cry arose,
"Behold, the bridegroom is coming,
  go forth to meet Christ the Lord." (P.T.
    Alleluia.)**

IV. FOR A VIRGIN ONLY

INTROIT   Ps. 44, 13, 15. 16. 2   [*Triumph*]

**All the rich among the people seek Your favor.
Behind her the virgins of her train are brought
    to the King.**

Her neighbors are brought to You with
gladness and joy. (P.T. Alleluia, alleluia.)

(Ps.) My heart overflows with a goodly theme;
as I sing my ode to the King.

Glory be to the Father, etc.

Repeat: All the rich, etc., *as far as* (Ps.).

GRADUAL Ps. 44, 12. 11 [*Beloved by the King*]

The King shall desire your beauty,
for He is the Lord your God.
Hear, O daughter, and see;
and turn your ear.

Alleluia, alleluia. [*A Wise Virgin*]
This is a wise virgin,
and one of the number of the prudent.
Alleluia.

*After Septuagesima, the Alleluia and versicle are
omitted and the following Tract is said:*

TRACT Ps. 44, 12, 13. 10. 15-16 [*Triumph before the King*]

For the King shall desire your beauty.
All the rich among the people seek Your favor;
the daughters of kings come in Your honor.
Behind her the virgins of her train are brought
to the King;
her neighbors are brought to you.
They are brought with gladness and joy;
they enter the palace of the King.

*During Paschaltime, the Gradual is omitted and the
following Alleluia is said:*

Alleluia, alleluia.   Wis. 4, 1   [Beauty of the Chaste]

This is a wise virgin,
  and one of the number of the prudent.
Alleluia. O how beautiful is the chaste generation with glory! Alleluia.

OFFERTORY   Ps. 44, 15-16   [Glory of Virgins]

Behind her the virgins of her train are brought
  to the King;
Her neighbors are brought to You with gladness and joy;
  they enter the palace of the Lord, the King.
  (P.T. Alleluia.)

COMMUNION   Matt. 13, 45-46 [Pearl of Great Price]

The kingdom of heaven is like a merchant
  in search of fine pearls.
When he finds a single pearl of great price,
  he sells all that he has and buys it. (P.T.
  Alleluia.)

COMMON OF HOLY WOMEN

I. FOR A HOLY WOMAN MARTYR

INTROIT   Ps. 118, 95-96. 1   [Fidelity to God]

Sinners wait to destroy me,
  but I pay heed to Your decrees, O Lord.
I see that all fulfillment has its limits;
  broad indeed is Your command. (P.T. Alleluia, alleluia.)
(Ps.) Happy are they whose way is blameless,
  who walk in the law of the Lord.

Glory be to the Father, etc.

Repeat: **Sinners wait,** etc., *as far as* (Ps.).

GRADUAL   Ps. 44, 8   [*Oil of Gladness*]

You love justice and hate wickedness.
  Therefore God, your God, has anointed you
  with the oil of gladness.
Alleluia, alleluia.   Ps. 44, 5   [*Triumph*]
In your splendor and your beauty
  ride on triumphant, and reign. Alleluia.

*After Septuagesima, the Alleluia and versicle are
omitted and the following Tract is said:*

TRACT   Ps. 44, 8. 5   [*Receive the Crown*]

Come, O spouse of Christ,
  receive forever the crown
Which the Lord has prepared for you:
  for Whose love you shed your blood.
You love justice and hate wickedness;
  therefore God, your God, has anointed you
  with the oil of gladness above your fellows.
In your splendor and your beauty
  ride on triumphant, and reign.

*During Paschaltime, the Gradual is omitted and the
following Alleluia is said:*

Alleluia, alleluia.   Ps. 44, 5   [*Spiritual Success*]
In your splendor and your beauty
  ride on triumphant, and reign.
Alleluia. Because of truth, and meekness, and
    justice;
  may your right hand show you wondrous
    deeds. Alleluia.

OFFERTORY   Ps. 44, 3   [*Grace*]

Grace is poured out upon your lips;
  thus God has blessed you forever, and ever.
    (P.T. Alleluia.)

COMMUNION   Ps. 118, 161-162

[*Joy in God's Promises*]

Princes persecute me without cause,
  but my heart stands in awe of Your words.
I rejoice at Your promise,
  as one who has found rich spoil. (P.T.
    Alleluia.)

————————

II. FOR A HOLY WOMAN NOT A MARTYR

INTROIT   Ps. 118, 75. 120. 1   [*Fidelity*]

I know, O Lord, that Your ordinances are just,
  and in Your faithfulness You have afflicted
    me.
Pierce my flesh with your fear;
  I fear Your ordinances. (P.T. Alleluia,
    alleluia.)
(Ps.) Happy are they whose way is blameless,
  who walk in the law of the Lord.
Glory be to the Father, etc.
Repeat: I know, etc., *as far as* (Ps.).

GRADUAL   Ps. 44, 3. 5   [*Grace*]

Grace is poured out upon your lips;
  thus God has blessed you forever.

Because of truth, and meekness, and justice;
    may your right hand show you wondrous
        deeds.

Alleluia, alleluia. Ps. 44, 5   [*Triumph*]

In your splendor and your beauty
    ride on triumphant, and reign. Alleluia.

*After Septuagesima, the Alleluia and versicle are
omitted and the following Tract is said:*

TRACT   Ps. 44, 8. 5   [*Receive the Crown*]

Come, O spouse of Christ,
    receive the crown

Which the Lord has prepared for you forever;
    for the love of Whom you shed your blood.

You love justice and hate wickedness;
    therefore God, your God, has anointed you
    with the oil of gladness above your fellows.

In your splendor and your beauty
    ride on triumphant, and reign.

*During Paschaltime, the Gradual is omitted and the
following Alleluia is said:*

Alleluia, alleluia. Ps. 44, 5   [*Victory*]

In your splendor and your beauty
    ride on triumphant, and reign.

Alleluia. Because of truth, and meekness, and
    justice;
    may your right hand show you wondrous
        deeds. Alleluia.

OFFERTORY   Ps. 44, 3   [*God's Blessing*]

Grace is poured out upon your lips;
    thus God has blessed you forever and ever.
    (P.T. Alleluia.)

COMMUNION   Ps. 44, 8   [*Oil of Gladness*]

You love justice and hate wickedness;
    therefore God, your God, has anointed you
    with the oil of gladness above your fellows.
      (P.T. Alleluia.)

COMMON OF THE DEDICATION
OF A CHURCH

INTROIT   Gen. 28, 17; Ps. 83, 2-3   [*House of the Lord*]

How awesome is this place!
    This is none other than the house of God;
This is the gate of heaven;
    and it shall be called the court of God. (P.T.
      Alleluia, alleluia.)
(Ps.) How lovely is Your dwelling place,
    O Lord of Hosts!
My soul yearns and pines
    for the courts of the Lord.
Glory be to the Father, etc.
Repeat: How awesome, etc., *as far as* (Ps.).

GRADUAL   [*Priceless Mystery*]

This place was made by God, a priceless
    mystery;
    it is without reproof.
O God, before Whom stands the choir of angels,
    hear the prayers of Your servants.

Alleluia, alleluia.   Ps. 137, 2   [*Worship*]
I will worship at Your holy temple
    and give thanks to Your Name. Alleluia.

After Septuagesima, the Alleluia and versicle are omitted and the following Tract is said:

TRACT   Ps. 124, 1-2   [God with His People]

They who trust in the Lord are like Mount Sion,
    which is immovable; which forever stands.
Mountains are round about Jerusalem;
    so the Lord is round about His people,
    both now and forever.

During Paschaltime, the Gradual is omitted and the following Alleluia is said:

Alleluia, alleluia.   Ps. 137, 2   [Founded Firmly]
I will worship at Your holy temple
    and give thanks to Your Name.
Alleluia. The house of the Lord is well founded
    upon a firm rock. Alleluia.

After Septuagesima "Alleluia" is omitted at the end of the following Antiphon.

OFFERTORY   1 Par. 29, 17. 18   [Total Offering]

O Lord God, in the simplicity of my heart
    I have joyfully offered all these things;
And I have seen with great joy Your people
    which is here present:
O God of Israel,
    keep this will. Alleluia.

COMMUNION   Matt. 21, 13   [House of Prayer]

"My house shall be called a house of prayer,"
    says the Lord;
"In it everyone who asks receives:
    and he who seeks finds,
And to him who knocks,
    it shall be opened."(P.T. Alleluia.)

COMMON OF FEASTS OF
THE BLESSED VIRGIN MARY

INTROIT   Ps. 44, 2   [*Queen of Heaven*]

**Hail, holy Mother, who gave birth to the King
   Who rules heaven and earth forever and ever.
      (P.T. Alleluia, alleluia.)**

(Ps.) **My heart overflows with a goodly theme;
   as I sing my ode to the King.**

Glory be to the Father, etc.

Repeat: **Hail, holy Mother,** etc., *as far as* (Ps.).

GRADUAL   [*Virgin and Mother*]

**Blessed and venerable are you,
   O Virgin Mary;
For without stain to your virginity
   you became the Mother of the Savior.
O Virgin Mother of God,
   He Whom the whole world cannot contain,
Being made Man,
   shut Himself up within your womb.**

Alleluia, alleluia.   [*Ever Virgin*]
**After childbirth you still remained an inviolate
      virgin:
   O Mother of God, intercede for us. Alleluia.**

*In Advent the Alleluia and the versicle are omitted
and the following Alleluia is said:*

Alleluia, alleluia. Luke 1, 28   [*Full of Grace*]

Hail, Mary, full of grace,
  the Lord is with you;
Blessed are you among women. Alleluia.

*After Septuagesima, the Alleluia and versicle are
omitted and the following Tract is said:*

TRACT   [*Virgin Most Faithful*]

Rejoice, O Virgin Mary,
  for alone you have destroyed all heresies.
You believed the words
  of the Archangel Gabriel.
As a virgin, you brought forth God and man;
  and after childbirth you remained an inviolate
    virgin.
O Mother of God, intercede for us.

*During Paschaltime, the Gradual is omitted and the
following Alleluia is said:*

Alleluia, alleluia. Luke 1, 28   [*Fruitful Virgin*]

The rod of Jesse has blossomed:
  a Virgin has brought forth God and man:
God has given peace,
  reconciling in Himself the lowest with the
    highest.
Alleluia. Hail, Mary, full of grace,
  the Lord is with you;
Blessed are you among women. Alleluia.

OFFERTORY   Luke 1, 28. 42   [*Greatest of Women*]

Hail, Mary, full of grace,
  the Lord is with you;
Blessed are you among women

and blessed is the fruit of your womb. (P.T.
Alleluia.)

COMMUNION   [God's Mother]

Blessed is the womb of the Virgin Mary,
which bore the Son of the eternal Father.
(P.T. Alleluia.)

MASSES OF THE
BLESSED VIRGIN ON SATURDAY

I. IN ADVENT

INTROIT   Isa. 45, 8; Ps. 84, 2   [Mother of a Savior]

Drop down dew, you heavens, from above,
and let the clouds rain the Just;
let the earth be opened and bud forth a
Savior.

(Ps.) You have favored, O Lord, Your land;
You have restored the well-being of Jacob.

Glory be to the Father, etc.

Repeat: **Drop down dew,** etc., *as far as* (Ps.)

GRADUAL   Ps. 23, 7. 3-4   [The Lord Is Coming]

Lift up, O gates, your lintels;
reach up, ancient portals,
that the King of glory may come in!

Who can ascend the mountain of the Lord?
or who may stand in His holy place?

He whose hands are sinless, whose heart is
clean.

Alleluia, alleluia. Luke 1, 28   [Blessed Among Women]

Hail, Mary, full of grace,

the Lord is with you;
blessed are you among women. Alleluia.

OFFERTORY   Luke 1, 28. 42   [*Fruitful Virgin*]

Hail, Mary, full of grace,
the Lord is with you;
Blessed are you among women,
and blessed is the fruit of your womb.

COMMUNION   Isa. 7, 14   [*Virgin and Child*]

Behold, a Virgin shall be with child and bear
a Son,
and shall name Him Emmanuel.

II. FROM CHRISTMAS TO THE PURIFICATION

INTROIT   Ps. 44, 13, 15. 16. 2   [*Queen Mother*]

All the rich among the people seek Your favor.
Behind her the virgins of her train are brought
to the King.
Her neighbors are brought to You with glad-
ness and joy.
(Ps.) My heart overflows with a goodly theme;
as I sing my ode to the King.
Glory be to the Father, etc.
Repeat: **All the rich,** etc., *as far as* (Ps.).

GRADUAL   Ps. 44, 3. 2   [*Song of Love*]

Fairer in beauty are you than the sons of men;
grace is poured out upon your lips.

My heart overflows with a goodly theme;
    as I sing my ode to the King,
    my tongue is nimble as the pen of a skillful
       scribe.

Alleluia, alleluia.   [Ever Virgin]

After childbirth, you still remained an inviolate
    virgin:
    O Mother of God, intercede for us. Alleluia.

*In Votive Masses after Septuagesima, the Alleluia
and versicle are omitted and the following Tract is said:*

TRACT   [Virgin Most Faithful]

Rejoice, O Virgin Mary;
    for alone you have destroyed all heresies.
You believed the words
    of the Archangel Gabriel.
As a virgin, you brought forth God and man;
    and after childbirth you remained an inviolate
       virgin.
O Mother of God, intercede for us.

OFFERTORY   [Joy of God's Mother]

For you are happy, O holy Virgin Mary,
    and most worthy of all praise;
For from you has risen the sun of justice,
    Christ our God.

COMMUNION   [God's Mother]

Blessed is the womb of the Virgin Mary,
    which bore the Son of the eternal Father.

III. FEBRUARY 3 TO WEDNESDAY IN HOLY WEEK

INTROIT   Ps. 44, 2   [*Queen of Heaven*]

Hail, holy Mother, who gave birth to the King
    Who rules heaven and earth forever.

(Ps.) My heart overflows with a goodly theme;
    as I sing my ode to the King.

Glory be to the Father, etc.

Repeat: **Hail, holy Mother,** etc., *as far as* (Ps.).

GRADUAL   [*Virgin and Mother*]

Blessed and venerable are you,
    O Virgin Mary;
For without stain to your virginity
    you became the Mother of the Savior.
O Virgin Mother of God,
    He Whom the whole world cannot contain,
Being made man,
    shut Himself up within your womb.

Alleluia, alleluia.   [*Fruitful Virgin*]
The rod of Jesse has blossomed:
    a Virgin has brought forth God and man:
God has given peace,
    reconciling in Himself the lowest with the
      highest. Alleluia.

*After Septuagesima, the Alleluia and versicle are
omitted and the following Tract is said:*

TRACT   [*Virgin Most Faithful*]

Rejoice, O Virgin Mary,
    for alone you have destroyed all heresies.

You believed the words of the Archangel
   Gabriel.
As a virgin, you brought forth God and man;
   and after childbirth you remained an inviolate
   virgin.
O Mother of God, intercede for us.

OFFERTORY   [*Joy of God's Mother*]

You are happy, O holy Virgin Mary,
   and most worthy of all praise.
Since from you has risen the sun of justice,
   Christ our God.

COMMUNION   [*God's Mother*]

Blessed is the womb of the Virgin Mary,
   which bore the Son of the eternal Father.

IV. PASCHALTIME

INTROIT   Ps. 44, 2   [*Queen of Heaven*]

Hail, holy Mother, who gave birth to the King
   Who rules heaven and earth forever, alleluia.
   alleluia.
(Ps.) My heart overflows with a goodly theme
   as I sing my ode to the King.
Glory be to the Father, etc.
Repeat: Hail, holy Mother, etc., *as far as* (Ps.).

Alleluia, alleluia.   Luke 1, 28   [*Fruitful Virgin*]
The rod of Jesse has blossomed:
   a Virgin has brought forth God and man:
God has given peace,

reconciling in Himself the lowest with the
   highest.
Alleluia. Hail, Mary, full of grace,
   the Lord is with you;
   blessed are you among women. Alleluia.

OFFERTORY   [Mother of the Creator]

Blessed are you, O Virgin Mary,
   who bore the Creator of all things;
you brought forth Him Who made you,
   and you remain forever a virgin. Alleluia.

COMMUNION   [God's Mother]

Blessed is the womb of the Virgin Mary,
   which bore the Son of the eternal Father,
   alleluia.

V. FROM TRINITY SUNDAY TO
SATURDAY BEFORE ADVENT

INTROIT   Ps. 44, 2   [Queen of Heaven]

Hail, holy Mother, who gave birth to the King
   Who rules heaven and earth forever.
(Ps.) My heart overflows with a goodly theme;
   as I sing my ode to the King.
Glory be to the Father, etc.
Repeat: Hail, holy Mother, etc., *as far as* (Ps.).

GRADUAL   [Virgin and Mother]

Blessed and venerable are you, O Virgin Mary;
For without stain to your virginity
   you became the Mother of the Savior.

O Virgin Mother of God,
He Whom the whole world cannot contain,
Being made man,
    shut Himself up within your womb.

Alleluia, alleluia.   [*Virgin and Mother*]
After childbirth you remained a pure virgin.
    O Mother of God, intercede for us. Alleluia.

OFFERTORY   Luke 1, 28. 42   [*Greatest of Women*]

Hail, Mary, full of grace,
    the Lord is with you.
Blessed are you among women
    and blessed is the fruit of your womb.

COMMUNION   [*God's Mother*]

Blessed is the womb of the Virgin Mary,
    which bore the Son of the eternal Father.

PLAN OF THE MASS

The people's parts are in **bold type.**

LITURGY OF THE WORD OF GOD

— Entrance Rite —

1. Introit   **2. Kyrie**
3. Gloria   4. Prayer

— The Word of God —

5. Epistle   **6. Gradual**   **7. Alleluia**
8. Gospel   9. Homily   **10. Creed**

LITURGY OF THE EUCHARIST

— Preparation of the Gifts —

11. Prayer of the Faithful   **12. Offertory Verse**
13. Prayer over the Gifts

— The Eucharistic Prayer —

14. Introduction to the Preface
15. Acclamation - "Holy, holy, holy."
16. Sacred Canon
17. The Great Amen

— The Eucharistic Banquet —

18. Our Father   **19. Lamb of God**
20. Communion Verse
21. Postcommunion Prayer
22. The Dismissal Rite

ORDINARY OF THE MASS

Liturgy of  the WORD of God

— ENTRANCE RITE —

The Prayers at the Foot of the Altar are the Priest's private preparation for Mass.

♪♪ *Entrance Hymn* may be sung here.
The people then recite the Introit.

● *Turn to -* **INTROIT** *- Today's Mass* ●

THE KYRIE   *[Plea for Mercy]*

PRIEST: Lord, have mercy.
PEOPLE: Lord, have mercy.
PRIEST: Lord, have mercy.
PEOPLE: Christ, have mercy.
PRIEST: Christ, have mercy.
PEOPLE: Christ, have mercy.
PRIEST: Lord, have mercy.
PEOPLE: Lord, have mercy.
PRIEST: Lord, have mercy.

THE GLORIA   [Hymn of Praise]

PRIEST: Glory to God in the highest.

PEOPLE: **And on earth peace to men of good will.** *

We praise You. We bless You. We worship You. We glorify You. *

We give You thanks for Your great glory. *

Lord God, heavenly King, God the Father almighty. *

Lord Jesus Christ, the Only-begotten Son. *

Lord God, Lamb of God, Son of the Father. *

You, Who take away the sins of the world, * **have mercy on us.** *

You, Who take away the sins of the world, * **receive our prayer.** *

You, Who sit at the right hand of the Father, *

have mercy on us. *

For You alone are holy. *

You alone are Lord. *

You alone, O Jesus Christ, are most high, * **With the Holy Spirit, in the glory of God the Father. Amen.**

THE PRAYER

[Petition to God]

PRIEST:	Dominus vobiscum.	The Lord be with you.
PEOPLE:	**Et cum spiritu tuo.**	**And with your spirit.**
PRIEST:	Oremus.	Let us pray.
	. . . per omnia sae-cula saeculorum	. . . forever and ever.
PEOPLE:	**Amen.**	**Amen.**

— THE WORD OF GOD —

SIT   **THE EPISTLE**

We listen to the proclamation of the Word of God.

● *Turn to* —

The GRADUAL and ALLELUIA or TRACT

— *Today's Mass* ●

STAND   **THE GOSPEL**

We listen to the proclamation of the Word of God.

PRIEST: The Lord be with you.

PEOPLE: **And with your spirit.**

PRIEST: ✠ A reading from the holy Gospel according to N . . .

PEOPLE: **Glory to You, O Lord.**

SIT   **THE HOMILY**

We listen to the explanation of the Word of God.

THE CREED

STAND   [*Our Profession of Faith*]

PRIEST: I believe in one God.

PEOPLE: **The Father almighty, Maker of heaven and earth, ***

and of all things visible and invisible. *

And I believe in one Lord, Jesus Christ, *
the Only-begotten Son of God. *

Born of the Father before all ages. *

God of God, Light of Light, true God of true God. *

Begotten, not made, *
of one substance with the Father. *

By Whom all things were made. *

Who for us men and for our salvation came
    down from heaven. *

And He became flesh by the Holy Spirit of the
    Virgin Mary: *
    and was made Man. *

He was also crucified for us, *
    suffered under Pontius Pilate, and was
    buried. *

And on the third day He rose again, according
    to the Scriptures. *

He ascended into heaven and sits at the right
    hand of the Father. *

He will come again in glory to judge the
    living and the dead. *

And of His kingdom there will be no end. *

And I believe in the Holy Spirit, the Lord and
    Giver of life, *
    Who proceeds from the Father and the Son. *

Who together with the Father and the Son
    is adored and glorified, *
    and Who spoke through the prophets. *

And one holy, Catholic, and Apostolic Church. *

I confess one baptism for the forgiveness of
    sins. *

And I await the resurrection of the dead. *
    And the life of the world to come. Amen.

Liturgy of the EUCHARIST

— PREPARATION OF THE GIFTS —

PRIEST: The Lord be with you.
PEOPLE: And with your spirit.
PRIEST: Let us pray.

"Prayer of the Faithful" may be said here.

● *Turn to* - **OFFERTORY VERSE** - *Today's Mass* ●

♪♩ *Offertory Hymn* may be sung here.
The Priest prepares the gifts of bread and wine.

SIT . . . after Offertory verse and/or Hymn.

The people join in the intentions of the prayer which the Priest is offering in their name, then ratify that prayer with "Amen!"

PRIEST: . . . per omnia sæcula sæculorum.	. . . forever and ever.
PEOPLE: Amen.	**Amen.**

— THE EUCHARISTIC PRAYER —

STAND   **PREFACE — CANON**

PRIEST: Dominus vobiscum.	The Lord be with you.
PEOPLE: Et cum spiritu tuo.	**And with your spirit.**
PRIEST: Sursum corda.	Lift up your hearts.
PEOPLE: Habemus ad Dominum.	**We have lifted them up to the Lord.**
PRIEST: Gratias agamus Domino Deo nostro.	Let us give thanks to the Lord our God.
PEOPLE: Dignum et iustum est.	**It is fitting and just.**

PREFACE FOR SUNDAYS *
[*Our Prayer of Thanksgiving*]

IT IS fitting indeed and just,
   right and helpful to salvation,
   for us always and everywhere
   to give thanks to You, O Lord,
   holy Father, almighty and eternal God.
With Your Only-begotten Son
   and the Holy Spirit
   You are one God, one Lord;
   not in the unity of a single person,
   but in the trinity of a single nature.
For that which we believe
   on Your revelation concerning Your glory,
   that same we believe of Your Son,
   that same of the Holy Spirit,
   without difference or discrimination.
So that in confessing
   the true and everlasting Godhead,
   we shall adore distinction in Persons,
   oneness in being, and equality in Majesty.
This the Angels and Archangels,
   the Cherubim, too,
   and the Seraphim do praise;
   day by day they cease not to cry out
   as with one voice, saying:

THE SANCTUS [*Our Hymn of Praise*]

PEOPLE: **Holy, holy, holy Lord God of Hosts.** *
Heaven and earth are filled with Your glory. *
Hosanna in the highest. *
**Blessed is He Who comes in the Name of the
   Lord.** * **Hosanna in the highest.**   *KNEEL*

---

* *Proper Prefaces for Weekdays and Feasts, pp. 293-298.*

The people may read the Canon while the Priest prays it quietly.

[We Pray for the Church]

THEREFORE, most gracious Father,
  we humbly beg of You
  and entreat You
  through Jesus Christ
  Your Son, our Lord.

Hold acceptable and bless
  these gifts, these offerings,
  these holy and unspotted oblations
  which, in the first place, we offer You
  for Your Holy Catholic Church.

Grant her peace and protection,
  unity and guidance
  throughout the world,
  together with Your servant N., our Pope,
  and N., our Bishop;
  and all true believers who cherish
  the Catholic and Apostolic Faith.

[We Pray for the Living]

REMEMBER, O Lord,
  Your servants and handmaids, N. and N.,
  (name them)
  and all here present,
  whose faith and devotion
  are known to You.

On whose behalf we offer to You,
   or who themselves offer to You,
   this sacrifice of praise
   for themselves, families and friends,
   for the good of their souls,
   for their hope of salvation
   and deliverance from all harm,
   and who offer their homage to You,
   eternal, living and true God.

[*Our Union with the Saints*]

IN THE unity of holy fellowship
   we observe the memory, first of all,
   of the glorious and ever Virgin Mary,
   Mother of our Lord and God Jesus Christ.

Next, we observe the memory of Blessed Joseph,
   Spouse of the same Virgin,
   and of Your Blessed Apostles and Martyrs,
   Peter and Paul, Andrew, James, John,
   Thomas, James, Philip, Bartholomew,
   Matthew, Simon and Thaddeus;
   of Linus, Cletus, Clement,
   Sixtus, Cornelius,
   Cyprian, Lawrence, Chrysogonus,
   John and Paul, Cosmas and Damian,
   and of all Your Saints.

By their merits and prayers
   grant that we may be always fortified
   by the help of Your protection.

Through the same Christ our Lord. Amen.

[We Renew Our Offering]

GRACIOUSLY accept, then,
we beseech You, O Lord,
this service of our worship
and that of all Your household.

Provide that our days be spent in Your peace,
save us from everlasting damnation,
and cause us to be numbered
in the flock You have chosen.
Through Christ our Lord. Amen.

[We Ask God to Bless Our Offering]

O GOD, deign to bless what we offer,
and make it approved, effective, right,
and wholly pleasing in every way,
that it may become for our good,
the Body and Blood
of Your dearly beloved Son,
Jesus Christ our Lord.

[Consecration of the Bread]

WHO, the day before He suffered,
took bread into His holy and venerable
hands,
and having raised His eyes to heaven,
to You, O God, His almighty Father,
giving thanks to You,
He blessed it, broke it,
and gave it to His disciples, saying:
All of you take and eat of this:

FOR THIS IS MY BODY.

[Consecration of the Wine]

IN LIKE manner,
    when the supper was done,
taking also this goodly chalice
into His holy and venerable hands,
again giving thanks to You,
He blessed it,
and gave it to His disciples, saying:
All of you take and drink of this:

FOR THIS IS THE CHALICE OF MY BLOOD
OF THE NEW AND ETERNAL COVENANT:
        THE MYSTERY OF FAITH:
    WHICH SHALL BE SHED FOR YOU
            AND FOR MANY
    UNTO THE FORGIVENESS OF SINS.

As often as you shall do these things,
    in memory of Me shall you do them.

[Memorial of Passion and Resurrection]

MINDFUL, therefore, O Lord,
    not only of the blessed Passion
of the same Christ, Your Son, our Lord,
but also of His Resurrection from the dead,
and finally of His glorious Ascension into
    heaven,
we, Your ministers, as also Your holy people,
offer to Your supreme Majesty,
of the gifts bestowed upon us,
the pure Victim, the holy Victim,
the all-perfect Victim:
the holy Bread of life eternal
and the Chalice of unending salvation.

[Memorial of Sacrifices of Old]

AND this deign to regard
with gracious and kindly attention
and hold acceptable, as You deigned to accept
the offerings of Abel, Your just servant,
and the sacrifice of Abraham our patriarch,
and that which Your chief priest Melchisedec
offered to You,
a holy sacrifice and a spotless victim.

[Banquet of Heaven]

MOST humbly we implore You,
almighty God,
bid these offerings to be brought by the hands
of Your holy Angel to Your altar above,
before the face of Your Divine Majesty.
And may those of us who by sharing
in the Sacrifice of this altar
shall receive the Most Sacred Body and
Blood of Your Son,
be filled with every grace
and heavenly blessing.
Through the same Christ our Lord. Amen.

[We Pray for the Dead]

REMEMBER also, O Lord,
Your servants and handmaids, *N.,* and *N.,*
who have gone before us
with the sign of faith,
and rest in the sleep of peace.
To these, O Lord, and to all who rest in Christ,
we beseech You to grant of Your goodness,
a place of comfort, light and peace.
Through the same Christ our Lord. Amen.

[We Pray for Eternal Happiness]

TO US sinners also, Your servants,
   trusting in the greatness of Your mercy,
deign to grant some part and fellowship
with Your Holy Apostles and Martyrs:
with John, Stephen, Matthias, Barnabas,
Ignatius, Alexander, Marcellinus, Peter,
Felicitas, Perpetua, Agatha, Lucy,
Agnes, Cecilia, Anastasia,
and all Your Saints.

Into their company,
   we implore You to admit us,
   not weighing our merits,
   but freely granting us pardon.
Through Christ our Lord.

[We Pray for Eucharistic Blessings]

THROUGH Whom, O Lord,
   You always create,
sanctify,
fill with life,
bless,
and bestow upon us all good things.

[We Praise God in Union with Christ]

THROUGH Him,
   and with Him,
   and in Him,
   is to You, God the Father almighty,
   in the unity of the Holy Spirit,
   all honor and glory.

PRIEST: . . . per omnia saecula saeculorum.

PEOPLE: Amen.   (. . . forever and ever.)

STAND — THE EUCHARISTIC BANQUET —

PRIEST: Let us pray: Taught by our Savior's command and formed by the word of God, we dare to say:

PEOPLE: **Our Father, Who art in heaven, ***
hallowed be Thy Name; *
Thy kingdom come; *
Thy will be done on earth as it is in heaven. *
Give us this day our daily bread; *
and forgive us our trespasses *
as we forgive those who trespass against us; *
and lead us not into temptation, *
but deliver us from evil.

DELIVER us, we beseech You, O Lord, from all evils, past, present, and to come; and by the intercession of the Blessed and glorious Mary, ever Virgin, Mother of God, together with Your Blessed Apostles Peter and Paul, and Andrew, and all the Saints, grant of Your goodness, peace in our days, that aided by the riches of Your mercy, we may be always free from sin and safe from all disturbance.

THROUGH the same Jesus Christ, Your Son, our Lord, Who lives and reigns with You in the unity of the Holy Spirit, God,

PRIEST: . . . per omnia sæcula sæculorum.

. . . forever and ever.

PEOPLE: **Amen.**

Amen.

PRIEST: Pax Domini sit semper vobiscum.

May the Peace of the Lord be always with you.

PEOPLE: **Et cum spiritu tuo.**

And with your spirit.

THE AGNUS DEI

PEOPLE: [Our Prayer for Forgiveness and Peace]

Lamb of God, Who take away the sins of the world, * have mercy on us. *

Lamb of God, Who take away the sins of the world, * have mercy on us. *

Lamb of God, Who take away the sins of the world, * grant us peace.

(In requiem Masses: . . . grant them rest . . . grant them rest . . . grant them eternal rest.)

COMMUNION OF THE FAITHFUL

KNEEL

PRIEST: Behold the Lamb of God * behold Him Who takes away the sins of the world.
PEOPLE:

Lord, I am not worthy that You should come under my roof. *

Speak but the word and my soul will be healed. *

Lord, I am not worthy that You should come under my roof. *

Speak but the word and my soul will be healed. *

Lord, I am not worthy that You should come under my roof. *

Speak but the word and my soul will be healed.

PRIEST: The Body of Christ. Communicant: **Amen.**

♪♩ *Communion Hymn* may be sung here. *STAND*
After the distribution of Holy Communion. . . *SIT*

● *Turn to* - COMMUNION VERSE - *Today's Mass* ●

THE POSTCOMMUNION PRAYER

STAND

PRIEST:	Dominus vobiscum.	The Lord be with you.
PEOPLE:	**Et cum spiritu tuo.**	**And with your spirit.**
PRIEST:	Oremus.	Let us pray.
	. . . per omnia sæcula sæculorum.	. . . forever and ever.
PEOPLE:	**Amen.**	**Amen.**

THE DISMISSAL RITE

PRIEST: The Lord be with you.
PEOPLE: And with your spirit.
PRIEST: Go, the Mass is ended.
PEOPLE: Thanks be to God.

(In Requiem Masses)

PRIEST: May they rest in peace. PEOPLE: **Amen.**

(When a procession follows the Mass)

PRIEST: Let us bless the Lord. PEOPLE: **Thanks be to God**

KNEEL **THE BLESSING**

MAY Almighty God bless you, the Father, and the Son, and the Holy Spirit.

PEOPLE: Amen.

♪♪ *Recessional Hymn may be sung here.*

PROPER PREFACES

Preface for Weekdays

This Common Preface is said on all Feasts and weekdays (ferias) during the year that have no Proper Preface.

It is fitting indeed and just, right and helpful to salvation, for us always and everywhere to give thanks to You, O Lord, holy Father, almighty and everlasting God, through Christ our Lord. Through Him the Angels praise Your Majesty, the Dominations adore it, the Powers are in awe. The heavens and the heavenly hosts, and the blessed Seraphim, join together in celebrating their joy. With these, we pray You, join our own voices also, while we say with lowly praise: ➤ **Holy, holy, holy,** etc., p. 283.

Preface for Christmas

It is fitting indeed and just, right and helpful to salvation, for us always and everywhere to give thanks to You, O Lord, holy Father, almighty and everlasting God. Because by the mystery of the Word made flesh the new light of Your glory has shone upon the eyes of our mind: that while we acknowledge Him to be God seen by men, we may be drawn by Him to the love of things unseen. And therefore with Angels and Archangels, with Thrones and Dominations, and with the whole host of the heavenly army, we sing a hymn to Your glory, saying again and again: ➤ **Holy, holy, holy,** etc., p. 283.

Preface of the Epiphany

It is fitting indeed and just, right and helpful to salvation, for us always and everywhere to give thanks to You, O Lord, holy Father, almighty and everlasting God; for when Your Only-begotten Son showed Himself in the substance of our mortal nature, He restored us by the new light of His own immortality. And therefore with Angels and Archangels, with Thrones and Dominations, and with the whole host of the heavenly army we sing a hymn to Your glory, saying again and again: ➤ **Holy, holy, holy,** etc., p. 283.

Preface for Lent

It is fitting indeed and just, right and helpful to salvation, for us always and everywhere to give thanks to You, O Lord, holy Father, almighty and everlasting God, Who by this bodily fast extinguish our vices, elevate our understanding, bestow on us virtue and its reward, through Christ our Lord. Through Whom the Angels praise Your Majesty, the Dominations adore it, the Powers are in awe. The heavens and the heavenly hosts, and the blessed Seraphim, join together in celebrating their joy. With these, we pray You, join our own voices also, while we say with lowly praise: ➤ **Holy, holy, holy,** etc., p. 283.

Preface of the Holy Cross

It is fitting indeed and just, right and helpful to salvation, for us always and everywhere to give thanks to You, O Lord, holy Father, almighty and everlasting God; Who set the salvation of mankind upon the tree of the Cross, so that whence came death, thence also life might rise again, and he that overcame by the tree, by the tree also might be overcome: through Christ our Lord. Through Whom the Angels praise Your Majesty, the Dominations worship it, and the Powers are in awe. The heavens and the heavenly hosts, and the blessed Seraphim join together in celebrating their joy. With these, we pray You, join our own voices also, while we say with lowly praise: ➤ **Holy, holy, holy,** etc., p. 283.

Preface for Easter

It is fitting indeed and just, right and helpful to salvation for us always to praise You, O Lord, but more gloriously on this day (*after the Octave say*: at this time) above others when Christ our Pasch was sacrificed. For He is the true Lamb Who has taken away the sins of the world: Who by dying has destroyed our death; and by rising again has restored us to life. And therefore with Angels and Archangels, with Thrones and Dominations, and with the whole host of the heavenly army, we sing a hymn to Your glory, saying again and again: ➤ **Holy, holy, holy,** etc., p. 283.

Preface for the Ascension

It is fitting indeed and just, right and helpful to salvation, for us always and everywhere to give thanks to You, O Lord, holy Father, almighty and everlasting God; through Christ our Lord. Who, after His Resurrection, appeared openly to all His disciples, and, while they looked on, was taken up into heaven, that He might grant us to be sharers in His own divinity. And therefore, with Angels and Archangels, with Thrones and Dominations, and with the whole host of the heavenly army, we sing a hymn to Your glory, saying again and again: ➤ **Holy, holy, holy,** etc., p. 283.

Preface for Pentecost

It is fitting indeed and just, right and helpful to salvation, for us always and everywhere to give thanks to You, O Lord, holy Father, almighty and everlasting God: through Christ our Lord. Who ascending above all the heavens, and sitting at Your right hand, *on this day* sent forth the Holy Spirit, as He had promised, on the children of adoption. Wherefore does the whole world rejoice with exceeding great joy; and the hosts above and the angelic powers also join in singing a hymn to Your glory, saying again and again: ➤ **Holy, holy, holy,** etc., p. 283.

Preface of the Sacred Heart

It is fitting indeed and just, right and helpful to salvation, always and everywhere to give thanks to You, O Lord, holy Father, almighty and everlasting God, Who willed that Your Only-begotten Son should be pierced by the soldier's lance as He hung upon the Cross; that the Heart thus opened, the sanctuary of divine bounty, should pour out on us an abundance of mercy and grace, and as it never ceases to burn with love for us, it may be for the devout a haven of rest, and for the penitent an ever-open refuge of salvation. And therefore, with Angels and Archangels, with Thrones and Dominations, and with the whole host of the heavenly army, we sing a hymn to Your glory, saying again and again: ➤ **Holy, holy, holy,** etc., p. 283.

Preface of Christ the King

It is fitting indeed and just, right and helpful to salvation, for us always and everywhere to give thanks to You, O Lord, holy Father, almighty and everlasting God. Who with the oil of gladness have anointed Your Only-begotten Son, our Lord Jesus Christ, as eternal High Priest and universal King; that, offering Himself on the altar of the Cross as an immaculate and peaceful oblation, He might complete the pledges of human redemption; and all creation being made subject to His dominion, He might deliver into the hands of Your infinite Majesty an eternal and universal kingdom: a kingdom of truth and life, a kingdom of holiness and grace, a kingdom of justice, love and peace. And therefore with Angels and Archangels, with Thrones and

Dominations, and with the whole host of the heavenly army, we sing a hymn to Your glory, saying again and again: ➤ **Holy, holy, holy,** etc., p. 283.

Preface of the Blessed Virgin

On all Feasts of Our Blessed Lady, the name of the occurring Feast is inserted in the Preface: Annunciation, Visitation, Assumption, Nativity, Presentation, Immaculate Conception, Transfixion, Commemoration; on all other Feasts: Festivity; on Saturday: Veneration.

It is fitting indeed and just, right and helpful to salvation, for us always and everywhere to give thanks to You, O Lord, holy Father, almighty and everlasting God, and that we should praise, bless, and proclaim You in the Immaculate Conception (*Assumption* or *Annunciation,* etc.) of the Blessed Mary, ever Virgin; for she conceived Your Only-begotten Son by the overshadowing of the Holy Spirit, and, while the glory of her virginity remained, brought forth to the world the Eternal Light, Jesus Christ, our Lord. Through Whom the Angels praise Your Majesty, the Dominations adore it, the Powers are in awe. The heavens and the heavenly hosts and the blessed Seraphim join together in celebrating their joy. With these, we pray You, join our own voices also, while we say with lowly praise: ➤ **Holy, holy, holy,** etc., p. 283.

Preface of St. Joseph

It is fitting indeed and just, right and helpful to salvation, for us always and everywhere to give thanks to You, O Lord, holy Father, almighty and everlasting God; and to magnify You with due praise, bless and proclaim You *on the feast of* Blessed Joseph; who, as a just man, was given by You to be the spouse of the Virgin Mother of God, and, as a faithful and prudent servant, was set over Your family, that with fatherly care he might guard Your Only-begotten Son, Jesus Christ our

Lord, conceived by the overshadowing of the Holy Spirit. Through Whom the Angels praise Your Majesty, the Dominations adore it, the Powers are in awe. The heavens and the heavenly hosts and the blessed Seraphim join together in celebrating their joy. With these, we pray You, join our own voices also, while we say with lowly praise:

➤ **Holy, holy, holy,** etc., p. 283.

Preface of the Apostles

It is fitting indeed and just, right and helpful to salvation, to entreat You humbly, O Lord, that You would not desert Your flock, O everlasting Shepherd, but, through Your Blessed Apostles, would keep it under Your constant protection; that it may be governed by those same rulers, whom, as vicars of Your work, You set over it to be its pastors. And therefore, with Angels and Archangels, with Thrones and Dominations, and with the whole host of the heavenly army, we sing a hymn to Your glory, saying again and again:

➤ **Holy, holy, holy,** etc., p. 283.

Preface for the Dead

It is fitting indeed and just, right and helpful to salvation, for us always and everywhere to give thanks to You, O Lord, holy Father, almighty and everlasting God, through Christ our Lord. In Whom the hope of a blessed resurrection has shone upon us, that those whom the certainty of dying afflicts may be consoled by the promise of future immortality. For to Your faithful, O Lord, life is changed, not taken away; and the abode of this earthly sojourn being dissolved, an eternal dwelling is prepared in heaven. And therefore with Angels and Archangels, with Thrones and Dominations, and with the whole host of the heavenly army, we sing a hymn to Your glory, saying again and again:

➤ **Holy, holy, holy,** etc., p. 283.

PROPER OF THE SAINTS

Nov. 29 — ST. SATURNINUS, Martyr

Mass: Of a Martyr not a Bishop, p. 237.

Nov. 30 — ST. ANDREW, Apostle

INTROIT Ps. 138, 17. 1-2   [*Glory of God's Friends*]

To me, Your friends, O God, are made exceed-
ingly honorable;
  their principality is exceedingly strengthened.
(Ps.) O Lord, You have probed me and You
know me;
  You know when I sit and when I stand.
Glory be to the Father, etc.
Repeat: To me, etc., *as far as* (Ps.).

GRADUAL   Ps. 44, 17-18   [*Princes*]

You shall make them princes through all the
land;
  they shall remember Your name, O Lord.
The place of Your fathers Your sons shall have;
  therefore shall nations praise You.
Alleluia, alleluia.   [*Andrew the Beloved*]
The Lord loved Andrew in an odor of sweetness.
Alleluia.

OFFERTORY   Ps. 138, 17   [*Apostolic Rulers*]

To me, your friends, O God, are made exceedingly honorable;
  their principality is exceedingly strengthened.

COMMUNION   Matt. 4, 19-20   [Follow Me]

"Come, follow Me,
  and I will make you fishers of men."
And at once they left the nets.
  and followed the Lord.

Dec. 2 — ST. BIBIAN, Virgin, Martyr

Mass: Of a Virgin Martyr, p. 257.

Dec. 3 — ST. FRANCIS XAVIER, Confessor

INTROIT   Ps. 118, 46-47; 116, 1-2   [Francis, the Witness]

I will speak of Your decrees before kings
  without being ashamed.
And I will delight in Your commands,
  which I love exceedingly.
(Ps.) **Praise the Lord, all you nations;**
  glorify Him, all you peoples!
For steadfast is His kindness toward us,
  and the fidelity of the Lord endures forever.
Glory be to the Father, etc.
Repeat: **I will speak,** etc., *as far as* (Ps.).

GRADUAL   Ps. 91, 13. 14. 3   [The Just Man Flourishes]

The just man shall flourish like the palm tree,
  like a cedar of Lebanon shall he grow
  in the house of the Lord.
To proclaim Your kindness at dawn,
  and Your faithfulness throughout the night.

Alleluia, alleluia.   James 1, 12   [Crown of Life]
Blessed is the man who endures temptation;

for when he has been tried,
he will receive the crown of life. Alleluia.

OFFERTORY   Ps. 88, 25   [Exalted in Christ]

My faithfulness and My kindness shall be with
him,
and through My Name shall his horn be
exalted.

COMMUNION   Matt. 24, 46-47   [Watching Servant]

Blessed is that servant, whom his master,
when he comes, shall find watching.
Amen I say to you,
he will set him over all his goods.

Dec. 4 — ST. PETER CHRYSOLOGUS
Bishop, Confessor and Doctor of the Church

INTROIT   Sir. 15, 5; Ps. 91, 2   [Teacher of Wisdom]

In the midst of the assembly He opened his
mouth;
And the Lord filled him with the spirit of wis-
dom and understanding;
He clothed him with a robe of glory.
(Ps.) It is good to give thanks to the Lord,
to sing praise to Your Name, Most High.
Glory be to the Father, etc.
Repeat: **In the midst,** etc., *as far as* (Ps.).

GRADUAL   Sir. 44, 16.20   [The Great Priest]

Behold a great priest,
who in his days pleased God.

There was not found the like to him,
  who kept the law of the Most High.

Alleluia, alleluia.   Ps. 109, 4   [*Priest Forever*]
You are a priest forever, according to the order
  of Melchisedec. Alleluia.

OFFERTORY   Ps. 91, 13   [*Growth*]
The just man shall flourish like the palm tree,
  like a cedar of Lebanon shall he grow.

COMMUNION   Matt. 25, 20. 21   [*Well Done*]
"Master, You delivered to me five talents:
  behold I have gained other five over and
    above."
"Well done, good and faithful servant;
Because you have been faithful over a few
    things,
  I will set you over many;
Enter into the joy of your Master."

Dec. 5 — ST. SABBA, Abbot

Mass: Of a Holy Abbot, p. 253.

Dec. 6 — ST. NICHOLAS, Bishop, Confessor

INTROIT   Sir. 45, 30; Ps. 131, 1   [*A Priestly Prince*]
The Lord made a covenant of friendship with
    him,
  and made him a prince,
    that he should possess the dignity of priest-
      hood forever.

(Ps.) **Remember, O Lord, David
and all his meekness.**

Glory be to the Father, etc.

Repeat: **The Lord,** etc., *as far as* (Ps.).

GRADUAL   Ps. 88, 21-23   [*Anointed*]

**I have found David, My servant;
with My holy oil I have anointed him,
That My hand may be always with him,
and that My arm may make him strong.
No enemy shall have an advantage over him,
nor shall the son of iniquity have power to
hurt him.**

Alleluia, alleluia. Ps. 91, 13   [*Strength of a Cedar*]
**The just man shall flourish like the palm tree,
like a cedar of Lebanon shall he grow. Alleluia.**

OFFERTORY   Ps. 88, 25   [*Exalted Love*]

**My faithfulness and My kindness shall be with
him,
and through My Name shall his horn be
exalted.**

COMMUNION   Ps. 88, 36-38   [*The Glory of Charity*]

**Once, by My holiness, have I sworn;
His posterity shall continue forever,
and his throne shall be like the sun before
Me;
Like the moon, which remains forever —
a faithful witness in the sky.**

Dec. 7 — ST. AMBROSE
Bishop, Confessor and Doctor of the Church

INTROIT   Sir. 15, 5; Ps. 91, 2   [*Teacher of Wisdom*]

In the midst of the assembly he opened his
   mouth;
And the Lord filled him with the spirit of wisdom and understanding;
   He clothed him with a robe of glory.

(Ps.) Is is good to give thanks to the Lord,
   to sing praise to Your Name, Most High.

Glory be to the Father, etc.

Repeat: In the midst, etc., *as far as* (Ps.).

GRADUAL   Sir. 44, 16. 20   [*Great Priest*]

Behold a great priest,
   who in his days pleased God.
There was not found the like to him,
   who kept the law of the Most High.

Alleluia, alleluia. Ps. 109, 4   [*Priest Forever*]

The Lord has sworn, and He will not repent:
   "You are a priest forever, according to the
   order of Melchisedec." Alleluia.

OFFERTORY   Ps. 88, 25   [*Exalted Love*]

My faithfulness and My kindness shall be with
   him,
   and through My Name shall his horn be
   exalted.

COMMUNION   Ps. 88, 36-38   [*The Glory of Charity*]

Once, by My holiness, have I sworn;
   His posterity shall continue forever,

and his throne shall be like the sun before
    Me;
Like the moon, which remains forever —
    a faithful witness in the sky.

Dec. 8—IMMACULATE CONCEPTION OF B.V.M.

INTROIT   Isa. 61, 10; Ps. 29, 2   [*Like a Bride*]

I will heartily rejoice in the Lord,
    in my God is the joy of my soul;
For He has clothed me with a robe of salvation,
    and wrapped me in a mantle of justice,
    like a bride bedecked with her jewels.
(Ps.) I will extol You, O Lord, for You drew me
    clear
    and did not let my enemies rejoice over me.
Glory be to the Father, etc.
Repeat: I will heartily, etc., *as far as* (Ps.).

GRADUAL   Judith 13, 23; 15, 10   [*Our Glory*]

Blessed are you, O Virgin Mary,
    by the Lord the most high God,
    above all women upon the earth.
You are the glory of Jerusalem,
    you are the joy of Israel,
    you are the honor of our people.

Alleluia, alleluia.   Cant. 4, 7   [*No Stain*]
You are all-beautiful, O Mary,
    and there is in you no stain of original sin.
    Alleluia.

OFFERTORY   Luke 1, 28   [*Blessed among Women*]

Hail, Mary, full of grace,
   the Lord is with you;
Blessed are you among women, alleluia.

COMMUNION   [*Mighty Lord*]

Glorious things are said of you, O Mary,
   because He Who is mighty has done great
   things for you.

Dec. 10 — ST. MELCHIADIS, Pope, Martyr

Mass: Of One or More Popes, p. 231.

Dec. 11 — ST. DAMASUS I, Pope, Confessor

Mass: Of One or More Popes, p. 231.

Dec. 12 — OUR LADY OF GUADALUPE

INTROIT   Ps. 44, 2   [*The King's Mother*]

Hail, holy Mother, who gave birth to the King
   Who rules heaven and earth forever and ever.
(Ps.) My heart overflows with a goodly theme;
   as I sing my ode to the King.
Glory be to the Father, etc.
Repeat: Hail, holy Mother, etc., *as far as* (Ps.).

GRADUAL   Cant. 6, 9; Sir. 50, 8   [*Resplendent*]

Who is this that comes forth like the dawn,
   as beautiful as the moon, as resplendent as
   the sun?

Like the rainbow appearing in the cloudy sky;
    like the blossoms on the branches in spring-
        time.

Alleluia, alleluia. Cant. 2, 12   [*Springtime*]

The flowers appear on the earth,
    the time of pruning the vines has come.
        Alleluia.

OFFERTORY 2 Par. 7, 16   [*Sanctified Place*]

I have chosen and have sanctified this place,
    that my name may be there
    and my eyes and my heart may remain there
        forever.

COMMUNION Ps. 147, 20   [*Special Patroness*]

He has not done this for any other nation;
    His ordinances He has not made known to
        them.

Dec. 13 — ST. LUCY, Virgin, Martyr

INTROIT Ps. 44, 8. 2   [*Innocence*]

You love justice and hate wickedness;
    therefore God, your God, has anointed you
    with the oil of gladness above your fellows.

(Ps.) My heart overflows with a goodly theme;
    as I sing my ode to the King.

Glory be to the Father, etc.

Repeat: You love justice, etc., *as far as* (Ps.).

GRADUAL Ps. 44, 8   [*Anointed*]

You love justice and hate wickedness.
    Therefore, God, your God, has anointed you
    with the oil of gladness.

Alleluia, alleluia.   Ps. 44, 3   [Grace]

Grace is poured out upon your lips;
  thus God has blessed you forever. Alleluia.

OFFERTORY   Ps. 44, 15. 16   [Glory]

Behind her the virgins of her train are brought
  to the King.
Her neighbors are brought to You with gladness
  and joy;
  they enter the palace of the Lord, the King.

COMMUNION Ps. 118, 161-162   [Joy in God's Promise]

Princes persecute me without cause,
  but my heart stands in awe of Your word.
I rejoiced at Your promise,
  as one who has found rich spoil.

———————

Dec. 16 — ST. EUSEBIUS, Bishop, Martyr

Mass: Of a Martyr Bishop, p. 234.

———————

Dec. 21 — ST. THOMAS, Apostle

INTROIT   Ps. 138, 17. 1-2   [Glory of God's Friends]

To me, Your friends, O God, are made exceedingly honorable;
  their principality is exceedingly strengthened.
(Ps.) O Lord, You have probed me and You
  know me;
  You know when I sit and when I stand.
Glory be to the Father, etc.

Repeat: **To me,** etc., *as far as* (Ps.).

GRADUAL   Ps. 138, 17-18   [*God's Saints*]

Your friends, O God, are made exceedingly honorable:
  their principality is exceedingly strengthened.
I will number them
  and they will outnumber the sands.

Alleluia, alleluia.   Ps. 32, 1   [*Praise from the Just*]
Exult, you just, in the Lord;
  praise from the upright is fitting. Alleluia.

OFFERTORY   Ps. 18, 5   [*Voice throughout the World*]

Through all the earth their voice resounds,
  and to the ends of the world, their message.

COMMUNION   John 20, 27   [*Faith*]

Put in your hand and know the place of the nails,
  and be not unbelieving,
  but believing.

Jan. 14 — ST. HILARY
Bishop, Confessor and Doctor of the Church

Mass: Of a Doctor, p. 248.

Jan. 15 — ST. PAUL, FIRST HERMIT, Confessor

INTROIT   Ps. 91, 13-14   [*The Just Man Flourishes*]

The just man shall flourish like the palm tree,
  like a cedar of Lebanon shall he grow:

Planted in the house of the Lord,
   in the courts of the house of our God.
(Ps.) **It is good to give thanks to the Lord,**
   to sing praise to Your Name, Most High.
Glory be to the Father, etc.
Repeat: **The just man,** etc., *as far as* (Ps.).

GRADUAL   Ps. 91, 13. 14. 3   *[Flourishing]*

The just man shall flourish like the palm tree,
   like a cedar of Lebanon shall he grow
   in the house of the Lord.
To proclaim Your kindness at dawn
   and Your faithfulness throughout the night.
Alleluia, alleluia.   Osee 14, 6   *[Like the Lily]*
The just man shall blossom like the lily,
   and flourish forever before the Lord. Alleluia.

OFFERTORY   Ps. 20, 2-3   *[Joy in the Lord]*

O Lord, in Your strength the just man is glad;
   in Your victory how greatly he rejoices!
You have granted him his heart's desire.

COMMUNION   Ps. 63, 11   *[Praise for the Just]*

The just man is glad in the Lord and takes
   refuge in Him;
   all the upright of heart shall be praised.

Jan. 16 — ST. MARCELLUS I, Pope, Martyr

Mass: Of One or More Popes, p. 231.

Jan. 17 — ST. ANTHONY, Abbot

Mass: Of a Holy Abbot, p. 253.

Jan. 18 — ST. PRISCA, Virgin, Martyr

Mass: Of a Virgin Martyr, p. 257.

Jan. 19 — STS. MARIUS, MARTHA, AUDIFAX AND ABACHUM, Martyrs

INTROIT   Ps. 67, 4. 2   [*Joy of the Just*]

The just rejoice and exult before God;
   they are glad and rejoice.
(Ps.) God arises; His enemies are scattered,
   and those who hate Him flee before Him.
Glory be to the Father, etc.
Repeat: **The just,** etc., *as far as* (Ps.).

GRADUAL   Wis. 3, 1. 2. 3   [*God's Glory*]

The souls of the just are in the hand of God,
   and no torment shall touch them.
They seemed, in the view of the foolish, to be
    dead;
   but they are in peace.
Alleluia, alleluia.   Ps. 67, 36   [*Souls at Peace*]
Our God is wonderful in His saints. Alleluia.

   After Septuagesima, the Alleluia and versicle are
omitted and the Tract, p. 239, is said.

OFFERTORY   Ps. 123, 7   [*Freedom*]

We were rescued like a bird
   from the fowlers' snare;
Broken was the snare, and we were freed.

COMMUNION   Luke 12, 4   [*Salvation*]

But I say to you, My friends:
   Do not be afraid of those who persecute you.

Jan. 20 — STS. FABIAN, Pope
AND SEBASTIAN, Martyrs

INTROIT Ps. 78, 11. 12. 10. 1 [*Avenge the Martyrs*]

Let the prisoners' sighing come before You,
   O Lord;
Repay our neighbors sevenfold into their
   bosoms;
    avenge the blood of Your saints which has
    been shed.
(Ps.) O God, the nations have come into Your
   inheritance;
    they have defiled Your holy temple,
    they have made Jerusalem as a place to
    keep fruit.
Glory be to the Father, etc.
Repeat: Let the prisoners', etc., *as far as* (Ps.).

GRADUAL Ex. 15, 11. 6 [*Glory to God*]

God is glorious in His saints,
   wonderful in majesty, a worker of wonders.
Your right hand, O Lord, is magnificent in
   power;
   Your right hand has shattered the enemy.

Alleluia, alleluia. Ps. 144, 10-11 [*Glorious Kingdom*]
Let Your faithful ones bless You, O Lord.
   Let them discourse of the glory of Your
   kingdom. Alleluia.

*After Septuagesima, the Alleluia and versicle are
omitted and the Tract, p. 239, is said.*

OFFERTORY   Ps. 31, 11   [*Joy of the Just*]

Be glad in the Lord, and rejoice you just;
   exult, all you upright of heart.

COMMUNION   Luke 6, 18. 19   [*Almighty Power*]

A multitude of sick,
   and those who were troubled with unclean
     spirits,
   came to Him;
For power went forth from Him and healed all.

Jan. 21 — ST. AGNES, Virgin, Martyr

INTROIT   Ps. 118, 95-96. 1   [*Love of God's Law*]

Sinners wait to destroy me,
   but I pay heed to Your decrees, O Lord.
I see that all fulfillment has its limits;
   broad indeed is Your command.
(Ps.) Happy are they whose way is blameless,
   who walk in the law of the Lord.
Glory be to the Father, etc.
Repeat: **Sinners wait,** etc., *as far as* (Ps.).

GRADUAL   Ps. 44, 3. 5   [*Grace*]

Grace is poured out upon your lips;
   thus God has blessed you forever.
Because of truth, and meekness, and justice;
   may your right hand show you wondrous
     deeds.

Alleluia, alleluia.   Matt. 25, 4. 6   [*Ever Watchful*]
The five wise virgins took oil in their vessels
   with the lamps;
   and at midnight a cry arose,

"Behold the bridegroom is coming,
    go forth to meet Christ our Lord." Alleluia.

*After Septuagesima, the Alleluia and versicle are
omitted and the Tract, p. 256, is said.*

OFFERTORY   Ps. 44, 15. 16   [*Triumph of Christ*]

Behind her the virgins of her train are brought
    to the King.

Her neighbors are brought to You with
    gladness and joy;
    they enter the palace of the Lord, the King.

COMMUNION   Matt. 25, 4. 6 [*Meet the Bridegroom*]

The five wise virgins took oil in their vessels
    with the lamps;
    and at midnight a cry arose,
"Behold the bridegroom is coming,
    go forth to meet Christ our Lord."

Jan. 22 — STS. VINCENT AND ANASTASIUS
Martyrs

Mass: Of Several Martyrs, p. 238.

Jan. 23 — ST. RAYMUND OF PENNAFORT
Confessor

Mass: Of a Confessor not a Bishop, p. 250.

Jan. 24 — ST. TIMOTHY, Bishop, Martyr

Mass: Of a Martyr Bishop, p. 233.

Jan. 25 — CONVERSION OF ST. PAUL, Apostle

INTROIT   2 Tim. 1, 12; Ps. 138, 1-2   [*Full Confidence*]

I know Whom I have believed,
   and I am certain
That He is able to guard the trust
   committed to me against that day,
   being a just Judge.
(Ps.) **O Lord, You have probed me and You
   know me;**
   You know when I sit and when I stand.
Glory be to the Father, etc.
Repeat: **I know,** etc., *as far as* (Ps.).

GRADUAL   Gal. 2, 8. 9   [*God's Grace in Paul*]

He Who worked in Peter for the apostleship,
   worked also in me among the Gentiles,
And they recognized the grace of God
   that was given to me.
The grace of God in me has not been fruitless;
   but His grace always remains in me.

Alleluia, alleluia.   [*Paul's Throne*]
The great Saint Paul, a vessel of election,
   is indeed worthy to be glorified,
For he was made worthy
   to sit upon the twelfth throne. Alleluia.

*After Septuagesima, the Alleluia and versicle are
omitted and the following Tract is said:*

TRACT   [*Teacher*]

O holy Apostle Paul, you are a vessel of election
   and indeed worthy to be glorified.

You are the preacher of truth
and teacher of the Gentiles in faith and truth.
Through you all nations
have known the grace of God.
Intercede for us with God,
Who chose you.

OFFERTORY   Ps. 138, 17   [*Honor of God's Friends*]

To me, Your friends, O God, are made exceedingly honorable;
their principality is exceedingly strengthened.

COMMUNION   Matt. 19, 28. 29   [*Reward*]

Amen, I say to you,
that you who have left all things, and followed Me,
Shall receive a hundredfold,
and shall possess life everlasting.

***

Jan. 26 — ST. POLYCARP, Bishop, Martyr

Mass: Of a Martyr Bishop, p. 234.

***

Jan. 27 — ST. JOHN CHRYSOSTOM
Bishop, Confessor and Doctor of the Church

INTROIT   Sir. 15, 5; Ps. 91, 2   [*Wisdom*]

In the midst of the assembly He opened his mouth;
And the Lord filled him with the spirit of wisdom and understanding;
He clothed him with a robe of glory.
(Ps.) It is good to give thanks to the Lord,
to sing praise to Your Name, Most High.

Glory be to the Father, etc.
Repeat: **In the midst,** etc., *as far as* (Ps.).

GRADUAL   Sir. 44, 16. 20   [*The Great Priest*]

Behold, a great priest,
  who in his days pleased God.
There was not found the like to him,
  who kept the law of the Most High.

Alleluia, alleluia.   James 1, 12   [*Crown of Life*]
Blessed is the man who endures temptation;
  for when he has been tried,
  he will receive the crown of life. Alleluia.

*After Septuagesima, the Alleluia and versicle are
omitted and the following Tract is said:*

TRACT   Ps. 111, 1-3   [*Almighty Family*]

Happy the man who fears the Lord,
  who greatly delights in His commands.
His posterity shall be mighty upon the earth;
  the upright generation shall be blessed.
Wealth and riches shall be in his house;
  his generosity shall endure forever.

OFFERTORY   Ps. 91, 13   [*Growth*]

The just man shall flourish like the palm tree
  like a cedar of Lebanon shall he grow.

COMMUNION   Luke 12, 42   [*Faithful Servant*]

The faithful and prudent servant
  whom the Master will set over His household
  to give them their ration of grain in due time.

Jan. 28 — ST. PETER NOLASCO, Confessor

Mass: Of a Confessor not a Bishop, p. 251.

Jan. 29 — ST. FRANCIS DE SALES
Bishop, Confessor and Doctor of the Church

Mass: Of a Doctor, p. 248.

Jan. 30 — ST. MARTINA, Virgin, Martyr

Mass: Of a Virgin Martyr, p. 255.

Jan. 31 — ST. JOHN BOSCO, Confessor

INTROIT   3 Kgs. 4, 29; Ps. 112, 1   [*A Great Heart*]

**God gave him wisdom and understanding ex-
    ceeding much,**
**and largeness of heart as the sand that is on
    the seashore.**
(Ps.) **Praise, you servants of the Lord,
    praise the Name of the Lord.**
Glory be to the Father, etc.
Repeat: **God gave,** etc., *as far as* (Ps.).

GRADUAL   Ps. 36, 3-5   [*Delight in the Lord*]

**Trust in the Lord and do good,
    that you may dwell in the land and be fed
        with its riches.**
**Take delight in the Lord,
    and He will grant you your heart's requests.**
**Commit to the Lord your way;
    trust in Him, and He will act.**

Alleluia, alleluia.   Ps. 73, 21   [*Praise from the Poor*]
**The afflicted and the poor shall praise your
    name. Alleluia.**

After Septuagesima, the Alleluia and versicle are omitted and the following Tract is said:

TRACT   Ps. 60, 4-6   [*God the Protector*]

You are my refuge, O Lord,
   a tower of strength against the enemy.
Oh, that I might lodge in your tent forever,
   take refuge in the shelter of your wings!
You indeed, O God, have accepted my vows;
    You granted me the heritage of those who
     fear Your Name.

OFFERTORY   Ps. 33, 12   [*Call of the Teacher*]

Come, children, hear me;
   I will teach you the fear of the Lord.

COMMUNION   Rom. 4, 18   [*Spiritual Fatherhood*]

Hoping against hope he believed,
   so that he became father of many nations,
   according to what was said to him.

Feb. 1 — ST. IGNATIUS, Bishop and Martyr

INTROIT   Gal. 6, 14; Ps. 131, 1   [*Only the Cross*]

But as for me,
   God forbid that I should glory
   save in the cross of our Lord Jesus Christ,
Through Whom the world is crucified to me,
   and I to the world.
(Ps.) Remember, O Lord, David
   and all his meekness.
Glory be to the Father, etc.
Repeat: But, etc., *as far as* (Ps.).

GRADUAL   Sir. 44, 16. 20   [*The Great Priest*]

Behold, a great priest
  who in his days pleased God.
There was not found the like to him,
  who kept the law of the Most High.

Alleluia, alleluia.   Gal. 2, 19-20   [*Life in Christ*]
With Christ I am nailed to the Cross.
It is now no longer I that live,
  but Christ lives in me. Alleluia.

After Septuagesima, the Alleluia and versicle are omitted and the following Tract is said:

TRACT   Ps. 20, 3-4   [*Crowned with Glory*]

You have granted him his heart's desire;
  You refused not the wish of his lips.
For You welcomed him with goodly blessings.
  You placed on his head a crown of precious
    stones.

OFFERTORY   Ps. 8, 6-7   [*Crown of Glory*]

O Lord, You crowned him with glory and honor
  and You have given him rule over the works
    of Your hands.

COMMUNION   [*Wheat of Christ*]

I am the wheat of Christ;
May I be ground by the teeth of beasts,
  that I may be found pure bread.

Feb. 2 — PURIFICATION OF THE B.V.M.

DISTRIBUTION OF CANDLES

ANTIPHON Luke 2, 32 [The Light Has Come]

A light of revelation to the Gentiles,
  and a glory for Your people Israel.

CANTICLE Luke 2, 29-31

Now you dismiss Your servant, O Lord,
  according to Your word, in peace.
  The Antiphon is repeated.
A light of revelation to the Gentiles,
  and a glory for Your people Israel.
Because my eyes have seen
  Your salvation.
  The Antiphon is repeated.
A light of revelation to the Gentiles,
  and a glory for Your people Israel.
Which You have prepared
  before the face of all peoples.
  The Antiphon is repeated.
A light of revelation to the Gentiles,
  and a glory for Your people Israel.
Glory be to the Father, and to the Son,
  and to the Holy Spirit.
  The Antiphon is repeated.
A light of revelation to the Gentiles,
  and a glory for Your people Israel.
As it was in the beginning, is now, and ever
    shall be,
  world without end. Amen.

The Antiphon is repeated.

A light of revelation to the Gentiles,
   and a glory for Your people Israel.

THE PROCESSION

ANTIPHON   [*King of Light*]

Adorn your bridal chamber, Sion,
   and welcome Christ the King;
Embrace Mary, who is the gate of heaven,
   for she carries the glorious King of the new
      light.
She remains a virgin,
   bearing in her hands the Son begotten before
      the daystar.
Holding Him in his arms,
   Simeon proclaimed to the peoples,
He is the Lord of life and death
   and the Savior of the world.

ANOTHER ANTIPHON   Luke 2, 26. 27. 28-29

It had been revealed to Simeon by the Holy
      Spirit
   that he should not see death
   before he had seen the Christ of the Lord.
And when they brought the Child into the
      temple,
   he received Him into his arms
And blessed God, saying:
   Now You dismiss Your servant, O Lord, in
      peace.
When His parents brought in the Child Jesus,
   to do for Him according to the custom of the
      Law,
   he received Him into his arms.

When the procession re-enters the church, the Choir sings:
[*The Presentation of the Lord*]

They offered for Him to the Lord
a pair of turtledoves or two young pigeons,
As it is written in the Law of the Lord.

After the days of Mary's purification were fulfilled,
according to the Law of Moses,

They took Jesus up to Jerusalem
to present Him to the Lord.
As it is written in the Law of the Lord.

Glory be to the Father, and to the Son,
and to the Holy Spirit.
As it is written in the Law of the Lord.

THE MASS

INTROIT   Ps. 47, 10-11. 2   [*Pondering God's Love*]

O God, we ponder Your kindness
within Your temple.

As Your Name, O God, so also Your praise
reaches to the ends of the earth.

Of justice Your right hand is full.

(Ps.) Great is the Lord, and wholly to be praised
in the city of our God, His holy mountain.

Glory be to the Father, etc.

Repeat: **O God,** etc., *as far as* (Ps.).

GRADUAL   Ps. 47, 10-1. 9   [*The Expected Has Come*]

O God, we ponder Your kindness
within Your temple.

As Your Name, O God, so also Your praise
reaches to the ends of the earth.

As we have heard, so have we seen,
in the city of our God, in His holy mountain.

Alleluia, alleluia.   [*The Mighty Child*]
The old man carried the Child:
  but the Child governed the old man. Alleluia.

*After Septuagesima, the Alleluia and versicle are
omitted and the following Tract is said:*

TRACT   Luke 2, 29-32   [*Salvation Is Here*]

Now You dismiss Your servant, O Lord,
  according to Your word, in peace.
Because my eyes have seen Your salvation.
  Which You have prepared before the face
    of all peoples.
A light of revelation to the Gentiles,
  and a glory for Your people Israel.

OFFERTORY   Ps. 44, 3   [*Blessed Forever*]

Grace is poured out upon your lips;
  thus God has blessed you forever and ever.

COMMUNION   Luke 2, 26   [*Seeing the Lord*]

It was revealed to Simeon
  by the Holy Spirit
That he should not see death
  before he had seen the Christ of the Lord.

.Feb. 3 — ST. BLASE, Bishop, Martyr

Mass: Of a Martyr Bishop, p. 234.

Feb. 4 — ST. ANDREW CORSINI
Bishop, Confessor

Mass: Of a Confessor Bishop, p. 245.

Feb. 5 — ST. AGATHA, Virgin, Martyr

INTROIT   Ps. 44, 2   [Angels Rejoice]

Let us all rejoice in the Lord,
 celebrating the feast in honor of blessed
  Agatha, Virgin and Martyr,
For whose passion the Angels rejoice
 and praise the Son of God.
(Ps.) My heart overflows with a goodly theme;
 as I sing my ode to the King.
Glory be to the Father, etc.
Repeat: **Let us all,** etc., *as far as* (Ps.).

GRADUAL   Ps. 45, 6. 5   [Consolation of God's Presence]

God will help her with His countenance;
 God is in her midst, she shall not be disturbed.
There is a stream whose runlets gladden the
  city of God;
 the Most High has sanctified His dwelling.

Alleluia, alleluia.   Ps. 118, 46   [Unafraid]

I will speak of Your decrees before kings
 without being ashamed. Alleluia.

*After Septuagesima, the Alleluia and versicle are
omitted and the following Tract is said:*

TRACT   Ps. 125, 5-6   [Joy at the End]

Those that sow in tears
 shall reap rejoicing.
Going, they went and wept,
 casting their seeds.
But coming, they shall come with joyfulness
 carrying their sheaves.

OFFERTORY   Ps. 44, 15   [*Triumph*]

Behind her the virgins of her train are brought
　　to the King.
　　Her neighbors are brought to You.

COMMUNION   [*Call on God's Power*]

I invoke Him, the living God,
　　Who deigned to cure me of every wound,
　　and to restore my breast to my body.

Feb. 6 — ST. TITUS, Bishop, Confessor

Mass: Of a Confessor Bishop, p. 245.

Feb. 7 — ST. ROMUALD, Abbot

Mass: Of a Holy Abbot, p. 253.

Feb. 8 — ST. JOHN OF MATHA, Confessor

Mass: Of a Confessor not a Bishop, p. 250.

Feb. 9 — ST. CYRIL OF ALEXANDRIA
Confessor and Doctor of the Church

Mass: Of a Doctor, p. 248.

Feb. 10 — ST. SCHOLASTICA, Virgin

Mass: Of a Virgin Only, p. 259.

Feb. 11 — THE APPARITION OF THE BLESSED VIRGIN MARY AT LOURDES

INTROIT   Apoc. 21, 2; Ps. 44, 2 [Heaven Let down to Earth]

I saw the holy city, New Jerusalem,
   coming down out of heaven from God,
   made ready as a bride adorned for her
      husband.

(Ps.) My heart overflows with a goodly theme;
   as I sing my ode to the King.

Glory be to the Father, etc.

Repeat: **I saw,** etc., *as far as* (Ps.).

GRADUAL   Cant. 2, 12. 10. 14   [Spiritual Springtime]

The flowers appear in our land,
   the time of pruning has come,
   the song of the dove is heard in our land.
Arise, my beloved, my beautiful one,
   and come!
O my dove, in the clefts of the rock,
   in the secret recesses of the cliff.

Alleluia, alleluia.   [Beloved]

Show me your face,
   let me hear your voice,
For your voice is sweet
   and your face is beautiful. Alleluia.

After Septuagesima, the Alleluia and versicle are omitted and the following Tract is said:

TRACT   Judith 15, 10; Cant. 4, 7   [Our Lady's Glory]

You are the glory of Jerusalem,
   you are the joy of Israel,
   you are the honor of our people.

You are all-beautiful, O Mary,
   and there is in you no stain of original sin.
Happy are you, O holy Virgin Mary,
   and most worthy of all praise,
For with your virgin foot
   you have crushed the serpent's head.

OFFERTORY   Luke 1, 28   [*Blessed among Women*]

Hail, full of grace,
   the Lord is with you.
Blessed are you among women.

COMMUNION   Ps. 64, 10   [*A Fruitful Coming*]

You have visited the land and watered it;
   greatly have you enriched it.

Feb. 12 — SEVEN HOLY FOUNDERS OF THE ORDER OF SERVITES OF THE B. V. M.

INTROIT   Wis. 10, 20-21; Ps. 8, 2

[*Wonders of God's Conquest*]

The just sang, O Lord, Your holy Name
   and praised in unison Your conquering
      hand—
Because wisdom opened the mouths of the
      dumb,
   and gave ready speech to infants.
(Ps.) O Lord, our Lord,
   how glorious is Your Name over all the earth!
Glory be to the Father, etc.
Repeat: **The just,** etc., *as far as* (Ps.).

GRADUAL Isa. 65, 23; Sir. 44, 14 [*The Names Live On*]

My elect shall not toil in vain,
  nor beget children for sudden destruction;
For a race blessed by the Lord
  are they and their offspring.
Their bodies are buried in peace,
  and their name lives on and on.

Alleluia, alleluia. Sir. 44, 15 [*Their Wisdom*]

At gatherings their wisdom is retold,
  and the assembly sings their praises. Alleluia.

*After Septuagesima, the Alleluia and versicle are
omitted and the Tract, p. 325, is said:*

OFFERTORY Isa. 56, 7 [*Glorified by God*]

I will bring them to My holy mountain,
  and make them joyful in My house of prayer;
Their holocausts and sacrifices
  will be acceptable on My altar.

COMMUNION John 15, 16 [*Bearing Fruit*]

I have chosen you from the world
  that you should go and bear fruit,
  and that your fruit should remain.

Feb. 14 — ST. VALENTINE, Priest, Martyr

Mass: Of a Martyr not a Bishop, p. 235.

Feb. 15 — STS. FAUSTINUS AND JOVITA
Martyrs

Mass: Of Several Martyrs, p. 241.

Feb. 18 — ST. SIMEON, Bishop, Martyr

Mass: Of a Martyr Bishop, p. 233.

Feb. 22 — CHAIR OF ST. PETER

INTROIT   Sir. 45, 30; Ps. 131, 1   [*Priestly Dignity*]

**The Lord made a covenant of friendship with
    him,
    and made him a prince;
    that he should possess the dignity of priest-
        hood forever.**

**(Ps.) Remember, O Lord, David
    and all his meekness.**

Glory be to the Father, etc.

Repeat: **The Lord,** etc., *as far as* (Ps.).

GRADUAL   Ps. 106, 32. 31   [*Thanksgiving*]

**Let them extol him in the assembly of the
    people
    and praise him in the council of the elders.
Let them give thanks to the Lord for His
    kindness
    and His wondrous deeds to the children of
        men.**

TRACT   Matt. 16, 18-19   [*The Rock*]

**You are Peter,
    and upon this rock I will build My Church.
And the gates of hell
    shall not prevail against it.
And I will give you
    the keys of the kingdom of heaven.**

And whatever you shall bind on earth
   shall be bound in heaven.
And whatever you shall loose on earth
   shall be loosed in heaven.

OFFERTORY   Matt. 16, 18-19   [*The Keys*]

You are Peter,
   and upon this rock I will build My Church,
And the gates of hell
   shall not prevail against it.
And I will give you
   the keys of the kingdom of heaven.

COMMUNION Matt. 16, 18 [*Foundation of the Church*]

You are Peter,
   and upon this rock I will build My Church.

Feb. 23 — ST. PETER DAMIAN
Bishop, Confessor and Doctor of the Church

Mass: Of a Doctor, p. 248.

Feb. 24 or 25 — ST. MATTHIAS, Apostle

INTROIT   Ps. 138, 17; 1-2   [*Honor God's Friends*]

To me, Your friends, O God, are made exceed-
   ingly honorable;
   their principality is exceedingly strengthened.
(Ps.) O Lord, You have probed me and You
   know me;
   You know when I sit and when I stand.
Glory be to the Father, etc.
Repeat: **To me,** etc., *as far as* (Ps.).

GRADUAL Ps. 138, 17-18[*Numberless Friends of God*]

Your friends, O God, are made exceedingly
    honorable;
  their principality is exceedingly strengthened.
Were I to recount them, they would outnumber
    the sands.

TRACT   Ps. 20, 3-4   [*Crown of Glory*]

You have granted him his heart's desire;
  You refused not the wish of his lips.
For You welcomed him with goodly blessings.
  You placed on his head a crown of precious
    stones.

OFFERTORY   Ps. 44, 17-18   [*Princes*]

You shall make them princes through all the
    land;
  they shall remember Your Name, O Lord,
    through all generations.

COMMUNION   Matt. 19, 28   [*Judges*]

You who have followed Me shall sit on thrones
  judging the twelve tribes of Israel.

Feb. 27 or 28 — ST. GABRIEL OF
OUR LADY OF SORROWS, Confessor

INTROIT   Sir. 11, 13; Ps. 72, 1   [*Raised by God*]

The eye of God looks favorably upon him;
  He raises him free of the vile dust;
And lifts his head to the amazement of the
    many
  who glorify God.

(Ps.) **How good is God to Israel,**
   to those who are clean of heart!

Glory be to the Father, etc.

Repeat: **The eye,** etc., *as far as* (Ps.).

GRADUAL   Ps. 30, 20   [*Refuge in God*]

How great is the goodness, O Lord,
   which You have in store for those who fear
      you.
And which, toward those who take refuge in
   You, You show in the sight of men.

TRACT   Ps. 83, 6-7, 11. 13   [*Happy in God's House*]

Happy the man whose strength You are!
   his heart is set upon the pilgrimage in the
      vale of tears,
   in the place he has set.
I had rather lie at the threshold of the house
   of my God
   than dwell in the tents of the wicked.
He withholds no good things
   from those who walk in sincerity.
O Lord of Hosts,
   happy the man who trusts in You!

OFFERTORY   Ps. 115, 16-17   [*Sacrificial Offering*]

O Lord, I am Your servant,
   the son of Your handmaid;
   You have loosed my bonds.
To You I will offer sacrifice of thanksgiving.

COMMUNION   Apoc. 3, 20   [*Union with Christ*]

Behold, I stand at the door and knock.
   If any man listens to My voice and opens the
      door to Me,

I will come in to him and will sup with him, and he with Me.

Mar. 4 — ST. CASIMIR, Confessor

Mass: Of a Confessor not a Bishop, p. 250.

Mar. 6 — STS. PERPETUA AND FELICITAS Martyrs

Mass: Of a Holy Woman Martyr, p. 262.

Mar. 7 — ST. THOMAS AQUINAS Confessor and Doctor of the Church

Mass: Of a Doctor, p. 248.

Mar. 8 — ST. JOHN OF GOD, Confessor

Mass: Of a Confessor not a Bishop, p. 250.

Mar. 9 — ST. FRANCES OF ROME, Widow

Mass: Of a Holy Woman not a Martyr, p. 264.

Mar. 10 — FORTY HOLY MARTYRS

INTROIT   Ps. 33, 18. 2   [*Cry of the Just*]

When the just cry out, the Lord hears them and from all their distress He rescues them.
(Ps.) I will bless the Lord at all times; His praise shall be ever in my mouth.

Glory be to the Father, etc.

Repeat: **When,** etc., *as far as* (Ps.).

GRADUAL Ps. 132, 1-2   [*Brotherhood*]

Behold, how good it is, and how pleasant.
  where brethren dwell at one!

It is as when the precious ointment upon the
    head
  runs down over the beard, the beard of
    Aaron.

TRACT Ps. 125, 5-6   [*Final Joy*]

Those that sow in tears
  shall reap rejoicing.

Going, they went and wept,
  casting their seeds.

But coming, they shall come with joyfulness,
  carrying their sheaves.

OFFERTORY Ps. 31, 11   [*True Joy*]

Be glad in the Lord, and rejoice you just;
  exult, all you upright of heart.

COMMUNION Matt. 12, 50   [*Christ's Own*]

"For whoever does the will of My Father in
    heaven,
  he is My brother and sister and mother,"
    says the Lord.

Mar. 12 — ST. GREGORY I
Pope, Confessor and Doctor of the Church

Mass: Of One or More Popes, p. 231.

Mar. 17 — ST. PATRICK, Bishop, Confessor

Mass: Of a Confessor Bishop, p. 245.

Mar. 18 — ST. CYRIL OF JERUSALEM
Bishop, Confessor, Doctor of the Church

Mass: Of a Doctor, p. 248.

Mar. 19 — ST. JOSEPH, Spouse of the B. V. M.
Confessor and Patron of the Universal Church

INTROIT   Ps. 91, 13-14. 2   [*Growth of the Just*]

**The just man shall flourish like the palm tree,
  like a cedar of Lebanon shall he grow:
Planted in the house of the Lord,
  in the courts of the house of our God. (P.T.
    Alleluia, alleluia.)**

(Ps.) It is good to give thanks to the Lord,
  to sing praise to Your Name, Most High.

Glory be to the Father, etc.

Repeat: **The just,** etc., *as far as* (Ps.).

GRADUAL   Ps. 20, 4-5   [*Crown of Glory*]

O Lord, You welcomed him with goodly
  blessings,
  You placed on his head a crown of precious
    stones.
He asked life of You; You gave him
  length of days forever and ever.

TRACT   Ps. 111, 1-3   [*Glory of the Just Man*]

Happy the man who fears the Lord,
  who greatly delights in His commands.
His posterity shall be mighty upon the earth;
  the upright generation shall be blessed.
Wealth and riches shall be in his house;
  his generosity shall endure forever.

*During Paschaltime, the Gradual and Tract are
omitted and the following Alleluia is said:*

Sir. 45, 9; Osee 14, 6

Alleluia, alleluia.   [*The Just Man Flourishes*]

The Lord loved him, and adorned him;
  He clothed him with a robe of glory.
Alleluia. The just man shall blossom as the lily;
  and shall flourish forever before the Lord.
    Alleluia.

OFFERTORY   Ps. 88, 25   [*Exaltation*]

My faithfulness and My kindness shall be with
    him,
  and through My Name shall his horn be
    exalted. (P.T. Alleluia.)

COMMUNION   Matt. 1, 20   [*Take Mary*]

"Do not be afraid, Joseph, son of David,
  to take to you Mary your wife,
For that which is begotten in her
  is of the Holy Spirit." (P.T. Alleluia.)

Mar. 21 — ST. BENEDICT, Abbot

Mass: Of a Holy Abbot, p. 253.

Mar. 24 — ST. GABRIEL, Archangel

INTROIT   Ps. 102, 20. 1   [Angelic Praise]

Bless the Lord, all you His angels,
   you mighty in strength, who do his bidding,
   obeying His spoken word.

(Ps.) Bless the Lord, O my soul;
   and all my being, bless His holy Name.

Glory be to the Father, etc.

Repeat: **Bless,** etc., *as far as* (Ps.).

GRADUAL   Ps. 102, 20. 1   [Bless the Lord]

Bless the Lord, all you His angels,
   you mighty in strength, who do His bidding.
Bless the Lord, O my soul;
   and, all my being, bless His holy Name.

TRACT   Luke 1, 28, 42, 31. 35   [Mother of God]

Hail, Mary, full of grace,
   the Lord is with you.
Blessed are you among women
   and blessed is the fruit of your womb.
And behold, you shall conceive and shall bring
         forth a Son,
   and you shall call His Name Emmanuel.
The Holy Spirit shall come upon you
   and the power of the Most High shall over-
         shadow you.
And therefore the Holy One to be born
   shall be called the Son of God.

OFFERTORY   Apoc. 8, 3. 4   [Angelic Minister]

An angel stood before the altar of the temple,
  having a golden censer in his hand;
And there was given to him much incense:
  and the smoke of the incense went up before
  God.

COMMUNION   Dan. 3, 58 [All Angels Bless the Lord]

Angels of the Lord, bless the Lord,
  sing a hymn, and exalt Him above all forever.

Mar. 25 — ANNUNCIATION OF THE B. V. M.

INTROIT   Ps. 44, 13, 15. 16. 2   [Glory of Mary]

All the rich among the people seek Your favor.
Behind her the virgins of her train are brought
  to the King.
  Her neighbors are brought to you with glad-
  ness and joy. (P.T. Alleluia, alleluia.)
(Ps.) My heart overflows with a goodly theme;
  as I sing my ode to the King.
Glory be to the Father, etc.
Repeat: **All the rich,** etc., *as far as* (Ps.).

GRADUAL   Ps. 44, 3. 5   [Grace in Mary]

Grace is poured out upon your lips;
  thus God has blessed you forever.
Because of truth, and meekness, and justice;
  may your right hand show you wondrous
  deeds.

TRACT Ps. 44, 11. 12. 13. 10. 15-16 [*Beloved of the King*]

Hear, O daughter, and see; turn your ear;
for the King shall desire your beauty.

All the rich among the people seek Your favor;
the daughters of kings come to meet You.

Behind her the virgins of her train are brought
to the King;
her neighbors are brought to You.

They are brought with gladness and joy;
they enter the palace of the King.

During Paschaltime, the Gradual and Tract are
omitted and the following Alleluia is said:

Alleluia, alleluia. Luke 1, 28 [*Blossoming of the Root*]

Hail, Mary, full of grace,
the Lord is with you;
blessed are you among women.

The rod of Jesse has blossomed:
a Virgin has brought forth God and man:

God has given peace,
reconciling in Himself the lowest with the
highest. Alleluia.

OFFERTORY Luke 1, 28. 42 [*Fruit of Mary*]

Hail, Mary, full of grace,
the Lord is with you.

Blessed are you among women
and blessed is the fruit of your womb. (P.T.
Alleluia.)

COMMUNION Isa. 7, 14 [*A Virgin's Son*]

Behold, a Virgin shall be with child, and bear
a Son,
and shall name Him Emmanuel. (P.T. alleluia.)

Mar. 27 — ST. JOHN DAMASCENE
Confessor and Doctor of the Church

INTROIT   Ps. 72, 24. 1   [*God's Guidance*]

You have hold of my right hand;
With Your counsel You guide me,
    and You will receive me in glory.
(Ps.) How good God is to Israel,
    to those who are clean of heart!
Glory be to the Father, etc.
Repeat: **You have,** etc., *as far as* (Ps.).

GRADUAL   Ps. 17, 33. 35   [*Strength from God*]

The God Who girded me with strength
    and kept my way unerring.
Who trained my hands for war
    and my arms to bend a bow of brass.

TRACT   Ps. 17, 38, 39. 50   [*Praise for God's Help*]

I pursued my enemies and overtook them.
I smote them, and they could not rise;
    they fell beneath my feet.
Therefore will I proclaim You, O Lord, among
        the nations,
    and I will sing praise to Your Name.

OFFERTORY   Job 14, 7   [*New Life in God*]

For a tree there is hope,
    if it be cut down,
That it will sprout again
    and that its tender shoots will not cease.

COMMUNION   Ps. 36, 17   [The Just Supported]

The power of the wicked shall be broken,
  but the Lord supports the just.

Mar. 28 — ST. JOHN CAPISTRAN, Confessor

INTROIT   Hab. 3, 18-19; Ps. 80, 2   [Rejoice in the Lord]

Yet will I rejoice in the Lord
  and exult in my saving God;
  the Lord God is my strength.
(Ps.) Sing joyfully to God our strength;
  acclaim the God of Jacob.
Glory be to the Father, etc.
Repeat: Yet will I, etc., as far as (Ps.).

GRADUAL   Ps. 21, 24-25   [Praise the Lord]

You who fear the Lord, praise Him;
  all you descendants of Jacob, give glory to
    Him!
  Revere Him, all you descendants of Israel!
For He has not spurned nor disdained
  the wretched man in his misery.

TRACT   Ex. 15, 2. 3; Judith 16, 3   [God, My Savior]

My strength and my courage is the Lord,
  and He has been my Savior.
  He is my God, I praise Him.
The Lord is a warrior,
  almighty is His Name.
The Lord Who breaks battles;
  the Lord is His name.

OFFERTORY   Sir. 46, 6   [*God Hears Him*]

He called upon the Most High God
  when his enemies beset him on all sides,
  and the great and holy God heard him.

COMMUNION   Wis. 10, 20   [*Sing of Truth*]

They sang, O Lord, Your holy Name
  and praised Your conquering hand.

Friday after the First Sunday of the Passion

SEVEN SORROWS OF THE BLESSED MOTHER

Mass: As on Sept. 15, p. 422.

Apr. 2 — ST. FRANCIS OF PAULA, Confessor

Mass: Of a Confessor not a Bishop, p. 251.

Apr. 4 — ST. ISIDORE
Bishop, Confessor and Doctor of the Church

Mass: Of a Doctor, p. 248.

Apr. 5 — ST. VINCENT FERRER, Confessor

Mass: Of a Confessor not a Bishop, p. 250.

Apr. 11 — ST. LEO I
Pope, Confessor and Doctor of the Church

Mass: Of One or More Popes, p. 231.

Apr. 13 — ST. HERMENEGILD, Martyr

In Paschaltime:

Mass: Of One Martyr, p. 243.

Outside Paschaltime:

Mass: Of a Martyr not a Bishop, p. 235.

Apr. 14 — ST. JUSTIN, Martyr

INTROIT   Ps. 118, 85. 46. 1   [*Preacher of Truth*]

The wicked have told me fables,
  but not as Your law.
I will speak of Your decrees before kings
  without being ashamed. (P.T. Alleluia,
    alleluia.)
(Ps.) **Happy are they whose ways is blameless,**
  who walk in the law of the Lord.
Glory be to the Father, etc.
Repeat: **The wicked,** etc., *as far as* (Ps.).

In Paschaltime:

1 Cor. 3, 19. 20; Phil. 3, 8
[*Christ the Real Truth*]

Alleluia, alleluia.
The wisdom of this world
  is foolishness with God.
For it is written,
  "The Lord knows the thoughts of the wise,
    that they are empty."
Alleluia. Nay more, I count everything loss,
  because of the excelling knowledge of Jesus
    Christ, my Lord. Alleluia.

Outside Paschaltime:

GRADUAL   1 Cor. 3, 19. 20; 1, 19   [*The Wisdom*]

The wisdom of this world
  is foolishness with God.
For it is written,
  "The Lord knows the thoughts of the wise,
  that they are empty."
"I will destroy the wisdom of the wise,
  and the prudence of the prudent I will reject."

TRACT   1 Cor. 2, 2. 7-8   [*Knowing Only Christ*]

I determined not to know anything among you,
  except Jesus Christ and Him crucified.
We speak the wisdom of God, mysterious,
  hidden,
  which God foreordained before the world
  unto our glory.
Which none of the rulers of this world has
  known;
  for had they known it,
  they would never have crucified the Lord of
  glory.

OFFERTORY   1 Cor. 2, 2   [*Only Christ Crucified*]

For I determined not to know anything among
  you,
  except Jesus Christ and Him crucified. (P.T.
  Alleluia.)

COMMUNION   2 Tim. 4, 8   [*The Crown*]

There is laid up for me a crown of justice,
  which the Lord, the just Judge,
  will give to me in that day. (P.T. Alleluia.)

Apr. 17 — ST. ANICETUS, Pope, Martyr

Mass: Of One or More Popes, p. 231.

Apr. 21 — ST. ANSELM

Bishop, Confessor and Doctor of the Church

Mass: Of a Doctor, p. 248.

Apr. 22 — STS. SOTER AND CAIUS
Popes, Martyrs

Mass: Of One or More Popes, p. 231.

Apr. 23 — ST. GEORGE, Martyr

Mass: Of One Martyr, p. 243.

Apr. 24 — ST. FIDELIS SIGMARINGEN, Martyr

Mass: Of One Martyr, p. 243.

Apr. 25 — ST. MARK, Evangelist

INTROIT   Ps. 63, 3. 2   [God's Protection]

You have sheltered me, O God, against the
    council of malefactors, alleluia,
against the multitude of the workers of in-
    iquity, alleluia, alleluia.

(Ps.) **Hear, O God, my voice in lament;**
  from the dread enemy preserve my life.

Glory be to the Father, etc.

Repeat: **You have,** etc., *as far as* (Ps.).

Ps. 88, 6; 20, 4

Alleluia, alleluia.   [*Proclaim the Lord's Wonders*]

The heavens proclaim Your wonders, O Lord,
  and Your faithfulness in the assembly of the
    holy ones.

Alleluia. You placed on his head, O Lord,
  a crown of precious stones. Alleluia.

OFFERTORY   Ps. 88, 6   [*The Heavens Are Witness*]

The heavens proclaim Your wonders, O Lord,
  and Your faithfulness in the assembly of the
    holy ones, alleluia, alleluia.

COMMUNION   Ps. 63, 11   [*Refuge of the Just*]

The just man is glad in the Lord and takes
  refuge in Him;
  all the upright of heart shall be praised,
    alleluia, alleluia.

Apr. 26 — STS. CLETUS AND MARCELLINUS
Popes, Martyrs

Mass: Of One or More Popes, p. 231.

Apr. 27 — ST. PETER CANISIUS
Confessor and Doctor of the Church

Mass: Of a Doctor, p. 248.

Apr. 28 — ST. PAUL OF THE CROSS, Confessor

INTROIT   Gal. 2, 19-20; Ps. 40, 2   [*Christ Lives in Me*]

With Christ I am nailed to the cross.

It is now no longer I that live,
but Christ lives in me.

I live in the faith of the Son of God,
Who loved me and gave Himself up for me.
(P.T. Alleluia, alleluia.)

(Ps.) **Happy is he who has regard for the lowly**
and the poor;
in the day of misfortune the Lord will deliver
him.

Glory be to the Father, etc.

Repeat: **With Christ,** etc., *as far as* (Ps.).

ALLELUIA   2 Cor. 5, 15; Rom. 8, 17

Alleluia, alleluia.   [*We Live in Christ's Death*]

Christ died for all,
in order that they who are alive may live
no longer for themselves,
but for Him Who died for them and rose
again.

Alleluia. If we are sons, we are heirs also:
heirs indeed of God and joint heirs with
Christ,

Provided, however, we suffer with Him,
that we may also be glorified with Him.
Alleluia.

OFFERTORY   Eph. 5, 2   [*Love*]

Walk in love, as Christ also loved us,
   and delivered Himself up for us,
An offering and a sacrifice to God,
   in fragrant odor. (P.T. Alleluia.)

COMMUNION   1 Pet. 4, 13   [*Glory after Suffering*]

Rejoice in as far as you are partakers of the
   sufferings of Christ,
   that you may also rejoice with exultation in
   the revelation of His glory. (P.T. Alleluia.)

Apr. 29 — ST. PETER, Martyr

Mass: Of One Martyr, p. 243.

Apr. 30 — ST. CATHERINE OF SIENA, Virgin

Mass: Of a Virgin Only, p. 259.

May 1 — ST. JOSEPH THE WORKER
Spouse of the Blessed Virgin Mary, Confessor

INTROIT   Wis. 10, 17; Ps. 126, 1   [*The Reward of Labor*]

Wisdom gave the holy ones the recompense of
   their labors,
   and conducted them by a wondrous road,
And became a shelter for them by day
   and a starry flame by night. (P.T. Alleluia
   alleluia.)

(Ps.) **Unless the Lord build the house,**
   they labor in vain who build it.

Glory be to the Father, etc.

Repeat: **Wisdom,** etc., *as far as* (Ps.).

   In Paschaltime:

Alleluia, alleluia.   [*Joseph's Patronage*]
In whatever trouble they shall call upon me,
   I will hear them,
      and I will always be their protector.

Alleluia. Obtain for us grace to lead an innocent
   life, O Joseph;
      and may it ever be secure under your
      protection. Alleluia.

   In Votive Masses outside Paschaltime:

GRADUAL   Ps. 127, 1-2   [*Glory of Work*]

Happy are you who fear the Lord,
   who walk in His ways!
You shall eat the fruit of your handiwork
   and you shall be favored.

Alleluia, alleluia.   [*Patronage*]
Obtain for us grace to lead an innocent life,
   O Joseph;
      and may it ever be secure under your
      protection. Alleluia.

   After Septuagesima, the Alleluia and versicle are
   omitted and the Tract, p. 337, is said.

OFFERTORY   Ps. 89, 17   [*Prosper Us*]

May the gracious care of the Lord our God
   be ours;
      prosper the work of our hands for us!
      Prosper the work of our hands! (P.T. Alleluia.)

COMMUNION　Matt. 13, 54, 55　[*Family of Jesus*]

Where did He get this wisdom and these
　miracles?
Is not this the carpenter's Son?
　Is not His Mother called Mary? (P.T. Alleluia.)

May 2 — ST. ATHANASIUS
Bishop, Confessor and Doctor of the Church

INTROIT　Sir. 15, 5; Ps. 91, 2　　　[*Wisdom*]

In the midst of the assembly He opened his
　mouth;
And the Lord filled him with the spirit of wis-
　dom and understanding;
　He clothed him with a robe of glory. (P.T.
　Alleluia, alleluia.)

(Ps.) It is good to give thanks to the Lord,
　to sing praise to Your Name, Most High.

Glory be to the Father, etc.

Repeat: In the midst, etc., *as far as* (Ps.).

ALLELUIA　Ps. 109, 4; James 1, 12　[*Priestly Crown*]

Alleluia, alleluia.
You are a priest forever, according to the order
　of Melchisedec.
Alleluia. Blessed is the man who endures
　temptation;
　for when he has been tried,
　he will receive the crown of life. Alleluia.

OFFERTORY　Ps. 88, 21-22　　　[*Anointed*]

I have found David, My servant;
　with My holy oil I have anointed him,

That My hand may be always with him,
   and that My arm may make him strong. (P.T.
   Alleluia.)

COMMUNION　　Matt. 10, 27　　　[*True Doctrine*]

"What I tell you in darkness,
   speak it in the light," says the Lord;
"And what you hear whispered,
   preach it on the housetops." (P.T. Alleluia.)

May 3 — STS. ALEXANDER, EVENTIUS
AND THEODULUS, Martyrs
AND JUVENAL, Bishop, Confessor

Mass: Of Several Martyrs, p, 244.

May 4 — ST. MONICA, Widow

Mass: Of a Holy Woman not a Martyr, p. 264.

May 5 — ST. PIUS V, Pope, Confessor

Mass: Of One or More Popes, p. 231.

May 7 — ST. STANISLAUS, Bishop, Martyr

Mass: Of One Martyr, p. 243.

May 9 — ST. GREGORY NAZIANZEN
Bishop, Confessor and Doctor of the Church

Mass: Of a Doctor, p. 248.

May 10 — ST. ANTONINE, Bishop, Confessor

Mass: Of a Confessor Bishop, p. 245.

May 11 — STS. PHILIP AND JAMES, Apostles

INTROIT   2 Esd. 9, 27; Ps. 32, 1   [*Rejoice in the Lord*]

**In the time of their tribulation they cried to
    You, O Lord,
    and You heard them from heaven, alleluia,
    alleluia.**
(Ps.) **Exult, you just, in the Lord;
    praise from the upright is fitting.**

Glory be to the Father, etc.

Repeat: **In the time,** etc., *as far as* (Ps.).

ALLELUIA Ps. 88, 6; John 14, 9 [*Christ and His Father*]

Alleluia, alleluia.
**The heavens proclaim Your wonders, O Lord,
    and Your faithfulness, in the assembly of the
    holy ones.**
**Alleluia. Have I been so long a time with you,
    and you have not known Me?**
**Philip, he who sees Me, sees also My Father.
    Alleluia.**

OFFERTORY   Ps. 88, 6   [*The Wonders of God*]

**The heavens proclaim Your wonders, O Lord,
    and Your faithfulness, in the assembly of the
    holy ones, alleluia, alleluia.**

COMMUNION   John 14, 9. 10 [*One with the Father*]

**Have I been so long a time with you,
    and you have not known Me?
Philip, he who sees Me
    sees also My Father, Alleluia.
Do you not believe that I am in the Father
    and the Father in Me? Alleluia, alleluia.**

May 12 — STS. NEREUS, ACHILLEUS
DOMITILLA, Virgin
AND PANCRATIUS, Martyrs

INTROIT   Ps. 32, 18, 19. 20. 1   [*Protection of the Lord*]

**But see, the eyes of the Lord are upon those
    who fear Him,
    upon those who hope in His kindness, alleluia:
To deliver them from death;
    for He is our help and our shield, alleluia.**

**(Ps.) Exult, you just, in the Lord;
    praise from the upright is fitting.**

Glory be to the Father, etc.

Repeat: **But see,** etc., *as far as* (Ps.).

ALLELUIA   [*The Brotherhood*]

**Alleluia, alleluia.
This is the true brotherhood,
    which overcame the wickedness of the world;**

It followed Christ,
  attaining the glorious kingdom of heaven.
Alleluia. The white-robed army of Martyrs
  praises You, O Lord. Alleluia.

OFFERTORY   Ps. 88, 6   [God's Wonders]

The heavens proclaim Your wonders, O Lord,
  and Your faithfulness, in the assembly of
  the holy ones, alleluia, alleluia.

COMMUNION   Ps. 32, 1   [Exult]

Exult, you just, in the Lord, alleluia;
  praise from the upright is fitting, alleluia.

May 13 — ST. ROBERT BELLARMINE
Bishop, Confessor and Doctor of the Church

INTROIT   Sir. 15, 5; Ps. 91, 2   [Wisdom]

In the midst of the assembly He opened his
  mouth;
And the Lord filled him with the spirit of wis-
  dom and understanding;
  He clothed him with a robe of glory. **(P.T.
  Alleluia, alleluia.)**
(Ps.) It is good to give thanks to the Lord,
  to sing praise to Your Name, Most High.
Glory be to the Father, etc.
Repeat: **In the midst,** etc., *as far·as* (Ps.).

ALLELUIA   Dan. 12, 3   [A Shining Light]
Alleluia, alleluia.
The wise shall shine brightly
  like the splendor of the firmament.

Alleluia. Those who led the many to justice, shall be like the stars forever. Alleluia.

OFFERTORY   Ps. 72, 28   [*Proclaiming God*]

But for me, to be near God is my good;
    to make the Lord God my refuge,
I shall declare all Your works
    in the gates of the daughter of Sion. (P.T. Alleluia.)

COMMUNION   Matt. 5, 14. 16   [*Light*]

You are the light of the world.
    Even so, let your light shine before men,
In order that they may see your good works
    and give glory to your Father in heaven. (P.T. Alleluia.)

May 14 — ST. BONIFACE, Martyr

In Paschaltime — Mass: Of One Martyr, p. 243.

Outside Paschaltime — Mass: Of a Martyr not a Bishop, p. 235.

May 15 — ST. JOHN BAPTIST DE LA SALLE Confessor

Mass: Of a Confessor not a Bishop, p. 250.

May 16 — ST. UBALDUS, Bishop, Confessor

Mass: Of a Confessor Bishop, p. 245.

May 17 — ST. PASCHAL BAYLON, Confessor

Mass: Of a Confessor not a Bishop, p. 250.

May 18 — ST. VENANTIUS, Martyr

In Paschaltime — Mass: Of One Martyr, p. 243.

Outside Paschaltime — Mass: Of a Martyr not a Bishop, p. 235.

May 19 — ST. PETER CELESTINE
Pope, Confessor

Mass: Of One or More Popes, p. 231.

May 20 — ST. BERNARDINE OF SIENA
Confessor

Mass: Of a Confessor not a Bishop, p. 250.

May 25 — ST. GREGORY VII, Pope, Confessor

Mass: Of One or More Popes, p. 231.

May 26 — ST. PHILIP NERI, Confessor

INTROIT   Rom. 5, 5; Ps. 102, 1   [*Indwelling Spirit*]

The charity of God is poured forth in our hearts, by His spirit dwelling within us. (P.T. Alleluia, alleluia.)

(Ps.) Bless the Lord, O my soul; and, all my being, bless His holy Name.

Glory be to the Father, etc.
Repeat: **The charity,** etc., *as far as* (Ps.).

In Paschaltime:

Alleluia, alleluia.   Lam. 1, 13; Ps. 38, 4   [*Zeal*]

From on high He sent fire into my very frame
  and instructed me.
Alleluia. Hot grew my heart within me;
  in my thoughts, a fire blazed forth. Alleluia.

Outside Paschaltime:

GRADUAL   Ps. 33, 12. 6   [*Joy*]

Come, children, hear Me;
  I will teach you the fear of the Lord.
Look to Him that you may be radiant with joy,
  and your faces may not blush with shame.

Alleluia, alleluia.   Lam. 1, 13   [*Zeal*]

From on high He sent a fire into my very frame,
  and instructed me. Alleluia.

OFFERTORY   Ps. 118, 32   [*Love of Obedience*]

I will run the way of Your commands
  when You enlarge my heart. (P.T. Alleluia.)

COMMUNION   Ps. 83, 3   [*Longing for God*]

My heart and my flesh
  cry out for the living God. (P.T. Alleluia.)

May 27 — ST. BEDE THE VENERABLE
Confessor and Doctor of the Church

Mass: Of a Doctor, p. 248.

May 28 — ST. AUGUSTINE OF CANTERBURY
Bishop, Confessor

Mass: Of a Confessor Bishop, p. 246.

May 29 — ST. MARY MAGDALEN OF PAZZI
Virgin

Mass: Of a Virgin Only, p. 259.

May 30 — ST. FELIX I, Pope, Martyr

Mass: Of One or More Popes, p. 231.

May 31 — QUEENSHIP OF THE BLESSED VIRGIN MARY

INTROIT   Ps. 44, 2   [*Heavenly Queen*]

Let us all rejoice in the Lord,
    celebrating a feast in honor of the Queen-
    ship of the Blessed Virgin Mary,
On whose solemnity the angels rejoice
    and give praise to the Son of God. (P.T.
    Alleluia, alleluia.)
(Ps.) My heart overflows with a goodly theme;
    as I sing my ode to the King.
Glory be to the Father, etc.
Repeat: Let us, etc., *as far as* (Ps.).

In Paschaltime:

Alleluia, alleluia.   [*Reigning with Christ*]
Blessed are You, O Virgin Mary,
    who stood beneath the cross of the Lord.

Alleluia. **Now with Him you reign forever. Alleluia.**

Outside Paschaltime:

GRADUAL   Apoc. 19, 16; Ps. 44, 10   [Coronation]

He has on His garment and on His thigh a
      name written:
   "King of kings and Lord of lords."
The Queen takes her place at His right hand in
      gold of Ophir.

Alleluia, alleluia.   [Receive Us]
Hail, Queen of mercy,
      protect us from the enemy,
      and receive us at the hour of death. Alleluia.

OFFERTORY   [Royal Lady]

Sprung from a royal line,
      Mary shines with glory.
We devoutly plead to be helped by her prayers
      in mind and in heart. (P.T. Alleluia.)

COMMUNION   [Queen of All]

Most worthy Queen of the world,
      Mary ever Virgin,
You bore Christ the Lord,
      the Savior of all men.
Intercede for our peace and salvation. (P.T.
      Alleluia.)

June 1 — ST. ANGELA MERICI, Virgin

Mass: Of a Virgin Only, p. 259.

June 2 — STS. MARCELLINUS, PETER AND ERASMUS, Bishop and Martyrs

Outside Paschaltime:

INTROIT   Ps. 33, 18. 2   [God Hears Them]

When the just cry out, the Lord hears them,
  and from all their distress He rescues them.

(Ps.) I will bless the Lord at all times;
  His praise shall be ever in my mouth.

Glory be to the Father, etc.

Repeat: When the just, etc., *as far as* (Ps.).

GRADUAL   Ps. 33, 18-19   [God Loves the Humble]

When the just cry out, the Lord hears them,
  and from all their distress He rescues them.
The Lord is close to the brokenhearted
  and those who are crushed in spirit He saves.

Alleluia, alleluia.   John 15, 16   [Bear Fruit]

I have chosen you out of the world,
  that you should go, and bear fruit,
  and that your fruit should remain. Alleluia.

OFFERTORY   Ps. 31, 11   [Rejoice]

Be glad in the Lord, and rejoice, you just;
  exult, all you upright of heart.

COMMUNION   Wis. 3, 1. 2. 3   [Peace]

The souls of the just are in the hand of God,
  and no torment shall touch them.
They seemed, in the view of the foolish, to be
    dead;
  but they are in peace.

In Paschaltime:

INTROIT   Ps. 144, 10. 11. 1   [*Glory of the Kingdom*]

Let Your faithful ones bless You, O Lord;
  let them discourse of the glory of Your king-
    dom, alleluia, alleluia.

(Ps.) I will extol You, O my God and King,
  and I will bless Your Name forever and ever.

Glory be to the Father, etc.

Repeat: Let Your faithful, etc., *as far as* (Ps.).

ALLELUIA   John 5, 16; Ps. 115, 15   [*Bear Fruit*]

Alleluia, alleluia.
I have chosen you out of the world,
  that you should go and bear fruit,
    and that your fruit should remain.
Alleluia. Precious in the eyes of the Lord
  is the death of His saints. Alleluia.

OFFERTORY   Ps. 31, 11   [*Joy of the Just*]

Be glad in the Lord, and rejoice, you just;
  and exult, all you upright of heart, alleluia,
    alleluia.

COMMUNION   Ps. 32, 1   [*Exult*]

Exult you just, in the Lord, alleluia;
  praise from the upright is fitting, alleluia.

June 4 — ST. FRANCIS CARACCIOLO
Confessor

INTROIT   Ps. 21, 15; 68, 10; 72, 1   [*Fire of Love*]

My heart has become like wax
  melting away within my bosom,

Because zeal for Your house consumes me.
(P.T. Alleluia, alleluia.)

(Ps.) How good God is to Israel,
   to those who are clean of heart!

Glory be to the Father, etc.

Repeat: My heart has, etc., *as far as* (Ps.).

GRADUAL   Ps. 41, 2. 3   [Longing Soul]

As the hind longs for the running waters,
   so my soul longs for You, O God.
Athirst is my soul for the strong living God.

Alleluia, alleluia.   Ps. 72, 26   [Hunger for God]
My flesh and my heart waste away;
   God is the God of my heart and my portion
      forever. Alleluia.

*During Paschaltime, the Gradual is omitted and the
following Alleluia is said:*

Alleluia, alleluia.   Ps. 64, 5; 111, 9   [Generous]
Happy the man You choose and bring
   to dwell in Your courts.
Alleluia. Lavishly he gives to the poor;
   his generosity shall endure forever. Alleluia.

OFFERTORY   Ps. 91, 13   [Growth]

The just man shall flourish like the palm tree,
   like a cedar of Lebanon shall he grow. (P.T.
      Alleluia.)

COMMUNION   Ps. 30, 20   [Reward]

How great is the goodness, O Lord,
   which You have in store for those who fear
      You. (P.T. Alleluia.)

June 5 — ST. BONIFACE, Bishop, Martyr

INTROIT   Isa. 65, 19. 23; Ps. 43, 2   [*A Saved People*]

I will rejoice in Jerusalem
  and exult in My people.
No longer shall the sound of weeping be heard
    there,
  or the sound of crying.
My elect shall not toil in vain,
  nor beget children for sudden destruction;
For a race blessed by the Lord are they
  and their offspring. (P.T. Alleluia, alleluia.)

(Ps.) O God, our ears have heard,
  our fathers have declared to us,
  the deeds You did in their days.

Glory be to the Father, etc.

Repeat: I will rejoice, etc., *as far as* (Ps.).

GRADUAL   1 Pet. 4, 13-14 [*Glory and Power of God*]

In as far as you are partakers
  of the sufferings of Christ,
Rejoice that you may also rejoice with
    exultation
  in the revelation of His glory.
If you are upbraided for the Name of Christ,
  blessed will you be,
Because the honor, the glory and the power of
    God, and His Spirit
  rest upon you.

Alleluia, alleluia.   Isa. 66, 12   [*Prosperity*]
I will spread prosperity over him like a river,
  and glory like an overflowing torrent. Alleluia.

During Paschaltime, the Gradual is omitted and the following Alleluia is said:

Alleluia, alleluia.   Isa. 66, 10. 14   [*Joyful Heart*]

Rejoice with Jerusalem and be glad because of her, all you who love the Lord.

Alleluia. You shall see and your heart shall rejoice;

and the Lord's power shall be known to His servants. Alleluia.

OFFERTORY   Ps. 15, 7. 8   [*God's Presence*]

I bless the Lord who counsels me;

I set God ever before me;

with Him at my right hand I shall not be disturbed. (P.T. Alleluia.)

COMMUNION   Apoc. 3, 21   [*Victory*]

He who overcomes,

I will permit him to sit with Me upon My throne;

As I also have overcome

and have sat with My Father on His throne (P.T. Alleluia.)

June 6 — ST. NORBERT, Bishop and Confessor

Mass: Of a Confessor Bishop, p. 245.

June 9 — STS. PRIMUS AND FELICIAN, Martyrs

INTROIT   Sir. 44, 15. 14; Ps. 32, 1   [*Everlasting Memory*]

At gatherings the wisdom of the saints is retold, and the assembly sings their praises;

Their name lives on and on.

(Ps.) **Exult, you just, in the Lord;**
  praise from the upright is fitting.

Glory be to the Father, etc.

Repeat: **At gatherings,** etc., *as far as* (Ps.).

GRADUAL   Ps. 88, 6. 2   [God's Wonders]

The heavens proclaim Your wonders, O Lord,
  and Your faithfulness, in the assembly of the
    holy ones.

The favors of the Lord I will sing forever;
  through all generations.

Alleluia, alleluia.   [*True Brotherhood*]
This is the true brotherhood
  which overcame the wickedness of the world;
It followed Christ,
  attaining the glorious kingdom of heaven.
    Alleluia.

OFFERTORY   Ps. 67, 36   [God's Saints]

God is wonderful in his saints;
  the God of Israel is He Who gives power and
    strength to His people.
  Blessed be God. Alleluia.

COMMUNION   John 15, 16   [Bearing Fruit]

I have chosen you out of the world,
  that you should go and bear fruit,
    and that your fruit should remain.

June 10 — ST. MARGARET, Queen and Widow

Mass: Of a Holy Woman not a Martyr, p. 264.

June 11 — ST. BARNABAS, Apostle

INTROIT   Ps. 138, 17. 1-2   [*Honor God's Friends*]

To me, Your friends, O God, are made exceed-
    ingly honorable;
  their principality is exceedingly strengthened.
(Ps.) **O Lord, You have probed me and You
    know me;**
  You know when I sit and when I stand.
Glory be to the Father, etc.
Repeat: **To me, Your friends,** etc., *as far as* (Ps.).

GRADUAL   Ps. 18, 5. 2   [*Apostolic Voices*]

Through all the earth their voice resounds,
  and to the ends of the world, their message.
The heavens declare the glory of God,
  and the firmament proclaims His handiwork.

Alleluia, alleluia.   John 15, 16   [*Bearing Fruit*]
I have chosen you out of the world,
  that you should go and bear fruit,
    and that your fruit should remain. Alleluia.

OFFERTORY   Ps. 44, 17-18   [*Princes*]

You shall make them princes through all the
    land;
  they shall remember Your Name, O Lord,
    through all generations.

COMMUNION   Matt. 19, 28   [*Thrones*]

You who have followed Me shall sit on thrones
  judging the twelve tribes of Israel.

In Paschaltime — Mass: As on Apr. 25, p. 346.

June 12 — ST. JOHN OF SAN FACONDO
Confessor

Mass: Of a Confessor not a Bishop, p. 250.

June 13 — ST. ANTHONY OF PADUA
Confessor and Doctor of the Church

Mass: Of a Doctor, p. 248.

June 14 — ST. BASIL THE GREAT
Bishop, Confessor and Doctor of the Church

INTROIT   Sir. 15, 5; Ps. 91, 2   [*Glory in the Church*]

**In the midst of the assembly He opened his
  mouth;**
**And the Lord filled him with the spirit of wis-
  dom and understanding;**
  He clothed him with a robe of glory.
**(Ps.) It is good to give thanks to the Lord,
  to sing praise to Your Name, Most High.**
Glory be to the Father, etc.
Repeat: **In the midst,** etc., *as far as* (Ps.).

GRADUAL   Ps. 36, 30-31   [*Law of God*]

**The mouth of the just tells of wisdom
  and his tongue utters what is right.**
**The law of his God is in his heart,
  and his steps do not falter.**

Alleluia, alleluia. Ps. 88, 21   [*Anointed*]
I have found David, My servant;

with My holy oil I have anointed him. Alleluia.

OFFERTORY Ps. 88, 25 [*Glory in Christ*]

My faithfulness and My kindness shall be with
  him,
  and through My Name shall his horn be
  exalted.

COMMUNION Luke 12, 42 [*Fidelity*]

The faithful and prudent servant
  whom the Master will set over His household
  to give them their ration of grain in due time.

June 15 — STS. VITUS, MODESTUS, CRESCENTIA, Martyrs

INTROIT Ps. 33, 20-21. 2 [*Protection*]

Many are the troubles of the just,
  but out of them all the Lord delivers them;
The Lord watches over all their bones;
  not one of them shall be broken.
(Ps.) I will bless the Lord at all times;
  His praise shall be ever in my mouth.
Glory be to the Father, etc.
Repeat: **Many are,** etc., *as far as* (Ps.).

GRADUAL Ps. 149, 5. 1 [*New Song*]

Let the faithful exult in glory;
  let them sing for joy upon their couches.
Sing to the Lord a new song
  of praise in the assembly of the faithful.

Alleluia, alleluia. Ps. 144, 10-11   [Glorious Kingdom]
Let Your faithful ones bless you, O Lord;
Let them discourse of the glory of Your
    kingdom. Alleluia.

OFFERTORY   Ps. 67, 36   [Glory of God's People]

God is wonderful in His saints;
    the God of Israel is He Who gives power
        and strength to His people.
    Blessed be God!

COMMUNION   Wis. 3, 1-2. 3   [Peace]

The souls of the just are in the hand of God,
    and no torment shall touch them.
They seemed, in the view of the foolish, to be
    dead,
    but they are in peace.

June 17 — ST. GREGORY BARBADICUS
Bishop and Confessor

Mass: Of a Confessor Bishop, p. 245.

June 18 — ST. EPHREM THE SYRIAN
Deacon, Confessor and Doctor of the Church

Mass: Of a Doctor, p. 248.

June 19 — ST. JULIANA FALCONIERI, Virgin

Mass: Of a Virgin Only, p. 259.

June 20 — ST. SILVERIUS, Pope and Martyr

Mass: Of One or More Popes, p. 231.

June 21 — ST. ALOYSIUS GONZAGA, Confessor

INTROIT   Ps. 8, 6; 148, 2   [*Angelic*]

You have made him little less than the angels,
  and crowned him with glory and honor.

(Ps.) **Praise the Lord, all you His angels,
  praise Him, all you His hosts.**

Glory be to the Father, etc.

Repeat: **You have made him** etc., *as far as* (Ps.).

GRADUAL Ps. 70, 5-6; 40, 13 [*God's Love for the Good*]

O Lord, You are my trust from my youth;
I have been strengthened by You from birth;
  from my mother's womb You are my
    protector.
But because of my integrity You sustain me
  and You establish me in Your sight forever.

Alleluia, alleluia. Ps. 64, 5   [*Dwelling with God*]
**Happy the man You choose and take to
  Yourself.**
  He shall dwell in Your courts. Alleluia.

OFFERTORY   Ps. 23, 3-4   [*Sinlessness*]

Who can ascend the mountain of the Lord?
  or who may stand in His holy place?
He whose hands are sinless, whose heart is
  clean.

COMMUNION   Ps. 77, 24-25   [Bread of Angels]

He gave them the bread of heaven;
   man ate the bread of angels.

June 22 — ST. PAULINUS, Bishop, Confessor

INTROIT   Ps. 131, 9-10. 1   [Garments of Justice]

May Your priests, O Lord, be clothed with
      justice;
   let Your faithful ones shout merrily for joy.
For the sake of David Your servant,
   reject not the plea of Your anointed.
(Ps.) Remember, O Lord, David
   and all his meekness.
Glory be to the Father, etc.
Repeat: **May Your priests,** etc., *as far as* (Ps.).

GRADUAL   Sir. 44, 16. 20   [Great Priest]

Behold a great priest,
   who in his days pleased God.
There was not found the like to him,
   who kept the law of the Most High.

Alleluia, alleluia.   Ps. 109, 4   [Priest Forever]
You are a priest forever, according to the order
   of Melchisedec. Alleluia.

OFFERTORY   Ps. 88, 21-22   [Anointed Servant]

I have found David, My servant;
   with My holy oil I have anointed him,
That My hand may be always with him,
   and that My arm may make him strong.

COMMUNION   Luke 12, 42   [Reward]

The faithful and prudent servant
  whom the Master will set over His household
  to give them their ration of grain in due time.

June 23 — VIGIL OF THE BIRTH OF ST. JOHN THE BAPTIST

INTROIT   Luke 1, 13. 15. 14; Ps. 20, 2   [Son Named John]

Do not be afraid, Zachary,
  your petition has been heard,
And your wife Elizabeth shall bear you a son,
  and you shall call his name John;
And he shall be great before the Lord,
  and shall be filled with the Holy Spirit
  even from his mother's womb;
And many will rejoice at his birth.
(Ps.) O Lord, in Your strength the king is glad;
  in Your salvation how greatly he rejoices!
Glory be to the Father, etc.
Repeat: Do not be afraid, etc., *as far as* (Ps.).

GRADUAL   John 1, 6-7   [Witness]

There was a man, one sent from God,
  whose name was John.
This man came to bear witness concerning the
  light,
  to prepare for the Lord a perfect people.

OFFERTORY   Ps. 8, 6-7   [Crowned]

You crowned him with glory and honor.
You have given him rule over the works of
  Your hands, O Lord.

COMMUNION   Ps. 20, 6   [Splendor]

Great is his glory in Your salvation;
   majesty and splendor You conferred upon
   him, O Lord.

June 24 — THE BIRTH OF
ST. JOHN THE BAPTIST

INTROIT   Isa. 49, 1. 2; Ps. 91, 2   [A Sword]

From my mother's womb the Lord called me
   by my name,
   and made my mouth a sharp-edged sword;
He concealed me in the shadow of His hand,
   and made me a chosen arrow.

(Ps.) It is good to give thanks to the Lord,
   to sing praise to Your Name, Most High.

Glory be to the Father, etc.

Repeat: **From,** etc., *as far as* (Ps.).

GRADUAL   Jer. 1, 5. 9   [Dedicated]

Before I formed you in the womb, I knew you,
   and before you were born, I dedicated you.
The Lord extended His hand, and touched my
   mouth,
   and said to me.

Alleluia, alleluia. Luke 1, 76   [Prophet]

You, child, shall be called the prophet of the
   Most High;
   you shall go before the Lord to prepare His
   ways. Alleluia.

OFFERTORY   Ps. 91, 13   [*The Just Flourishes*]

The just man shall flourish like the palm tree;
   like a cedar of Lebanon shall he grow.

COMMUNION   Luke 1, 76   [*Prepare His Ways*]

You, child, shall be called the prophet of the
   Most High;
      for you shall go before the face of the Lord
      to prepare His ways.

June 25 — ST. WILLIAM, Abbot

Mass: Of a Holy Abbot, p. 253.

June 26 — STS. JOHN AND PAUL, Martyrs

INTROIT   Ps. 33, 20-21. 2   [*Protection of the Lord*]

Many are the troubles of the just;
   but out of them all the Lord delivers them;
The Lord watches over all their bones;
   not one of them shall be broken.
(Ps.) I will bless the Lord at all times;
   His praise shall be ever in my mouth.
Glory be to the Father, etc.
Repeat: **Many are,** etc., *as far as* (Ps.).

GRADUAL   Ps. 132, 1-2   [*Dwelling in Unity*]

Behold, how good it is and how pleasant,
   where brethren dwell at one!
It is as when the precious ointment upon the
   head
      runs down over the beard, the beard of
      Aaron.

Alleluia, alleluia.   [*Brotherhood*]

This is the true brotherhood,
  which overcame the wickedness of the world;
It followed Christ,
  attaining the glorious kingdom of heaven.
    Alleluia.

OFFERTORY   Ps. 5, 12-13   [*Shield of Good Will*]

All who love Your Name shall glory in You,
  for You, O Lord, bless the just man;
O Lord, you surround us with the shield of
  Your good will.

COMMUNION   Wis. 3, 4, 5. 6   [*Gold*]

For if before men they were punished,
  God tried them;
As gold in the furnace He proved them,
  and as sacrificial offerings He took them to
    Himself.

June 28 — VIGIL OF STS. PETER AND PAUL
Apostles

INTROIT   John 21, 18-19; Ps. 18, 1   [*Led to Sacrifice*]

The Lord said to Peter,
  "When you were young you girded yourself
  and walked where you would.
But when you are old you will stretch forth
    your hands,
  and another will gird you,
  and lead you where you would not."
Now this He said to signify
  by what manner of death he should glorify
    God.

(Ps.) **The heavens declare the glory of God,
and the firmament proclaims His handiwork.**

Glory be to the Father, etc.

Repeat: **The Lord said,** etc., *as far as* (Ps.).

GRADUAL   Ps. 18, 5. 2   [*Voice of Apostles*]

**Through all the earth their voice resounds,
and to the ends of the world, their message.
The heavens declare the glory of God,
and the firmament proclaims His handiwork.**

OFFERTORY   Ps. 138, 17   [*Honored Friends of God*]

**To me, Your friends, O God, are made exceedingly honorable;
their principality is exceedingly strengthened.**

COMMUNION   John 21, 15. 17   [*Greatest Love*]

**Simon, son of John,
do you love Me more than these do?
Lord, You know all things;
You know, Lord, that I love You.**

June 29 — STS. PETER AND PAUL, Apostles

INTROIT   Acts 12, 11; Ps. 138, 1-2   [*Rescue*]

**Now I know for certain
that the Lord has sent His angel
And rescued me from the power of Herod
and from all that the Jewish people were
expecting.**

(Ps.) **O Lord, You have probed me and You
know me;
You know when I sit and when I stand.**

Glory be to the Father, etc.

Repeat: **Now I know,** etc., *as far as (Ps.).*

GRADUAL   Ps. 44, 17-18   [*Princes*]

**You shall make them princes through all the
    land;**
  they shall remember Your Name, O Lord.
The place of Your fathers Your sons shall have;
  therefore shall nations praise You.

Alleluia, alleluia.   Matt. 16, 18   [*Rock*]
You are Peter,
  and upon this rock I will build My Church.
  Alleluia.

OFFERTORY Ps. 44, 17-18 [*Unforgettable Name of God*]

**You shall make them princes through all the
    land;**
  **they shall remember Your Name, O Lord,
    through all generations.**

COMMUNION   Matt. 16, 18   [*Foundation*]

You are Peter,
  and upon this rock I will build My Church.

June 30 — COMMEMORATION OF
ST. PAUL THE APOSTLE

INTROIT   2 Tim. 1, 12; Ps. 138, 1-2   [*Full Confidence*]

I know Whom I have believed,
  and I am certain that He is able
To guard the trust committed to me
  against that day, being a just Judge.
(Ps.) O Lord, You have probed me and You

know me;
You know when I sit and when I stand.
Glory be to the Father, etc.
Repeat: I know, etc., *as far as* (Ps.).

GRADUAL Gal. 2, 8-9; 1 Cor. 15, 10 [*God's Grace in Paul*]

He Who worked in Peter for the apostleship,
　worked also in Me among the Gentiles,
And they recognized the grace of God,
　that was given to me.
The grace of God in me has not been fruitless;
　but His grace always remains in me.
Alleluia, alleluia.　　　　　　　　[*Pray for Us*]
Holy Apostle Paul,
　preacher of truth and teacher of the Gentiles,
　intercede for us. Alleluia.

OFFERTORY Ps. 138, 17 　 [*Honor of God's Friends*]

To me, Your friends, O God, are made exceed-
　ingly honorable;
　their principality is exceedingly strengthened.

COMMUNION Matt. 19, 28. 29 　　　　 [*Reward*]

Amen I say to you
　that you who have left all things and fol-
　　lowed Me,
Shall receive a hundredfold,
　and shall possess life everlasting.

July 1 — FEAST OF THE PRECIOUS BLOOD

INTROIT Apoc. 5, 9-10; Ps. 88, 2 　　　　[*Redemption*]

You have redeemed us, O Lord, with Your
　Blood,

out of every tribe and tongue and people
  and nation,
and have made us for our God a kingdom.

(Ps.) The favors of the Lord I will sing forever;
  through all generations my mouth shall proclaim Your faithfulness.

Glory be to the Father, etc.

Repeat: **You have redeemed**, etc., *as far as* (Ps.).

GRADUAL   1 John 5, 6. 7-8   [Witness]

This is He Who came in water and in blood,
  Jesus Christ;
Not in the water only,
  but in the water and in the blood.
There are three that bear witness in heaven:
  the Father, the Word, and the Holy Spirit;
  and these three are one.
And there are three that bear witness on earth:
  the Spirit, the water, and the blood;
  and these three are one.

Alleluia, alleluia. 1 John 5, 9   [Testimony of God]
If we receive the testimony of men,
  the testimony of God is greater. Alleluia.

OFFERTORY   1 Cor. 10, 16   [Cup of Salvation]

The cup of blessing that we bless,
  is it not the sharing of the Blood of Christ?
And the bread that we break,
  is it not the partaking of the Body of the
  Lord?

COMMUNION   Heb. 9, 28   [*The Redeemed*]

Christ was offered once
  to take away the sins of many;
The second time He will appear
  with no part in sin
  to those who wait for Him unto salvation.

July 2 — VISITATION OF THE B. V. M.

INTROIT   Ps. 44, 2   [*Mother of the Redeemer*]

Hail, holy Mother, who gave birth to the King
  Who rules heaven and earth forever and ever.
(Ps.) My heart overflows with a goodly theme;
  as I sing my ode to the King.
Glory be to the Father, etc.
Repeat: **Hail, holy Mother,** etc., *as far as* (Ps.).

GRADUAL   [*Maiden and Mother*]

Blessed and venerable are you,
  O Virgin Mary,
For without stain to your virginity,
  you became the Mother of the Savior.
O Virgin, Mother of God,
  He Whom the whole world cannot contain,
Being made man,
  shut Himself up within your womb.

Alleluia, alleluia.   [*Sun of Justice*]
Happy are you, O holy Virgin Mary,
  and most worthy of all praise;
For out of you has risen the sun of justice,
  Christ our God. Alleluia.

OFFERTORY   [*Creator's Mother*]

Blessed are you, O Virgin Mary
  who bore the Creator of all things;
you brought forth Him Who made you,
  and you remain forever a virgin.

COMMUNION   [*Blessed Womb*]

Blessed is the womb of the Virgin Mary,
  which bore the Son of the eternal Father.

July 3 — ST. IRENAEUS, Bishop, Martyr

INTROIT   Mal. 2, 6; Ps. 77, 1   [*Teaching from God*]

The law of truth was in his mouth,
  and iniquity was not found on his lips.
He walked with Me in peace, and in equity,
  and turned many away from evil.
(Ps.) Hearken, My people, to My law;
  incline your ears to the words of My mouth.
Glory be to the Father, etc.
Repeat: The law of truth, etc., *as far as* (Ps.).

GRADUAL   Ps. 121, 8; Ps. 36, 37   [*Men of Peace*]

Because of my relatives and friends
  I will say, "Peace be within you!"
Keep innocence, and behold equity;
  for there is a future for the man of peace.

Alleluia, alleluia.   Sir. 6, 35   [*Learning Wisdom*]

Stand in the multitude of the prudent priests
  and from your heart join yourself to their
    wisdom
That you may hear every discourse of God.
  Alleluia.

OFFERTORY   Sir. 24, 44   [*Spread of the Truth*]

I send My teachings forth to all shining like
the dawn,
  and I will make them known afar off.

COMMUNION   Sir. 24, 47   [*Laboring for Truth*]

See that I have not labored for myself only,
  but for all who seek the truth.

July 5 — ST. ANTHONY MARY ZACCARIA
Confessor

INTROIT   1 Cor. 2, 4; Ps. 110, 1   [*Power in the Spirit*]

My speech and my preaching
  were not in the persuasive words of human
    wisdom,
But in the demonstration of the Spirit
  and of the power.
(Ps.) I will give thanks to You, O Lord, with
    all my heart
  in the company and assembly of the just.
Glory be to the Father, etc.
Repeat: My speech, etc., *as far as* (Ps.).

GRADUAL   Phil. 1, 8-9. 10   [*Apostolic Charity*]

God is my witness how I long for you all
  in the heart of Christ Jesus.
And this I pray,
  that your charity may more and more abound
  in knowledge and all discernment.
That you may approve the better things,

that you may be upright and without offense
unto the day of Christ.

Alleluia, alleluia. Phil. 1, 11   [*Fruits of Justice*]
Filled with the fruit of justice,
   through Jesus Christ,
   to the glory and praise of God. Alleluia.

OFFERTORY Ps. 137, 1-2 [*Giving Praise and Thanks*]

In the presence of the angels I will sing Your
   praise;
I will worship at Your holy temple
   and give thanks to Your Name.

COMMUNION   Phil. 3, 17   [*Pattern*]

Brethren, be imitators of me,
   and mark those who walk after the pattern
   you have in us.

July 7 — STS. CYRIL AND METHODIUS
Bishops, Confessors

INTROIT Ps. 131, 9-10. 1   [*Priestly Justice*]

May Your priests, O Lord, be clothed with
   justice;
   let Your faithful ones shout merrily for joy.
For the sake of David, Your servant,
   reject not the plea of Your anointed.
(Ps.) Remember, O Lord, David
   and all his meekness.
Glory be to the Father, etc.
Repeat: **May Your priests,** etc., *as far as* (Ps.).

GRADUAL   Ps. 131, 16-17   [*A Saving Priesthood*]

Her priests I will clothe with salvation,
  and her faithful ones shall shout merrily for
  joy.
In her will I make a horn to sprout forth for
  David;
  I will place a lamp for My anointed.

Alleluia, alleluia.   Ps. 109, 4   [*Priest Forever*]
The Lord has sworn, and He will not repent:
  "You are a priest forever, according to the
  order of Melchisedec." Alleluia.

OFFERTORY   Ps. 67, 36 [*God's Power in His Saints*]

God is wonderful in His saints;
  the God of Israel gives power and strength
  to His people.
Blessed be God!

COMMUNION   Matt. 10, 27   [*Preach Openly*]

"What I tell you in darkness, speak it in the
  light,"
  says the Lord,
"And what you hear whispered,
  preach it on the housetops."

July 8 — ST. ELIZABETH, Queen, Widow

Mass: Of a Holy Woman not a Martyr, p. 264.

July 10—SEVEN HOLY BROTHERS. Martyrs and STS. RUFINA and SECUNDA, Virgins, Martyrs

INTROIT   Ps. 112, 1. 9. 2   [*Praise from Children*]

Praise the Lord. you children,
  praise the Name of the Lord.
He established in her home the barren wife
  as the joyful mother of children.
(Ps.) **Blessed be the Name of the Lord**
  both now and forever.
Glory be to the Father, etc.
Repeat: **Praise the Lord,** etc., *as far as* (Ps.).

GRADUAL   Ps. 123, 7-8   [*Release*]

We were rescued like a bird
  from the fowlers' snare.
Broken was the snare,
  and we were freed.
Our help is in the name of the Lord,
  Who made heaven and earth.

Alleluia, alleluia.   [*True Brotherhood*]
This is the true brotherhood,
  which overcame the wickedness of the world;
It followed Christ,
  attaining the glorious kingdom of heaven.
    Alleluia.

OFFERTORY   Ps. 123, 7   [*Freedom*]

We were rescued like a bird
  from the fowlers' snare;
Broken was the snare,
  and we were freed.

COMMUNION   Matt. 12, 50   [*Christ's Will*]

"Whoever does the will of My Father in heaven,
  he is my brother and sister and mother,"
  says the Lord.

July 11 — ST. PIUS I, Pope, Martyr

Mass: Of One or More Popes, p. 231.

July 12 — ST. JOHN GUALBERT, Abbot

Mass: Of a Holy Abbot, p. 253.

JULY 14 — ST. BONAVENTURE
Bishop, Confessor and Doctor of the Church

INTROIT   Sir. 15, 5; Ps. 91, 2   [*Wisdom*]

In the midst of the assembly He opened his
    mouth;
And the Lord filled him with the spirit of wis-
    dom and understanding;
  He clothed him with a robe of glory.
(Ps.) It is good to give thanks to the Lord,
  to sing praise to Your Name, Most High.
Glory be to the Father, etc.
Repeat: In the midst, etc., *as far as* (Ps.).

GRADUAL   Ps. 36, 30-31   [*Law of God*]

The mouth of the just man tells of wisdom,
  and his tongue utters what is right.
The law of his God is in his heart,
  and his steps do not falter.

Alleluia, alleluia. Ps. 109, 4 [*A Priest Forever*]

The Lord has sworn, and He will not repent:
   "You are a priest forever, according to the order of Melchisedec." Alleluia.

OFFERTORY Ps. 88, 25 [*Exaltation*]

My faithfulness and My kindness shall be with him,
   and through My Name shall his horn be exalted.

COMMUNION Luke 12, 42 [*Faithful Servant*]

The faithful and prudent servant
   whom the Master will set over His household
   to give them their ration of grain in due time.

July 15 — ST. HENRY, Emperor, Confessor

Mass: Of a Confessor not a Bishop, p. 250.

July 16 — OUR LADY OF MOUNT CARMEL

INTROIT Ps. 44, 2 [*Rejoice*]

Let us all rejoice in the Lord,
   celebrating a feast in honor of the Blessed Virgin Mary,
For whose solemnity the angels rejoice
   and join in praising the Son of God.
(Ps.) My heart overflows with a goodly theme;
   as I sing my ode to the King.
Glory be to the Father, etc.
Repeat: **Let us all rejoice,** etc., *as far as* (Ps.).

GRADUAL   [*Virgin Mother*]

Blessed and venerable are you,
  O Virgin Mary;
For without stain to your virginity
  you became the Mother of the Savior.
O Virgin Mother of God,
  He Whom the whole world cannot contain,
Being made man,
  shut Himself up within your womb.

Alleluia, alleluia.   [*New Life*]
Mother of God, the life that had been lost
  was given us through you,
Who received your offspring from heaven,
  and brought forth a Savior into the world.
    Alleluia.

OFFERTORY   Jer. 18, 20   [*Speak for Us*]

Be mindful, O Virgin Mother,
  to speak good things for us in the sight of
    the Lord,
  so that He may turn away His anger from us.

COMMUNION   [*Queen of All*]

Most worthy Queen of the world,
  Mary ever Virgin,
You brought forth Christ the Lord,
  the Savior of all men.
Intercede for our peace and salvation.

July 17 — ST. ALEXIUS, Confessor

Mass: Of a Confessor not a Bishop, p. 250.

July 18—ST. CAMILLUS OF LELLIS, Confessor

INTROIT   John 15, 13; Ps. 40, 2   [*Supreme Love*]

Greater love than this no one has,
  that one lay down his life for his friends.
(Ps.) Happy is he who has regard for the lowly
      and the poor;
  in the day of misfortune the Lord will deliver
  him.
Glory be to the Father, etc.
Repeat: Greater love, etc., *as far as* (Ps.).

GRADUAL   Ps. 36, 30-31   [*True Wisdom*]

The mouth of the just man tells of wisdom,
  and his tongue utters what is right.
The law of his God is in his heart,
  and his steps do not falter.

Alleluia, alleluia.   Ps. 111, 1   [*Law of Love*]
Happy the man who fears the Lord,
  who greatly delights in His commands.
      Alleluia.

OFFERTORY   Ps. 20, 2-3   [*Reward from God*]

O Lord, in Your strength the just man is glad;
  in Your victory how greatly he rejoices;
You have granted him his heart's desire.

COMMUNION   Matt. 25, 36. 40   [*Done for Christ*]

I was sick and you visited Me.
Amen, amen, I say to you,
  as long as you did it for one of these the
  least of My brethren,
  you did it for Me.

July 19 — ST. VINCENT DE PAUL, Confessor

Mass: Of a Confessor not a Bishop, p. 251.

July 20 —ST. JEROME EMILIAN, Confessor

INTROIT   Lam. 2, 11; Ps. 112, 1   [*Love for Children*]

My gall is poured out on the ground
    because of the downfall of the daughter of
      my people,
As child and infant faint away
   in the open spaces of town.
(Ps.) Praise the Lord, you servants,
    praise the Name of the Lord.
Glory be to the Father, etc.
Repeat: **My gall is poured,** etc., *as far as* (Ps.).

GRADUAL   Prov. 5, 16; Ps. 111, 5-6   [*The Generous Man*]

Let your water sources be dispersed abroad,
    and in the streets divide your waters.
Well for the man who is gracious and lends,
    who conducts his affairs with justice;
He shall never be moved.

Alleluia, alleluia. Ps. 111, 9   [*The Giver*]
Lavishly he gives to the poor;
    his generosity shall endure forever. Alleluia.

OFFERTORY   Tob. 12, 12   [*Prayer of the Generous*]

When you prayed with tears,
    and buried the dead,
And left your dinner,
    and hid the dead by day in your house,

And buried them by night,
  I offered your prayer to the Lord.

COMMUNION   James 1, 27   [*True Religion*]

Religion pure and undefiled
  before God the Father, is this:
To give aid to orphans and widows in their
    tribulation,
  and to keep oneself unspotted from this
    world.

July 21 — ST. LAWRENCE OF BRINDISI
Confessor and Doctor of the Church

Mass: Of a Doctor, p. 248.

July 22 — ST. MARY MAGDALEN, Penitent

INTROIT   Ps. 118, 95-96. 1   [*Fidelity to God*]

Sinners wait to destroy me,
  but I pay heed to Your decrees, O Lord.
I see that all fulfillment has its limits;
  broad indeed is Your command.
(Ps.) Happy are they whose way is blameless,
  who walk in the law of the Lord.
Glory be to the Father, etc.
Repeat: Sinners wait, etc., *as far as* (Ps.).

GRADUAL   Ps. 44, 8   [*Anointed by Love*]

You love justice and hate iniquity.
  Therefore God, your God, has anointed you
  with the oil of gladness.

Alleluia, alleluia.　Ps. 44, 3　　　　[*Grace*]

Grace is poured out upon your lips;
  thus God has blessed you forever. Alleluia.

OFFERTORY　Ps. 44, 10　　　　[*Glory*]

The daughters of kings come in Your honor;
  the queen takes her place at Your right hand
  in gold and colored clothing.

COMMUNION　Ps. 118, 121, 122. 128

[*The Way of the Beloved*]

I have fulfilled just ordinances, O Lord;
  let not the proud oppress me.
For in all Your precepts I go forward;
  every false way I hate.

July 23 — ST. APOLLINARIS, Bishop, Martyr

INTROIT　Dan. 3, 84. 87. 57　　　[*Priestly Praise*]

Priests of the Lord, bless the Lord;
  holy men of humble heart, praise God.

(Ps.) Bless the Lord, all you works of the Lord,
  praise and exalt Him above all forever.

Glory be to the Father, etc.

Repeat: **Priests of the Lord,** etc., *as far as* (Ps.).

GRADUAL　Ps. 88, 21-23　　　　[*Anointed*]

I have found David, My servant;
  with My holy oil I have anointed him,
That My hand may be always with him,
  and that My arm may make him strong.
No enemy shall have an advantage over him,

nor shall the son of iniquity have power to
hurt him.

Alleluia, alleluia.   Ps. 109, 4   [*A Priest Forever*]
The Lord has sworn, and He will not repent:
"You are a priest forever, according to the
order of Melchisedec." Alleluia.

OFFERTORY   Ps. 88, 25   [*Exaltation*]

My faithfulness and My kindness shall be with
him,
and through My Name shall his horn be
exalted.

COMMUNION   ‾Matt. 25, 20. 21   [*Enter into Joy*]

"Master, You delivered to me five talents;
behold, I have gained other five over and
above."
"Well done, good and faithful servant;
because you have been faithful over a few
things,
I will set you over many;
enter into the joy of your Master."

July 24 — ST. CHRISTINA, Virgin, Martyr

Mass: Of a Virgin Martyr, p. 257.

July 25 — ST. JAMES, Apostle

INTROIT   Ps. 138, 17. 1-2   [*Friends of God*]

To me, Your friends, O God, are made exceedingly honorable;
their principality is exceedingly strengthened.

(Ps.) **O Lord, You have probed me and You
know me;**

You know when I sit and when I stand.

Glory be to the Father, etc.

Repeat: **To me, Your** etc., *as far as* (Ps.).

GRADUAL   Ps. 44, 17-18   [*Princes*]

**You shall make them princes through all the
land;**

they shall remember Your Name, O Lord.

**The place of Your fathers Your sons shall have;
therefore shall nations praise You.**

Alleluia, alleluia.,   John 15, 16   [*Bearing Fruit*]

**I have chosen you out of the world,
that you should go and bear fruit,
and that your fruit should remain. Alleluia.**

OFFERTORY   Ps. 18, 5   [*Apostolic Voices*]

**Through all the earth their voice resounds,
and to the ends of the world, their message.**

COMMUNION   Matt. 19, 28   [*Kings*]

**You who have followed Me shall sit on thrones,
judging the twelve tribes of Israel.**

July 26 — ST. ANN
Mother of the Blessed Virgin Mary

INTROIT   Ps. 44, 2   [*Honor to Ann*]

**Let us all rejoice in the Lord,
celebrating a feast in honor of blessed Anne,**

On whose solemnity the angels rejoice
  and give praise to the Son of God.
(Ps.) My heart overflows with a goodly theme;
  as I sing my ode to the King.
Glory be to the Father, etc.
Repeat: Let us all rejoice, etc., *as far as* (Ps.).

GRADUAL   Ps. 44, 8   [Anointed]

You love justice and hate wickedness.
  Therefore God, your God, has anointed you
  with the oil of gladness.

Alleluia, alleluia.   Ps. 44, 3   [Grace]
Grace is poured out upon your lips;
  thus God has blessed you forever. Alleluia.

OFFERTORY   Ps. 44, 10   [Glory]

The daughters of kings come in Your honor;
  the queen takes her place at Your right hand
  in gold and colored clothing.

COMMUNION   Ps. 44, 3   [Blessed Forever]

Grace is poured out upon your lips;
  thus God has blessed you forever and ever.

July 27 — ST. PANTALEON, Martyr

Mass: Of a Martyr not a Bishop, p. 237.

July 28—STS. NAZARIUS and CELSUS, Martyrs
ST. VICTOR I, Pope, Martyr
ST. INNOCENT I, Pope, Confessor

Mass: Of Several Martyrs, p. 238.

July 29 — ST. MARTHA, Virgin

Mass: Of a Virgin Only, p. 259.

July 30 — STS. ABDON and SENNEN, Martyrs

INTROIT   Ps. 78, 11, 12. 10.1   *[Avenge the Saints]*

Let the prisoners' sighing come before You,
    O Lord;
Repay our neighbors sevenfold into their
    bosoms;
    avenge the blood of Your saints which has
    been shed.

(Ps.) O God, the nations have come into Your
    inheritance;
    they have defiled Your holy temple,
    they have made Jerusalem as a place to keep
    fruit.

Glory be to the Father, etc.

Repeat: Let the prisoners', etc., *as far as* (Ps.).

GRADUAL   Ex. 15, 11.6

             [The Glory of God in the Saints]
God is glorious in His saints,
    wonderful in majesty, a worker of wonders.
Your right hand, O Lord, is magnificent in
    power;

Your right hand has shattered the enemy.

Alleluia, alleluia. Wis. 3, 1   [*Peace*]
The souls of the just are in the hand of God,
    and no torment shall touch them. Alleluia.

OFFERTORY   Ps. 67, 36   [*Glory to God*]

God is wonderful in His saints;
    the God of Israel is He Who gives power and
        strength to His people.
    Blessed be God!

COMMUNION   Ps. 78, 2. 11   [*Persecution*]

They have given the corpses of Your servants,
    O Lord,
    as food to the birds of heaven,
    the flesh of Your faithful ones to the beasts
        of the earth.
With Your great power free those doomed to
    death.

July 31 — ST. IGNATIUS LOYOLA, Confessor

INTROIT   Phil. 2, 10-11; Ps. 5, 12-13   [*Name of Jesus*]

At the Name of Jesus every knee should bend
    of those in heaven, on earth and under the
        earth,
And every tongue should confess
    that the Lord Jesus Christ is in the glory of
        God the Father.
(Ps.) All who love Your Name shall glory in
    You,
    for You bless the just man.

Glory be to the Father, etc.

Repeat: **At the Name,** etc., *as far as* (P^c).

GRADUAL   Ps. 91, 13. 14. 3   [*Holy Men Flourish*]

**The just man shall flourish like the palm tree,
  like a cedar of Lebanon shall he grow
  in the house of the Lord.**
**To proclaim Your kindness at dawn
  and Your faithfulness throughout the night.**

Alleluia, alleluia.   James 1, 12   [*Crown of Glory*]

**Blessed is the man who endures temptation;
  for when he has been tried,
  he will receive the crown of life. Alleluia.**

OFFERTORY   Ps. 88, 25   [*Exaltation*]

**My faithfulness and My kindness shall be with
  him,
  and through My Name shall his horn be
  exalted.**

COMMUNION   Luke 12, 49   [*Casting Fire*]

**I have come to cast fire upon the earth,
  and what will I but that it be kindled?**

Aug. 1 — THE HOLY MACHABEES, Martyrs

INTROIT   Ps. 33, 18. 2   [*Cry of the Just*]

**The just cry out and the Lord hears them,
  and from all their distress He rescues them.**
**(Ps.) I will bless the Lord at all times;
  His praise shall be ever in my mouth.**
Glory be to the Father, etc.

Repeat: **The just cry,** etc., *as far as* (Ps.).

GRADUAL   Ps. 132, 1-2   [Brotherhood]

Behold, how good it is, and how pleasant,
  where brethren dwell at one!
It is as when the precious ointment upon the
    head
    runs down over the beard, the beard of
      Aaron.

Alleluia, alleluia.   [Attaining the Kingdom]
This is the true brotherhood
  which overcame the wickedness of the world;
It followed Christ,
  attaining the glorious kingdom of heaven.
    Alleluia.

OFFERTORY   Ps. 149, 5-6   [Exult]

Let the faithful exult in glory;
  let them sing for joy upon their couches;
  let the high praises of God be in their throats.
    Alleluia.

COMMUNION   Luke 12, 4   [Be Unafraid]

But I say to you, My friends:
  Do not be afraid of those who persecute you.

Aug. 2 — ST. ALPHONSUS MARY LIGUORI
Bishop, Confessor and Doctor of the Church

INTROIT   Luke 4, 18; Ps. 77, 1   [Spirit of the Lord]

The Spirit of the Lord is upon me,
  because He has anointed me;
To bring good news to the poor, He has sent
    me,
    to heal the contrite of heart.

(Ps.) **Hearken, My people, to My teachings;**
   incline your ears to the words of My mouth.

Glory be to the Father, etc.

Repeat: **The Spirit,** etc., *as far as* (Ps.).

GRADUAL   Ps. 118, 52-53; Ps. 39, 11   [*God's Law*]

I remember Your ordinances of old, O Lord,
   and I am comforted.

Indignation seizes me because of the wicked
   who forsake Your law.

Your justice I kept not hid within my heart;
   Your faithfulness and Your salvation I have
      spoken of.

Alleluia, alleluia.   Sir. 49, 3-4   [*Virtue*]

He was directed by God to the repentance of
   the nation,
   and he took away the abominations of
      wickedness,

He turned to God with his whole heart,
   and though times were evil, he practiced
      virtue. Alleluia.

OFFERTORY   Prov. 3, 9. 27   [*Do Good*]

Honor the Lord with your wealth,
   and give Him the first fruits of all your
      produce.

Do not withhold him from doing good who is
   able:
   if you are able, do good yourself also.

COMMUNION   Sir. 50, 1.9   [*Like a Bright Fire*]

A great priest,
   who in his time renovated the house,

And in his days reinforced the temple,
  as a bright fire,
    and frankincense burning in the fire.

Aug. 4 — ST. DOMINIC, Confessor

INTROIT   Ps. 36, 30-31. 1   [*Wisdom*]

The mouth of the just man tells of wisdom,
  and his tongue utters what is right.
The law of his God is in his heart.
(Ps.) Be not vexed over evildoers,
  nor jealous of those who do wrong.
Glory be to the Father, etc.
Repeat: The mouth, etc., *as far as* (Ps.).

GRADUAL   Ps. 91, 13. 14. 3   [*The Just Man Flourishes*]

The just man shall flourish like the palm tree,
  like a cedar of Lebanon shall he grow
    in the house of the Lord.
To proclaim Your kindness at dawn
  and Your faithfulness throughout the night.

Alleluia, alleluia.   Osee, 14, 6   [*Beauty*]
The just man shall blossom like the lily,
  and flourish forever before the Lord. Alleluia.

OFFERTORY   Ps. 88, 25   [*Exaltation*]

My faithfulness and My kindness shall be with
  him,
    and through My Name shall his horn be
    exalted.

COMMUNION   Luke 12, 42   [*Faithful and Prudent*]

The faithful and prudent servant
  whom the Master will set over his household
  to give them their ration of grain in due time.

Aug. 5 — DEDICATION OF THE CHURCH OF OUR LADY OF THE SNOWS

Mass: Of the Blessed Virgin Mary, p. 268.

Aug. 6 — TRANSFIGURATION OF OUR LORD

INTROIT   Ps. 76, 19; 83, 2-3   [*Light*]

Your lightning illumined the world;
  the earth quivered and quaked.

(Ps.) How lovely is Your dwelling place,
  O Lord of Hosts!
My soul yearns and pines
  for the courts of the Lord.

Glory be to the Father, etc.

Repeat: **Your lightning,** etc., *as far as* (Ps.).

GRADUAL   Ps. 44, 3. 2   [*Full of Beauty*]

Fairer in beauty are You than the sons of men;
  grace is poured out upon Your lips.
My heart overflows with a goodly theme;
  as I sing my ode to the King.

Alleluia, alleluia.   Wis. 7, 26   [*Spotless Image*]
He is the refulgence of eternal light,
  the spotless mirror,
  and the image of His goodness. Alleluia.

OFFERTORY   Ps. 111, 3   [*Spiritual Wealth*]

Glory and wealth are in His house;
His generosity shall endure forever. Alleluia.

COMMUNION   Matt. 17, 9   [*Prevue*]

Tell the vision you have seen to no one,
till the Son of Man has risen from the dead.

Aug. 7 — ST. CAJETAN, Confessor

Mass: Of a Confessor not a Bishop, p. 250.

Aug. 8 — ST. JOHN MARY VIANNEY, Confessor

Mass: Of a Confessor not a Bishop, p. 250.

Aug. 9 — VIGIL OF ST. LAWRENCE, Martyr

INTROIT   Ps. 111, 9. 1   [*Exalted in Glory*]

Lavishly he gives to the poor;
his generosity shall endure forever;
his horn shall be exalted in glory.
(Ps.) Happy the man who fears the Lord,
who greatly delights in His commands.
Glory be to the Father, etc.
Repeat: **Lavishly he gives,** etc., *as far as* (Ps.).

GRADUAL   Ps. 111, 9. 2   [*Unforgotten*]

Lavishly he gives to the poor;
his generosity shall endure forever.
His posterity shall be mighty upon the earth;
the upright generation shall be blessed.

OFFERTORY   <small>Job 16, 20</small>   [*God, My Judge*]

My prayer is pure, and therefore I ask
    that a place may be given to my voice in
      heaven;
For there is my judge,
    and He Who knows my conscience is on
      high.
Let my prayer ascend to the Lord.

COMMUNION   <small>Matt. 16, 24</small>   [*Denial of Self*]

He who wishes to come after Me,
    let him deny himself,
    and take up his cross, and follow Me.

Aug. 10 — ST. LAWRENCE, Martyr

INTROIT   <small>Ps. 95, 6. 1</small>   [*Exaltation*]

Splendor and majesty go before Him;
    praise and grandeur are in His sanctuary.
(Ps.) Sing to the Lord a new song;
    sing to the Lord, all you lands.
Glory be to the Father, etc.
Repeat: **Splendor,** etc., *as far as* (Ps.).

GRADUAL   <small>Ps. 16, 3</small>   [*Ever Faithful*]

Though You test my heart, O Lord, searching
    it in the night.
    Though You try me with fire, You shall find
      no malice in me.

Alleluia, alleluia.   [*Miracles*]
The Levite Lawrence performed a good work.
    By the sign of the Cross, he gave sight to
      the blind. Alleluia.

OFFERTORY   Ps. 95, 6   [*Grandeur*]

**Splendor and majesty go before Him:
praise and grandeur are in His sanctuary.**

COMMUNION   John 12, 26   [*Faithful Follower*]

**If anyone serve Me,
let him follow Me;
And where I am
there also shall My servant be.**

Aug. 11 — STS. TIBURTIUS and SUSANNA
Virgin, Martyrs

Mass: Of Several Martyrs, p. 241.

Aug. 12 — ST. CLARE, Virgin

Mass: Of a Virgin Only, p. 259.

Aug. 13 — STS. HIPPOLYTUS and CASSIAN
Martyrs

Mass: Of Several Martyrs, p. 241.

Aug. 14 — VIGIL OF THE ASSUMPTION OF THE BLESSED VIRGIN MARY

INTROIT   Ps. 44, 13. 15-16. 2 [*Solemn Entry into Glory*]

**All the rich among the people seek Your favor.
Behind her the virgins of her train are brought
to the King.
Her neighbors are brought to You with gladness and joy.**

(Ps.) My heart overflows with a goodly theme;
   as I sing my ode to the King.

Glory be to the Father, etc.

Repeat: **All the rich,** etc., *as far as* (Ps.).

GRADUAL   [*Virgin and Mother*]

Blessed and venerable are you,
   O Virgin Mary;
For without stain to your virginity
   you became the Mother of the Savior.
O Virgin Mother of God,
   He Whom the whole world cannot contain,
Being made man,
   shut Himself up within your womb.

OFFERTORY   [*Creator's Mother*]

Blessed are you, O Virgin Mary,
   you who bore the Creator of all things;
You brought forth Him Who made you,
   and you remain forever a Virgin.

COMMUNION   [*Blessed Womb*]

Blessed is the womb of the Virgin Mary,
   which bore the Son of the eternal Father.

Aug. 15 — FEAST OF THE ASSUMPTION OF THE BLESSED VIRGIN MARY

INTROIT   Apoc. 12, 1; Ps. 97, 1   [*The Sign in Heaven*]

A great sign appeared in heaven:
   a woman clothed with the sun,
And the moon was under her feet,
   and upon her head a crown of twelve stars.

(Ps.) **Sing to the Lord a new song,**
   for He has done wondrous deeds.
Glory be to the Father, etc.
Repeat: **A great sign,** etc., *as far as* (Ps.).

GRADUAL   Ps. 44, 11-12. 14   [*Her Beauty*]

Hear, O daughter, and see; turn your ear;
   for the King shall desire your beauty.
All glorious is the King's daughter as she enters;
   her raiment is threaded with spun gold.

Alleluia, alleluia.   [*Rejoice*]
Mary has been taken up into heaven;
   the choirs of the angels rejoice. Alleluia.

OFFERTORY   Gen. 3, 15   [*Protectress*]

I will put enmity between you and the Woman,
   between your seed and her seed.

COMMUNION   Luke 1, 48-49   [*Great Things*]

All generations shall call me blessed;
Because He Who is mighty has done great
   things for me.

Aug. 16 — ST. JOACHIM, Father of the Blessed Virgin Mary, Confessor

INTROIT   Ps. 111, 9. 1   [*Total Giving*]

Lavishly he gives to the poor;
   his generosity shall endure forever;
   his horn shall be exalted in glory.
(Ps.) **Happy the man who fears the Lord,**
   who greatly delights in His commands.

Glory be to the Father, etc.

Repeat: **Lavishly,** etc., *as far as* (Ps.).

GRADUAL   Ps. 111, 9. 2   [*Unforgotten*]

Lavishly he gives to the poor;
  his generosity shall endure forever.
His posterity shall be mighty upon the earth;
  the upright generation shall be blessed.

Alleluia, alleluia.   [*Help to Save Us*]

O Joachim, husband of St. Anne,
  father of the kind Virgin,
  help your servants to save their souls,
  Alleluia.

OFFERTORY   Ps. 8, 6-7   [*Crowned*]

You crowned him with glory and honor.
You have given him rule over the works of
  Your hand, O Lord.

COMMUNION   Luke 12, 42   [*Faithful Servant*]

The faithful and prudent servant
  whom the Master will set over His household
  to give them their ration of grain in due time.

Aug. 17 — ST. HYACINTH, Confessor

Mass: Of a Confessor not a Bishop, p. 250.

Aug. 18 — ST. AGAPITUS, Martyr

Mass: Of a Martyr not a Bishop, p. 237.

Aug. 19 — ST. JOHN EUDES, Confessor

Mass: Of a Confessor not a Bishop, p. 250.

Aug. 20 — ST. BERNARD
Abbot and Doctor of the Church

Mass: Of a Doctor, p. 248.

Aug. 21 — ST. JANE FRANCES DE CHANTAL
Widow

Mass: Of a Holy Woman not a Martyr, p. 264.

Aug. 22 — FEAST OF THE IMMACULATE HEART OF MARY

This Mass may be said on First Saturday of the month.

INTROIT Heb. 4, 16; Ps. 44, 2   [*Throne of Grace*]

**Let us draw near with confidence
  to the throne of grace,
That we may obtain mercy
  and find grace to help in time of need. (P.T.
    Alleluia, alleluia.)**

**(Ps.) My heart overflows with a goodly theme;
  as I sing my ode to the King.**

Glory be to the Father, etc.

Repeat: **Let us draw,** etc., *as far as* (Ps.).

GRADUAL Ps. 12, 6; 44, 18
                [*All Generations Shall Remember*]

**Let my heart rejoice in Your salvation;
  let me sing to the Lord, "He has been good
    to me."
Yes, I will sing to the Name of the Lord, Most
  High.
They shall remember Your Name throughout
  all generations;**

therefore shall nations praise You forever and ever.

Alleluia, alleluia. Luke 1, 46-47   [Rejoice in God]

My soul magnifies the Lord,
  and my spirit rejoices in God my Savior. Alleluia.

In Votive Masses after Septuagesima, the Alleluia and versicle are omitted and the following Tract is said:

TRACT   Prov. 8, 32, 35   [Life in God's Law]

So now, O children, listen to me.
  Happy those who keep my ways.
Hear instruction, and be wise,
  and do not reject it.
Happy the man who hears me,
  watching daily at my gates,
  waiting at my doorposts.
For he who finds me finds life,
  and wins favor from the Lord.

During Paschaltime, the Gradual is omitted and the following Alleluia is said:

Alleluia, alleluia. Luke 1, 46-48   [Magnificat]

My soul magnifies the Lord,
  and my spirit rejoices in God my Savior.
Alleluia. All generations shall call me blessed,
  because God has regarded His humble handmaid. Alleluia.

OFFERTORY   Luke 1, 47. 49   [Great Things]

My spirit rejoices in God my Savior;
Because He Who is mighty has done great things for me,
  and holy is His Name. (P.T. Alleluia.)

COMMUNION   John 19, 26-27   [*True Mother*]

Jesus said to His Mother,
  "Woman, behold your Son."
Then He said to the disciple,
  "Behold your mother."
And from that hour
  the disciple took her into his home. (P.T.
    Alleluia, alleluia.)

Aug. 23 — ST. PHILIP BENIZI, Confessor

Mass: Of a Confessor not a Bishop, p. 251.

Aug. 24 — ST. BARTHOLOMEW, Apostle

INTROIT   Ps. 138, 17. 1-2   [*God's Friends*]

To me, Your friends, O God, are made exceed-
    ingly honorable;
  their principality is exceedingly strengthened.
(Ps.) O Lord, You have probed me and You
    know me;
  You know when I sit and when I stand.
Glory be to the Father, etc.
Repeat: To me, etc., *as far as* (Ps.).

GRADUAL   Ps. 44, 17-18   [*Princes*]

You shall make them princes through all the
    land;
  they shall remember Your Name, O Lord.
The place of Your fathers Your sons shall have;
  therefore shall nations praise You.

Alleluia, alleluia.　　　　　　[*Apostolic Choir*]
The glorious choir of Apostles praises You,
　O Lord. Alleluia.

OFFERTORY　Ps. 138, 17　[*Honor of God's Friends*]

To me, Your friends, O God, are made exceed-
　ingly honorable,
　their principality is exceedingly strengthened.

COMMUNION　Matt. 19, 28　　　[*Thrones*]

"You who have followed Me shall sit on thrones
　judging the twelve tribes of Israel," says the
　O Lord. Alleluia.

Aug. 25 — ST. LOUIS, King, Confessor

Mass: Of a Confessor not a Bishop, p. 250.

Aug. 26 — ST. ZEPHYRINUS, Pope, Martyr

Mass: Of One or More Popes, p. 231.

Aug. 27 — ST. JOSEPH CALASANCTIUS
Confessor

INTROIT　Ps. 33, 12. 2　　　[*The True Teacher*]

Come, children, hear me;
　I will teach you the fear of the Lord.
(Ps.) I will bless the Lord at all times;
　His praise shall be ever in my mouth.
Glory be to the Father, etc.
Repeat: **Come, children,** etc., *as far as* (Ps.).

GRADUAL   Ps. 36, 30-31   [*Wisdom and Truth*]

The mouth of the just man tells of wisdom,
  and his tongue utters what is right.
The law of his God is in his heart,
  and his steps do not falter.

Alleluia, alleluia.   James 1, 12   [*Crown of Life*]
Blessed is the man who endures temptation;
  for when he has been tried,
  he will receive the crown of life. Alleluia.

OFFERTORY   Ps. 9, 17   [*Prayers of Affliction*]

The desire of the afflicted the Lord hears.
  You pay heed to the strengthening of their
  hearts.

COMMUNION   Mark 10, 14   [*Call for Children*]

Let the little children come to Me,
  and do not hinder them,
  for of such is the kingdom of God.

Aug. 28 — ST. AUGUSTINE
Bishop, Confessor and Doctor of the Church

INTROIT   Sir. 15, 5; Ps. 91, 2   [*Wisdom*]

In the midst of the assembly He opened his
  mouth;
and the Lord filled him with the spirit of wis-
  dom and understanding;
  He clothed him with a robe of glory.
(Ps.) It is good to give thanks to the Lord,
  to sing praise to Your Name, Most High.
Glory be to the Father, etc.
Repeat: **In the midst,** etc., *as far as* (Ps.).

GRADUAL Ps. 36, 30-31 [*Law of God*]

The mouth of the just man tells of wisdom,
  and his tongue utters what is right.
The law of his God is in his heart,
  and his steps do not falter.

Alleluia, alleluia. Ps. 88, 21 [*Anointed*]

I have found David, My servant,
  with My holy oil I have anointed him. Alleluia.

OFFERTORY Ps. 91, 13 [*Growth*]

The just man shall flourish like the palm tree,
  like a cedar of Lebanon shall he grow.

COMMUNION Luke 12, 42 [*Faithful Servant*]

The faithful and prudent servant
  whom the Master will set over His household
  to give them their ration of grain in due time.

Aug. 29 — THE BEHEADING OF ST. JOHN THE BAPTIST

INTROIT Ps. 118, 46-47; 91, 2 [*Fearless*]

I will speak of Your decrees before kings
  without being ashamed.
And I will delight in Your commands,
  which I love exceedingly.
(Ps.) It is good to give thanks to the Lord,
  to sing praise to Your Name, Most High.
Glory be to the Father, etc.
Repeat: **I will speak,** etc., *as far as* (Ps.).

GRADUAL Ps. 91, 13. 14. 3 [*Just Man Flourishes*]

The just man shall flourish like the palm tree,
  like a cedar of Lebanon shall he grow
  in the house of the Lord.

To proclaim Your kindness at dawn
   and Your faithfulness throughout the night.

Alleluia, alleluia.   Osee 14, 6   [*Growth in Beauty*]
The just man shall blossom like the lily,
   and flourish forever before the Lord. Alleluia.

OFFERTORY   Ps. 20, 2-3   [*God with the Just*]

O Lord, in Your strength the just man is glad;
   in Your victory how greatly he rejoices!
You have granted him his heart's desire.

COMMUNION   Ps. 20, 4   [*The Crown*]

You placed on his head, O Lord,
   a crown of precious stones.

Aug. 30 — ST. ROSE OF LIMA, Virgin

Mass: Of a Virgin Only, p. 259.

Aug. 31 — ST. RAYMUND NONNATUS Confessor

Mass: Of a Confessor not a Bishop, p. 250.

Sept. 1 — ST. GILES, Abbot
Mass: Of a Holy Abbot, p. 253.

Sept. 2 — ST. STEPHEN, King, Confessor
Mass: Of a Confessor not a Bishop, p. 250.

Sept. 3 — ST. PIUS X, Pope, Confessor

INTROIT   Ps. 88, 20-22. 2   [The Chosen One]

I have raised up the chosen one from the people;
   with My holy oil I have anointed him,
That My hand may be always with him,
   and that My arm may make him strong.
(Ps.) The favors of the Lord I will sing forever;
   through all generations my mouth shall proclaim Your faithfulness.
Glory be to the Father, etc.
Repeat: **I have raised,** etc., *as far as* (Ps.).

GRADUAL   Ps. 39, 10-11   [Witnessing the Lord]

I announced Your justice in the vast assembly;
   I did not restrain my lips as You, O Lord,
   know.
Your justice I kept not hid within my heart;
   Your faithfulness and Your salvation I have
   spoken of.
Alleluia, alleluia.   Ps. 22, 5-6   [Heavenly Banquet]
You spread the table before me;
You anoint my head with oil;
   my cup overflows. Alleluia.

OFFERTORY   Ps. 33, 12   [Love for Children]

Come, children, hear me;
   I will teach you the fear of the Lord.

COMMUNION   John 6, 56-57   [Communion]

My Flesh is food indeed,
   and My Blood is drink indeed.
He who eats My Flesh and drinks My Blood,
   abides in Me and I in him.

Sept. 5 — ST. LAWRENCE JUSTINIAN
Bishop, Confessor

Mass: Of a Confessor Bishop, p. 245.

Sept. 8 — NATIVITY OF THE BLESSED
VIRGIN MARY

Mass: Same as on July 2, p. 381.

Sept. 9 — ST. PETER CLAVER, Confessor

INTROIT   Ps. 106, 9-10. 8   [*Deliverance*]

The Lord has satisfied the longing soul;
Those who sit in darkness and in the shadow
    of death,
    bondsmen in want and in chains.
(Ps.) Let them give thanks to the Lord for His
    kindness
    and His wondrous deeds to the children of
    men.
Glory be to the Father, etc.
Repeat: The Lord has, etc., *as far as* (Ps.).

GRADUAL   Ps.-71, 12-14   [*Rescuer of the Poor*]

He shall rescue the poor man from the powerful,
    and the poor man when he has no one to
    help him.
He shall have pity for the poor and the needy,
    and the lives of the poor he shall save.
From fraud and wickedness he shall redeem
    their lives,
    and honorable shall be their name in his sight.

Ps. 9, 33. 35

Alleluia, alleluia.   [*Helper of the Helpless*]

Rise, O Lord! O God, lift up Your hand!
    Forget not the afflicted.
On You the poor man depends,
    of the fatherless You are the helper. Alleluia.

OFFERTORY   Job 29, 12-13. 15-16   [*True Father*]

I rescued the poor who cried out for help,
    the orphans, and the unassisted;
The blessing of those in extremity came upon
    me,
    and the heart of the widow I made joyful.
I was eyes to the blind,
    and feet to the lame;
I was a father to the needy.

COMMUNION   Ezech. 34, 15-16 [*The Good Shepherd*]

I Myself will pasture My sheep;
    I Myself will give them rest,
    says the Lord God.
The lost I will seek out.
    The strayed I will bring back,
The injured I will bind up,
    and the sick I will heal.

Sept. 10 — ST. NICHOLAS OF TOLENTINE
Confessor

Mass: Of a Confessor not a Bishop, p. 251.

Sept. 11 — STS. PROTUS AND HYACINTH
Martyrs

Mass: Of Several Martyrs, p. 241.

Sept. 12 — THE MOST HOLY NAME OF MARY

INTROIT Ps. 44, 13, 15. 16. 2 [*Glory Be to the Great King*]

All the rich among the people seek Your favor.
Behind her the virgins of her train are brought
    to the King.
  Her neighbors are brought to You with glad-
    ness and joy.
(Ps.) My heart overflows with a goodly theme;
  as I sing my ode to the King.
Glory be to the Father, etc.
Repeat: **All the rich,** etc., *as far as* (Ps.).

GRADUAL   [*Virgin and Mother*]

Blessed and venerable are you,
  O Virgin Mary;
For without stain to your virginity
  you became the Mother of the Savior.
O Virgin Mother of God,
  He Whom the whole world cannot contain,
Being made man,
  shut Himself up within your womb.

Alleluia, alleluia.   [*Mother of God*]
After childbirth you still remained an inviolate
    Virgin:
  O Mother of God, intercede for us. Alleluia.

OFFERTORY   Luke 1, 28. 42   [*Full of Grace*]

Hail, Mary, full of grace,
  the Lord is with you;
Blessed are you among women,
  and blessed is the fruit of your womb.

COMMUNION [*Blessed Fruit*]

Blessed is the womb of the Virgin Mary,
  which bore the Son of the eternal Father.

Sept. 14 — EXALTATION OF THE HOLY CROSS

INTROIT Gal. 6, 14; Ps. 66, 2 [*Glory in the Cross*]

But it behooves us to glory
  in the Cross of our Lord Jesus Christ;
In Whom is our salvation, life, and resurrection;
  by Whom we are saved and delivered.
(Ps.) May God have pity on us and bless us;
  may He let His face shine upon us;
  and may He have pity on us.
Glory be to the Father, etc.
Repeat: But it behooves, etc., *as far as* (Ps.).

GRADUAL Phil. 2, 8. 9 [*Obedient to Death*]

Christ became obedient for us to death,
  even to death on a cross.
Therefore God has also exalted Him,
  and has bestowed upon Him
  the Name that is above every name.

Alleluia, alleluia. [*Blessed Cross*]

Sweet the wood, sweet the nails,
  sweet the load that hangs on you!
You alone were worthy
  to bear up the King and Lord of heaven.
    Alleluia.

OFFERTORY [*The Cross, Our Protection*]

Protect Your people, O Lord,
  through the sign of the Holy Cross,
  from the snares of their enemies,

That we may pay You a pleasing service,
   and our sacrifice may be acceptable to You.
      Alleluia.

COMMUNION   [Sign of the Cross]

O our God, through the sign of the Cross,
   deliver us from our enemies.

Sept. 15 — SEVEN SORROWS OF THE BLESSED VIRGIN MARY

INTROIT   John 19, 25. 26-27   [Mother of Sorrows]

There were standing by the Cross of Jesus
   His Mother, and His Mother's sister, Mary
      of Cleophas,
   and Salome, and Mary Magdalene.
(Ps.) "Woman, behold your son," said Jesus;
   and to the disciple, "Behold your mother."
Glory be to the Father, etc.
Repeat: There were, etc., *as far as* (Ps.).

GRADUAL   [Standing at the Cross]

You are sorrowful and tearful, O Virgin Mary,
   standing by the Cross of the Lord Jesus,
      your Son and Redeemer.
O Virgin Mother of God,
   He Whom the whole earth does not contain,
The Author of life made Man,
   bears this torture of the cross.

Alleluia, alleluia.   [Sorrowful Mother]

Holy Mary, the Queen of heaven and Mistress
   of the world,
      filled with sorrow,
      stood by the Cross of our Lord Jesus Christ.
In Votive Masses the word Alleluia is added.

After Septuagesima, the Alleluia and versicle are omitted and the following Tract is said:

TRACT   Lam. 1, 12   [Attend and See]

**Holy Mary, the Queen of heaven and Mistress
    of the world,**

    filled with sorrow,

    stood by the Cross of our Lord Jesus Christ.

O all you that pass by the way,

    **look and see if there be any suffering like
    my suffering.**

*During Paschaltime, the Gradual is omitted and the
following Alleluia is said:*

Alleluia, alleluia. Lam. 1, 12   [At the Cross]

**Holy Mary, the Queen of heaven and Mistress
    of the world,**

    filled with sorrow,

    stood by the Cross of our Lord Jesus Christ.

Alleluia. O all you that pass by the way,

    **look and see if there be any suffering like
    my suffering. Alleluia.**

In Votive Masses the following Sequence is not said.

SEQUENCE

[*Hymn of a Mother's Sorrow*]

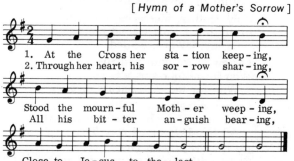

1. At the Cross her sta-tion keep-ing,
2. Through her heart, his sor-row shar-ing,

Stood the mourn-ful Moth-er weep-ing,
All his bit-ter an-guish bear-ing,

Close to Je-sus to the last.
Now at length the sword has passed. A - men.

Oh, how sad and sore distressed
Was that Mother highly blessed
   of the sole begotten One!

Christ above in torment hangs,
She beneath beholds the pangs
   Of her dying, glorious Son.

Is there one who would not weep
'Whelmed in miseries so deep
   Christ's dear Mother to behold?

Can the human heart refrain
From partaking in her pain,
   In that mother's pain untold?

Bruised, derided, cursed, defiled,
She beheld her tender Child,
   All with bloody scourges rent.

For the sins of His own nation
Saw Him hang in desolation
   Till His spirit forth He sent.

O sweet Mother! fount of love,
Touch my spirit from above,
   Make my heart with yours accord.

Make me feel as you have felt;
Make my soul to glow and melt
   With the love of Christ, my Lord.

Holy Mother, pierce me through,
In my heart each wound renew
   Of my Savior crucified.

Let me share with you His pain,
Who for all our sins was slain,
   Who for me in torments died.

Let me mingle tears with you
Mourning Him who mourned for me,
   All the days that I may live.

By the Cross with you to stay,
There with you to weep and pray,
   Is all I ask of you to give.

Virgin of all virgins blest!
Listen to my fond request:
  Let me share your grief divine.

Let me, to my latest breath
In my body bear the death
  Of that dying Son of yours.

Wounded with His every wound,
Steep my soul till it has swooned
  In His very blood away.

Be to me, O Virgin, nigh,
Lest in flames I burn and die,
  In His awful judgment day.

Christ, when You shall call me hence,
Be Your Mother my defense,
  Be Your Cross my victory.

While my body here decays,
May my soul Your goodness praise,
  Safe in heaven eternally.
Amen. Alleluia.

OFFERTORY   Jer. 18, 20   [Speak for Us]

Be mindful, O Virgin Mother of God,
  when you stand in the sight of the Lord,
To speak good things for us,
  and turn away His wrath from us.

COMMUNION   [Martyr]

Happy the Heart of the Blessed Virgin Mary,
  which, without dying,
Earned the palm of martyrdom
  beneath the Cross of our Lord.

———

Sept. 16 — STS. CORNELIUS, Pope, AND CYPRIAN, Bishop, Martyrs

Mass: Of Several Martyrs, p. 238.

Sept. 17 — STIGMATA OF ST. FRANCIS
Confessor

Mass: As on Oct. 4, p. 435.

Sept. 18 — ST. JOSEPH OF CUPERTINO
Confessor

INTROIT   Sir. 1, 14-15; Ps. 83, 2   [*True Wisdom*]

The love of God is honorable wisdom
  and they to whom she shall show herself,
Love her by the sight
  and by the knowledge of her great works.
(Ps.) **How lovely is Your dwelling place,**
  O Lord of Hosts!
My soul yearns and pines
  for the courts of the Lord.
Glory be to the Father, etc.
Repeat: **The love,** etc., *as far as* (Ps.).

GRADUAL   Ps. 20, 4-5   [*Everlasting Crown*]

O Lord, You welcomed him with goodly
  blessings,
  You placed on his head a crown of precious
  stones.
He asked life of You and You gave him
  length of days forever and ever.

Alleluia, alleluia. Sir. 11, 13   [*Glorified*]

The eye of God looks favorably upon him;
   He raises him free of the vile dust
   and lifts up his head. Alleluia.

OFFERTORY   Ps. 34, 13   [*Expiation*]

But I, when they were ill, put on sackcloth.
   I afflicted myself with fasting
   and poured forth my prayers within my
     bosom.

COMMUNION   Ps. 68, 30-31   [*Glorify God*]

I am afflicted and in pain;
   let Your saving help, O God, protect me.
I will praise the Name of God in song,
   and will glorify Him with thanksgiving .

Sept. 19 — STS. JANUARIUS, Bishop AND COMPANIONS, Martyrs

Mass: Of Several Martyrs, p. 241.

Sept. 20 — STS. EUSTACE AND COMPANIONS, Martyrs

Mass: Of Several Martyrs, p. 240.

Sept. 21 — ST. MATTHEW, Apostle, Evangelist

INTROIT   Ps. 36, 30-31. 1   [*Apostolic Wisdom*]

The mouth of the just man tells of wisdom
   and his tongue utters what is right.
The law of his God is in his heart.

(Ps.) **Be not vexed by evildoers,**
  nor jealous of those who do wrong.
Glory be to the Father, etc.
Repeat: **The mouth,** etc., *as far as* (Ps.).

GRADUAL   Ps. 111, 1-2   [*Fear of the Lord*]

Happy the man who fears the Lord,
  who greatly delights in His commands.
His posterity shall be mighty upon the earth;
  the upright generation shall be blessed.
Alleluia, alleluia.   [*Apostolic Choir*]
The glorious choir of Apostles
  praises You, O Lord. Alleluia.

OFFERTORY   Ps. 20, 4-5   [*Golden Crown*]

O Lord, You placed on his head
  a crown of precious stones;
He asked life of You,
  and You gave it to him, alleluia.

COMMUNION   Ps. 20, 6   [*Splendor*]

Great is his glory in Your victory;
  majesty and splendor You conferred upon
  him, O Lord.

Sept. 22 — ST. THOMAS OF VILLANOVA
Bishop, Confessor

Mass: Of a Confessor Bishop, p. 245.

Sept. 23 — ST. LINUS, Pope, Martyr

Mass: Of One or More Popes, p. 231.

Sept. 24 — OUR LADY OF MERCY

Mass: Of the Blessed Virgin Mary, p. 268.

Sept. 26 — STS. ISAAC JOGUES, JOHN DE BREBEUF AND COMPANIONS, Martyrs

INTROIT   Apoc. 7, 14; Ps. 116, 1   [*Martyrs*]

These are they
  who have come out of the great tribulation,
And have washed their robes
  and made them white in the Blood of the
    Lamb.
(Ps.) **Praise the Lord, all you nations;**
  glorify Him, all you peoples.
Glory be to the Father, etc.
Repeat: **These are they,** etc., *as far as* (Ps.).

GRADUAL   Ps. 123, 7-8   [*Rescue*]

Our life was rescued like a bird
  from the fowlers' snare.
Broken was the snare,
  and we were freed.
Our help is in the Name of the Lord,
  Who made heaven and earth.

Alleluia, alleluia.   2 Cor. 1, 5   [*Suffering and Comfort*]

As the sufferings of Christ abound in us,
  so also through Christ does our comfort
    abound. Alleluia.

OFFERTORY   Wis. 3, 6   [*Proved*]

As gold in the furnace, the Lord proved them,
  and as sacrificial offerings He took them to
    Himself.

COMMUNION   Phil. 1, 20-21   [*To Live Is Christ*]

Christ will be glorified in my body,
  whether through life or through death:
For to me to live is Christ
  and to die is gain.

Sept. 27 — STS. COSMAS AND DAMIAN
Martyrs

INTROIT   Sir. 44, 15. 14; Ps. 32, 1   [*Wisdom of the Saints*]

At gatherings the wisdom of the saints is retold,
  and the assembly sings their praises;
Their name lives on and on.

(Ps.) Exult, you just, in the Lord;
  praise from the upright is fitting.

Glory be to the Father, etc.

Repeat: At gatherings, etc., *as far as* (Ps.).

GRADUAL   Ps. 33, 18-19   [*The Lord Hears the Just*]

When the just cry out, the Lord hears them,
  and from all their distress He rescues them.
The Lord is close to the brokenhearted,
  and those who are crushed in spirit He saves.

Alleluia, alleluia.   [*True Brotherhood*]
This is the true brotherhood
  which overcame the wickedness of the world;
It followed Christ,
  holding fast to the glorious heavenly
    kingdom. Alleluia.

OFFERTORY   Ps. 5, 12-13   [*Glory in God*]

All who love Your Name shall glory in You,
  for You, O Lord, bless the just man.
O Lord, You surround us
  with the shield of Your good will.

COMMUNION   Ps. 78, 2. 11   [*Crown of Martyrdom*]

They have given the corpses of Your servants,
    O Lord,
  as food to the birds of heaven,
  the flesh of Your faithful ones to the beasts
    of the earth.
With Your great power free those doomed to
  death.

Sept. 28 — ST. WENCESLAUS, Duke, Martyr

Mass: Of a Martyr not a Bishop, p. 235.

Sept. 29 — DEDICATION OF ST. MICHAEL THE ARCHANGEL

INTROIT   Ps. 102, 20. 1   [*God's Angels*]

Bless the Lord, all you His angels,
  you mighty in strength, who do His bidding,
  obeying His spoken word.
(Ps). Bless the Lord, O my soul;
  and all my being, bless His holy Name.
Glory be to the Father, etc.
Repeat: **Bless the Lord,** etc., *as far as* (Ps.).

GRADUAL Ps. 102, 20. 1   [*Angelic Servants*]

Bless the Lord, all you His angels,
  you mighty in strength, who do His bidding.
Bless the Lord, O my soul;
  and all my being, bless His holy Name.

Alleluia, alleluia.   [*Defend Us in Battle*]
St. Michael the Archangel, defend us in battle,
  that we may not perish in the dreadful
  judgment. Alleluia.

OFFERTORY Apoc. 8, 3. 4   [*Angelic Ministers*]

An Angel stood before the altar of the temple,
  having a golden censer in his hand,
And there was given to him much incense;
  and the smoke of the spices ascended before
  God. Alleluia.

COMMUNION Dan. 3, 58 [*All Angels, Bless the Lord*]

All you angels of the Lord,
  bless the Lord,
Sing a hymn,
  and exalt Him above all forever.

Sept. 30 — ST. JEROME
Priest, Confessor and Doctor of the Church

Mass: Of a Doctor, p. 248.

Oct. 1 — ST. REMIGIUS, Bishop, Confessor

Mass: Of a Confessor Bishop, p. 245.

Oct. 2 — THE HOLY GUARDIAN ANGELS

INTROIT   Ps. 102, 20. 1   [Angel Servants]

Bless the Lord, all you His angels,
  you mighty in strength, who do His bidding,
  obeying His spoken word.
(Ps.) Bless the Lord, O my soul;
  and all my being, bless His holy Name.
Glory be to the Father, etc.
Repeat: **Bless the Lord,** etc., *as far as* (Ps.).

GRADUAL   Ps. 90, 11-12   [Guarding Us]

To His angels God has given command about
  you,
  that they guard you in all your ways.
Upon their hands they shall bear you up,
  lest you dash your foot against a stone.

Alleluia, alleluia.   Ps. 102, 21   [Lord's Ministers]
Bless the Lord, all you His hosts,
  His ministers, who do His will. Alleluia.

OFFERTORY   Ps. 102, 20. 21   [Obedient Angels]

Bless the Lord, all you His angels,
  His ministers, who do His will,
  obeying His spoken word.

COMMUNION   Dan. 3, 58   [Angelic Hymns]

All you angels of the Lord, bless the Lord,
  sing a hymn, and exalt Him above all forever.

Oct. 3 — ST. THERESA OF THE CHILD JESUS
Virgin

INTROIT   Cant. 4, 8-9   [Christ's Bride]

Come from Lebanon, My bride,
  come from Lebanon, come!
You have ravished My heart, My sister, My
    bride;
  you have ravished My heart.
(Ps.) **Praise the Lord, you children,**
  praise the Name of the Lord.
Glory be to the Father, etc.
Repeat: **Come from,** etc., *as far as* (Ps.).

GRADUAL   Matt. 11, 25; Ps. 70, 5   [The Little Ones]

I praise You, Father,
  Lord of heaven and earth,
That You did hide these things from the wise
    and prudent,
  and did reveal them to little ones.
You are my trust, O Lord,
  from my youth.

Alleluia, alleluia. Sir. 39, 17-19   [Little Flowers]
Open up your petals,
  like roses planted near running waters;
Send up a sweet odor like Lebanon.
  Break forth in blossoms like the lily,
  and yield a smell.
And bring forth leaves in grace.
  And praise with canticles
  and bless the Lord in His works. Alleluia.

OFFERTORY   Luke 1, 46-48. 49   [Lowliness]

My soul magnifies the Lord,
    and my spirit rejoices in God my Savior;
Because He has regarded the lowliness of His
       handmaid.
He Who is mighty has done great things for me.

COMMUNION   Deut. 32, 10-12   [God's Special One]

He led her about and taught her,
    and He guarded her as the apple of His eye.
As an eagle He spread His wings to receive her
    and bore her up on his pinions.
The Lord alone was her leader.

Oct. 4 — ST. FRANCIS OF ASSISI, Confessor

INTROIT   Gal. 6, 14; Ps. 141, 2   [Only the Cross]

But as for me, God forbid that I should glory,
    save in the cross of our Lord Jesus Christ,
Through Whom the world is crucified to me,
    and I to the world.
(Ps.) With a loud voice I cry out to the Lord;
    with a loud voice I beseech the Lord.
Glory be to the Father, etc.
Repeat: **But as,** etc., *as far as* (Ps.).

GRADUAL   Ps. 36, 30-31   [God's Law in the Heart]

The mouth of the just man tells of wisdom,
    and his tongue utters what is right.
The law of his God is in his heart,
    and his steps do not falter.

Alleluia, alleluia.   [The Poor Man Now Rich]

Francis, poor and humble, enters heaven a rich
    man,
        and he is welcomed with celestial hymns.
            Alleluia.

OFFERTORY   Ps. 88, 25   [Exaltation]

My faithfulness and My kindness shall be with
    him,
        and through My Name shall his horn be
            exalted.

COMMUNION   Luke 12, 42   [Faithful Servant]

The faithful and prudent servant
    whom the Master will set over His household
    to give them their ration of grain in due time.

Oct. 5 — STS. PLACIDUS AND COMPANIONS
Martyrs

Mass: Of Several Martyrs, p. 241.

Oct. 6 — ST. BRUNO, Confessor

Mass: Of a Confessor not a Bishop, p. 250.

Oct. 7 — THE BLESSED VIRGIN MARY
OF THE MOST HOLY ROSARY

INTROIT   Ps. 44, 2   [Rejoice]

Let us all rejoice in the Lord,
    celebrating a feast in honor of the Blessed
        Virgin Mary,

For whose solemnity the angels rejoice
   and join in praising the Son of God.

(Ps.) My heart overflows with a goodly theme;
   as I sing my ode to the King.

Glory be to the Father, etc.

Repeat: Let us all, etc., *as far as* (Ps.).

GRADUAL   Ps. 44, 5. 11. 12   [A Daughter's Beauty]

Because of truth and mercy and for the sake of
      justice:
   may your right hand show you wondrous
      deeds.
Hear, O daughter, and see; turn your ear;
   for the King shall desire your beauty.

Alleluia, alleluia.   [Royal Lady]
The solemnity of the glorious Virgin Mary,
   of the seed of Abraham,
Sprung from the tribe of Juda,
   of the noble line of David. Alleluia.

OFFERTORY   Sir. 24, 25; 39, 17   [Like a Rose]

In me is all grace of the way and of the truth,
   in me is all hope of life and of virtue.
Like a rose planted near running waters
   I have budded forth.

COMMUNION   Sir. 39, 19   [Flowering Mystery]

Break forth in blossoms like the lily,
   and yield a smell.
And bring forth leaves in grace.
   And praise with canticles
   and bless the Lord in His works.

Oct. 8 — ST. BRIDGET, Widow

Mass: Of a Holy Woman not a Martyr, p. 264.

Oct. 9 — ST. JOHN LEONARD, Confessor

INTROIT   Sir. 42, 15-16; Ps. 95, 1   *[Glory of the Lord]*

At the Lord's word were His works brought
   into being.
As the rising sun is clear to all,
   so the glory of the Lord shines upon all His
   works.
(Ps.) Sing to the Lord a new song;
   sing to the Lord, all you lands.
Glory be to the Father, etc.
Repeat: At the Lord's, etc., *as far as* (Ps.).

GRADUAL   Ps. 72, 21; 68, 10; Isa. 49, 2   *[Zeal for God]*

My heart was embittered
   and my soul was pierced.
Zeal for your house consumed me.
He made my mouth a sharp-edged sword
   and concealed me in the shadow of His arm.
He made me a polished arrow.

Alleluia, alleluia.   Ps. 70, 7   *[Refuge]*
A portent am I to many,
   but You are my strong refuge! Alleluia.

OFFERTORY   Col. 1, 25   *[Full Preaching]*

I have become a minister of Christ
   in virtue of the office that God has given me,
   for I am to fulfill the word of God.

COMMUNION   Phil. 3, 7   [*No Personal Gain*]

The things that were gain to me,
  these, for the sake of Christ, I have counted
    loss.

Oct. 10 — ST. FRANCIS BORGIA, Confessor

Mass: Of a Holy Abbot, p. 253.

Oct. 11 — MATERNITY OF THE B. V. M.

INTROIT   Isa. 7, 14; Ps. 97, 1   [*Emmanuel*]

Behold, the virgin shall be with child and bear
    a Son,
  and shall name Him Emmanuel.
(Ps.) Sing to the Lord a new song,
  for He has done wondrous deeds.
Glory be to the Father, etc.
Repeat: Behold, etc., *as far as* (Ps.).

GRADUAL   Isa. 11, 1-2   [*Root of Jesse*]

A shoot shall sprout from the stump of Jesse,
  and from his roots a bud shall blossom.
And the Spirit of the Lord
  shall rest upon Him.

Alleluia, alleluia.   [*Virgin and Mother*]
O Virgin, Mother of God,
  He Whom the whole world cannot contain,
Being made man,
  shut Himself up within your womb. Alleluia.

OFFERTORY   Matt. 1, 18   [With Child]

When Mary His Mother had been betrothed to
    Joseph,
    she was found to be with child by the Holy
        Spirit.

COMMUNION   [Mother of God]

Blessed is the womb of the Virgin Mary,
    which bore the Son of the eternal Father.

Oct. 13 — ST. EDWARD, King, Confessor

Mass: Of a Confessor not a Bishop, p. 250.

Oct. 14 — ST. CALLISTUS I, Pope, Martyr

Mass: Of One or More Popes, p. 231.

Oct. 15 — ST. TERESA, Virgin

Mass: Of a Virgin Only, p. 259.

Oct. 16 — ST. HEDWIG, Widow

Mass: Of a Holy Woman not a Martyr, p. 264.

Oct. 17 — ST. MARGARET MARY ALACOQUE
Virgin

INTROIT   Cant. 2, 3; Ps. 83, 2-3   [Joy in God]

I delight to rest in His shadow,
    and His fruit is sweet to my mouth.

(Ps.) **How lovely is Your dwelling place,**
** O Lord of Hosts!**
My soul yearns and pines
** for the courts of the Lord.**

Glory be to the Father, etc.

Repeat: **I delight,** etc., *as far as* (Ps.).

GRADUAL   Cant. 8, 7; Ps. 72, 26   [Love Unquenchable]

Deep waters cannot quench love,
** nor floods sweep it away.**
My flesh and my heart waste away;
** God is the God of my heart and my portion**
** forever.**

Alleluia, alleluia.   Cant. 7, 10   [Fullness of Love]
I belong to my Lover
** and for me He yearns. Alleluia.**

OFFERTORY   Zach. 9, 17   [Beauty]

What wealth is His, and what beauty!
** grain that makes the chosen ones flourish,**
** and new wine, the maidens!**

COMMUNION   Cant. 6, 2   [Union]

I belong to my Lover and my Lover to me;
** He browses among the lilies.**

Oct. 18 — ST. LUKE, Evangelist

INTROIT   Ps. 138, 17. 1-2   [God's Friends]

To me, Your friends, O God, are made exceed-
** ingly honorable;**
** their principality is exceedingly strengthened.**

(Ps.) **O Lord, You have probed me and You know me;**

You know when I sit and when I stand.

Glory be to the Father, etc.

Repeat: **To me,** etc., *as far as* (Ps.).

GRADUAL   Ps. 18, 5. 2   [Apostolic Voices]

Through all the earth their voice resounds,
    and to the ends of the world, their message.
The heavens declare the glory of God,
    and the firmament proclaims His handiwork.

Alleluia, alleluia.   John 15, 16   [Bearing Fruit]
I have chosen you out of the world,
    that you should go and bear fruit,
    and that your fruit should remain. Alleluia.

OFFERTORY   Ps. 138, 17   [Princes]

To me, Your friends, O God, are made exceedingly honorable;
    their principality is exceedingly strengthened.

COMMUNION   Mt. 19, 28   [Thrones]

You who have followed Me shall sit upon thrones,
    judging the twelve tribes of Israel.

Oct. 19 — ST. PETER OF ALCANTARA
Confessor

Mass: Of a Confessor not a Bishop, p. 251.

Oct. 20 — ST. JOHN CANTIUS, Confessor

INTROIT Sir. 18, 12-13; Ps. 1, 1 [God's Mercy]

Man may be merciful to his fellow man,
  but God's mercy reaches all flesh.
He has mercy, teaches and guides,
  as a shepherd does his flock.
(Ps.) Happy the man who follows not
  the counsel of the wicked
Nor walks in the way of sinners,
  nor sits in the company of the insolent.
Glory be to the Father, etc.
Repeat: **Man may be,** etc., *as far as* (Ps.).

GRADUAL Ps. 06, 8-9 [Filling the Hungry]

Let them give thanks to the Lord for His
    kindness
  and His wondrous deeds to the children of
    men.
Because He satisfied the longing soul
  and filled the hungry soul with good things.

Alleluia, alleluia. Prov. 31, 20 [Help for the Poor]
He extends His arms to the needy,
  and reaches out His hands to the poor.
    Alleluia.

OFFERTORY Job 29, 14-16 [True Father]

I wore my honesty like a garment;
  justice was my robe and my turban.
I was eyes to the blind,
  and feet to the lame was I;
I was a father to the needy.

COMMUNION   Luke 6, 38   [*Give and Receive*]

Give, and it shall be given to you;
    good measure, pressed down, shaken to-
        gether, running over,
    shall they pour into your lap.

Oct. 21 — ST. HILARION, Abbot

Mass: Of a Holy Abbot, p. 253.

Oct. 23 — ST. ANTHONY MARY CLARET
Bishop, Confessor

Mass: Of a Confessor Bishop, p. 246.

Oct. 24 — ST. RAPHAEL THE ARCHANGEL

INTROIT   Ps. 102, 20   [*God's Angels*]

Bless the Lord, all you His angels,
    you mighty in strength, who do His bidding,
    obeying His spoken word.
(Ps.) Bless the Lord, O my soul;
    and, all my being, bless his holy Name.
Glory be to the Father, etc.
Repeat: Bless the Lord, etc., *as far as* (Ps.).

GRADUAL   Tob. 8, 3; Ps. 146, 5   [*Angelic Power*]

The angel of the Lord, Raphael,
    took and bound the devil.
Great is our Lord and mighty in power.

Alleluia, alleluia. Ps. 137, 1-2 [*Praise with the Angels*]
In the presence of the angels I will sing Your
   praise;
I will worship at Your holy temple
   and give thanks to Your Name, O Lord.
   Alleluia.

OFFERTORY   Apoc. 8, 3. 4   [*Angelic Ministers*]

An angel stood before the altar of the temple,
   having a golden censer in his hand;
And there was given to him much incense:
   and the smoke of the spices went up before
   God.

COMMUNION   Dan. 3, 58 [*All Angels Bless the Lord*]

All you Angels of the Lord, bless the Lord;
   sing a hymn, and exalt Him above all forever.

Oct. 25 — ST. ISIDORE THE FARMER
Confessor

Mass: Of a Confessor not a Bishop, p. 251.

Oct. 26 — ST. EVARISTUS, Pope, Martyr

Mass: Of One or More Popes, p. 231.

Oct. 28 — STS. SIMON AND JUDE, Apostles

INTROIT   Ps. 138, 17. 1-2   [*God's Friends*]

To me, Your friends, O God, are made exceedingly honorable;
   their principality is exceedingly strengthened.

(Ps.) **O Lord, You have probed me and You
    know me;**
  You know when I sit and when I stand.
Glory be to the Father, etc.
Repeat: **To me,** etc., *as far as* (Ps.).

GRADUAL   Ps. 44, 17-18   [*Princes*]

**You shall make them princes through all the
    land;**
  they shall remember Your Name, O Lord.
The place of Your fathers Your sons shall have;
  therefore shall nations praise You.

Alleluia, alleluia.   Ps. 138, 17   [*Friends of God*]
**Your friends, O God, are made exceedingly
    honorable;**
  their principality is exceedingly strengthened.
  Alleluia.

OFFERTORY   Ps. 18, 5   [*Apostolic Voices*]

Through all the earth their voice resounds,
  and to the ends of the world, their message.

COMMUNION   Matt. 19, 28   [*Thrones*]

You who have followed Me shall sit on thrones,
  judging the twelve tribes of Israel.

Nov. 1 — FEAST OF ALL SAINTS

INTROIT   Ps. 32, 1   [*Glory of the Saints*]

Let us all rejoice in the Lord,
  **celebrating a feast-day in honor of all the
    Saints,**

On whose solemnity the Angels rejoice,
   and join in praising the Son of God.

(Ps). Exult, you just, in the Lord;
   praise from the upright is fitting.

Glory be to the Father, etc.

Repeat: Let us all, etc., *as far as* (Ps.).

GRADUAL   Ps. 33, 10. 11   [*The Lord Our Reward*]

Fear the Lord, all you His holy ones,
   for nought is lacking to those who fear Him.
But those who seek the Lord want for no good
      thing.

Alleluia, alleluia.   Matt. 11, 28   [*Refreshment*]

Come to Me, all you who labor and are
      burdened,
   and I will give you rest. Alleluia.

OFFERTORY   Wis. 3, 1, 2. 3   [*Peace at Last*]

The souls of the just are in the hand of God,
   and no torment shall touch them.
They seemed, in view of the foolish, to be
      dead;
   but they are in peace. Alleluia.

COMMUNION   Matt. 5, 8-10   [*The Kingdom*]

Blessed are the pure of heart,
   for they shall see God.
Blessed are the peacemakers,
   for they shall be called children of God.
Blessed are they who suffer persecution for
      justice' sake,
   for theirs is the kingdom of heaven.

Nov. 2 — ALL SOUL'S DAY

Mass: For the Dead, p. 456. (Sequence must be said in First Mass.)

Nov. 4 — ST. CHARLES BORROMEO
Bishop, Confessor

Mass: Of a Confessor Bishop, p. 245.

Nov. 8 — FOUR HOLY CROWNED MARTYRS

Mass: Of Several Martyrs, p. 238.

Nov. 9 — DEDICATION OF THE BASILICA OF OUR SAVIOR

Mass: Of the Dedication of a Church, p. 266.

Nov. 10 — ST. ANDREW AVELLINO, Confessor

Mass: Of a Confessor not a Bishop, p. 250.

Nov. 11 — ST. MARTIN, Bishop, Confessor

INTROIT   Sir. 45, 30; Ps. 131, 1   [*Priestly Dignity*]

The Lord made a covenant of friendship with him,
And made him a prince,
    that he should possess the dignity of priesthood forever.

(Ps.) **Remember, O Lord, David
   and all his meekness.**

Glory be to the Father, etc.

Repeat: **The Lord made,** etc., *as far as* (Ps.).

GRADUAL   Sir. 44, 16. 20   [*The Noble Priest*]

**Behold, a great priest,
   who in his days pleased God.
There was not found the like to him, who kept
   the law of the Most High.**

Alleluia, alleluia.   [*Triumph*]

**The blessed man, St. Martin, Bishop of Tours,
   has gone to rest;
Angels and archangels, thrones, dominations,
   and powers
have received him. Alleluia.**

OFFERTORY   Ps. 88, 25   [*Exalted*]

**My faithfulness and My kindness shall be with
   him,
   and through My Name shall his horn be
   exalted.**

COMMUNION   Matt. 24, 46-47   [*Watchfulness*]

**Blessed is that servant whom his Master,
   when He comes, shall find watching.
Amen I say to you,
   He will set him over all His goods.**

Nov. 12 — ST. MARTIN, Pope, Martyr

Mass: Of One or More Popes, p. 231.

Nov. 13 — ST. FRANCES XAVIER CABRINI
Virgin

INTROIT   Ps. 72, 24. 1   [*God's Guidance*]

You have hold of my right hand;
With Your counsel You guide me,
   and in the end You will receive me in glory.
(Ps.) **How good God is to Israel,**
   to those who are clean of heart.
Glory be to the Father, etc.
Repeat: **You have hold,** etc., *as far as* (Ps.).

GRADUAL   Ps. 17, 33-34   [*Strength from God*]

The God Who girded me with strength
   and kept my way unerring.
Who made my feet swift as those of hinds
   and set me on the heights.

Alleluia, alleluia. 1 Cor. 9, 22   [*To Save All Men*]
I became all things to all men,
   that I might save all. Alleluia.

OFFERTORY   Ps. 72, 78   [*Near God*]

But for me, to be near God is my good;
   to make the Lord God my refuge.
I shall declare all Your works
   in the gates of the daughter of Sion.

COMMUNION   Matt. 11, 28   [*Rest*]

Come to Me, all you who labor and are
      burdened,
   and I will give you rest.

Nov. 14 — ST. JOSAPHAT, Bishop, Martyr

INTROIT   Ps. 32, 1   [Rejoice]

Let us all rejoice in the Lord,
  celebrating a feast-day in honor of the Bles-
    sed Martyr Josaphat,
At whose martyrdom the Angels rejoice
  and give praise to the Son of God.

(Ps.) Exult, you just, in the Lord;
  praise from the upright is fitting.

Glory be to the Father, etc.

Repeat: **Let us all,** etc., *as far as* (Ps.).

GRADUAL   Ps. 88, 21-23   [Anointed]

I have found David, My servant,
  with My holy oil I have anointed him,
That My hand may be always with him,
  and that My arm may make him strong.
No enemy shall have an advantage over him,
  nor shall the son of iniquity have power to
    hurt him.

Alleluia, alleluia.   [Great Priest]
This is the priest whom the Lord has crowned.
  Alleluia.

OFFERTORY   John 15, 13   [Supreme Love]

Greater love than this no one has,
  that one lay down his life for his friends.

COMMUNION   John 10, 14   [Strong Faith]

I am the Good Shepherd,
  and I know My sheep, and Mine know Me.

Nov. 15 — ST. ALBERT THE GREAT
Bishop, Confessor and Doctor of the Church

Mass: Of a Doctor, p. 248.

Nov. 16 — ST. GERTRUDE, Virgin

Mass: Of a Virgin Only, p. 259.

Nov. 17 — ST. GREGORY THE
WONDERWORKER, Bishop, Confessor

Mass: Of a Confessor Bishop, p. 245.

Nov. 18 — DEDICATION OF THE BASILICAS
OF STS. PETER AND PAUL

Mass: Of the Dedication of a Church, p. 266.

Nov. 19 — ST. ELIZABETH, Widow

Mass: Of a Holy Woman not a Martyr, p. 264.

Nov. 20 — ST. FELIX OF VALOIS, Confessor

Mass: Of a Confessor not a Bishop, p. 251.

Nov. 21 — THE PRESENTATION OF
THE BLESSED VIRGIN MARY

Mass: Of the Blessed Virgin Mary, p. 268.

Nov. 22 — ST. CECILIA, Virgin, Martyr

INTROIT   Ps. 118, 46-47. 1   [*Joyful Witness*]

I will speak of Your decrees before kings
   without being ashamed.
And I will delight in Your commands,
   which I love exceedingly.
(Ps.) Happy are they whose way is blameless,
   who walk in the law of the Lord.
Glory be to the Father, etc.
Repeat: **I will speak,** etc., *as far as* (Ps.).

GRADUAL   Ps. 44, 11. 12. 5   [*Reigning in Glory*]

Hear, O daughter, and see; turn your ear;
   for the King shall desire your beauty.
In your splendor and your beauty
   ride on triumphant, and reign.

Alleluia, alleluia.   Matt. 25, 4. 6   [*The Bridegroom*]
The five wise virgins took oil in their vessels
   with the lamps:
   and at midnight a cry arose,
"Behold the Bridegroom is coming,
   go forth to meet Christ the Lord." Alleluia.

OFFERTORY   Ps. 44, 15. 16   [*Triumph*]

Behind her the virgins of her train are brought
   to the King.
Her neighbors are brought to You with gladness and joy;
   they enter the palace of the Lord, the King.

COMMUNION   Ps. 118, 78. 80   [Judgment of God]

Let the proud be put to shame for oppressing
　　me unjustly;
I will meditate on Your precepts, on Your
　　statutes,
　　that I be not put to shame.

Nov. 23 — ST. CLEMENT, Pope, Martyr

INTROIT   Isa. 59, 21; 56, 7; Ps. 111, 1   [Accepted Gifts]

The Lord says,
"My words that I have put into your mouth,
　　shall never leave your mouth;
　　and your gifts shall be accepted upon My
　　altar."
(Ps.) Happy the man who fears the Lord,
　　who greatly delights in His commands.
Glory be to the Father, etc.
Repeat: **The Lord says,** etc., *as far as* (Ps.).

GRADUAL   Ps. 106, 32, 31   [Praise from the Church]

Let them extol Him in the assembly of the
　　people;
　　and praise Him in the council of the elders.
Let them give thanks to the Lord for His
　　kindness
　　and His wondrous deeds to the children of
　　men.

Alleluia, alleluia.   Matt. 16, 18   [The Rock]
You are Peter,
　　and upon this rock I will build My Church.
　　Alleluia.

OFFERTORY   Jer. 1, 9.10   [Authority]

See, I place My words in your mouth:
    behold, I set you over nations and over
       kingdoms,
To root up and to tear down,
    and to build and to plant.

COMMUNION   Matt. 16, 18   [The Rock]

You are Peter,
    and upon this rock I will build My Church.

Nov. 24 — ST. JOHN OF THE CROSS
Confessor and Doctor of the Church

Mass: Of a Doctor, p. 248.

Nov. 25 — ST. CATHERINE, Virgin, Martyr

Mass: Of a Virgin Martyr, p. 255.

Nov. 26 — ST. SYLVESTER, Abbot

Mass: Of a Holy Abbot, p. 253.

MASSES FOR DEAD

REQUIEM MASS ON THE DAY OF DEATH OR BURIAL

BEFORE MASS

RESPONSORY

Come to his (her) aid,   [Receive This Soul]
   O saints of God;
Hasten to meet him (her),
   angels of the Lord;
Taking up his (her) soul,
   presenting it in the sight of the Most High.
May you be received by Christ, Who has called
   you:
   and may the Angels bring you into the bosom
   of Abraham.
Taking up his (her) soul,
   presenting it in the sight of the Most High.
Eternal rest grant unto him (her), O Lord:
   and let perpetual light shine upon him (her).
Presenting his (her) soul in the sight of the
   Most High.

THE MASS

INTROIT   4 Esdras 2, 34. 35   [Light and Rest]

Eternal rest grant unto them, O Lord:
   and let perpetual light shine upon them.
(Ps.) To You we owe our hymn of praise,
   O God, in Sion;

To You must vows be fulfilled
  in Jerusalem.
Hear my prayer;
  to You all flesh must come.

Repeat: **Eternal rest,** etc., *as far as* (Ps.).

GRADUAL   4 Esdras 2, 34. 35; Ps. 111, 7

[The Just Are Not Forgotten]

Eternal rest grant unto them, O Lord:
  and let perpetual light shine upon them.
The just man shall be in everlasting remembrance;
  an evil report he shall not fear.

TRACT   *[Forgive and Grant Bliss]*

Absolve, O Lord, the souls of all the faithful departed
  from every bond of sin.
And by the help of Your grace
  may they deserve to escape the judgment of vengeance.
And to enjoy the blessedness of light eternal.

SEQUENCE

[Song of Judgment]

Day of wrath! O day of mourning!
See fulfilled the prophets' warning,
Heav'n and earth in ashes burning!

O what fear man's bosom rendeth
When from heav'n the judge descendeth,
On whose sentence all dependeth!

Wondrous sound the trumpet flingeth;
Through earth's sepulchers it ringeth;
All before the throne it bringeth.

Death is struck, and nature quaking,
All creation is awaking,
To its judge an answer making.

Lo! the book, exactly worded,
Wherein all hath been recorded:
Thence shall judgment be awarded.

When the judge his seat attaineth
And each hidden deed arraigneth,
Nothing unavenged remaineth.

What shall I, frail man, be pleading?
Who for me be interceding,
When the just are mercy needing?

King of majesty tremendous,
Who dost free salvation send us,
Fount of pity, then befriend us!

Think, good Jesus, my salvation
Cost thy wondrous incarnation;
Leave me not to reprobation!

Faint and weary, thou hast sought me,
On the cross of suff'ring bought me.
Shall such grace be vainly brought me?

Righteous judge! for sin's pollution
Grant thy gift of absolution,
Ere the day of retribution.

Guilty, now I pour my moaning,
All my shame with anguish owning;
Spare, O God, thy suppliant groaning!

Thou the sinful woman savedst;
Thou the dying thief forgavest;
And to me a hope vouchsafest.

Worthless are my prayers and sighing,
Yet, good Lord, in grace complying,
Rescue me from fires undying!

With thy favored sheep, O place me
Nor among the goats abase me,
But to thy right hand upraise me.

While the wicked are confounded,
Doomed to flames of woe unbounded,
Call me with Thy saints surrounded.

Low I kneel, with heart submission:
See, like ashes, my contrition;
Help me in my last condition.

Ah! that day of tears and mourning!
From the dust of earth returning,

Man for judgment must prepare him;
Spare, O God, in mercy spare him!

Lord, all pitying, Jesus blest,
Grant them thine eternal rest. Amen.

OFFERTORY   [*Deliver the Souls of the Faithful*]

Lord Jesus Christ, King of glory,
   deliver the souls of all the faithful departed
   from the pains of hell and the deep pit;
Deliver them from the lion's mouth,
   may hell not swallow them up,
   nor may they fall into darkness,
But may Michael, the holy standard-bearer,
   bring them into the holy light:
   Which You once promised to Abraham and
     to his seed.
We offer You, O Lord,
   sacrifices and prayers of praise;

Receive them for the souls
   whom we remember this day.

Grant, O Lord, that they may pass from death
   to life.
   Which You once promised to Abraham and
   to his seed.

COMMUNION   4 Esdras 2, 35. 34   [Perpetual Light]

May light eternal shine upon them, O Lord:
   With Your saints forever, for You are
   merciful.

Eternal rest grant unto them, O Lord;
   and let perpetual light shine upon them.
   With Your saints forever, for You are
   merciful.

ABSOLUTION AFTER MASS

RESPONSORY
[Save Them from Eternal Death]

Deliver me, O Lord, from everlasting death
   on that day of terror:
when the heavens and the earth will be shaken.
   As You come to judge the world by fire.
I am in fear and trembling
   at the judgment and the wrath that is to
   come.
When the heavens and the earth will be shaken.
That day will be a day of wrath, of misery, and
   of ruin:
   a day of grandeur and great horror:
   As You come to judge the world by fire.
Eternal rest grant unto them, O Lord,
   and let perpetual light shine upon them.

**Deliver me, O Lord, from everlasting death
  on that day of terror:**
**When the heavens and the earth will be shaken.
  As You come to judge the world by fire.**
Lord, have mercy.
Christ, have mercy.

Then all together:
Lord, have mercy.

Next the priest says in a high voice:
Our Father.

And lead us not into temptation.
But deliver us from evil.
From the gate of hell.
Rescue his (her) soul, O Lord.
May he (she) rest in peace.
Amen.
O Lord, hear my prayer.
And let my cry come to You.
The Lord be with you.
And with your spirit.

ANNIVERSARY MASS FOR THE DEAD

Same as Mass on the Day of Death or Burial,
p. 456; Sequence is optional.

DAILY MASS FOR THE DEAD

Same as Mass on the Day of Death or Burial,
p. 456; Sequence is optional.

THE NUPTIAL MASS

INTROIT Tob. 7, 15. 8, 19; Ps. 127, 1 [*May God Join You*]

May the God of Israel join you together;
    and may He be with you, Who was merciful
        to two only children:
and now, O Lord,
    make them bless You more fully. (P.T. Alle-
        luia, alleluia.)

(Ps.) Blessed are all who fear the Lord,
    who walk in his ways.

Glory be to the Father, etc.

Repeat: **May the God,** etc., *as far as* (Ps.).

GRADUAL   Ps. 127, 3   [*Fruitful Union*]

Your wife shall be like a fruitful vine
    in the recesses of your home.
Your children like olive plants
    around your table.

Alleluia, alleluia. Ps. 19, 3   [*Help from God*]
May the Lord send you help from the sanctuary,
    from Sion may He sustain you. Alleluia.

After Septuagesima, the Alleluia and versicle are
omitted and the following Tract is said:

TRACT   Ps. 127, 4-6   [*Prosperity*]

Behold, thus is the man blessed
    who fears the Lord.
The Lord bless you from Sion:

may you see the prosperity of Jerusalem
all the days of your life.
May you see your children's children.
Peace be upon Israel!

*During Paschaltime, the Gradual is omitted and the
following Alleluia is said:*

Alleluia, alleluia. Ps. 19, 3; 133, 3   [*Help from God*]
May the Lord send you help from the sanctuary,
from Sion may He sustain you.
Alleluia. May the Lord bless you from Sion,
the Maker of heaven and earth. Alleluia.

OFFERTORY Ps. 30, 15-16 [*Future in God's Keeping*]

My trust is in You, O Lord;
I say, "You are my God."
In Your hands is my destiny. (P.T. Alleluia.)

COMMUNION Ps. 127, 4. 6   [*Blessing*]

Behold, thus is the man blessed
who fears the Lord;
May you see your children's children.
Peace be upon Israel! (P.T. Alleluia.)

VOTIVE MASSES

*In all Masses of feasts during Paschaltime (P.T.)
two "Alleluias" are to be added (unless already added
in the Missal) to the Introit before the Psalm-verse
(Ps.), and one "Alleluia" to the Offertory and Communion verses. (Masses of Apostles and Martyrs add
two "Alleluias.") In addition, the Gradual is replaced
by two versicles with four "Alleluias" as indicated for
each Mass.*

MONDAY

MASS OF THE HOLY TRINITY

Mass: As on Trinity Sunday, p. 170, except:

*After Septuagesima, the Alleluia and versicle are
omitted and the following Tract is said:*

TRACT   [*Praise to the Triune God*]

**With all our hearts we confess You,
we praise You, we bless You,
God the Father unbegotten,
the only-begotten Son,
the Holy Spirit, the Consoler,
Holy and undivided Trinity.
For You are great and do wonderful things;
You alone are God.
To You be praise,
to You glory,
To You thanksgiving for eternal ages,
O blessed Trinity.**

*During Paschaltime, the Gradual is omitted and the
following Alleluia is said:*

[*Glory to the Three Persons*]

Alleluia, alleluia. Dan. 3, 52

Blessed are you, O Lord, the God of our fathers, and praiseworthy forever.

Alleluia. Let us bless the Father and the Son with the Holy Spirit. Alleluia.

TUESDAY

MASS OF THE HOLY ANGELS

INTROIT   Ps. 102, 20. 1   [*God's Angels*]

Bless the Lord, all you His angels,
  you mighty in strength, who do His bidding,
  obeying His spoken word. (P.T. Alleluia, alleluia.)

(Ps.) Bless the Lord, O my soul;
and, all my being,
  bless His holy Name.

Glory be to the Father, etc.

Repeat: **Bless the Lord,** etc., *as far as* (Ps.).

GRADUAL   Ps. 148, 1-2   [*Angelic Praise*]

Praise the Lord from the heavens,
  praise Him in the heights.
Praise Him, all you His angels,
  praise Him, all you His hosts.

Alleluia, alleluia. Ps. 137, 1-2 [*Praise with the Angels*]
In the presence of the Angels I will sing Your praise;

I will worship at Your holy temple
and give thanks to Your Name. Alleluia.

*After Septuagesima, the Alleluia and versicle are
omitted and the following Tract is said:*

TRACT   Ps. 102, 20. 21. 22   [Glory from the Angels]

Bless the Lord, all you His Angels,
you mighty in strength, who do His bidding.
Bless the Lord, all you His hosts,
His ministers, who do His will.
Bless the Lord, all His works,
everywhere in His domain.
Bless the Lord, O my soul!

*During Paschaltime, the Gradual is omitted and the
following Alleluia is said:*

Alleluia, alleluia. Ps. 137, 1-2; Matt. 28, 2 [Angelic Service]
In the presence of the Angels I will sing Your
praise;
I will worship at Your holy temple
and give thanks to Your Name.
Alleluia. An angel of the Lord came down from
heaven,
and drawing near rolled back the stone,
and sat upon it. Alleluia.

OFFERTORY   Apoc. 8,3. 4   [Angelic Ministers]

An angel stood near the altar of the temple,
having a golden censer in his hand,
and there was given to him much incense:
and the smoke of the perfumes ascended
before God. (P.T. Alleluia.)

COMMUNION   [*Praise from Angels*]

Angels, archangels, thrones and dominations,
   principalities, and powers, the virtues of the
      heavens,
Cherubim and seraphim,
   bless the Lord forever. (P.T. Alleluia.)

WEDNESDAY

MASS OF ST. JOSEPH

INTROIT   Ps. 32, 20-21; 79, 2   [*Guide of the Flock*]

The Lord is our help and our shield;
In Him our hearts rejoice;
   in His holy Name we trust. (P.T. Alleluia,
      alleluia.)
(Ps.) O Shepherd of Israel, hearken,
   O Guide of the flock of Joseph!
Glory be to the Father, etc.
Repeat: The Lord, etc., *as far as* (Ps.).

GRADUAL   Ps. 20, 4-5   [*Crowned*]

O Lord, You welcomed him with goodly
   blessings,
   You placed on his head a crown of precious
      stones.
He asked life of You: You gave him
   length of days forever and ever.

Alleluia, alleluia.   [*Growth*]
Make us lead, O Joseph, an innocent life;
   and may it ever be safe under your patronage.
      Alleluia.

After Septuagesima, the Alleluia and versicle are omitted and the following Tract is said:

TRACT Ps. 111, 1-3 [Glory of the Just]

Happy the man who fears the Lord,
 who greatly delights in His commands.
His posterity shall be mighty upon the earth;
 the upright generation shall be blessed.
Wealth and riches shall be in his house;
 his generosity shall endure forever.

During Paschaltime, the Gradual is omitted and the following Alleluia is said:

Alleluia, alleluia. [Joseph's Patronage]

In whatever tribulation they shall cry to me,
 I will hear them,
  and be their protector always.
Alleluia. Make us lead, O Joseph, an innocent
  life;
 and may it ever be safe under your patronage.
  Alleluia.

OFFERTORY Ps. 147, 12. 13 [Blessed Children]

Glorify the Lord, O Jerusalem,
For He has strengthened the bars of your gates,
 He has blessed your children within you.
  (P.T. Alleluia.)

COMMUNION Matt. 1, 16 [Mary's Spouse]

And Jacob begot Joseph the husband of Mary,
 and of her was born Jesus Who is called
  Christ. (P.T. Alleluia.)

THURSDAY

MASS OF THE HOLY SPIRIT

Mass: As on Pentecost Sunday, p. 161 (omitting Sequence), except:

From Pentecost to Septuagesima the Alleluia on p. 162, is omitted and the following is said:

GRADUAL   Ps. 32, 12. 6   [Creator, Bless]

Happy the nation whose God is the Lord,
   the people He has chosen for His own
      inheritance.
By the word of the Lord the heavens were
   made;
   by the breath of His mouth all their hosts.

Alleluia, alleluia.   [Come Holy Spirit]

Come, O Holy Spirit, fill the hearts of Your
   faithful;
And kindle in them the fire of Your love.
   Alleluia.

After Septuagesima, the Alleluia and versicle are omitted and the following Tract is said:

TRACT   Ps. 103, 30   [Enkindle Our Hearts]

Send forth Your Spirit, and they shall be
   created;
   and You shall renew the face of the earth.
O Lord, how good and sweet
   is Your spirit within us!
Come, O Holy Spirit, fill the hearts of Your
   faithful;
   and kindle in them the fire of Your love.

ALSO ON THURSDAY

MASS OF THE BLESSED SACRAMENT

INTROIT   Ps. 80, 17. 2   [*Food for God's People*]

He fed them with the best of wheat;
   and filled them with honey from the rock.
   (P.T. alleluia, alleluia.)

(Ps.) **Sing joyfully to God our strength;
   acclaim the God of Jacob.**

Glory be to the Father, etc.

Repeat: **He fed them,** etc., *as far as* (Ps.).

GRADUAL   Ps. 144, 15-16   [*Hope*]

The eyes of all look hopefully to You, O Lord;
   and You give them their food in due season.
You open Your hand;
   and satisfy the desire of every living thing.

Alleluia, alleluia.   John 6, 56. 57 [*The Heavenly Food*]
My Flesh is food indeed,
   and My Blood is drink indeed.
He who eats My flesh, and drinks My Blood,
   abides in Me and I in him. Alleluia.

*After Septuagesima, the Alleluia and versicle are
omitted and the following Tract is said:*

TRACT   Mal. 1, 11; Prov. 9, 5   [*Perpetual Sacrifice*]

From the rising of the sun, even to its setting,
   My Name is great among the nations.
And everywhere they bring sacrifice to My
      Name,
   and a pure offering;
For great is My Name among the nations.

Come, eat of my bread,
   and drink of the wine I have mixed for you.

During Paschaltime, the Gradual is omitted and the following Alleluia is said:

Luke 24, 35; John 6, 56-57

Alleluia, alleluia.   [*Life from the Eucharist*]
The disciples recognized the Lord Jesus
   in the breaking of the bread.
Alleluia. My Flesh is food indeed,
   and My Blood is drink indeed.
He who eats My Flesh, and drinks My Blood,
   abides in Me and I in him. Alleluia.

OFFERTORY   Lev. 21, 6   [*Solemn Liturgy*]

The priests of the Lord
   offer incense and loaves to God,
And therefore they shall be sacred to their God
   and not profane His Name. (P.T. Alleluia.)

COMMUNION   1 Cor. 11, 26-27   [*Divine Command*]

As often as you shall eat this bread
   and drink the cup,
You proclaim the death of the Lord,
   until He comes.
Therefore whoever eats this bread
   or drinks the cup of the Lord unworthily,
Will be guilty
   of the Body and Blood of the Lord. (P.T.
   Alleluia.)

ALSO ON THURSDAY

JESUS THE ETERNAL HIGH PRIEST

INTROIT   Ps. 109, 4. 1   *[Eternal High Priest]*

The Lord has sworn and He will not repent:
   "You are a priest forever, according to the
      order of Melchisedec." (P.T. Alleluia,
      alleluia.)

(Ps.) **The Lord said to my Lord:**
   "Sit at My right hand."

Glory be to the Father, etc.

Repeat: **The Lord has,** etc., *as far as* (Ps.).

GRADUAL   Luke 4, 18   *[Anointed]*

The Spirit of the Lord is upon Me
   because He has anointed Me.
To bring good news to the poor He has sent
      Me,
   to heal the contrite of heart.

Alleluia, alleluia.   Heb. 7, 24   *[Forever a Priest]*
But Jesus, because He continues forever,
   has an everlasting priesthood. Alleluia.

*After Septuagesima, the Alleluia and versicle are
omitted and the following Tract is said:*

TRACT   Ps. 9, 34-36   *[Protector]*

Rise, O Lord! O God, lift up Your hand!
   Forget not the afflicted!
You do see, for You behold misery and sorrow.
   On You the unfortunate man depends;
   of the fatherless You are the helper.

*During Paschaltime, the Gradual is omitted and the
following Alleluia is said:*

Heb. 7, 24; Luke 4, 18

Alleluia, alleluia.   [Good News and Healing]

But Jesus, because he continues forever,
   has an everlasting priesthood.

Alleluia. The Spirit of the Lord is upon Me
   because He has anointed Me;
    to bring good news to the poor He has sent
    Me,
    to heal the contrite of heart. Alleluia.

OFFERTORY   Heb. 10, 12-14   [One Sacrifice]

Christ, having offered one sacrifice for sins,
   has taken His seat forever at the right hand
   of God;

For by one offering He has perfected forever
   those who are sanctified. (P.T. Alleluia.)

COMMUNION   1 Cor. 11, 24-25   [Do This]

"This is the Body
   which shall be given up for you.

This cup is the new covenant in My Blood,"
   says the Lord.

"Do this as often as you drink it,
   in remembrance of Me." (P.T. Alleluia.)

FRIDAY

MASS OF THE PASSION

INTROIT   Phil. 2, 8-9; Ps. 88, 2   [Triumph of Obedience]

The Lord Jesus Christ humbled Himself unto
   death,
   even to death on a Cross;

Therefore God also exalted Him
and has bestowed upon Him
the Name that is above every name. (P.T.
Alleluia, alleluia.)

(Ps.) The favors of the Lord I will sing forever;
through all generations.

Glory be to the Father, etc.

Repeat: The Lord Jesus, etc., *as far as* (Ps.).

GRADUAL Ps. 68, 21-22 [No One to Comfort Him]

Insult has broken My heart, and I am weak;
I looked for sympathy, but there was none;
for comforters, and I found none.
Rather they put gall in My food,
and in My thirst they gave Me vinegar to
drink.

Alleluia, alleluia.
Hail, our King; [Obedient King]
You alone pitied our errors;
Obedient to the Father, You were led to be
crucified
like a meek lamb to the slaughter. Alleluia.

*After Septuagesima, the Alleluia and versicle are
omitted and the following Tract is said:*

TRACT Isa. 53, 4-5 [Pierced and Crushed]

Yet it was our infirmities that He bore,
our sufferings that He endured.
While we thought of Him as stricken,
as One smitten by God and afflicted.
But He was pierced for our offenses,
crushed for our sins.

Upon Him was the chastisement that makes us
    whole,
    by His stripes we were healed.

*During Paschaltime, the Gradual is omitted and the
following Alleluia is said:*

Alleluia, alleluia.   [Victorious Lamb]
Hail, our King:
    You alone pitied our errors;
Obedient to the Father, You were led to be
    crucified
    like a meek lamb to the slaughter.
Alleluia. Glory to You,
    to You hosanna;
To You triumph and victory;
    to You the crown of highest praise and
    honor! Alleluia.

OFFERTORY   [Mockery]

Wicked men rose up against Me;
    pitilessly they sought to slay Me without
    mercy;
    And they did not spare to spit in My face;
With lances they wounded Me,
    and all My bones are shattered. (P.T. Alleluia.)

COMMUNION   Ps. 21, 17-18   [Pierced]

They have pierced My hands and My feet:
    they have numbered all My bones. (P.T.
    Alleluia.)

ALSO ON FRIDAY

MASS OF THE SACRED HEART

INTROIT　Ps. 32, 11. 19. 1　　　　[*Love for All*]

The thoughts of His heart are to all generations:
To deliver them from death
　and preserve them in spite of famine. (P.T.
　　Alleluia, alleluia.)

(Ps.) Exult, you just, in the Lord;
　praise from the upright is fitting.

Glory be to the Father, etc.

Repeat: **The thoughts,** etc., *as far as* (Ps.).

GRADUAL　　Ps. 24, 8-9　　　　　[*The Guide*]

Good and upright is the Lord;
　thus He shows sinners the way.
He guides the humble to justice;
　He teaches the humble His way.

Alleluia, alleluia.　Matt. 11, 29　　　　[*Learn*]

Take My yoke upon you, and learn from Me,
　for I am meek, and humble of Heart:
　　and you will find rest for your souls. Alleluia.

After Septuagesima, the Alleluia and versicle are
omitted and the following Tract is said:

TRACT　Ps. 102, 8-10　　　　[*Forgiving Lord*]

Merciful and gracious is the Lord,
　slow to anger and abounding in kindness.
He will not always chide,
　nor does He keep His wrath forever.
Not according to our sins does He deal with us,
　nor does He requite us according to our
　　crimes.

During Paschaltime, the Gradual is omitted and the following Alleluia is said:

Alleluia, alleluia.   Matt. 11, 29. 28   [Learn of Me]

Take My yoke upon you and learn from Me,
 for I am meek and humble of Heart;
 and you will find rest for your souls.
Alleluia. Come to Me, all you who labor and are
 burdened,
 and I will give you rest. Alleluia.

OFFERTORY   Ps. 68, 21   [No One to Comfort]

My heart expected reproach and misery;
 I looked for sympathy, but there was none;
 and for comforters, and I found none.

During Paschaltime, substitute the following:

OFFERTORY   Ps. 39, 7-9   [Obedient Love]

Holocausts or sin-offerings You sought not;
 then said I: "Behold I come;
 in the written scroll it is prescribed for Me;
To do Your will, O my God, is My delight,
 and your law is within My Heart!" Alleluia.

COMMUNION   John 19, 34   [Blood and Water]

One of the soldiers opened His side with a
 lance,
 and immediately there came out blood and
 water.

During Paschaltime, substitute the following:

COMMUNION   John 7, 37   [Thirst No More]

If anyone thirst,
 let him come to Me and drink, alleluia,
 alleluia.

SATURDAY

MASS OF OUR LADY

The Common of the Feasts of the B.V.M., p. 268.

ON FIRST SATURDAY

MASS OF THE IMMACULATE HEART OF MARY

One Mass as on the Feast, p. 410, may be celebrated.

VARIOUS VOTIVE MASSES

ON THE DAY OF RELIGIOUS PROFESSION OF MEN

INTROIT   Ps. 39, 8-9. 2   [*Delight in God's Law*]

In the written scroll it is prescribed for Me:
To do Your will, O my God, is my delight,
    and Your law is within my heart. (P.T. Alleluia, alleluia.)

(Ps.) **I have waited, waited for the Lord,**
    and He stooped toward me.

Glory be to the Father, etc.

Repeat: **In the written,** etc., *as far as* (Ps.).

GRADUAL   Ps. 65, 13-14. 16   [*Vows*]

I will bring holocausts to Your house;
    to You I will fulfill the vows
    which my lips uttered.

Hear now, all you who fear God,
   while I declare what He has done for me.

Gal. 6, 14

Alleluia, alleluia.   [*With Christ on the Cross*]
But as for me,
   God forbid that I should glory,
   save in the Cross of our Lord Jesus Christ,
Through Whom the world is crucified to me,
   and I to the world. Alleluia.

After Septuagesima, the Alleluia and versicle are omitted and the following Tract is said:

TRACT   Ps. 62, 2; 50, 12   [*Longing for God*]

O God, my God, to You do I watch at break
   of day.
For You my flesh pines and my soul thirsts.
A clean heart create for me, O God,
   and a steadfast spirit renew within me.

During Paschaltime, the Gradual and Tract are omitted and the following Alleluia is said:

Gal. 6, 14; Ps. 132, 4

Alleluia, alleluia.   [*Dwelling Together in Christ*]
But as for me,
   God forbid that I should glory,
   save in the Cross of our Lord Jesus Christ,
Through Whom the world is crucified to me,
   and I to the world.
Alleluia. Behold, how good it is and how
   pleasant,
   where brethren dwell at one! Alleluia.

OFFERTORY 1 Par. 29, 17-18 [*Joyful Offering*]

O Lord God, in the simplicity of my heart
  I have joyfully offered all these things:
O God of Israel, keep forever this will. (P.T.
  Alleluia.)

COMMUNION Ps. 33, 9 [*Happy in the Lord*]

Taste and see how good the Lord is:
  happy the man who takes refuge in Him.
    (P.T. Alleluia.)

ON THE DAY OF RELIGIOUS PROFESSION
OF WOMEN

INTROIT Ps. 44, 11-12. 2 [*Follow the King*]

Hear, O daughter, and see: turn your ear,
  forget your people and your father's house;
And the King shall desire your beauty. (P.T.
  Alleluia, alleluia.)

(Ps.) My heart overflows with a goodly theme;
  as I sing my ode to the King.

Glory be to the Father, etc.

Repeat: **Hear, O daughter,** etc., *as far as* (Ps.).

GRADUAL Ps. 44, 2 [*For Love of Christ*]

I hold the kingdom of this world and all its
    allurements
  in contempt for the love of my Lord Jesus
    Christ,
Whom I have seen, Whom I have loved,
  and in Whom is my belief and my delight.
My heart overflows with a goodly theme;
  as I sing my ode to the King.

Alleluia, alleluia. Cant. 2, 16   [Union]

My Lover belongs to me and I to Him;
   He browses among the lilies. Alleluia.

After Septuagesima, the Alleluia and versicle are omitted and the following Tract is said:

TRACT   Ps. 26, 7-8. 10   [Seeking the Lord]

Hear, O Lord, the sound of my call;
   have pity on me, and answer me.
Of You my heart speaks, You my glance seeks;
   Your presence, O Lord, I seek.
You are my helper: cast me not off,
   forsake me not, O God my Savior.

During Paschaltime, the Gradual is omitted and the following Alleluia is said: Cant. 2, 16; Ps. 83, 5

Alleluia, alleluia.   [Happy in God's House]

My Lover belongs to me and I to Him;
   He browses among the lilies.

Alleluia. Happy they who dwell in Your house,
   O Lord;
   continually they praise You. Alleluia.

OFFERTORY   Ps. 115, 16-17   [Thanksgiving]

You have loosed, O Lord, my bonds;
To You will I offer the sacrifice of thanksgiving
   and I will call upon the Name of the Lord.
   (P.T. Alleluia.)

COMMUNION   Ps. 72, 28   [Near to God]

But for me, to be near God is my good;
   to make the Lord God my refuge. (P.T.
   Alleluia.)

---

482 VOCATIONS TO THE CLERICAL STATE

FOR VOCATIONS TO THE CLERICAL STATE

INTROIT   Matt. 4, 18-19; Ps. 18, 2   [*The Call*]

By the sea of Galilee, the Lord saw two
   brothers,
   Peter and Andrew;
And He called them,
   "Come, follow Me, and I will make you
   fishers of men." (P.T. Alleluia, alleluia.)
(Ps.) The heavens declare the glory of God,
   and the firmament proclaims His handiwork.
Glory be to the Father, etc.
Repeat: By the sea, etc., *as far as* (Ps.).

GRADUAL   Ps. 26, 4   [*To Dwell with the Lord*]

One thing I ask of the Lord;
   this I seek:
To dwell in the house of the Lord
   all the days of my life.
That I may gaze on the loveliness of the Lord
   and contemplate His temple.

Alleluia, alleluia.   Ps. 83, 5   [*In God's House*]
Happy they who dwell in Your house, O Lord!
   Continually they praise You! Alleluia.

*After Septuagesima, the Alleluia and versicle are
omitted and the following Tract is said:*

TRACT   Ps. 83, 2-4   [*Longing for God*]

How lovely is your dwelling place,
   O Lord of Hosts!
My soul yearns and pines
   for the courts of the Lord.
My heart and my flesh
   cry out for the living God.

Even the sparrow finds a home,
    and the swallow a nest
    in which she puts her young:
Your altars, O Lord of Hosts,
    my King and my God.

During Paschaltime, the Gradual is omitted and the following Alleluia is said:

Alleluia, alleluia.   Ps. 83, 5; Sir. 39, 19   [*New Life*]
Happy they who dwell in Your house, O Lord!
    Continually they praise You.

Alleluia. Break forth in blossoms like the lily,
    and yield a smell.
And bring forth leaves in grace.
    And praise with canticles
    and bless the Lord in His works. Alleluia.

OFFERTORY   Ps. 15, 5   [*My Portion*]

O Lord, my allotted portion and my cup,
    You it is Who hold fast my lot. (P.T. Alleluia.)

COMMUNION   Ps. 65, 16   [*What God Has Done*]

Hear now, all you who fear God, while I declare
    what He has done for me. (P.T. Alleluia.)

TO OBTAIN AND FOSTER RELIGIOUS VOCATIONS

INTROIT   Ps. 79, 15-16. 2   [*Preserve the Vine*]

Look down from heaven, and see,
Take care of this vine,
    and protect what your right hand has planted.
        (P.T. Alleluia, alleluia.)

(Ps.) **Shepherd of Israel, hearken,**
  O Guide of the flock of Joseph.

Glory be to the Father, etc.

Repeat: **Look down,** etc., *as far as* (Ps.).

GRADUAL   Ps. 99, 2-3   [*Joyful Service*]

Serve the Lord with gladness;
  come before Him with joyful song.
Know that the Lord is God;
  He made us, His we are.

Alleluia, alleluia.   Ps. 113, 15   [*Blessed by the Lord*]
May you be blessed by the Lord,
  Who made heaven and earth. Alleluia.

After Septuagesima, the Alleluia and versicle are omitted and the following Tract is said:

TRACT   Ps. 121, 6, 8-9   [*Peace*]

Pray for the peace of Jerusalem!
  May those who love you prosper!
Because of my relatives and friends
  I will say, "Peace be within you!"
Because of the house of the Lord, our God,
  I will pray for your good.

During Paschaltime, the Gradual and Tract are omitted and the following Alleluia is said:

Alleluia, alleluia.   Ps. 113, 15; 32, 12   [*God's Family*]
May you be blessed by the Lord,
  Who made heaven and earth.

Alleluia. Happy the nation whose God is the Lord,
  the people He has chosen for His own inheritance. Alleluia.

OFFERTORY   Ps. 42, 4   [Gladness in My Youth]

I will go in to the altar of God,
   the God of my gladness and joy. (P.T.
   Alleluia.)

COMMUNION   Ps. 132, 1. 3   [Brethren Together]

Behold, how good it is, and how pleasant,
   where brethren dwell at one!
For there the Lord has pronounced His blessing. (P.T. Alleluia.)

PROPAGATION OF THE FAITH

INTROIT   Ps. 66, 2-3. 4   [Salvation for All]

May God have pity on us and bless us;
   may He let His face shine upon us;
   and may He have pity on us.
So may Your ways be known upon earth;
   among all nations, Your salvation. (P.T. Alleluia, alleluia.)
(Ps.) May the peoples praise You, O God;
   may all the peoples praise You!
Glory be to the Father, etc.
Repeat: **May God have,** etc., *as far as* (Ps.).

GRADUAL   Ps. 66, 6-8   [Universal Praise]

May the peoples praise You, O God;
   may all the peoples praise you!
The earth has yielded its fruits.
   God, our God, has blessed us.
May God bless us,
   and may all the ends of the earth fear Him!

Alleluia, alleluia. Ps. 99, 1   [All Lands]

Sing joyfully to God, all you lands;
    serve the Lord with gladness;
    come before Him with joyful song. Alleluia.

After Septuagesima, the Alleluia and versicle are omitted and the following Tract is said:

TRACT Ps. 95, 3-5   [Proclaim God]

Tell the glory of the Lord among the nations;
    among all peoples, His wondrous deeds.
For great is the Lord and highly to be praised;
    awesome is He, beyond all gods.
For all the gods of the nations are devils,
    but the Lord made the heavens.

During Paschaltime, the Gradual is omitted and the following Alleluia is said:

Alleluia, alleluia. Ps. 99, 1-2   [The One Lord]

Sing joyfully to God, all you lands;
    serve the Lord with gladness;
    come before Him with joyful song.
Alleluia. Know that the Lord is God;
    He made us, His we are. Alleluia.

OFFERTORY Ps. 95, 7-9   [Worship the Lord]

Give to the Lord, you families of nations,
    give to the Lord glory and praise;
    give to the Lord the glory due His Name!
Bring gifts, and enter His courts;
    worship the Lord in His holy court. (P.T.
    Alleluia.)

COMMUNION Ps. 116, 1-2 [All Nations Praise the Lord]

Praise the Lord, all you nations;
    glorify Him, all you peoples!

For steadfast is His kindness toward us,
  and the fidelity of the Lord endures forever.
    (P.T. Alleluia.)

FOR CHURCH UNITY

INTROIT   Ps. 105, 47. 1   [Gather Us]

Save us, O Lord, our God,
  and gather us from among the nations,
That we may give thanks to Your holy Name
  and glory in praising you. (P.T. Alleluia,
    alleluia.)
(Ps.) Give thanks to the Lord, for He is good,
  for His kindness endures forever!
Glory be to the Father, etc.
Repeat: **Save us,** etc., *as far as* (Ps.).

GRADUAL   Ps. 121, 6-7   [Peace]

Pray for the peace of Jerusalem!
  May those who love You prosper!
May peace be within your walls,
  prosperity in your buildings.

Alleluia, alleluia.   Ps. 147, 12   [Glorify God]
Glorify the Lord, O Jerusalem;
  praise your God, O Sion. Alleluia.

After Septuagesima, the Alleluia and versicle are
omitted and the following Tract is said:

TRACT   Ps. 75, 2-4   [City of Peace]

God is renowned in Juda;
  in Israel great is His Name.
In the city of peace is His abode;
  his dwelling is in Sion.

There he shattered the flashing shafts of the
  bow,
    shield and sword, and weapons of war.

*During Paschaltime, the Gradual is omitted and the
following Alleluia is said:*

Alleluia, alleluia. Ps. 147, 12. 14   [Spiritual Food]

Glorify the Lord, O Jerusalem;
  praise your God, O Sion.

Alleluia. He has granted peace in your borders;
  with the best of wheat he fills you. Alleluia.

OFFERTORY   Rom. 15, 5-6 [One in Mind and Spirit]

May God grant you
  to be of one mind toward one another;
That, one in spirit,
  you may with one mouth glorify our God.
    (P.T. Alleluia.)

COMMUNION   1 Cor. 10, 17   [One Body]

The Bread is one,
  and we though many, are one body,
All of us who partake of the one Bread,
  and of the one Chalice. (P.T. Alleluia.)

FOR PEACE

INTROIT   Sir. 36, 18; Ps. 121, 1   [Peace]

Give peace, O Lord,
  to those who have hoped in You,
  and let Your prophets be proved true.
Hear the prayers of Your servant,
  and of Your people Israel. (P.T. Alleluia,
    alleluia.)

(Ps.) **I rejoiced because they said to me,**
 "We will go up to the house of the Lord."

Glory be to the Father, etc.

Repeat: **Give peace,** etc., *as far as* (Ps.).

GRADUAL   Ps. 121, 6-7   [Peace]

Pray for the peace of Jerusalem!
 May those who love You prosper!
May peace be within your walls,
 prosperity in your buildings.

Alleluia, alleluia. Ps. 147, 12   [Glorify God]
Glorify the Lord, O Jerusalem;
 praise your God, O Sion. Alleluia.

After Septuagesima, the Alleluia and versicle are omitted and the following Tract is said:

TRACT   Ps. 75, 2-4   [City of Peace]

God is renowned in Juda;
 in Israel great is His Name.
In the city of peace is His abode;
 his dwelling is in Sion.
There he shattered the flashing shafts of the bow,
 shield and sword, and weapons of war.

During Paschaltime, the Gradual is omitted and the following Alleluia is said:

Alleluia, alleluia. Ps. 147, 12. 14   [Spiritual Food]
Glorify the Lord, O Jerusalem;
 praise your God, O Sion.
Alleluia. He has granted peace in your borders;
 with the best of wheat he fills you. Alleluia.

OFFERTORY   Ps. 134, 3. 6   ⌈ *Praise the Lord* ⌉

Praise the Lord, for He is good:
   sing to His Name, for it is sweet.
All that He wills He does
   in heaven and on earth. (P.T. Alleluia.)

COMMUNION   John 14, 27   [*My Peace*]

"Peace I leave with you,
   My peace I give to you," says the Lord. (P.T.
   Alleluia.)

FOR THE SICK

INTROIT   Ps. 54, 2-3. 4   [*Give Heed to Me*]

Hearken, O God, to my prayer;
   turn not away from my pleading;
   give heed to me, and answer me. (P.T. Alleluia,
   alleluia.)
(Ps.) **I rock with grief, and am troubled**
   at the voice of the enemy and the clamor of
   the wicked.
Glory be to the Father, etc.
Repeat: **Hearken, O God,** etc., *as far as* (Ps.).

GRADUAL   Ps. 6, 3-4   [*Pity*]

Have pity on me, O Lord, for I am languishing;
   heal me, O Lord. For my body is in terror;
My soul, too, is utterly terrified.

Alleluia, alleluia.   Ps. 101, 2   [*Hear Me*]
Lord, hear my prayer,
   and let my cry come to You. Alleluia.

After Septuagesima, the Alleluia and versicle are omitted and the following Tract is said:

TRACT   Ps. 30, 10-11   [Failing Strength]

Have pity on me, O Lord, for I am in distress;
   with sorrow my eye is consumed; my soul
     also, and my body.
For my life is spent with grief
   and my years with sighing.
My strength has failed through affliction,
   and my bones are consumed.

During Paschaltime, the Gradual is omitted and the following Alleluia is said:

Alleluia, alleluia.   Ps. 101, 2; 27, 7   [Trust]
Hear, O Lord, my prayer,
   and let my cry come to You.
Alleluia. In God my heart trusts, and I find help;
   then my flesh flourishes again and with my
     song I give Him thanks. Alleluia.

OFFERTORY   Ps. 54, 2-3   [Turn Not Away]

Hearken, O God, to my prayer;
   turn not away from my pleading;
     give heed to me and answer me. (P.T.
     Alleluia).

COMMUNION   Ps. 30, 17-18   [God's Kindness]

Let Your face shine upon Your servant;
   save me in Your kindness.
O Lord, let me not be put to shame, for I call
   upon You. (P.T. Alleluia.)

HYMNS and PSALMODY

ALPHABETICAL INDEX

LITURGICAL INDEX (Suggested Use)

HOLY SPIRIT, LORD OF LIGHT 1

Tr. Rev. E. Caswall

Samuel Webbe

1. Ho - ly Spir - it, Lord of Light,
2. Thou, of all con - sol - ers best,
3. Light im - mor - tal, Light di - vine,
4. Heal our wounds, our strength re - new;

1. From thy clear ce - les - tial height,
2. Thou the souls most wel - come Guest,
3. Vis - it Thou these hearts of Thine,
4. On our dry - ness pour Thy dew;

1. Thy pure beam - ing ra - diance give.
2. Dost re - fresh - ing peace be - stow.
3. And our in - most be - ing fill.
4. Wash the stains of guilt a - way.

1. Come, Thou Fa - ther of the poor;
2. Thou in toil art com - fort sweet;
3. If Thou take Thy grace a - way,
4. Bend the stub - born heart and will;

1. Come, with treas - ures which en - dure;
2. Plea - sant cool - ness in the heat;
3. Noth - ing pure in man will stay;
4. Melt the fro - zen, warm the chill;

1. Come, Thou Light of all that live.
2. So - lace in the midst of woe.
3. All his good is turned to ill.
4. Guide the steps that go a - stray.

- 495 -

2   A MIGHTY FORTRESS IS OUR GOD

Ann Hoeffer Pax 1965   M. Luther

1. A might-y for-tress is___ our God, A
2. There is a riv-er flow-ing strong, Of
3. Be-hold the la-bors of___ the Lord, He

bul-wark nev-er fail — ing,
liv-ing wa-ters deep and wide,
teach-es men His ways of peace,

Our help-er he___ a-bove the flood Of
Je-ru-sa-lem for thee we long, The
His might-y voice does melt the sword, And

earth-ly woe pre-vail — ing. And
dwell-ing place of God most high. Though
caus-es war and hate to cease. Be

though the earth should quake, And
kings and na-tions rage, And
still and know your God who

might-y moun-tains shake, Yet
bit-ter wars do wage, Yet
rules with gen-tle rod, For

we shall nev-er fear, The Lord of Hosts is
we shall nev-er fear, The Lord of Hosts is
we shall nev-er fear, The Lord of Hosts is

near, Our Fa-ther's hand pro - tects us.
near, The Son of God pro - tects us.
near, His Spir - it o - ver - flows us all.

FAITH OF OUR FATHERS 3

Frederick W. Faber

Henri F. Hemy
and James G. Walton

1. Faith of our fa - thers! liv - ing still,
2. Faith of our fa - thers! We will love
3. Faith of our fa - thers! Ma - ry's prayers

In spite of dun - geon, fire,___and sword:
Both friend and foe in all ___ our strife,
Shall keep our coun - try close___ to thee;

O how our hearts beat high with joy,
And preach thee too, as love knows how,
And through the truth that comes from God,

When-e'er we hear that glo - rious word!
By kind - ly words and vir - tuous life.'
O we shall pros - per and be free.

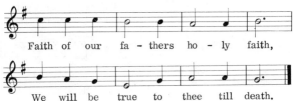

Faith of our fa - thers ho - ly faith,

We will be true to thee till death.

4   JESUS CHRIST IS RISEN TODAY

Tate and Brady   C Wesley   Lyra Davidica, 1708

1. Je - sus Christ is ris'n to - day, ____
2. Hymns of praise then let us sing, ____
3. But the pains which He en - dured, ____
4. Sing we to our God a - bove, ____

Al - le - lu - ia!

1. Our tri - um - phant
2. Un - to Christ our
3. Our sal - va - tion
4. Praise e - ter - nal

1. ho - ly day, ____
2. heav'n - ly King, ____
3. have se - cured, ____
4. as His love, ____

Al - . le -

1. Who did once up - on the cross,
2. Who en - dured the cross and grave,
3. Now in heav - en Christ our King,
4. Praise Him, all ye heav'n - ly host,

lu - ia!

Al - le - lu - ia!

1. Suf - fer to re -
2. Sin - ners to re -
3. Where the an - gels
4. Fa - ther, Son and

deem our loss,
deem and save,
ev - er sing,
Ho - ly Ghost,

Al - le - lu - ia!

NOW THANK WE ALL OUR GOD 5

Martin Rinkart, d. 1649
Tr. Catherine Winkworth, alt.

Johann Cruger

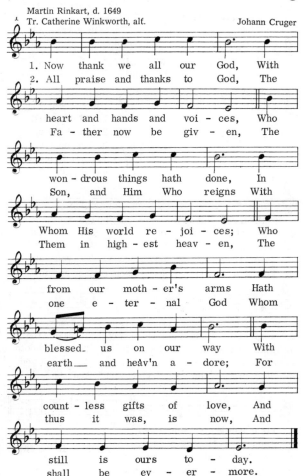

1. Now thank we all our God, With
2. All praise and thanks to God, The

heart and hands and voi - ces, Who
Fa - ther now be giv - en, The

won - drous things hath done, In
Son, and Him Who reigns With

Whom His world re - joi - ces; Who
Them in high - est heav - en, The

from our moth - er's arms Hath
one e - ter - nal God Whom

blessed us on our way With
earth and heav'n a - dore; For

count - less gifts of love, And
thus it was, is now, And

still is ours to - day.
shall be ev - er - more.

6 O SONS AND DAUGHTERS OF THE LORD

Jean Tisserand, O.F.M., 1494
Tr. John Neale

Adapted from Palestrina
By William H. Monk

Al - le - lu - ia! Al - le - lu -

ia! Al - le - lu - ia!

1. O sons and
2. On East-er
3. An an-gel
4. On this most
5. Glo - ry to

1. daugh-ters, let ___ us sing! The King of
2. morn, at break of day, The faith-ful
3. clad in white they see, Who sat and
4. ho - ly day ___ of days, To you our
5. Fa - ther and to Son, Who has for

1. heav'n, the glo - rious King, To - day is
2. wom - en went their way To seek the
3. spoke un - to ___ the three, "Your Lord doth
4. hearts and voice we raise, In laud and
5. us the vict - 'ry won And ho - ly

1. ris'n and tri - umph - ing.
2. tomb where Je - sus lay.
3. go to Gal - i - lee."
4. ju - bi - lee and praise.
5. Ghost; blest Three in One.

Al - le - lu - ia!

PRAISE THE LORD YE HEAVENS

7

Ps. 148 Foundling Hospital Collection

Rowland H. Prichard

1. Praise the Lord,___ ye heav'ns, a-
dore Him; Praise him, an-gels in___ the height;
Sun and moon re-joice be-fore___ him;
Praise him, all ye stars of light.
Praise the Lord, for he has spo-ken;
Worlds his might-y voice o-beyed;
Laws, which nev-er shall be bro-ken,
For their guid-ance he has made.

2. Praise the Lord,___ for he is
glo-rious, Nev-er shall his prom-ise fail;
God has made his saints vic-to-rious,
Sin and death shall not___ pre-vail.
Praise the God of our sal-va-tion;
Hosts on high, his power pro-claim;
Heav'n and earth and all cre-a-tion,
Praise and mag-ni-fy his name.

8   PRAISE TO THE LORD

Based on Ps. 103 and 150
Joachim Neander

Stralsund, 1665

1. Praise to the Lord, the Al - might - y the King of cre - a - tion; O my soul, praise him, for he is our health and sal - va - tion: Hear the great throng, Joy-ous with prais - es and song, Sound-ing in glad ad - o - ra - tion.

2. Praise to the Lord, who doth pros - per thy way and de - fend thee; Sure - ly his good-ness and mer - cy shall ev - er at - tend thee; Pon - der a - new What the Al - might - y can do, Who with his love doth be - friend thee.

3. Praise to the Lord, O let all that is in me a - dore him! All that hath breath join in our prais - es now to a - dore him! Let the "A - men" Sung by all peo - ple a - gain Sound as we wor - ship be - fore him. A - men.

WE PRAISE THEE O GOD OUR REDEEMER 9

Ps. 26:12
Tr. Julia B. Cady

E. Kremser

1. We praise Thee, O God, our Re-
2. We wor-ship Thee, God of our
3. With voic-es u - nit-ed our

deem-er, Cre - a-tor, In grate-ful de-
fa-thers, we bless Thee; Thro' trou-ble and
prais-es we of - fer, To Thee, great Je-

vo - tion our trib - ute we bring; We
tem - pest our Guide hast Thou been; When
ho - vah, glad an -thems we raise. Thy

lay it be-fore Thee, we kneel and a-
per - ils o'er-take us, es - cape Thou wilt
strong arm will guide us, our God is be-

dore Thee, We bless Thy ho - ly name, glad
make us, And with Thy help, O Lord, our
side us, To Thee, our great Re-deem - er for-

prais - es we sing.
bat - tles we win.
ev - er be praise. A - men.

10 YE WATCHERS AND YE HOLY ONES

Athelstan Riley, 1858-1945

Cologne, 1623

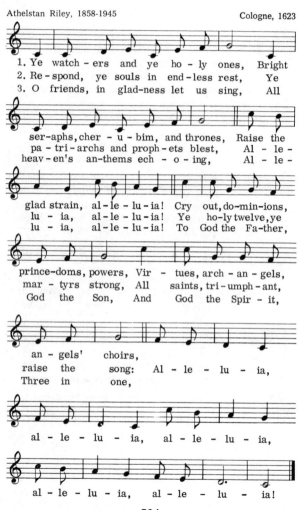

1. Ye watch-ers and ye ho-ly ones, Bright ser-aphs, cher-u-bim, and thrones, Raise the glad strain, al-le-lu-ia! Cry out, do-min-ions, prince-doms, powers, Vir-tues, arch-an-gels, an-gels' choirs, raise the song: Al-le-lu-ia, al-le-lu-ia, al-le-lu-ia, al-le-lu-ia, al-le-lu-ia!

2. Re-spond, ye souls in end-less rest, Ye pa-tri-archs and proph-ets blest, Al-le-lu-ia, al-le-lu-ia! Ye ho-ly twelve, ye mar-tyrs strong, All saints, tri-umph-ant, raise the song:

3. O friends, in glad-ness let us sing, All heav-en's an-thems ech-o-ing, Al-le-lu-ia, al-le-lu-ia! To God the Fa-ther, God the Son, And God the Spir-it, Three in one,

ACCEPT ALMIGHTY FATHER

11

Anonymous

J. Mohr

1. Ac - cept, Al-might - y Fa - ther, This
gift of bread and wine Which now thy priest
does of - fer To thee, O God be - nign,
In hum - ble rep - a - ra - tion For sins
and fail - ings dread, To win life ev - er -
last - ing For liv - ing and for dead.

2. O God, by this com - ming - ling Of
wa - ter and of wine, May he who took
our na - ture Give us his life di - vine.
Come, thou who mak - est ho - ly, And bless
this sac - ri - fice; Then shall our gift be
pleas - ing To thee a - bove the skies.

12 ACCEPT O GOD ETERNAL KING

Eugene Lindusky, O.S.C.

J. H. Schein

1. Ac - cept, O God, e - ter - nal King,
2. We place our-selves be - fore your throne:

This bread and wine, the gifts we bring;
Take all we are and all we own.

Though now the fruit of field and vine,
Our hearts, our lives are yours by right,

They soon shall be a gift di - vine;
Then make them pleas - ing in your sight,

For when the sa - cred words are done,
U - nite them all with Christ, your Son,

Our gift will be your on - ly Son.
That he and we may be as one.

1. Lord, ac - cept the gifts we of - fer
2. May our souls be pure and spot - less
3. Take our gifts, Al - might - y Fa - ther,

At this Eu - char - is - tic Feast.
As the Host of wheat so fine;
Liv - ing God, e - ter - nal, true,

Bread and wine to be trans-formed now
May all stain of sin be crushed out
Which we give through Christ, our Sav - ior,

Through the ac - tion of Thy priest.
Like the grape that forms the wine,
Plead - ing here for us a - new.

Take us, too, O Lord, trans-form us;
As we, too, be - come par - tak - ers
Grant sal - va - tion to all pres - ent

Be thy grace in us in - creased.
In this Sa - cri - fice di - vine.
And our faith and love re - new.

Anonymous

B. Helder, 1848

1. Re - ceive, O God this of - f'ring Now made in mem - o - ry Of Je - sus' death and pas - sion, And pas - chal vic - to - ry; In praise of Bless - ed Ma - ry, And John the Bap - tist great, Of Pet - er, Paul a - pos - tles, And Saints in glo - rious state.

2. This sac - ri - fice most ho - ly We pray O Tri - une God, A vail to their great hon - or Who this dark earth have trod; May they, whose mem - 'ry keep - ing, We ho - nor here be - low Now plead for us in heav - en, That Thou Thy mer - cy show.

English: John Ryan

Adapted

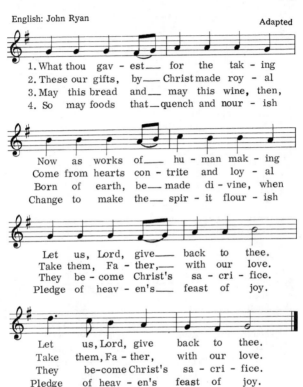

1. What thou gav - est___ for the tak - ing
2. These our gifts, by___ Christ made roy - al
3. May this bread and___ may this wine, then,
4. So may foods that___quench and nour - ish

Now as works of___ hu - man mak - ing
Come from hearts con - trite and loy - al
Born of earth, be___ made di - vine, when
Change to make the___ spir - it flour - ish

Let us, Lord, give___ back to thee.
Take them, Fa - ther,___ with our love.
They be - come Christ's sa - cri - fice.
Pledge of heav - en's___ feast of joy.

Let us, Lord, give back to thee.
Take them, Fa - ther, with our love.
They be - come Christ's sa - cri - fice.
Pledge of heav - en's feast of joy.

16 HUMBLY WE ADORE THEE

Melvin Farrell, S.S.   Paris Processional, 1697

1. Hum - bly we a - dore thee, Christ, Re - deem - er King; Thou art Lord of heav - en, thou to whom we sing.
2. Je - sus, Lord, we thank thee for this wond - rous Bread; In our land thou dwell - est, by thee we are fed.
3. Thou who died to save us liv - est as our Light; Though our eyes are blind - ed, yet our Faith gives sight.
4. Christ, our God and Broth - er, hear our hum - ble plea: By this ho - ly ban - quet keep us joined to thee.
5. Hail, thou Word In - car - nate, born from Mar - ry's womb; Hail, thou Strength im - mor - tal, ris - en from the tomb.
6. Christ, at his Last Sup - per, break - ing bread, de - creed: "This my Bod - y, take and eat" heav - 'nly Food in - deed!
7. Now with glad thanks-giv - ing, praise Christ glo - ri - fied, He in us is pres - ent; we in him a - bide.

1. God, the Might - y, thou hast come,
2. We who share __ this Mys - te - ry
3. Christ, do thou __ be mer - ci - ful,
4. Make us one __ in lov - ing thee,
5. Share with us __ thy vic - tor - y,
6. Then he blessed __ the cup of wine -
7. Mem - bers of __ his Bod - - y,

1. bear - ing gifts of grace;
2. in thee are made one:
3. Lamb for sin - ners slain,
4. one in mind and heart,
5. Sav - ior ev - er blest:
6. "Take ye this," he said:
7. we in him are One;

1. Son of Ad - am still thou art:
2. Ev - 'ry act we of - fer thee
3. We in grief con - fess our guilt.
4. Till in heav - en we are thine,
5. Live more ful - ly in our hearts;
6. "Drink the chal - ice of my Blood,
7. Hail this sa - cred Un - ion,

1. Sav - ior to our race.
2. in thy Name is done.
3. cleanse our souls of stain.
4. nev - er - more to part.
5. be our con - stant Guest.
6. soon for sin - ners shed."
7. heav'n on earth be - gun!

17   AT THAT FIRST EUCHARIST

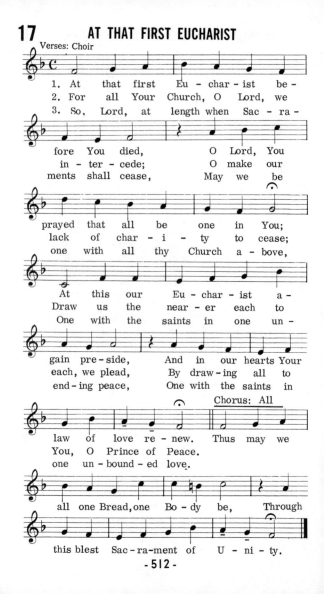

Verses: Choir

1. At that first Eucharist before You died, O Lord, You prayed that all be one in You; At this our Eucharist again preside, And in our hearts Your law of love re-new. Thus may we all one Bread, one Body be, Through this blest Sacrament of Unity.

2. For all Your Church, O Lord, we intercede; O make our lack of charity to cease; Draw us the nearer each to each, we plead, By drawing all to You, O Prince of Peace.

3. So, Lord, at length when Sacraments shall cease, May we be one with all thy Church above, One with the saints in one unending peace, One with the saints in one unbounded love.

Chorus: All

-512-

J. Conder   Verspoell's Gesangbuch, 1810

1. Bread of Heav'n, on Thee we feed,
For thy Flesh is food in-deed;
Ev - er may our souls be fed
With this true and liv - ing Bread,
Day by day with strength sup - plied,
Through the life of him who died.

2. Vine of Heav'n, thy Blood sup - plies
This blest Cup of Sac - ri - fice;
Lord, thy wounds our heal - ing give;
To thy Cross we look and live;
Je - sus, may we ev - er be
Graft - ed, root - ed, built in thee.

19 SING MY TONGUE THE SAVIOR'S GLORY

St. Thomas Aquinas
Tr. Rev. E. Caswall

Gregorian Chant

1. Sing my tongue, the Sav-ior's glo - ry,
2. Of a pure_ and spot-less Vir - gin
3. On the night_ of that last sup - per
4. Word made Flesh, the bread of na - ture
5. Down in ad - or - a - tion fall - ing,
6. To the ev - er-last-ing Fa - ther,

1. Of_ His flesh the mys-t'ry sing;____
2. Born_ for us on earth be - low,____
3. Seat - ed with His Chos-en band,____
4. By___ His word to Flesh He turns;___
5. Lo!_ the sa - cred Host we hail;_____
6. And_ the Son who reigns on high,____

1. Of the Blood all price ex - ceed - ing,
2. He, as Man, with man con - vers - ing,
3. He, the Pas - chal vic - tim eat - ing,
4. Wine in - to His Blood He chan - ges,
5. Lo! o'er an - cient forms de - part - ing,
6. With the Ho - ly Ghost pro - ceed - ing

1. Shed by our im - mor - tal King,____
2. Stayed, the seeds of truth to sow;___
3. First ful - fills the Law's com - mand;___
4. What though sense no change dis - cerns?_
5. New - er rites of grace pre - vail;___
6. Forth from Each e - ter - nal - ly,____

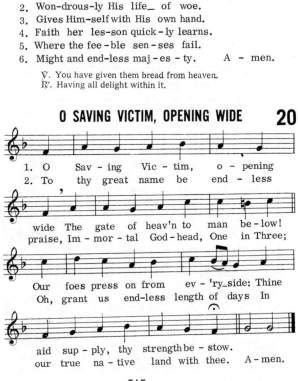

1. Des - tined for the world's re - demp-tion,
2. Then He closed in sol - emn or - der
3. Then as food to all His breth - ren
4. On - ly be the heart in ear - nest,
5. Faith for all de-fects sup - ply - ing
6. Be sal - va - tion, hon - or, bless - ing,

1. From a no - ble womb to spring.
2. Won-drous-ly His life_ of woe.
3. Gives Him-self with His own hand.
4. Faith her les-son quick - ly learns.
5. Where the fee - ble sen - ses fail.
6. Might and end-less maj - es - ty. A - men.

V. You have given them bread from heaven.
R. Having all delight within it.

O SAVING VICTIM, OPENING WIDE 20

1. O Sav - ing Vic - tim, o - pening
2. To thy great name be end - less

wide The gate of heav'n to man be - low!
praise, Im - mor - tal God-head, One in Three;

Our foes press on from ev - 'ry_side: Thine
Oh, grant us end-less length of days In

aid sup - ply, thy strength be - stow.
our true na - tive land with thee. A - men.

21 LET ALL MORTAL FLESH KEEP SILENCE

Gerald Moultrie

French, Traditional

1. Let all mor-tal flesh keep___ si-lence,
2. King of kings, yet born of ___ Mar - y,
3. Rank on rank the host of ___ heav - en
4. At his feet the six - winged___ ser - aph,

1. and with fear and trem - bling___ stand;
2. as of old on earth he ___ stood,
3. spreads its van-guard on the___ way,
4. cher - u - bim with sleep - less___ eye,

1. Pon - der noth - ing earth - ly - mind - ed
2. Lord of lords in hu - man___ ves - ture
3. As the Light of Light de - scend - eth
4. Veil their fac - es to the ___ Pres - ence,

1. for with bless-ing in his___ hand
2. in the Bod - y and the ___ Blood
3. from the realms of end - less___ day,
4. as with cease-less voice they___ cry,

1. Christ, our God, to earth de - scend -
2. He will give to all the faith -
3. That the powers of hell may van -
4. "Al - le - lu - ia, al - le - lu -

1. eth, our full hom - age to de - mand.
2. ful his own self for heav'n-ly___ food.
3. ish as the dark-ness clears a - way.
4. ia, al - le - lu - ia, Lord Most___ High!"

-516-

O FOOD THAT WEARY PILGRIMS LOVE 22

H. Isaac

1. O Food that wea-ry pil-grims love, O___
2. O fount of love,— O cleans-ing tide, Which
3. Lord Je-sus, Whom— by pow'r di-vine, Now___

Bread of an-gel hosts a-bove, O Man-na of the
from the Sav-ior's pierc-ed side, And Sa-cred Heart does
hid-den 'neath the out-ward sign, We wor-ship and a-

saints! The hun-gry soul_would feed on Thee, Ne'er
flow! Be ours to drink_from Thy pure rill, Which
dore; Grant, when the veil___ a-way is rolled, With

may the heart un-sol-aced be Which for_Thy sweet-ness faints.
on-ly can our spir-its fill, And all_we need be-stow.
o-pen face we may be-hold Thy-self for ev-er-more.

23 I LOVE THEE, O THOU LORD MOST HIGH

'Psalteriolum Cantionum Catholicarum', 1710
Tr. Rev. E. Caswall

Koln, 1695
'Symphonia Sirenum,

1. I love Thee, O Thou Lord most high, Be-cause Thou first hast lov-ed me; I seek no oth-er lib-er-ty But that of be-ing bound to Thee.

2. May mem-o-ry no thought sug-gest But shall to Thy pure glo-ry tend; May un-der-stand-ing find no rest, Ex-cept in Thee, its on-ly end.

3. All mine is Thine; say but the word, What-e'er Thou will-est shall be done; I know Thy love, all gra-cious Lord, I know it seeks my good a-lone.

4. A-part from Thee, all things are naught; Then grant, O ev-er bless-ed Bliss, Grant me to love Thee as I ought; Thou giv-est all in giv-ing this.

GOD FATHER PRAISE AND GLORY   24

Tr. Rothensteiner, 1936

Mainz Melody

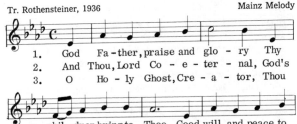

1. God   Fa-ther, praise and glo-ry   Thy
2. And Thou, Lord Co - e - ter - nal, God's
3. O   Ho-ly Ghost, Cre - a - tor, Thou

1. chil-dren bring to   Thee. Good will and peace to
2. sole be-got-ten Son;   O   Je-sus, King a-
3. Gift   of God most high; Life, love and sa-cred

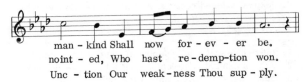

man - kind Shall   now   for - ev - er   be.
noint - ed, Who   hast   re - demp-tion   won.
Unc - tion Our   weak-ness Thou sup - ply.

Refrain

O   most Ho - ly   Trin - i - ty,

Un - di - vid - ed   U - ni - ty;   Ho - ly God,

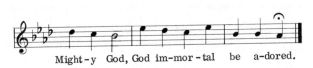

Might-y God, God im-mor-tal   be a-dored.

25 MY GOD HOW WONDERFUL THOU ART

Frederick W. Faber

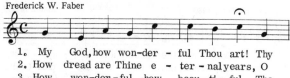

1. My God, how won-der-ful Thou art! Thy
2. How dread are Thine e-ter-nal years, O
3. How won-der-ful, how beau-ti-ful The
4. Oh, how I fear Thee, liv-ing God, With

1. Maj-es-ty how bright! How beau-ti-ful Thy
2. ev-er-last-ing Lord, By pros-trate spir-its
3. sight of Thee must be, Thine end-less wis-dom,
4. deep-est, ten-d'rest fears And wor-ship Thee with

1. mer-cy-seat In depths of burn-ing light!
2. day and night Un-ceas-ing-ly a-dored!
3. bound-less power And shin-ing pur-i-ty!
4. trem-bling hope And pen-i-ten-tial tears!

26 O GOD OUR HELP IN AGES PAST

1.
O God, our help in ages past,
Our hope for years to come,
Our shelter from the stormy blast,
And our eternal home.

2.
Under the shadow of Thy throne,
Thy saints have dwelt secure,
Sufficient is Thine arm alone,
And our defense is sure.

3.
A thousand ages in Thy sight,
Are like an evening gone:
Short as the watch that ends the night,
Before the rising sun.

4.
O God, our help in ages past,
Our hope for years to come,
Be Thou our guide while troubles last,
And our eternal home.

I. Watts.

All People That On Earth Do Dwell

v. 1. Thomas Ken
v. v. 2-4. William Kethe

Louis Bourgeois

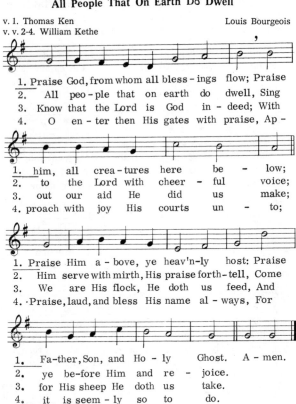

1. Praise God, from whom all bless-ings flow; Praise
2. All peo-ple that on earth do dwell, Sing
3. Know that the Lord is God in-deed; With
4. O en-ter then His gates with praise, Ap-

1. him, all crea-tures here be - low;
2. to the Lord with cheer - ful voice;
3. out our aid He did us make;
4. proach with joy His courts un - to;

1. Praise Him a-bove, ye heav'n-ly host: Praise
2. Him serve with mirth, His praise forth-tell, Come
3. We are His flock, He doth us feed, And
4. Praise, laud, and bless His name al-ways, For

1. Fa-ther, Son, and Ho - ly Ghost. A - men.
2. ye be-fore Him and re - joice.
3. for His sheep He doth us take.
4. it is seem - ly so to do.

28   HOLY, HOLY, HOLY

Reginald Heber, 1826   John B. Dykes, 1861

1. Ho - ly, ho - ly, ho - ly! Lord___ God Al -
2. Ho - ly, ho - ly, ho - ly! All the saints a -
3. Ho - ly, ho - ly, ho - ly! Though the dark - ness
4. Ho - ly, ho - ly, ho - ly! Lord___ God Al -

1. might - y! Ear - ly in the morn - ing our
2. dore thee, Cast - ing down their gold - en crowns a -
3. hide thee, Though the eye of sin - ful man thy
4. might - y! All thy works shall praise thy name in

1. song shall rise to thee: Ho - ly, ho - ly,
2. round the glass - y sea; Cher - u - bim and
3. glo - ry may not see, On - ly thou art
4. earth, and sky, and sea; Ho - ly, ho - ly,

1. ho - ly! Mer - ci - ful and might - y,
2. Ser - a - phim fall - ing down be - fore thee,
3. ho - ly; there is none be - side thee,
4. ho - ly! Mer - ci - ful and might - y,

1. God in three per - sons, bless - ed Trin - i - ty.
2. Who were and are and ev - er - more shall be.
3. Per - fect in power, in love, and pur - i - ty.
4. God in three per - sons, bless - ed Trin - i - ty.

WITHIN THY SACRED HEART 29

1. With - in Thy Sa - cred Heart, dear Lord, My
2. Say on - ly Thou hast par - doned me, Say

anx - ious thoughts shall rest I
on - ly I am Thine In

nei - ther ask for life nor death, Thou
all things else dis - pose of me, Thy

know - est what is best.
Ho - ly Will is mine.

STRENGTHEN, O GOD 30

ANT: Strength-en, O God, what You have wrought in us,

From Your holy temple, which is in Je - ru - sa - lem.

Glo - ry be to the Father, and to the Son,
As it was in the beginning
is now and ever shall be,

and to the - - - - - - - Ho - ly Spi - rit,
world with - - - - - - out end A - men.

ANT: Strength-en, O God what You have wrought in us,

From Your holy temple which is in Je - ru - sa - lem.

31   O LOVE WHO DREW FROM JESUS' SIDE

Anonymous, 1962

John B. Dykes, 1861

1. O Love, who drew from Je - sus' side, One Bod - y freed from Ad - am's shame, One Church sent forth to rule and guide, One faith con-firmed by gifts of flame: When world - ly schemes our hopes as - sail, king - dom come, thy truth pre - vail.

2. Round Pe - ter's throne may all u - nite; From blind - ed eyes the veil with-draw; The minds of rul - ers set a - right Who bind thy Church be - neath their law; Where faith grows dim and hearts are frail, Thy king - dom come, thy truth pre - vail.

3. While Chris-tians pray for u - ni - ty, Pour forth the light thy saints have seen; Dis - pel the dark of en - mi - ty: Make known to all what love can mean; Where brood - ing minds old wounds be-wail, king - dom come, thy truth pre - vail.

4. Spoiled chil - dren, we, so blest with sight Re - deemed by love sur - pass-ing all; Lest we who glo - ry in thy light Share not our gift, heed not thy call; In Chris - tian hearts that faint and fail, king - dom come, thy truth pre - vail.

CROWN HIM WITH MANY CROWNS   32

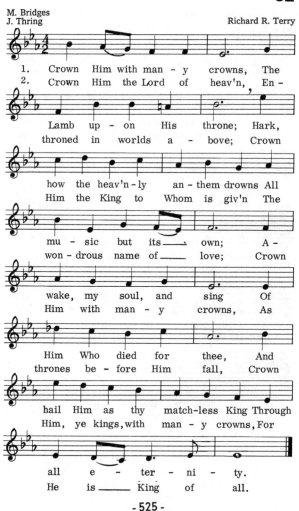

M. Bridges
J. Thring

Richard R. Terry

1. Crown Him with man - y crowns, The
2. Crown Him the Lord of heav'n, En -

Lamb up - on His throne; Hark,
throned in worlds a - bove; Crown

how the heav'n - ly an - them drowns All
Him the King to Whom is giv'n The

mu - sic but its___ own; A -
won - drous name of___ love; Crown

wake, my soul, and sing Of
Him with man - y crowns, As

Him Who died for thee, And
thrones be - fore Him fall, Crown

hail Him as thy match-less King Through
Him, ye kings, with man - y crowns, For

all e - ter - ni - ty.
He is___ King of all.

33　O KING OF MIGHT AND SPLENDOR

Dom Gregory Murray, O.S.B.　　　　　　J. Cruger, 1598-1662

1. O King of might and splen-dor, Cre-
a-tor most a-dored, This sac-ri-fice we
ren-der To thee as sov'-reign Lord. May
these our gifts be pleas-ing Unto thy Maj-es-ty, Man-kind from sin re-
leas-ing Who have of-fend-ed thee.

2. Thy Bod-y thou hast giv-en, Thy
Blood thou hast out-poured That sin might be for-
giv-en, O Je-sus, lov-ing Lord. As
now with love most ten-der Thy
death we cel-e-brate, Our lives in self-sur-
ren-der To thee we con-se-crate.

TO JESUS CHRIST OUR SOVEREIGN KING 34

Msgr. Martin B. Hellriegel

Mainz, 1870

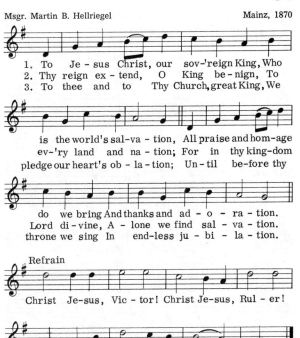

1. To Je - sus Christ, our sov-'reign King, Who
2. Thy reign ex - tend, O King be - nign, To
3. To thee and to Thy Church, great King, We

is the world's sal - va - tion, All praise and hom-age
ev - 'ry land and na - tion; For in thy king-dom
pledge our heart's ob - la - tion; Un - til be-fore thy

do we bring And thanks and ad - o - ra - tion.
Lord di - vine, A - lone we find sal - va - tion.
throne we sing In end-less ju - bi - la - tion.

Refrain

Christ Je-sus, Vic - tor! Christ Je-sus, Rul - er!

Christ Je - sus, Lord and Re - deem - er!

35 SING OF MARY, PURE AND LOWLY

Anonymous

Trier, 1695

1. Sing of Ma - ry, pure and low - ly,
2. Sing of Je - sus; son of Ma - ry,
3. Glo - ry be to God the Fa - ther,

Vir - gin - moth - er un - de - filed,
In the home at Na - za - reth.
Glo - ry be to God the Son;

Sing of God's own Son most ho - ly,
Toil and la - bor can - not wea - ry
Glo - ry be to God the Spir - it;

Who be - came her lit - tle child.
Love en - dur - ing un - to death.
Glo - ry to the Three in One.

Fair - est child of fair - est moth - er,
Con - stant was the love he gave her,
From the heart of bless - ed Ma - ry,

God the Lord who came to earth,
Though he went forth from her side,
From all saints the song as - cends,

Word made flesh, our ve - ry broth - er,
Forth to preach, and heal, and suf - fer,
And the Church the strain re - ec - hoes

Takes our na - ture by his birth.
Till on Cal - va - ry he died.
Un - to earth's re - mo - test ends.

THE GOD WHOM EARTH AND SEA AND SKY 36

Venantius Fortunatus, 609
Tr. J. M. Neale, alt.

J. S. Bach

1. The God whom earth and sea and sky A -
2. O Moth-er blest! the chos - en shrine Where-
3. Blest in the mes-sage Gab-riel brought; Blest
4. O Lord, the Vir - gin born, to thee E -

dore and laud and mag - ni - fy, Whose
in the Ar - chi - tect di - vine, Whose
by the work the Spir - it wrought; Most
ter - nal praise and glo - ry be, Whom

might they own, whose praise they tell, In
hand con - tains the earth and sky, Vouch -
blest, to bring to hu - man birth The
with the Fa - ther we a - dore And

Ma - ry's bo - dy deigned to dwell.
safed in hid - den guise to lie.
long de - sired of all the earth.
Ho - ly Ghost for ev - er - more.

37 IMMACULATE MARY

Immaculate Mary, thy praises we sing,
    Who reignest in splendor with Jesus, our King.
        — Refrain:
Ave, ave, ave, Maria! Ave, ave, Maria!

2. In heaven, the blessed thy glory proclaim,
    On earth, we thy children invoke thy fair name.
        — Refrain:

3. Thy name is our power, thy virtues our light,
    Thy love is our comfort, thy pleading our might.
        — Refrain:

4. We pray for our mother, the Church upon earth;
    And bless, dearest Lady, the land of our birth.
        — Refrain:

38 HAIL HOLY QUEEN ENTHRONED ABOVE

Hail, holy Queen, enthroned above, O Maria!
    Hail, Mother of mercy and of love, O Maria!
        — Refrain:
Triumph, all ye cherubim,
    Sing with us, ye seraphim,
Heav'n and earth resound the hymn.
    Salve, salve, salve Regina.

2. Our life, our sweetness here below, O Maria!
    Our hope in sorrow and in woe, O Maria!
        — Refrain:

3. To thee we cry, poor sons of Eve, O Maria!
    To thee we sigh, we mourn, we grieve, O Maria!
        — Refrain:

4. Turn, then, most gracious Advocate, O Maria!
    Toward us thine eyes compassionate, O Maria!
        — Refrain:

5. When this our exile's time is o'er, O Maria!
    Show us thy Son for evermore, O Maria!
        — Refrain:

GREAT ST. JOSEPH SON OF DAVID 39

Tr. Louis C. Casartelli

A. Stein, 1852

1. Great Saint Jo - seph, son of Da - vid,
Fos - ter - fa - ther___ of our Lord,
Spouse of Ma - ry, ev - er vir - gin,
Keep - ing o'er them watch and ward:
In the sta - ble thou didst guard them
With a fa - ther's lov-ing care; Thou by God's com-
mand didst save them From the cru - el Her-od's snare.

2. Three long days in grief and an - guish,
With that moth - er___ sweet and mild,
Ma - ry, Vir - gin, didst thou wan - der,
Seek - ing her be - lov - ed Child.
In the tem - ple thou didst find Him:
Oh, what joy then filled thy heart! In thy sor-rows,
in thy glad-ness, Grant us, Jo-seph, to have part.

3. Clasped in Je - sus' arms and Mar - ry's
When death gent - ly___ came at last,
Thy pure spir - it, sweet - ly sigh - ing,
From its earth - ly dwell - ing passed.
Dear Saint Jo - seph, by that pass - ing
May our death be like to thine, And with Je - sus,
Ma - ry, Jo-seph, May our souls for - ev - er shine.

40 FOR ALL THE SAINTS

William W. How

R. Vaughan Williams, 1872-1958

Moderately, in unison

1. For all the saints, who from their la-bors rest, Who Thee by faith be-fore the world con - fessed, Thy Name, O Je - sus, be for ev - er blest. Al -
2. O blest com - mu - nion! fel - low-ship di - vine! We fee - bly strug - gle, they in glo - ry shine; Yet all are one in Thee, for all are Thine.
3. But lo! there breaks a yet more glo - rious day; The saints tri - umph - ant rise in bright ar - ray; The King of glo - ry pass - es on His way.
4. From earth's wide bounds, from o - cean's far-thest coast, Through gates of pearl streams in the count - less host, Sing - ing to Fa - ther, Son and Ho - ly Ghost,

le - lu - ia, al - le - lu - ia!

O COME, O COME EMMANUEL   41

John M. Neale, Tr.

Melody adapted by T. Helmore

1. O come, O come, Em-man - u-el,
2. O come thou Day-spring come and cheer
3. O come, O come, thou Lord of might,

1. And ran-som cap-tive Is - ra-el,
2. Our spir-its by thine ad - vent here!
3. Who to the tribes on Si - nai's height

1. That mourns in low-ly ex - ile here,
2. Dis-perse the gloom-y clouds of night
3. In an-cient times you gave the law

1. Un-til the Son of God_____ ap-pear.
2. And death's dark shad-ows put _____ to flight.
3. In cloud and maj-es-ty. _____ and awe.

Refrain.

Re-joice! Re-joice! O Is - ra-
el, To thee shall come Em-ma - nu-el.

4. O come, thou Rod of Jesse free
   Thy own from Satan's tyranny
   From depths of hell thy people save,
   And give them vict'ry o'er the grave.—*Refrain.*

5. O come, thou Key of David, come,
   And open wide our heavn'ly home;
   Make safe the way that leads on high,
   And close the path to misery.—*Refrain.*

42
42-A

A CHILD IS BORN IN BETHLEHEM
THE MAGI KINGS

Verses: Choir

1. A Child is born in Beth-le-hem, al-
2. Our Broth-er in the Flesh is He, al-
3. By grace this Child is born a-gain, al-

1. The Ma-gi Kings come from a-far, al-
2. Gold, in-cense, myrrh they of-fer Him, al-

1. le - lu - ia;   Re-joice, re-joice Je-ru-
2. le - lu - ia;   Our King for all e-ter-
3. le - lu - ia;   In ev-'ry heart He frees

1. le - lu - ia;   Led on by faith in heav-
2. le - lu - ia;   And bend-ing low they wor-

1. sa - lem,   al - le - lu - ia, al - le - lu - ia.
2. ni - ty,   al - le - lu - ia, al - le - lu - ia.
3. from sin,   al - le - lu - ia, al - le - lu - ia.

1. en's star,   al - le - lu - ia, al - le - lu - ia.
2. ship Him,   al - le - lu - ia, al - le - lu - ia.

Responsory: All

Let grate-ful hearts now sing, A song

of joy and ho-ly praise to Christ the new-born King.

43
SILENT NIGHT

Silent night, holy night!
　All is calm, all is bright.
'Round yon Virgin Mother and
　　Child,
　Holy Infant so tender and mild:
Sleep in heavenly peace,
　Sleep in heavenly peace!

Silent night, holy night!
　Shepherds quake at the sight!
Glories stream from heaven afar,
Heav'nly hosts sing Alleluia:
Christ, the Savior is born,
　Christ, the Savior is born!

GOOD CHRISTIAN MEN REJOICE

44

In Dulci Jubilo
Tr. John Mason Neale

German, 14th cent.

1. Good Chris-tian men, re - joice_____ With heart and soul and voice;____ Give ye heed to what we say: Je - sus Christ is born to-day! Ox and ass be - fore him bow, And he is in the man - ger now. Christ is born to - day!____ Christ is born to - day!____

2. Good Chris-tian men, re - joice_____ With heart and soul and voice;____ Now ye hear of end-less bliss: Je - sus Christ was born for this! He has oped the heav - n'ly door, And man is bless - ed ev - er-more. Christ was born for this!____ Christ was born for this!____

3. Good Chris-tian men, re - joice_____ With heart and soul and voice;____ Now ye need not fear the grave: Je - sus Christ was born to save! Calls you one and calls you all To gain his ev - er - last - ing hall. Christ was born to save!____ Christ was born to save!____

45 HARK! THE HERALD ANGELS SING

Hark! The herald angels sing,
  "Glory to the new-born King,
Peace on earth, and mercy mild
  God and sinners reconciled."
Joyful all ye nations rise,
  Join the triumph of the skies.
With th' angelic host proclaim,
  "Christ is born in Bethlehem."

  —Refrain: Hark! The herald angels sing,
  "Glory to the new-born King."

2. Christ, by highest heaven adored,
  Christ, the everlasting Lord.
Late in time behold Him come,
  Off-spring of a virgin's womb.
Veiled in flesh, the God-head see;
  Hail th' incarnate Deity!
Pleased as Man with men to appear,
  Jesus, our Immanuel here! *— Refrain:*

46 O COME ALL YE FAITHFUL

O come, all ye faithful, joyful and triumphant,
O come ye, O come ye to Bethlehem;
  Come and behold Him, born, the King of angels;

  —Refrain: O come, let us adore Him,
  O come, let us adore Him,
O come, let us adore Him, Christ the Lord.

2. Sing, Choirs of angels, sing in exultation,
Sing, all ye citizens of heav'n above;
  Glory to God, in the highest: *— Refrain:*

47 THE FIRST NOEL

The first Noel the angel did say,
  Was to three poor shepherds in fields as they lay;
In fields where they lay keeping their sheep
  On a cold winter's night that was so deep.

  —Refrain: Noel, Noel, Noel, Noel,
  Born is the King of Israel.

2. They looked up and saw a star,
  Shining in the east, beyond them far,
And to the earth it gave great light,
  And so it continued both day and night *— Refrain:*

HOW BRIGHT APPEARS THE MORNING STAR 48

1. How bright ap-pears the Morn-ing Star, With
2. Re - joice, ye heav'ns; thou earth re - ply; With

mer - cy beam - ing from a - far; The
praise, ye sin - ners, fill the sky, For

host of heav'n re - joic - es; O
this his In - car - na - tion. In -

Right-eous Branch, O Jes - se's Rod! Thou
car - nate God, put forth your power, Ride

Son of Man and Son of God! We,
on, ride on, great Con - quer - or, Till

too, will lift our voic - es: Je - sus,
all know your sal - va - tion. A - men,

Je - sus! Ho - ly, ho - ly, yet most low - ly,
A - men! Al - le - lu - ia! Al - le - lu - ia!

Draw thou near us; Great Em - man - uel,
Praise be giv - en Ev - er - more, by

come and hear us.
earth and heav - en. A - men.

AS WITH GLADNESS MEN OF OLD

W. C. Dix, alt.

C. Kocher

1. As with gladness men of old
Did the guiding star behold,
As with joy they hailed its light,
Leading onward, beaming bright,
So, most gracious Lord, may we
Evermore be led to thee.

2. As with joyful steps they sped
To that lowly manger-bed,
There to bend the knee before
him, Whom heav'n and earth adore,
So may we, O Lord, this day
Unto thee our homage pay.

3. As they offered gifts most rare
At that manger, rude and bare,
So may we with humble heart
And the joy that you impart,
All our costly treasures bring,
Christ, to thee, our heav'n-ly King.

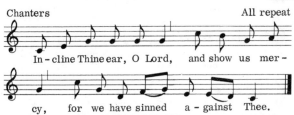

Chanters   All repeat

In - cline Thine ear, O Lord, and show us mer -

cy, for we have sinned a - gainst Thee.

LORD WHO THROUGHOUT THESE FORTY DAYS 51

Moderately   English Psalter,

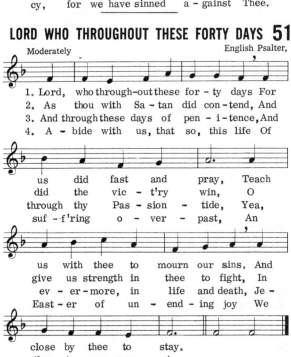

1. Lord, who through-out these for - ty days For
2. As thou with Sa - tan did con - tend, And
3. And through these days of pen - i - tence, And
4. A - bide with us, that so, this life Of

us did fast and pray, Teach
did the vic - t'ry win, O
through thy Pas - sion - tide, Yea,
suf - f'ring o - ver - past, An

us with thee to mourn our sins, And
give us strength in thee to fight, In
ev - er - more, in life and death, Je -
East - er of un - end - ing joy We

close by thee to stay.
thee to con - quer sin.
sus! with us a - bide.
may at - tain at last! A - men.

52   O SACRED HEAD SURROUNDED

Tr. Henry W. Baker   H. L. Hassler

1. O Sa-cred Head sur-round-ed By crown of pierc-ing thorn! O bleed-ing Head, so wound-ed, Re-viled, and put to scorn! Death's pal-lid hue comes o'er Thee, The glow of life de-cays, Yet an-gel-hosts a-dore Thee, And trem-ble as they gaze.

2. I see Thy strength and vig-or All fad-ing in the strife, And death with cru-el rig-or, Be-reav-ing Thee of life; O ag-o-ny and dy-ing! O love to sin-ners free! Je-sus, all grace sup-ply-ing, O turn Thy face on me.

COME HOLY GHOST, CREATOR BLEST 53

Louis Lambillotte, S.J.

1. Come, Holy Ghost, Creator blest, And in our hearts take up Thy rest; Come with Thy grace and heav'n-ly aid To fill the hearts which Thou hast made, To fill the hearts which Thou hast made.

2. O Comforter, to Thee we cry, Thou heav'n-ly Gift of God most high; Thou fount of life and fire of love And sweet a-noint-ing from a-bove, And sweet a-noint-ing from a-bove.

3. O Holy Ghost, through Thee a-lone Know we the Father and the Son; Be this our firm un-chang-ing creed: That Thou dost from Them both pro-ceed, That Thou dost from Them both pro-ceed.

4. Praise we the Father and the Son, And the blest Spir-it with Them one; And may the Son on us be-stow The gifts that from the Spir-it flow, The gifts that from the Spir-it flow.

54   O HOLY SPIRIT, COME TO US

Melvin Farrell, S.S.   T. Tallis

1. O Ho - ly Spir - it, come to us,
2. Thou art our Source of strength and might,
3. We thank thee for Thy gifts of grace,
4. Then come, Great Spir - it, to thy sons;
5. O Might - y Coun - sel, hear our prayer:
6. Show us the Fa - ther and the Son,

1. The chil - dren thou hast made:
2. Great gift from God a - bove:
3. O Prom - ised One of God:
4. Our hearts make pure and strong.
5. And teach us trust in thee;
6. O Spir - it, we im - plore,

1. In - flame our hearts and rule our minds
2. Thou art the Font of Truth and Light,
3. Thy won - drous Life be - comes our own,
4. Di - rect our wea - ry steps to thee,
5. For in thy love we place our hope
6. That in the God - head we may live

1. With thine un - fail - ing aid.
2. The Flame of hope and love.
3. Thy strength, our staff and rod!
4. And turn our wills from wrong.
5. To live e - ter - nal - ly.
6. Both now and ev - er - more.

ANTIPHONS

Gelineau, S.J.

PSALM 22

My ¦ shep-herd ¦ is the Lord, no-thing ¦ in-deed ¦ shall I want.

PSALM 122 **56**

The Lord_ is my shep-herd, nothing shall I want;
he
leads me by safe_ paths, nothing shall I fear.

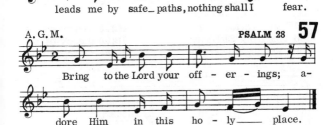

A. G. M.

PSALM 28 **57**

Bring to the Lord your off — er - ings; a-
dore Him in this ho - ly____ place.

Holy God, We Praise Thy Name

Holy God, we praise Thy Name!
Lord of all, we bow before Thee!
All on earth Thy sceptre claim,
All in heaven above adore Thee.
Infinite Thy vast domain,
Everlasting is Thy reign.

Repeat last two lines

2. Hark! the loud celestial hymn,
Angel choirs above are raising;
Cherubim and seraphim,
In unceasing chorus praising,
Fill the heavens with sweet accord;
Holy, holy, holy Lord!

Repeat last two lines

HYMN: "Sing my tongue, the Savior's Glory," p. 516.

Lord	have	mer	-	cy. ij.
Christ	have	mer	-	cy. ij.
Lord	have	mer	-	cy. ij.

Christ hear us. *ij.* Christ graciously hear us. *ij*

God the Father of   HEAV-en,   **Have mercy on us.**
God the Son, Redeemer
  OF the world,   **Have mercy on us.**
God the Holy SPIR-it,   **Have mercy on us.**
Holy Trinity, ONE God.   **Have mercy on us.**

Holy   Ma - ry,   Pray for   us.

Holy Mother OF God,
Holy Virgin of VIR-gins,
St. MI-chael,
St. GAB-ri-el,
St. RA-pha-el,
All you holy angels and
  arch-AN-gels,
All you holy ranks of
  blessed SPI-rits,
St. John the BAP-tist,
St. JO-seph
All you holy patriarchs
  and PRO-phets,
St. PE-ter,
St. PAUL,
St. AN-drew,
St. JOHN,
St. JAMES,
St. JOHN,
St. THOM-as,

St. JAMES,
St. PHIL-ip,
St. Bar-THOL-o-mew,
St. MAT-thew,
St. SI-mon,
St. THAD-deus,
St. Mat-THI-as,
St. LUKE,
St. MARK,
All you holy Apostles and
  E-VAN-ge-lists,
All you holy disciples of
  the LORD,
All you holy IN-no-cents,
St. STE-phen,
St. LAW-rence,
Ss. Fabian and Se-BAS-
  tian,
Ss. JOHN and PAUL,
Ss. Cosmas and DA-mi-an.

Ss. Gervase and PRO-tase
All you holy MAR-tyrs
St. Syl-VES-ter
St. GRE-go-ry,
St. AM-brose,
St. Au-GUS-tine,
St. JE-rome,
St. MAR-tin,
St. NI-cho-las,
All you holy Bishops and Con-FES-sors,
All you holy DOC-tors,
St. AN-tho-ny,
St. BEN-e-dict,
St. BER-nard,

St. DOM-i-nic,
St. FRAN-cis,
All you holy Priests, and LE-vites,
All you holy Monks and HER-mits,
St. AG-atha,
St. LU-cy,
St. AG-nes,
St. Ce-CIL-ia,
St. CATH-erine,
St. Anas-TA-si-a,
All you holy Virgins and WI-dows.

All you holy men and women, saints of God. **In-ter-cede for us.**

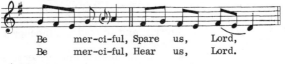

Be mer-ci-ful, Spare us, Lord,
Be mer-ci-ful, Hear us, Lord.

From ev-*er*-y E-vil, **De-liv-er us, Lord.**

From ev-*er*-y SIN,
From sudden and *un*-pro-VI-ded death,
From the snares *of* the DEV-il,
From anger, hatred *and* all ILL-will,
From the spirit of for-*ni*-CA-tion,
From light - *ning* and TEM-pest,
From plague, *fa* - mine AND war,
From threat-*en*-ing DAN-gers,
From Your WRATH.

From *e* - ver-LAST - ing death,
Through the mystery of Your holy *In*-car-NA-tion,
Through Your COM-ing,
Through YOUR birth,
Through Your baptism and *ho*-ly FAST-ing,
Through Your *cross* and PAS-sion,
Through Your *death* and BUR-i-al,
Through your holy *re*-sur-REC-tion,

Through Your wonder-*ful* as-CEN-sion,
Through the coming of | the Holy Spirit *the* Con-SO-ler,
In the *day* of JUDG-ment,

Sin-ners THAT we are.   **We ask You to hear us.**

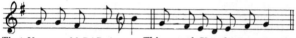

That You would PAR-don us. **This we ask You, hear our prayer.**

That You would bring us to *true* PEN-ance,

That You would govern and preserve *Your* HO-ly Church,

That You would preserve the Apostolic Pope and all ranks in the Church in holy *re*-LIG-ion,

That You would humble the enemies *of* HO-ly Church,

That You would give peace and true union of hearts to Christian Kings *and* RU-lers,

That You would vouchsafe to recall all wanderers to the unity of the Church, and to lead all unbelievers to the light of *the* GOS-pel,

That You would vouchsafe to confirm and preserve us in Your ho-*ly* SER-vice,

That You would lift up our minds to heavenly, *de*-SI-res,

That You would render eternal blessings to all our be-*ne*-FAC-tors,

That You would deliver our souls, and the souls of our brethren, relations and benefactors, from eternal *dam*-NA-tion,

That You would vouchsafe to give and preserve the fruits *of* THE earth,

That You would vouchsafe to grant eternal rest to all the faithful *de*-PAR-ted,

That You would vouchsafe graciously *to* HEAR us, Son *of* GOD.

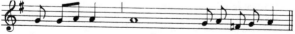

Lamb of God   Who take away the sins of the world

(Sung three times)

1. **Spare us Lord.**
2. **Hear us Lord.**

3. **Have mercy on us.**

Christ hear us. Christ gra-cious-ly hear us.

1. Lord, have mer - cy. 3. Lord,
2. Christ, have mer - cy.

have mer - cy. Our Fa-ther,

And lead us not into temptation. **But deliver us from evil.**

Deign, O God, to RES-cue me.

O Lord, make haste to help ME.

Let them be put to shame *and* con-FOUND-ed *
  who seek my LIFE.
Let them be *turned* back IN disgrace *
  who desire my RUIN.
Let them re-*tire* in THEIR shame *
  who say to me, Aha! AHA!
But may *all* who SEEK You *
  exult and be glad in YOU.
And may those who love *Your* sal-VA-tion *
  say ever, God be glori-FIED.
But I am af-*flic*-ted AND poor *
  O God hasten to ME!
You are my help and *my* de-LI-ver-er; *

O Lord, hold not BACK!

Glory be to the Father, *and* to THE Son, *
and to the Holy Spi-RIT.

As it was in the beginning, is now and *ever* SHALL be, *
world without end. A-men.

℣. Save Your ser-VANTS. ℟. Who trust in You, my
GOD.

℣. Be a tower of strength, for us, O LORD.

℟. Against the attack of the e-NEMY.

℣. Let not the enemy prevail against US.

℟. And let not the son of evil dare to harm US.

℣. O Lord, deal not with us according to our SINS.

℟. Neither requite us according to our ini-QUITIES.

℣. Let us pray for our Sovereign Pontiff, PAUL.

℟. The Lord preserve him, and give him *life,* † and
make him to be bless-*ed* up-ON the earth, * and
deliver him not up to the will of his e-NEMIES.

℣. Let us pray for our benefac-TORS.

℟. Vouchsafe, O Lord, for Your Name's *sake,* † to reward *with* e-TER-nal life * all those who do us
good. A-*men.*

℣. Let us pray for the faithful depart-ED.

℟. Eternal rest *grant* to THEM, O Lord, *
and let perpetual light shine upon THEM.

℣. May they rest in PEACE. ℟. Amen.

℣. For our absent breth-REN.

℟. Save Your servants who trust in You, my GOD.

℣. Send them help, O Lord, *from* Your SANC-tuary.

℟. And sustain them from SION.

℣. O Lord, hear my PRAYER. ℟. And let my cry come
to YOU.

OPENING CEREMONIES: ℣. The Lord be with You.

   ℟. And with your spi-RIT.

CLOSING CEREMONIES: ℣. You have given them bread
from heav-EN.

   ℟. Having all delight within IT.

Let us pray.

1. O God, Who in this wonderful sacrament left us a
memorial of Your Passion, grant, we implore You, that
we may so venerate the sacred mysteries of Your Body
and Blood as always to be conscious of the fruit of
Your Redemption.

2. *In Advent.* O God, Who willed that, at the message
of an Angel, Your Word should take flesh in the womb
of the Blessed Virgin Mary, grant to Your suppliant
people that we, who believe her to be truly the Mother
of God, may be helped by her intercession with You.

From Christmas to Purification. O God, Who by the fruitful virginity of Blessed Mary, bestowed upon the human race the rewards of eternal salvation, grant we beseech You, that we may feel the power of her intercession, through whom we have been made worthy to receive the Author of life, our Lord Jesus Christ Your Son.

In Paschaltime. O God, Who by the Resurrection of Your Son, our Lord Jesus Christ, were pleased to make glad the whole world, grant, we beseech You, that, through the intercession of the Virgin Mary, His Mother, we may attain the joys of eternal life.

At all other times. Grant to us, Your servants, we beseech You, O Lord God, perpetual health of mind and body, and, through the intercession of Blessed Mary ever Virgin, to be delivered from present sorrow and to enjoy the happiness of life everlasting.

3. Almighty, everlasting God, have mercy upon Your servant Paul, our Sovereign Pontiff, and direct him according to Your clemency into the way of everlasting salvation, that by Your grace he may desire those things that are pleasing to You, and perform them with all his strength.

4. O God, our refuge and our strength, the author of holiness, hear the devout prayers of Your Church, and grant that what we ask with faith we may obtain in deed.

5. Almighty and everlasting God, Who have dominion over the living and the dead, and are merciful to all whom You foreknow will be Yours by faith and good works; we humbly beseech You that those for whom we intend to pour forth our prayers, whether this present world still detain them in the flesh, or the world to come has already received them out of their bodies, may, through the intercession of all Your Saints, by the clemency of Your goodness, obtain the remission of all their sins. Through Christ our Lord. ℟. Amen.

Celebrant kneels and sings: ℣. O Lord, hear my prayer. ℟. And let my cry come to You.

Chanters: ℣. May the almighty and most merciful Lord graciously hear us.

℟. And may He always watch over us. A-men.

Celebrant, on one note at a lower pitch: ℣. May the souls of the faithful departed through the mercy of God rest in peace. ℟. A-men.

Psalm used for stripping of the altars

Antiphon: They divide My garments among them, and
for My vesture they cast lots.

My God, My God, why have You forsaken Me,
    far from My prayer, from the words of My cry?

O my God, I cry out by day, and You answer not;
    by night, and there is no relief for Me.

Yet You are enthroned in the holy place,
    O glory of Israel!

In You our fathers trusted;
    they trusted and You delivered them.

To You they cried, and they escaped;
    in you they trusted, and they were no put to shame.

But I am a worm, not a man!
    the scorn of men, despised by the people.

All who see Me scoff at Me;
    they mock Me with parted lips, they wag their heads:
"He relied on the Lord; let Him deliver Him,
    let Him rescue Him, if He loves Him."

You have been My guide since I was first formed,
    My security at My mother's breast.

To You I was committed at birth,
    From My mother's womb You are my God.

Be not far from Me, for I am in distress;
    be near, for I have no one to help Me.

Many bullocks surround Me;
    the strong bulls of Basan encircle Me.

They open their mouths against Me
    like ravening and roaring lions.

I am like water poured out;
    all My bones are racked.

My heart has become like wax
    melting away within My bosom.

My throat is dried up like baked clay,
    My tongue cleaves to My jaws;
    to the dust of death You have brought Me down.

Indeed, many dogs surround Me,
    a pack of evildoers closes in upon Me;

They have pierced My hands and My feet;
    I can count all My bones.

They look on and gloat over Me;
   they divide My garments among them,
   and for My vesture they cast lots.
But You, O Lord, be not far from Me;
   O My help, hasten to aid Me.
Rescue My soul from the sword,
   My loneliness from the grip of the dog.
Save Me from the lion's mouth;
   from the horns of the wild bulls, My wretched life.
I will proclaim Your Name to My brethren;
   in the midst of the assembly I will praise You:
"You who fear the Lord, praise Him;
   all you descendants of Jacob, give glory to Him;
   revere Him, all you descendants of Israel!
For He has not spurned nor disdained
   the wretched man in His misery,
Nor did He turn His face away from him,
   but when He cried out to Him, He heard Him."
So by Your gift will I utter praise in the vast assembly;
   I will fulfill My vows before those who fear Him.
The lowly shall eat their fill;
   they who seek the Lord shall praise Him:
   "May your hearts be ever merry!"

II

All the ends of the earth
   shall remember and turn to the Lord;
All the families of the nations
   shall bow down before Him.
For dominion is the Lord's,
   and He rules the nations.
To Him alone shall bow down
   all who sleep in the earth;
Before Him shall bend
   all who go down into the dust.
And to Him My soul shall live;
   My descendants shall serve Him.
Let the coming generation be told of the Lord
   that they may proclaim to a people yet to be born
   the justice He has shown.

Ant. They divide, etc.

———————

Jan Vermulst

Lord, have mer - cy. Lord, have mer - cy. Lord,

have mer - cy. Christ, have mer-cy. Christ,

have mer - cy. Christ, have mer - cy. Lord, have

mer - cy. Lord, have mer-cy. Lord, have mer - cy.

THE GLORIA

Priest: Glory to God in the highest.

PEOPLE:

And on earth peace to men of good will. We

praise_ you. We bless_ you. We wor-ship

you. We glo - ri - fy__ you. We give you

thanks for your great glo - ry. Lord God, heav-en-

ly__ King, God the Fa - ther Al - might-y.

Lord,— Je-sus Christ, the on-ly-be-got-ten Son.

Lord God, Lamb of — God, Son of the Fa-ther.

You, who take a-way the sins of the world, have

mer-cy on us. You, who take a-way the

sins of the world, re-ceive— our— prayer.

You, who sit at the right hand of the Fa-ther,

have mer-cy on us. For you a-lone are—

ho-ly. You a-lone are— Lord. You a-lone,

O Je-sus—Christ, are most—high. With the

Ho-ly— Spir-it, in the glo-ry of

God — the Fa-ther. A — men.

THE CREED

Priest:

I be - lieve____ in one God.

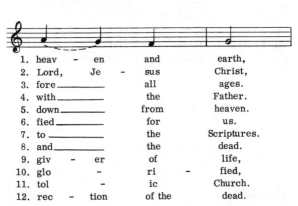

PEOPLE:

1. The Father almighty, maker of
2. And I believe in one
3. Born of the Father be -
4. Begotten, not made, / of one substance
5. Who for us men and for our salvation / came
6. He was also cruci -
7. And on the third day he rose again, / according
8. He will come again in glory / to judge the living
9. And I believe in the Holy Spirit, / the Lord and
10. Who together with the Father and the Son is adored and
11. And one holy, Catholic, and Apos -
12. And I await the resur -

1. heav - en   and   earth,
2. Lord, Je - sus   Christ,
3. fore____   all   ages.
4. with____   the   Father.
5. down____   from   heaven.
6. fied____   for   us.
7. to ____   the   Scriptures.
8. and____   the   dead.
9. giv - er   of   life,
10. glo -   ri -   fied,
11. tol -   ic   Church.
12. rec - tion   of the   dead.

1. and of all things
2. the only be -
3. God of God, Light of Light, / true
4. By whom
5. And he became flesh by the Holy Spirit of the Vir gin Mary:
6. suffered under Pontius
7. He ascended into heaven / and sits at the
8. And of his kingdom
9. who proceeds from the
10. and who
11. I confess one baptism for the for -
12. And the life of the

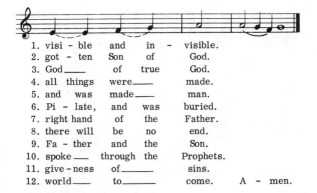

1. visi - ble	and	in -	visible.
2. got - ten	Son	of	God.
3. God____	of	true	God.
4. all things	were____		made.
5. and was	made____		man.
6. Pi - late,	and	was	buried.
7. right hand	of	the	Father.
8. there will	be	no	end.
9. Fa - ther	and	the	Son.
10. spoke ____	through	the	Prophets.
11. give - ness	of____		sins.
12. world____	to____		come. A - men.

THE SANCTUS

Ho - ly, ho - ly, ho - ly Lord God of hosts.

Heav - en and earth are filled_ with your glo - ry.

Ho - san - na___ in the high - est.

Bless - ed is he who comes in the name of the

Lord.   Ho - san - na___ in the high - est.

THE LAMB OF GOD

Lamb of God, who take a - way the sins of

the world, have mer - cy on us. Lamb of God,

who take a - way the sins of the world,

have mer - cy on us. Lamb of God, who take a -

way the sins of the world, grant us peace.

WHERE ABIDETH CHARITY AND LOVE 60-A

Antiphon

Where a - bid - eth char - i - ty
and love God is ev - er there.

1. All to - gether one in
   love of Christ our Bless-ed Lord,
2. Live we in holy
   fear and gentle love our life in God,
3. And whenever we
   come to-geth-er in mind and heart,
4. Cease all angry thoughts
   and bitter words all e-vils end,
5. And when we shall see the
   saints in heav-en, our broth-ers too,
6. O joy that knows
   no fear of end-ing at love so true;

1. let us sing in exaltation of one ac - cord.
2. and give we to one anoth-er our hearts in truth.
3. there is no fear of quar-
   reling among us to drive a - part.
4. and Christ our brother
   comes to live among us, our guest and friend.
5. there will Christ in glory
   shine among us our life a - new.
6. through all the ages
   of eternity world with-out end. A - men.

Thomas Reardon

Lord, have mer - cy. Lord, have mer - cy.

Lord, have mer - cy. Christ, have mer - cy.

Christ, have mer - cy. Christ, have mer - cy.

Lord, have mer - cy. Lord, have mer - cy.

Lord, have mer - cy.

THE GLORIA

Glo-ry to God in the high-est, and on earth peace

to men of good will. We praise you. We bless you.

We wor-ship you. We glo-ri- fy you. We give you

thanks for your great glo-ry. Lord God, hea-
ven-ly King, God the Fa-ther Al-migh-ty. Lord
Je-sus Christ, the on-ly be-got-ten Son.
Lord God, Lamb of God, Son of the Father. You, who take a-way the sins of the world,
have mer-cy on us. You, who take a-way the sins
of the world, re-ceive our prayer. You, who sit at
the right hand of the Fa-ther, have mer-cy on us.
For you a-lone are ho-ly. You a-lone are Lord.
You a-lone, O Je-sus Christ, are most high. With

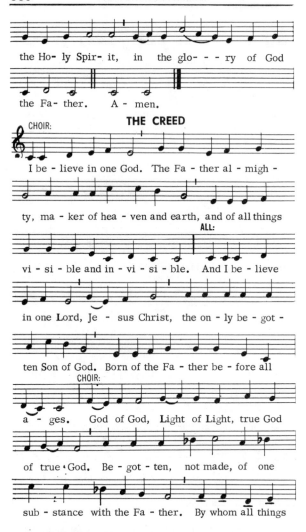

the Ho- ly Spir- it, in the glo - - - ry of God

the Fa- ther.   A - men.

THE CREED

CHOIR:

I be - lieve in one God. The Fa - ther al - migh -

ty, ma - ker of hea - ven and earth, and of all things

ALL:

vi - si - ble and in - vi - si - ble. And I be - lieve

in one Lord, Je - sus Christ, the on - ly be - got -

ten Son of God. Born of the Fa - ther be - fore all

CHOIR:

a - ges.   God of God, Light of Light, true God

of true God. Be - got - ten, not made, of one

sub - stance with the Fa - ther. By whom all things

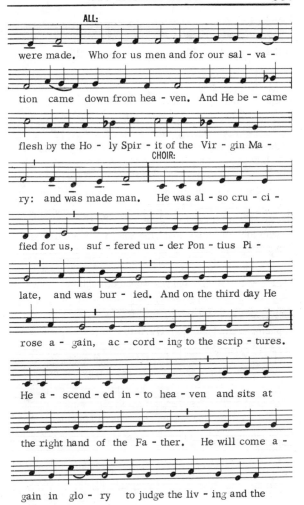

ALL: were made. Who for us men and for our sal - va - tion came down from hea - ven. And He be - came flesh by the Ho - ly Spir - it of the Vir - gin Ma - **CHOIR:** ry: and was made man. He was al - so cru - ci - fied for us, suf - fered un - der Pon - tius Pi - late, and was bur - ied. And on the third day He rose a - gain, ac - cord - ing to the scrip - tures. He a - scend - ed in - to hea - ven and sits at the right hand of the Fa - ther. He will come a - gain in glo - ry to judge the liv - ing and the

dead. And of His king - dom there will be no

ALL:

end. And I be - lieve in the Ho - ly Spir - it,

the Lord and Giv - er of life, who pro - ceeds

from the Fa - ther and the Son. Who to - geth - er

with the Fa - ther and the Son is a - dored and

glor - i - fied, and who spoke through the pro -

CHOIR:

phets. And one ho - ly, Cath - o - lic, and A -

pos - to - lic Church. I con - fess one bap -

ALL:

tism for the for - give - ness of sins. And

I a - wait the re - sur - rec - tion of the dead.

And the life of the world to come. A - men.

SANCTUS

Ho - ly, Ho - ly, Ho - ly Lord God of hosts.

Heav - en and earth are filled with your glo - ry.

Ho - san - na in the high - est. Bless - ed is He

who comes in the name of the Lord. Ho - san - na

in the high - est.

THE LAMB OF GOD

Lamb of God, who take a - way the sins of the

world, have mer - cy on us. Lamb of God,

who take a - way the sins of the world, have

mer - cy on us. Lamb of God, who take a - way

the sins of the world, grant us peace.

SEASONAL PSALMS

THE Psalms were the inspired Songs of the People of God under the Old Covenant. Christ, our eternal High Priest, used the Psalms when He instituted the Holy Eucharist, and when He offered Himself for us on the Cross. For the People of God in the New Covenant the Psalms have been retained as prayers of praise, thanksgiving, petition and offering, and form the heart of the Divine Office recited daily by priests and choir religious.

Antiphons prepare for and often echo the words and sentiments of the Psalms. Here we have compiled some of the Psalms according to the various seasons with suitable Antiphons, to serve as food for our meditations and help us to live according to the spirit of the liturgical Seasons on Sundays and Feast Days.

These Psalms may be used together with the Antiphons of the Mass at the Introit, Offertory and Communion as a processional hymn. In this case only as many verses are recited as is required.

ADVENT

PSALM 84 (85)

Prayer for Christ's Coming

*Ant. Behold the Lord shall come, * and with Him all His Saints: and there shall be a great light in that day. Alleluia.*

You have favored, O Lord, Your land:
You have restored the well-being of Jacob.

3 You have forgiven the guilt of Your people;
You have covered all their sins.

4 You have withdrawn all Your wrath;
You have revoked Your burning anger.

5 Restore us, O God our Savior,
and abandon Your displeasure against us.

6 Will You be ever angry with us,
prolonging Your anger to all generations?

7 Will You not instead give us life;
and shall not Your people rejoice in You?

8 Show us, O Lord, Your kindness,
and grant us Your salvation.

9 I will hear what God proclaims;
the Lord—for He proclaims peace

To His people, and to His faithful ones,
and to those who put in Him their hope.

10 Near indeed is His salvation to those who
fear Him,
glory dwelling in our land.

PSALM 79 (80)

Prayer for the Restoration of the Church

Ant. I will give to Sion salvation, and to Jerusalem My glory. Alleluia.

O shepherd of Israel, hearken,
  O guide of the flock of Joseph!

2 From Your throne upon the cherubim, shine forth

3   before Ephraim, Benjamin and Manasse.
  Rouse Your power,
    and come to save us.

4   O Lord of hosts, restore us;
      if Your face shine upon us, then
        we shall be safe.

5 O Lord of hosts, how long will You burn with anger
    while Your people pray?

6 You have fed them with the bread of tears
    and given them tears to drink in ample measure.

7 You have left us to be fought over by our neighbors,
    and our enemies mock us.

8   O Lord of hosts, restore us;
      if Your face shine upon us, then
        we shall be safe.

CHRISTMAS

PSALM 2

The Universal Reign of the Messia

*Ant. The Lord said * to Me: "You are My Son, this day I have begotten You.*

WHY do the nations rage *
   and the peoples utter folly?

2 The kings of the earth rise up,
   and the princes conspire together
   against the Lord and against His Anointed:

3 "Let us break their fetters
   and cast their bonds from us!"

4 He Who is throned in heaven laughs;
   the Lord derides them.

5 Then in anger He speaks to them;
   He terrifies them in His wrath:

6 "I Myself have set up My King
   on Sion, My holy mountain."

7 I will proclaim the decree of the Lord:
   The Lord said to Me, "You are My Son;
   this day I have begotten You.

8 Ask of Me and I will give You
   the nations for an inheritance
   and the ends of the earth for Your possession.

9 You shall rule them with an iron rod;
   You shall shatter them like an earthen dish."

PSALM 109 (110)

The Messia: King, Priest, and Conqueror

Ant. Yours is princely power in the day of Your birth, in holy splendor; before the daystar, like the dew, I have begotten You.

The Lord said to my Lord: "Sit at my right hand
till I make Your enemies Your footstool."

2 The scepter of Your power the Lord will stretch forth from Sion:
"Rule in the midst of Your enemies.

3 Yours is princely power in the day of Your birth, in holy splendor;
before the daystar, like the dew, I have begotten You."

4 The Lord has sworn, and He will not repent:
"You are a priest forever, according to the order of Melchisedec."

5 The Lord is at Your right hand;
He will crush kings on the day of His wrath.

6 He will do judgment on the nations,
heaping up corpses;
He will crush heads over the wide earth.

7 From the brook by the wayside He will drink;
therefore will He left up His head.

EPIPHANY

PSALM 71 (72)

The Kingdom of the Messia

*Ant. The Kings of Tharsis * and the isles shall offer gifts to the King Who is the Lord.*

O God, with Your judgment endow the King,
  and with Your justice, the king's Son;

2 He shall govern Your people with justice
  and Your afflicted ones with judgment.

3 The mountains shall yield peace for the people,
  and the hills justice.

4 He shall defend the afflicted among the people,
  save the children of the poor,
  and crush the oppressor.

5 May He endure as long as the sun,
  and like the moon through all generations.

6 He shall be like rain coming down on the meadow,
  like showers watering the earth.

7 Justice shall flower in His days,
  and profound peace, till the moon be no more.

10 The kings of Tharsis and the Isles shall offer gifts;
  the kings of Arabia and Saba shall bring tribute.

11 All kings shall pay Him homage,
  all nations shall serve Him.

SEPTUAGESIMA
PSALM 30 (31)
Trust in God

*Ant. But my trust is in You, O Lord; * I say,
"You are my God."*

In You, O Lord, I take refuge;
    let me never be put to shame.

2 In Your justice rescue me,
    incline Your ear to me,
    make haste to deliver me!

3 Be my rock of refuge,
    a stronghold to give me safety.

4 You are my rock and my fortress;
    for Your Name's sake You will lead and
      guide me.

5 You will free me from the snare they set
    for me,
    for You are my refuge.

6 Into Your hands I commend my spirit;
    You will redeem me, O Lord, O faithful
      God.

7 You hate those who worship vain idols,
    but my trust is in the Lord.

8 I will rejoice and be glad of Your kindness,
    when You have seen my affliction
    and watched over me in my distress,

9 Not shutting me up in the grip of the enemy
    but enabling me to move about at large.

10 Have pity on me, O Lord, for I am in distress;
    with sorrow my eye is consumed; my soul
      also, and my body.

LENT

PSALM 90 (91)

Security under God's Protection

*Ant. It is better * to trust in the Lord than to trust in princes.*

You who dwell in the shelter of the Most High,
    who abide in the shadow of the Almighty,

2 Say to the Lord, "My refuge and my fortress,
    my God, in Whom I trust."

3 For He will rescue you from the snare of the
    fowler,
    from the destroying pestilence.

4 With His pinions He will cover you,
    and under His wings you shall take refuge;
    His faithfulness is a buckler and a shield.

5 You shall not fear the terror of the night
    nor the arrow that flies by day;

6 Not the pestilence that roams in darkness
    nor the devastating plague at noon.

7 Though a thousand fall at your side,
    ten thousand at your right side,
    near you it shall not come.

8 Rather with your eyes shall you behold
    and see the requital of the wicked,

9 Because you have the Lord for your refuge;
    you have made the Most High your strong-
    hold.

10 No evil shall befall you,
    nor shall affliction come near your tent,

PSALM 24 (25)

Prayer for Guidance and Help

*Ant. To You I lift up my soul, * O Lord My God.*

To You I lift up my soul,
  O Lord, my God.
  In You I trust; let me not be put to shame,
    let not my enemies exult over me.

³ No one who waits for You shall be put to shame;
    those shall be put to shame who heedlessly break faith.

⁴ Your ways, O Lord, make known to me;
    teach me Your paths,

⁵ Guide me in Your truth and teach me,
    for You are God my Savior,
    and for You I wait all the day.

⁶ Remember that Your compassion, O Lord,
    and Your kindness are from of old.

⁷ The sins of my youth and my frailties remember not;
    in Your kindness remember me,
    because of Your goodness, O Lord.

EASTER

PSALM 117 (118)

Hymn of Thanksgiving to the Savior of Israel

Ant. Open to me the gates of justice; * I will enter them and give thanks to the Lord.

G ive thanks to the Lord, for He is good,
   for His mercy endures forever.

21 I will give thanks to You, for You have answered me
      and have been my Savior.

22 The stone which the builders rejected
      has become the cornerstone.

23 By the Lord has this been done;
      it is wonderful in our eyes.

24 This is the day the Lord has made;
      let us be glad and rejoice in it.

25 O Lord, grant salvation!
      O Lord, grant prosperity!

26 Blessed is He Who comes in the Name of the Lord;
      we bless you from the house of the Lord.

27 The Lord is God, and He has given us light.
   Join in procession with leafy boughs
      up to the horns of the altar.

28 You are my God, and I give thanks to You;
      O my God, I extol You.

29 Give thanks to the Lord, for He is good;
      for His kindness endures forever.

PSALM 113B (115)

The Greatness and Goodness of the True God

*Ant. But our God * is in heaven: whatever He wills, He does.*

A lleluia.

9 Not to us, O Lord, not to us
   but to Your Name give glory
   because of Your kindness, because of Your
      truth.

10 Why should the pagans say,
   "Where is their God?"

21 He will bless those who fear the Lord,
   both the small and the great.

22 May the Lord bless you more and more,
   both you and your children.

23 May you be blessed by the Lord,
   Who made heaven and earth.

24 Heaven is the heaven of the Lord,
   but the earth He has given to the children
      of men.

25 It is not the dead who praise the Lord,
   nor those who go down into silence;

26 But we bless the Lord,
   both now and forever.

PENTECOST

PSALM 67 (68)

God's Triumphal Procession

*Ant. Confirm, O God, * what You did for us in Your holy temple at Jerusalem, alleluia, alleluia.*

God arises; His enemies are scattered,
and those who hate Him flee before Him.

3 As smoke is driven away, so are they driven;
as wax melts before the fire,
so the wicked perish before God.

4 But the just rejoice and exult before God;
they are glad and rejoice.

5 Sing to God, chant praise to His Name,
extol Him Who rides upon the clouds,
Whose Name is the Lord;
exult before Him.

6 The father of orphans and the defender of widows
is God in His holy dwelling.

7 God gives a home to the forsaken;
He leads forth prisoners to prosperity;
only rebels remain in the parched land.

29 Show forth, O God, Your power,
the power, O God, with which You took our part;

30 For Your temple in Jerusalem
let the kings bring You gifts.

31 Rebuke the wild beast of the reeds,
the herd of strong bulls and the bullocks,
the nations.

Let them prostrate themselves with bars of
    silver;
    scatter the people who delight in war.

32 Let nobles come from Egypt;
    let Ethiopia extend its hands to God.

33 You kingdoms of the earth, sing to God,
    chant praise to the Lord

34   Who rides on the heights of the ancient
      heavens.
   Behold, His voice resounds, the voice of
      power:

35   "Confess the power of God!"
  Over Israel is His majesty;
    His power is in the skies.

The publisher extends sincere gratitude to the following
authors and copyright owners for their kind permission to
use the following hymns:

Burns & Oates, Ltd., from *Westminster Hymnal* 1940: Hymn
No. 33.

Rt. Rev. Msgr. Martin B. Hellriegel: Hymn No. 34.

Rev. Eugene Lindusky, O.S.C.: Hymn No. 12.

McLaughlin & Reilly Co., from *"Alverno Hymnal"*: Hymn
No. 11, from *Cantus Populi*: Text No. 14.

Oxford Univ. Press, from *English Hymnal*: Hymns Nos. 10
and 40.

Liturgical Press, from *"Our Parish Prays and Sings"*: Hymns
Nos. 42, 42A, 50, 13, and 17.

Frederick Pustet Co., Inc. from *Catholic Hymnal*: Text No. 37.

World Library of Sacred Music, from *"Peoples Mass Book"*:
Hymns Nos. 12, 15, 16, 18, 31, 41, 49, 54, and the Mass for
Christian Unity by Jan Vermulst.

Gregorian Institute of America, from *Hymnal of Christian
Unity*: Hymn No. 36. Also the Gelineau Antiphons, Nos. 55-57.

Ann Hoeffer Pax, words of Hymn No. 2.

To Rev. Thomas Reardon, Rev. Thomas Etten, and Sister
Mary David. O.S.B. for the original compositions used in
Holy Week, and "An English Mass."

THANKSGIVING PRAYERS AFTER MASS

Ant. Let us sing the Canticle of the Three Youths which these Saints sang in the fiery furnace, giving praise to the Lord. (P.T. Alleluia.)

Canticle of the Three Youths
Dan. 3, 57-88.56

Bless the Lord, all you works of the Lord,
  praise and exalt Him above all forever.

Angels of the Lord, bless the Lord,
  you heavens, bless the Lord;
All you waters above the heavens bless the
    Lord.
  All you hosts of the Lord, bless the Lord;
Sun and moon, bless the Lord;
  stars of heaven, bless the Lord.

Every shower and dew, bless the Lord;
  all you winds, bless the Lord;
Fire and heat, bless the Lord;
  cold and chill, bless the Lord;
Dew and rain, bless the Lord;
  frost and cold, bless the Lord;
Ice and snow, bless the Lord;
  nights and days, bless the Lord;
Light and darkness bless the Lord;
  lightnings and clouds, bless the Lord.

Let the earth, bless the Lord,
  praise and exalt Him above all forever.
Mountains and hills, bless the Lord;
  everything growing from the earth, bless the
    Lord;
You springs, bless the Lord;
  seas and rivers, bless the Lord;

You dolphins and all water creatures, bless the
Lord;
all you birds of the air, bless the Lord;
All you beasts, wild and tame, bless the Lord;
praise and exalt Him above all forever.

You sons of men, bless the Lord;
O Israel, bless the Lord;
Priests of the Lord, bless the Lord;
servants of the Lord, bless the Lord;
Spirits and souls of the just, bless the Lord;
holy men of humble heart, bless the Lord.

Ananias, Azarias, Misael, bless the Lord;
praise and exalt Him above all forever.
Let us bless the Father and the Son and the
Holy Spirit,
let us praise and exalt God above all forever.
Blessed are You, O Lord, in the firmament of
heaven,
praiseworthy and glorious forever;

Psálm 150

Praise the Lord in His sanctuary,
praise Him in the firmament of His strength.
Praise Him for His mighty deeds,
praise Him for His sovereign majesty.
Praise Him with the blast of the trumpet,
praise Him with lyre and harp,
Praise Him with timbrel and dance,
praise Him with strings and pipe.
Praise Him with sounding cymbals,
praise Him with clanging cymbals.
Let everything that has breath
praise the Lord.   Ps. (150)
Glory be to the Father, and to the Son,
and to the Holy Spirit.

As it was in the beginning is now and ever shall be,
world without end. Amen.

Ant. Let us sing the Canticle of the Three Youths which these Saints sang in the fiery furnace, giving praise to the Lord. (P.T. Alleluia.)

Lord, have mercy. Christ, have mercy, Lord, have mercy. Our Father (silently).

℣. And lead us not into temptation.

℞. **But deliver us from evil.**

℣. Let all Your works, O Lord, praise You.

℞. **And let Your saints bless You.**

℣. The saints shall exsult in glory.

℞. **They shall rejoice in their beds.**

℣. Not to us, O Lord, not to us.

℞. **But to Your Name give glory.**

℣. O Lord, hear my prayer.

℞. **And let my cry come to You.**

Let us pray.

O God, You allayed the flames of fire for the three youths; mercifully grant that the flame of sin may not consume us Your servants.

Direct, we beseech You, O Lord, our actions by Your holy inspirations, and carry them on by Your gracious assistance, that every prayer and work of ours may begin always with You, and through You be happily ended.

Grant us, we beseech You, almighty God, to extinguish within ourselves the flames of our vices even as You granted to Blessed Lawrence to overcome the fires of his torments.

℞. **Amen.**

BENEDICTION OF THE MOST BLESSED SACRAMENT

At the opening of Benediction any Eucharistic Hymn may be sung.

Hymn: **Down in adoration falling,**
     Lo! The sacred Host we hail;
  Lo! O'er ancient forms departing
     Newer rites of grace prevail;
  Faith for all defects supplying
     Where the feeble senses fail.

  To the everlasting Father
     And the Son Who reigns on high,
  With the Spirit blest proceeding
     Forth from each eternally,
  Be salvation, honor, blessing,
     Might, and endless majesty. Amen.

℣. **You have given them bread from heaven. (P.T. Alleluia.)**

℟. **Having all sweetness within it. (P.T. Alleluia.)**

Celebrant: Let us pray: O God, Who in this wonderful sacrament left us a memorial of Your passion, grant, we implore You, that we may so venerate the sacred mysteries of Your Body and Blood as always to be conscious of the fruit of Your redemption. You Who live and reign with God the Father in the unity of the Holy Spirit, God, forever and ever. ℟. **Amen.**

The Divine Praises

Blessed be God. * Blessed be His Holy Name. * Blessed be Jesus Christ, true God and true man. * Blessed be the Name of Jesus. * Blessed be His Most Sacred Heart. * Blessed be His Most Precious Blood. * Blessed be Jesus in the Most Holy Sacrament of the Altar. * Blessed be the Holy Spirit, the Paraclete. * Blessed be the great Mother of God, Mary most holy. * Blessed be her holy and Immaculate Conception. * Blessed be her glorious Assumption. * Blessed be the name of Mary, Virgin and Mother. * Blessed be St. Joseph, her most chaste spouse. * Blessed be God in His angels in His saints. Indulgence of 3 years